W9-BUC-220

*Under the General Editorship of*

JESSE W. MARKHAM, *Princeton University*

*Houghton Mifflin Adviser in Economics*

# PRICE THEORY

*Donald Stevenson Watson*

HOUGHTON MIFFLIN COMPANY · BOSTON

# AND ITS USES

THE GEORGE WASHINGTON UNIVERSITY

NEW YORK    ATLANTA    GENEVA, ILL.    DALLAS    PALO ALTO

ALSO BY THE SAME AUTHOR

*Economic Policy: Business and Government*

HOUGHTON MIFFLIN COMPANY • BOSTON

Printed in the U. S. A.

# Editor's Introduction

Price theory is the keystone of economics. Without it, the copious economic facts stored in the statistical depositories of the world would remain precisely what they are — a vast store of unrelated, uninterpreted facts. When organized and subjected to the analytical tools of price theory, they reveal with tolerable accuracy how components of an economy, such as industries and firms, function. Price theory, then, is not simply one of several means for training students to reason logically, although this attribute alone would surely merit its inclusion in the college curriculum. It is also practical, especially for a generation so preoccupied with the economic state of men and nations.

As the title of this book makes clear, Professor Watson not only presents price *theory,* but throughout points to its *uses.* This approach makes the study of theory a much more exciting venture. Interest may occasionally flag when the subject is presented as an uninterrupted stream of abstract models; interest is much more likely to be sustained when these same models are used to illuminate a variety of economic problems ranging from water shortages to agricultural surpluses, from decisions on economic policy to decisions of the business firm.

The level of mathematical understanding in our colleges is steadily rising, but some students of economics and business administration still have difficulties with price theory cast in mathematical terms. Professor Watson has taken account of the trend but avoided the difficulties by including a modest amount of elementary mathematical economics. Instructors and students so inclined will find the mathematical treatment here a useful supplement to many of the topics treated in the text proper. At all points, however, he formulates price theory verbally and presents it in terms of conventional geometric diagrams. This method of presentation allows for the optional omission of the mathematical supplements without loss of substance, continuity, or topical coverage.

Instructors and students will find here the standard materials of price theory and an excellent treatment of such recent developments as modern utility theory and linear programming. Professor Watson has developed the entire subject with freshness, vigor, and exemplary clarity — a clarity that comes from long teaching experience and directness of language that goes straight to the point of each topic. I commend it as an eminently teachable book.

JESSE W. MARKHAM

*Princeton, New Jersey*

v

# Preface

This book is intended as a text for the course in intermediate price theory, a course whose importance has been steadily growing. Besides those who major in economics, increasing numbers of students in business administration and in other curricula are including intermediate price theory in their programs. The intermediate level, however, is the highest reached by most of the students who take the course. To meet their needs, it is important to show them the relevance and uses of price theory.

Though their cultivation is fascinating for its own sake, price theory's techniques have many uses. The concepts and methods of analysis provide a way of thinking helpful in many kinds of business problems, in the appraisal of economic policies of government, and in serious reflection on the meaning of private enterprise in the world today. Much, though of course not all, of the theory that is used, and useful, in the analysis of actual problems belongs to the intermediate rather than to the advanced level. This book contains many short applications of price theory; they are always subordinate, however, to the exposition of the theory itself.

This text offers only the briefest discussion of methodology — where theory turns upon itself and chases its own tail. Methodology too often becomes a system of apologetics for theory. Although it does have limitations, price theory needs no defensive explanations. Teaching experience has induced me to bypass the preliminaries on methodology, to get on with the analysis, to unveil its methods as they are needed, and to open the course with the familiar and interesting subject of demand. Important uses of price theory can thus be demonstrated almost at once. Teaching experience has also shown me the wisdom of proceeding deliberately at first, and of taking it for granted that students usually remember little of the exact meanings of the concepts they encounter in the elementary course in economics. Familiarity with the manipulation of quantitative relations and with diagrams soon develops; then the pace can be quickened. So too in this book. After the first chapters, new concepts and techniques are introduced with much briefer explanations.

Exercises and problems are furnished for all chapters except the first. The selected references for each chapter are standard works in the field. They serve as suggestions for possible additional reading, and also help to keep footnotes to a minimum.

Only a limited amount of material can be covered in one semester. Selective rather than encyclopedic, this book includes those topics regarded as having the greatest importance and interest. The newer subjects of modern utility theory and of linear programming compelled me to devote less space to older and now less interesting subjects, such as the theory of distribution. Price theory deals with the allocation of scarce resources among competing ends. The scarce resources here are the pages that can be studied in one semester; the competing ends are all the topics that could be given full treatment. How far my allocation falls short of an optimum is for others to judge.

Except for a few simple equations, no algebra is used. In a nonmathematical exposition, I try to maintain the level of rigor appropriate to the intermediate course. The quantitative relations of price theory are displayed with arithmetic and with diagrams. Geometry, after all, is a branch of mathematics with its own rigor. Brief and mostly simple mathematical notes on certain topics are segregated in appendices to parts of the book. These notes are intended to show the illumination that elementary algebra and calculus can give. I hope that some readers will find them helpful.

To those who helped me put the manuscript into its final form, my gratitude is great. Because I did not take all the advice that was offered, mine is the responsibility for errors. Professor Edward Coen of the University of Minnesota painstakingly read the entire manuscript and made many suggestions for improving the clarity and accuracy of the materials. Professor Jesse W. Markham of Princeton University also gave useful advice. Professor Everett H. Johnson of The George Washington University assisted with the mathematical notes in the appendices; he prepared the first drafts of some of them and carefully scrutinized and corrected the first drafts prepared by me. Dr. Henry Solomon of the Navy Logistics Research Project at The George Washington University read the chapters on modern utility theory and linear programming and showed me how to improve them; the absence of mathematics in these chapters is my decision and his regret. After reading part of the manuscript and all of the proofs, Dr. Mary A. Holman gave much constructive criticism. For intelligent preparation of the manuscript I am indebted to Miss Margot Watson and Miss Wendy Watson, and especially to Mrs. Carmel Cassidy, who also offered suggestions on matters of form and substance. To my wife, Dr. Liselotte B. Watson, I owe thanks that cannot be adequately expressed. Finally, I gratefully acknowledge the cooperation of the editorial and art departments of Houghton Mifflin Company.

DONALD STEVENSON WATSON

*The George Washington University*

# Contents

PART   THREE

*The Theory of the Firm*

## PART FOUR

### *Competitive Pricing*

# PART FIVE

## *Monopoly Pricing*

# PART SIX

## *Pricing in Imperfect Competition*

# PART SEVEN

## *Incomes as Prices*

# PRICE THEORY AND ITS USES

# PART ONE

*Introduction*

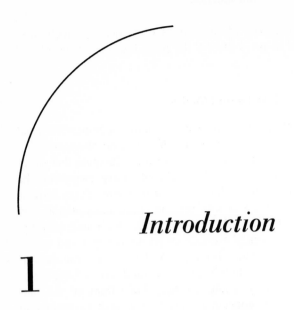

# *Introduction*

## 1

The flood of material things enjoyed by Americans does not make them contented. The desire for more, and still more, runs always ahead of the rising level of living. How to get more and how to make the best use of what is available is *the* economic problem, the everlasting problem of every family, every business firm, and every unit of government.

The economic problem is the subject of price theory. In a free economy, prices are the instruments that allocate resources — material things and human services — among the ends that they can serve. Prices determine what goods and services are produced, how they are produced, and who gets them.

In the 1950's, social critics began to aim their barbs at the "affluence," the "abundance," and the "waste" they thought they could see in the United States. Such censure was by no means new. It had appeared on and off again during the last century. Anyway, in the affluent society, consumers are said to indulge themselves with unnecessary gadgets bought under the influence of advertising, while government services are skimped. In their abundant society, Americans live at too high a standard, while hundreds of millions elsewhere in the world eke out their existences in abject poverty. In the wasteful economy, too many of the wrong things are produced.

Whatever might be the merits of these lines of criticism, which raise issues beyond the confines of price theory, the plain fact is that unsatisfied wants exist everywhere.

## Scarcity and Choice

If we look at what people do want, instead of passing judgment on what they ought to want, it is clear that there is no affluence, no abundance, no plenty, no embarrassment of riches. The test is simple. Imagine that every person in the United States was told that he could have everything he wants, and in any quantity. Imagine that every businessman, every farmer, every self-employed person was also told that he could have all the new equipment and all the personal services he wants, free, and in any quantity. Imagine that the heads of the armed services, of all the colleges and school systems, of the health services, police forces, and of the other multifarious public bodies and activities were told that they too could have all the materials, equipment, and people they would ask for. Then think of the sum total of the three lists — what consumers, producers, and governmental bodies would want. Who can doubt that the total would exceed, by many times, the amounts of material and human resources that are available?

Because they fall short of wants, resources are said to be scarce. The usual everyday meaning of scarcity is physical nonavailability; in a serious drought, water might not be available in customary quantities in some communities. But in economic literature, scarcity means availability in amounts less than sufficient to satisfy all wants or desires. The test of scarcity is price. Only goods that are not scarce, such as air, do not command a price. Resources have alternative uses. A consumer's resources are money and time. Both can be put to many uses, some more urgent than others. The consumer's economic choices allocate his limited amounts of money and time among his competing ends, or purposes. A business firm's resources are labor, materials, and equipment, which also have many uses of varying importance. The business firm's resources must also be allocated. Units of government use their budgets as the formal procedures for allocating their scarce resources among alternative ends.

## Price Theory and Income Theory

The two main branches of modern economic theory are price theory and income theory. Another name for price theory is micro-economics — the theory of the small, of the behavior of consumers, producers, and markets. The corresponding name for income theory is macro-economics — the theory of the large, of the behavior of hundreds of billions of dollars of consumer expenditures, business investments, and government purchases.

Price theory explains the composition, or allocation, of total production — why more of some things are produced than of others. Income theory explains the level of total production and why the level rises and falls.

For two centuries, price theory has been the center of attention of economists. In the eighteenth and nineteenth centuries, it was known as the theory of value. The theory of value played a leading role as one of the intellectual foundations of the new freedoms that came after 1776. The theory of value was also at the heart of the old controversies over capitalism and socialism. Karl Marx's critique of capitalism was based upon his special version of the theory of the value of commodities.

Many of the features of modern price theory were constructed by Alfred Marshall of Cambridge University. He established much of the terminology still in use, as well as several of the concepts and analytical techniques still employed. Other economists have added to and modified the corpus of price theory. Prominent among them are Edward H. Chamberlin of Harvard University, Mrs. Joan Robinson, also of Cambridge University, and J. R. Hicks of Oxford University. Income theory is based on the ideas of the best-known economist of the twentieth century, J. M. (Lord) Keynes, who also had a long association with Cambridge University.

The price theory presented in this book is the standard, established body of theory. Some parts are old, others are new. The logic of the theory has been tried and tested by many minds. On nearly all of it, economists substantially agree. Such disagreement as exists is on points of emphasis.

### Theory and Reality

Why bother with theory, why not go to the real word itself and study it? Why not get the facts?

There are two troubles with facts. It is not always easy to say just what a fact is. Anyone who has been in a laboratory or in a court of law can testify to that. The other trouble with the facts of economic life is that there are too many of them, too many hundreds of millions of them. Some 57 million families in the United States consume goods and services every day. In some way, each family differs from the others. Goods and services are provided by over 10 million producers; these too are all different from one another. Goods and services are exchanged for money in tens of thousands of markets. Obviously, it is quite impossible to get "all of the" facts of economic life.

Theory is the systematic description of reality. Theory selects the essential features and shows the connections among them. Theory consists of generalizations and of causal relationships.

## Models

Economic theory consists of the building and using of economic models, which are sets of interconnected economic relationships. Suppose that severe freezing weather damages most of the citrus crop. Everyone would then agree that the price of citrus fruits will go up. Here is an example of a model and its use. The model consists of what people think are the relations among demand, supply, and price. The bad weather affects supply. The model predicts the rise in price. This kind of economic model, which exists in just about everyone's mind, is not necessarily identical with the corresponding model of formal price theory. The models of theory are clear and exact. Their foundations are carefully specified, as are the relations among the variables. As simplifications of reality, models have their limitations which theory recognizes.

A model airplane lacks many of the features of a real airplane, but the model exhibits the essentials of what an airplane is and what it does. So too, economic models are stripped down to the essentials. A model of the pricing of beef does not include tens of thousands of the facts that have to do with beef. The demand-price relationship in the model does not have to mention whether more people prefer their steaks rare than well-done. Nor does the supply-price relationship in the model have to mention whether ranch hands prefer jeeps to horses. A model contains only the essential and the relevant relationships that can explain an aspect of how prices function in a private-enterprise economy.

Just because things are left out of them, there must be caution in using models. In a particular application, one of the omitted things might turn out to be crucially important. A model in which businessmen always act so as to maximize their profits has to be modified when it is applied in circumstances where businessmen don't.

Alert readers will be able to think of exceptions to many of the statements made in this book. But the exceptions will turn out to be complications or refinements of simple statements, rather than contradictions. More complicated models are needed to handle the exceptions. A feather blowing along in the breeze does not really contradict the law of gravity. An explanation of the movements of the feather has to be furnished by a model much more intricate than the standard and simple one for falling bodies.

The proper contrast, accordingly, is not between theory and the facts of real life. To select facts, to align them, to give them meaning is to theorize. The proper contrast is between good theory and bad theory, between useful theory and irrelevant theory.

## The Uses of Price Theory

The uses of price theory are many. Of these the greatest is the under-standing of the operation of the economy. The United States is usually said to have a mixed economy, a mixture of public and private enterprise. But the private-enterprise sector is still about four times as large as the public sector. Knowledge of price theory is indispensable to anyone who wants depth of understanding of how the private-enterprise sector of the economy functions. Such understanding is important as a foundation for an intelligent position on the ideological and political conflicts in the world in the present age.

When it confines itself to statements about causes and their effects and to statements of functional relations, theory is said to be positive. When, in contrast, it embraces norms or standards, mixing them with cause-effect analyses, theory is said to be normative. Positive economic theory con-sists of propositions of this type: If $A$, then $B$. Normative economic theory seeks rules for improving the working of the economy. The distinction is akin to that between pure science and applied science.

In fact, however, the distinction between positive and normative eco-nomic theory is never drawn as a clear line. In part this is due to language itself. To say, for example, that "the function of prices is . . ." is to confer some approval, however mild, on the work that prices do. Nor can the word "monopoly" be mentioned without some overtones of evil. The same thing is true in macro-economics, where no matter how technical the anal-ysis, it is always plain that full employment and stable growth are good, whereas unemployment, depression, and inflation are bad.

### Welfare Economics

Normative price theory is more commonly known as welfare economics. The subject of welfare economics is the economic well-being of persons as consumers and as producers, and the possible ways of improving that well-being, or welfare. Welfare economics proper has only a remote connection with "the welfare state," that vast complex of social-service activities of modern governments in providing for the aged, the blind, the disabled, the unemployed, and others who cannot care for themselves. The social-service activities embrace selected groups of the population, whose unique common characteristic is their low incomes.

In contrast, the theory of welfare economics examines the conditions of the economic welfare of all persons, considered as individuals. Economic welfare consists of the subjective satisfactions that individuals get from consuming goods and services, and from enjoying leisure. The force of the word "economic" is that economic welfare is confined to those subjective satisfactions that, in fact or in principle, can be put under the measuring rod of money. More economic welfare, or a higher level of economic welfare, means more satisfaction or a higher level of satisfaction.

Here is an illustration of what welfare economics does. Consider the price that a profit-hungry monopolist charges. Everyone would probably agree that the monopoly price is high and that the consumers who pay the price are injured. But the monopoly price is higher than what? And just how great is the injury to the consumers? Of what does it consist? Can it be measured? Is the injury to the consumers greater or less than the benefit the monopolist enjoys? The theory of welfare economics tries to answer these questions. It also goes on to make proposals for dealing with monopoly.

One of the main tasks of welfare economics is to define an ideal economy, which is one that would give the maximum of satisfactions to individuals from the resources available. The actual economy falls short of the ideal in many ways, though not hopelessly so. Thus, a companion task of welfare economics is to point to ways of bringing the actual closer to the ideal.

Much of welfare economics is highly abstract, as a discussion of the ideal must be. And welfare economics operates with an idealistic conception of government as an all-seeing Olympian intelligence. By doing so, welfare economics furnishes standards. Yet the economic controls actually exercised by government fall short of ideal standards in many ways. Forming no consistent pattern, the controls are a mixture of the wise and the foolish. Let them now be classified under the heading of economic policy. Another use of price theory is as a foundation of logical analysis for economic policy.

### Economic Policy

As was just indicated, economic policy means all of the actions of government — federal, state, and local — that are intended to influence the economy. The multitudes of economic controls that now exist have a wide range of objectives. One group of controls is aimed at stabilizing the economy. These controls rest on and can be evaluated by macro-economic theory. Other controls directly and indirectly cause changes in the allocation of resources. Government fixes some prices, and tries to influence others. Taxes, tariffs, loans, and subsidies all have various effects on prices and production.

Price theory furnishes the analytical tools for economic policies affecting prices and production. These tools are not always used by policy-makers in government; and when they are, they are often not used wisely. Price theory then becomes an apparatus of criticism, its standards of criticism being drawn from its view of the ideal economy.

## Managerial Economics

Still another use of price theory is the application of its methods of analysis to certain of the problems continually faced by business enterprises. Since the end of World War II, the business community has been drawing upon the organized knowledge and the analytical techniques of the social sciences to an extent far greater than ever before. Price theory in the service of business executives is known as managerial economics. Its main contributions to improved decision-making in business are in demand analysis, cost analysis, and in methods of calculating prices. Even though it might be supposed that businessmen always know what their profits are, events have shown that the consulting economist can often give useful advice to businessmen on how they should think about and measure their profits.

The postwar period has also seen the emergence of a powerful new analytical tool in price theory. This tool is linear programming, which is described in Chapter 12. Linear programming is a mathematical method that has already proved itself as a major innovation in theory and in the practical application of theory to business problems. The contribution of linear programming is that of finding actual numerical solutions to problems calling for optimum choices when the problems have to be solved within definite bounds.

Operations research, also known as operations analysis, has many affinities with managerial economics, and indeed overlaps it. Operations research was born during World War II, when physicists, mathematicians, and other specialists solved such problems as how best to lay mines to destroy enemy ships. Since the end of the war, operations research has grown much. The armed services continue to use operations research for new and difficult problems; so does industry. The special feature of operations research is its use of mathematical tools in tackling practical problems. Usually, also, operations research is conducted by teams of technicians with varied specializations — engineering, mathematics, statistics, psychology, economics. When it tackles economic problems, operations research draws upon the methods of price theory.

## Economy and Efficiency

What once was often said to be a weakness of price theory has turned out to be perhaps its greatest strength. The supposed weakness is the reliance on the notion that businessmen and consumers behave rationally — that they survey possible courses of action, measure the expected benefits and costs of each course of action, and then choose those promising the greatest surpluses of benefits over costs.

Even if it were true that many persons do not always behave rationally in making decisions about material things, it would still be important to know what rational behavior is, because rational behavior is the kind that results in the best uses of scarce resources. The best uses are what price theory demonstrates. They are the meaning of welfare economics, of managerial economics, and of linear programming. Another way to express the same thought is to say that price theory deals with decisions and their consequences on economy and efficiency. Economy, or economizing, means to achieve a given objective with the fewest resources — at the least costs. (Economizing does *not* mean doing things the cheap way. The least cost of a given objective might be very expensive — in the everyday sense.) Efficiency means to achieve the maximum possible benefits from given resources. Economy and efficiency are therefore mirrors of each other.

Since the end of World War II, the greatest single concentration of applied economic knowledge has been to the problems of the national defense. Clearly, the size of the gross national product is important to the national defense, and so is the stable growth of the gross national product. But the special contributions of economists in the many research organizations working directly and indirectly with the armed services have been to demonstrate how to attain economy and efficiency in the allocation of resources among defense programs and weapons systems.

Some economists believe that the next great application of economic knowledge will be to government activities generally. Much has been learned about improved economy and efficiency in the national defense. The new knowledge applies equally well in the growing civilian part of the public sector of the economy. It is not that economists have superior knowledge and wisdom on all government activities, but that they do have a tested way of thinking on economy and efficiency, on how to show decision-makers the means of achieving the best uses of scarce resources.

Price theory does not of course yield immediate solutions to real problems. Solutions require the hard work of gathering and interpreting facts and the still harder work of making estimates for an uncertain future. The essential role of theory is to tell what facts to look for and what to do with them once they have been found. Facts do not speak for themselves; they convey meaning only when they are selected, arranged, and interpreted by systematic thought.

### Summary

Price theory investigates *the* economic problem: how prices function so as to allocate scarce resources among competing, or alternative, purposes. Price theory, or micro-economics, is one of the two main branches of modern economic theory, the other being income theory, or macro-economics.

Price theory has many uses. The greatest of these is depth in understanding of how a free private-enterprise economy operates. When it is adapted to the task of stating the norms and standards of an ideal economy, price theory is called welfare economics, because an ideal economy provides the maximum of economic welfare — subjective satisfaction — obtainable from the economy's resources. Price theory also offers the analytical tools for evaluating and criticizing the everyday economic controls of government over prices and production. Price theory in the service of business is known as managerial economics. Because it is a tested way of thinking about economy and efficiency, price theory has wide uses in decision-making in the employment of resources in government programs.

## SELECTED REFERENCES

On scope and method: Lionel Robbins, *An Essay on the Nature and Significance of Economic Science,* 2d ed. (London: Macmillan, 1935). Philip H. Wicksteed, "The Scope and Method of Political Economy," *Economic Journal,* Vol. XXIV, 1914. Reprinted in George J. Stigler and Kenneth E. Boulding, eds., *Readings in Price Theory* (Homewood: Irwin, 1952).

An integration of modern theory with its origins: William Fellner, *Emergence and Content of Modern Economic Analysis* (New York: McGraw-Hill, 1960).

On the uses of micro-economic theory: Charles J. Hitch, "The Uses of Economics," in Brookings Dedication Lectures, *Research for Public Policy* (Washington, D.C.: Brookings Institution, 1961).

# PART TWO

## The Theory

## of Demand

# The Demand

# for a Commodity

## 2

THE DEMAND FUNCTION · DEMAND SCHEDULES AND DEMAND
CURVES · CHANGES IN DEMAND · SOME APPLICATIONS ·

People have been talking about demand and supply for centuries. They
still do, in everyday conversation as well as in such places as the financial
pages and the editorial columns of newspapers. It was long ago remarked,
however, that if the ups and downs of prices can be explained simply by
uttering the two words "demand" and "supply," economics could be taught
to parrots.

This chapter and the next five cover the theory of demand. Although
the economists of the eighteenth and nineteenth centuries went deep into
the subject of prices, they put most of their efforts into the analysis of
supply. Penetrating analysis of demand did not come until the end of the
nineteenth century. The modern theory of market demand still rests on
the structure built by Alfred Marshall (1842–1924). He taught at Cambridge University and through his *Principles of Economics*[1] molded the
thinking of his and the following generations of British and American
economists.

The subject of this chapter is the demand for a commodity in a market.
This demand is the total of the demands of the individual buyers in a

[1] London: Macmillan. 1st ed. 1890, 8th ed. 1920.

15

market. The voice of logic would say that the theory of the behavior of the individual consumer ought to come first. Because the theory of market demand is simpler, however, there are advantages in introducing the techniques of theoretical analysis with the simpler relations and problems.

### The Demand Function

Theory deals with concepts and functions. A function states the relation between two or more variables, such as prices and physical quantities. A function says how the variables depend on one another. Important in price theory are demand functions, cost functions, production functions, and supply functions. The word "function" is just a shorthand way of referring to the things that determine demand, cost, production, and supply.

In a given market in a given period of time, the demand function for a commodity is the relation between the various amounts of the commodity that might be bought and the determinants of those amounts. The determinants are (1) the possible prices of the commodity, (2) the incomes of the buyers, (3) their tastes, and (4) the prices of closely related commodities. (Note 2 in the Appendix to Part Two gives some examples of mathematical demand functions.)

The role of price will be taken up shortly. At this point, a few preliminary remarks will be made about the other determinants. Clearly, the incomes of buyers influence their purchases of a commodity. Though suitable enough for consumers making purchases at retail, the word "tastes" is hardly right for the state of mind of the purchasing agent of a business corporation. Presumably, the agent buys commodities on the basis of their specifications and of their estimated productivities for his company. The business demand for commodities is a *derived demand* — derived from consumer demand, and therefore immediately or ultimately dependent on it. Accordingly, a general analysis need not keep a high wall between consumer demand and business demand.

The commodities closely related to any one commodity are its substitutes and complements. In practical problems, the closely related commodities are nearly always easy to identify. Purchases of a commodity can be highly sensitive to changes in the prices of its substitutes and complements.[2] But the substitutes of a commodity have *their* substitutes, which in turn have *their* substitutes, etc. Much depends on how a commodity is defined.

#### Commodities, Markets, and Time

The word "commodity" can mean a broad or narrow class of objects, as well as some one unique object. The meaning of the word is nearly

---

[2] This point is elaborated in Chapter 7 under the heading of cross elasticity of demand.

always plain from its context. Whether the meaning is broad or narrow depends on the problem at hand. Thus, the demand for meat can be a subject of investigation; so can the demand for beef, and the demand for sirloin steaks. Tobacco, automobiles, and housing are other examples of broad classes of commodities that can be subdivided into narrower classes. When commodities are successively subdivided into narrower classes, their demands undergo changes, mainly because their substitutes take different forms. If the commodity is tobacco, it has no close substitutes. If the commodity is cigarettes, the substitutes are cigars and pipe tobacco. But if the commodity happens to be a brand of filter-tip cigarettes, then it has several even closer substitutes — the other brands.

How to define a commodity is by no means a problem thought up by academic hairsplitters. The problem comes up constantly in the enforcement of the antitrust laws. Millions of dollars can ride on the final decisions of the federal courts on how particular commodities should be defined. For example, suppose the commodity is baseballs. Should "the" commodity include *all* baseballs, those meeting major-league specifications as well as the cheap rubber-covered baseballs bought for children? Or should baseballs be divided into three or four groups, each one a separate commodity? Remember that a children's ball is not a substitute for a major-league ball, although a major-league ball is an enthusiastically accepted substitute for a children's ball. The importance of the legal definition can be illustrated in this hypothetical example: Suppose 50 companies make baseballs of all kinds and that two of them merge. A merger may be unlawful if it substantially lessens competition. If there are now 49 companies instead of 50, competition is not reduced much. But if the two companies that merge turn out to be the only ones making major-league baseballs, competition is not just substantially lessened; it is eliminated. If the courts decide that major-league balls, not baseballs generally, are a distinct commodity, they will prohibit such a merger, thus denying to the companies the possible profits from merging.

The word "commodity" need not mean only physical objects, or classes of them. Services, such as entertainment and medical care, can also be included as commodities. After all, what people want from physical objects are the services they render. This is obviously true of durable goods, which provide services to their owners over periods of time. But it is also true of nondurable goods; food is there to be eaten, clothes to be worn, and so on.

A note on terminology: Economic literature does not distinguish, unvaryingly, between "commodities" and "products." In some contexts the two words are interchangeable, but in others they convey different shades of meaning. In general, commodity is the broader term. Automobiles are commodities, but Chevrolets are products of General Motors Corporation.

That is, the outputs of industries are commodities, whereas the outputs of individual business firms are products. In the national income and product accounts, however, all final goods and services are known as "products." The items in the gross national product are distinguished from "intermediate goods" and from "factors." Labor and capital[3] are the factors that produce a typewriter, which is a final product, if it is a personal typewriter. The steel in the typewriter is an intermediate good.

The demand for a commodity exists in a market. The word "market" also has a flexible meaning, and markets can also be subdivided. In general, a market is a set of points of contact between buyers and sellers. A market can, but need not be, a definite geographical area. The market for college professors does not exist at any one place, nor is it confined within national boundaries. Where markets are primarily geographical, they can also be local, regional, national, and international.

The demand for a commodity in a market must also be specified for a period of time. It obviously makes a difference whether demand is for a day, or a month, or a year, or longer. Because commodities, markets, and time periods can each be specified in many ways, and because the idea of demand requires all three of them, it follows that demand can take on an endless number of forms. What can be said about "the" demand for "a" commodity in "a" market in "a" period of time consists of the generalizations that apply to demand in all of the forms it can take.

### Demand and Price

As a determinant of the demand for a commodity, price can have the simple meaning of money value per physical unit, e.g., ten cents per pound. The wider meaning of price is the terms on which the commodity is available. The more expensive consumer durable goods are available on terms that include not only the quoted price, but also such matters as down payments, trade-in allowances, financing charges, and lengths of loans. Such matters do exert an influence on demand; for the sake of simplicity they will be treated here as having a cash equivalent which is part of "price."

The relation between demand and price occupies the center of the stage of price theory. Demand schedules and demand curves, to be taken up next, are the techniques for describing the demand-price relation. The three other determinants of demand — tastes, incomes, and the prices of substitutes and complements — are held constant while attention focuses on demand and price.

---

[3] In this book, land is not treated as a separate factor of production. The tendency in modern theory is to subsume land under capital. See the opening pages of Chapter 25.

## Demand Schedules and Demand Curves

### Demand Schedules

A demand schedule, one of Alfred Marshall's many contributions to the techniques of price theory, is a list of prices and quantities. At each price, the corresponding quantity is the amount of the commodity that would be bought at that price. A simple demand schedule is shown in Table 2–1.

**TABLE 2–1**

A Demand Schedule

| Price | Quantity |
|-------|----------|
| 10¢ | 1,000 units |
| 9 | 2,000 units |
| 8 | 3,000 units |
| 7 | 4,000 units |

A demand schedule states the relation between the two variables of price and quantity. Economic theory employs many other relations between two variables; all are similar in form. The demand schedule in Table 2–1 should be read in this way: If the price were 10 cents, the quantity bought would be 1,000 units; if instead the price were 9 cents, the quantity bought would be 2,000 units, and so on. A demand schedule does not say what the price is. It only says what amounts would be bought at different possible prices. The lower the price, the larger is the quantity that is bought. Similarly, the higher the price, the smaller the quantity.

This inverse relationship between price and quantity is often called the "law of demand." The law rests upon firm logic (the theory of consumer behavior presented in Chapters 4 and 6). The law also stands confirmed by many empirical investigations.

### Demand Curves

The price–quantity relation can be illustrated with numbers as in Table 2–1. It can also be displayed geometrically. The demand schedule is then transformed into a demand curve. The demand curve is always so called, even when it happens to be a straight line.

Figure 2–1 shows a demand curve. Price is plotted on the vertical axis and quantity on the horizontal axis.[4] The little circles in Figure 2–1 are obtained by using the numbers in Table 2–1. The circle in the upper left shows the price of 10 cents and the 1,000 units that would be bought at that price. The next one, down and to the right, shows 9 cents and 2,000 units, and so on. The heavy line is drawn from one circle to the next. This line is the demand curve.

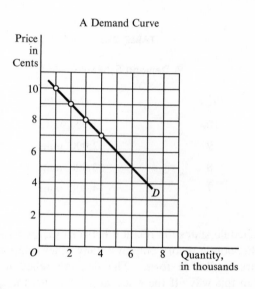

Fig. 2–1

Demand curves, supply curves, cost curves, and many others are used throughout economic theory. Once they are mastered, these visual aids become a convenient shorthand that can quickly and accurately portray the logic of economic relations. But demand curves, and the others, contain an important implicit assumption, namely, that price and quantity vary continuously. This assumption is not realistic, but it has the great advantages of simplicity and of convenience.[5]

---

[4] Some mathematical economists reverse the axes, on the ground that quantity is the dependent variable, which belongs on the *y*-axis. To put price on the *y*-axis and quantity on the *x*-axis is a convention established by Alfred Marshall.

[5] The assumption of continuity is easily justified for demand curves that are statistically constructed from prices that are averages of discrete individual quotations.

In Figure 2–2, a demand curve is constructed from bars instead of from the little circles in Figure 2–1. In Figure 2–2, the horizontal lengths of the bars represent the quantities bought at each of the prices shown. The vertical widths of the bars represent the gradations of price. The demand curve is drawn through the mid-points of the vertical widths at the right. The appearance of the bars suggests a set of steps. Imagine that the height of the steps becomes smaller and smaller — that the gradations of price become finer and finer. Ultimately, the height of the steps would become so small that the bars would become thin horizontal lines. The smooth curve would then give a perfect fit.

Another Demand Curve

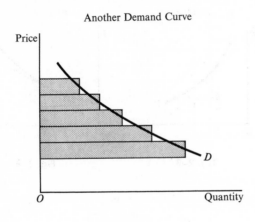

**Fig. 2–2**

### The Slope of a Curve

With unimportant exceptions to be noted later, a demand curve always goes downward from left to right. The slope of a demand curve is negative. The notion of the slope of a curve is important in economic theory; there are many other kinds of curves besides demand curves. Hence a few words are in order on the meaning of the slope of a curve.

Figures 2–3, 2–4, and 2–5 contain curves with different slopes. In these Figures, $P$ and $Q$ are price and quantity, but they could be any two other related variables. The curves *1, 2, 3,* and *4* show four of the possible relations between the two variables. Loosely speaking, the slope of a curve is its steepness. Strictly speaking, the slope of a curve has to be measured at a point on the curve. This is done by finding the slope of the tangent (i.e., the tangent line) to the curve at a point.

In Figure 2–3, curve *1* goes downhill from left to right. So does the tangent at point $A$. The actual slope at point $A$ is the line $AB$ divided by the line $BC$. The lengths of the two lines are equal, so that the slope at $A$

is 1 : 1, or unity. The slope of curve *1* is negative, because *P* decreases while *Q* increases.

In Figure 2–4, curve *2* goes up and to the right. Here the slope at point *A* is *AB* divided by *BC*. Since *AB* is half as long as *BC*, the slope at *A* is 1 : 2, or ½. The slope of curve *2* is positive, because *P* increases as *Q* increases.

In Figure 2–5, curves *3* and *4* are neither falling nor rising at their points *A*. Both tangents are horizontal; when they are, slopes are said to be zero.

The Slopes of Curves

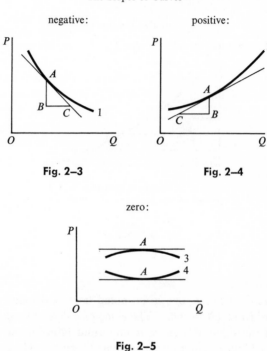

negative:                    positive:

Fig. 2–3                    Fig. 2–4

zero:

Fig. 2–5

The slope of a demand curve can vary from one point to another. But whether it is large or small, as measured by the slopes of tangents at different points, the slope of a demand curve is negative. Finally, if a demand curve is a straight line, it has the same negative slope at all points.

### Changes in Demand

A change in demand is a change in an entire demand schedule; it is a shift in a demand curve. When demand increases, all of the quantities opposite each of the prices become larger. Or to say the same thing in another way: When demand increases, buyers are willing to pay a higher price than before for any given quantity.

An increase in demand should not be confused with an increase in the quantity bought because of a fall in price. Consider the hypothetical data in Table 2–2. In Schedule A, the quantity bought at the price of 9 cents

### TABLE 2–2

#### Two Demand Schedules

| Schedule A | | Schedule B | |
|---|---|---|---|
| P | Q | P | Q |
| 10¢ | 1,000 units | 10¢ | 2,000 units |
| 9 | 2,000 units | 9 | 3,000 units |
| 8 | 3,000 units | 8 | 4,000 units |

is 2,000 units, and at 8 cents more is bought. But this is not an increase in demand. The demand remains the same — it is the whole schedule. But from Schedule A to Schedule B, the amount bought at 9 cents increases from 2,000 units to 3,000 units. And at each other price the amount increases. The meaning of an increase (or a decrease) in demand, then, is a change in the entire schedule.

Change in Demand

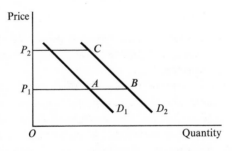

Fig. 2–6

The meaning of a change in demand is also shown in Figure 2–6. In the figure are two demand curves, $D_1$ and $D_2$. An increase in demand is a shift of the curve to the right. (That the two curves are parallel has no special meaning.) At the price $OP_1$, the amount bought with $D_1$ is the quantity $P_1A$. When the demand increases to $D_2$, the quantity $P_1B$ is bought at the same price. Observe also that the quantity $P_1A$, equal to $P_2C$, is bought at the higher price $OP_2$, when demand is $D_2$. All of this, of course, applies in reverse, if demand decreases from $D_2$ to $D_1$.

### Causes of Changes in Demand

A demand curve is like a still photograph. Behind the price–quantity relation are always the tastes of the buyers, their incomes, and the prices of substitute and complementary commodities. When they change, the demand curve changes, shifting to the right or to the left. Demand curves are thus in constant motion; motion pictures would be far better than still photographs.

The causes of changes in demand will be more fully discussed in the next few chapters. At this point, a brief summary statement can be made. It is contained in Table 2–3. The four causes of increases and decreases in demand can work in the same direction, or can offset one another. Each one can also have a different strength.

### TABLE 2–3

### Causes of Changes in Demand

| *Increase* | *Decrease* |
| --- | --- |
| Consumer desires become stronger | Consumer desires become weaker |
| Consumer incomes rise[a] | Consumer incomes fall[a] |
| Prices of substitutes rise | Prices of substitutes fall |
| Prices of complements fall | Prices of complements rise |

[a] Exceptions to this statement are treated in Chapters 6 and 7.

### Exceptions to the Law of Demand

Full proof of the inverse relation between price and quantity is postponed until later chapters. For the time being, let it simply be assumed that the law of demand is valid.

Only two possible exceptions to the law of demand have been discovered, both of them quite unimportant. One is associated with the name of Thorstein Veblen (1857–1929), the sharp-tongued social critic, and his doctrine of conspicuous consumption. If consumers measure the desirability of a commodity entirely by its price, and if nothing else influences consumers, then they will buy less of the commodity at a low price, and more at a high price. Diamonds are often mentioned as an example. Here the demand curve has to be consumer demand, not the industrial demand for diamonds as cutting edges in machine tools. The other exception is associated with the name of Sir Robert Giffen (1837–1910), who observed that a rise in the price of bread caused low-paid British wage earners, early in the nineteenth century, to buy more bread, not less. These wage earners subsisted on a diet of mainly bread. When its price rose, and when therefore they had to spend more money for a given quantity of bread, they could not afford to buy as much meat as before. To maintain their intake of food, they bought more bread at higher prices.

Other exceptions to the law of demand are apparent, not real. Suppose a local gasoline price war breaks out. Seeing prices fall, and expecting them to go down still more, motorists whose tanks still hold a few days' gasoline may wait for the expected low prices before they buy gasoline. Here the buyers are dominated, for a few days, by their price expectations. Reduced prices cause their demand curves to shift to the left, as still lower prices are expected. The reverse is also true — higher prices with the expectation of further rises cause demand curves to shift to the right, with increases in the amounts bought. Then too, the statistical data for many commodities show large amounts bought at high prices and small amounts at low prices over the course of the business cycle. But such data do not contradict the law of demand; they mean only that the demands for many commodities increase in times of prosperity because of rising incomes, and decrease in times of depression, when incomes are falling. Still another false exception is the article sold under two brand names at the same time. Consumers often buy more of the higher-priced brand than of the low-priced, even though the articles are otherwise identical. But consumers who act in this way *think* that the two brands are different. Hence the two brands must be analyzed as if they were two different commodities.

### Some Applications

The first and greatest use of the concept of the demand curve is in understanding part of the mechanism of a whole economy. The gross national product consists of many billion dollars' worth of many thousands of final products. What the products are and the relative amounts of each are decided in part by demand. Rattlesnake meat and beef are both foodstuffs; both are produced and sold. But much less of one is sold than of the other, the difference in demand being a sufficient — though only a partial — explanation.

#### Surpluses and Shortages

Surpluses and shortages of commodities appear here and there in the American economy much of the time. The word "surplus" is likely to suggest farm products and the problem of government when it tries to raise their prices. The word "shortage" may suggest one of the accompaniments of wartime price control. Even when there are no government price controls, temporary surpluses and shortages arise from mistakes in pricing by business firms. These surpluses and shortages can be illustrated by a simple application of the demand curve.

Figure 2–7 can be interpreted to show the meaning of both surpluses and shortages. Suppose that the amount of a commodity offered for sale in some period of time is $OB$. Suppose too that the prevailing price is $P_1A$. At the price $P_1A$, however, the consumers will buy only the amount $OA$, for this is the information conveyed by the demand curve $D$. The amount $AB$ is not sold — it is the surplus. The surplus remains on shelves or in warehouses during the time period in question. Unless the demand increases, so that at price $P_1A$ the whole amount $OB$ will be bought, the sellers of the commodity must either keep the unsold surplus or lower the price. If they had chosen the price $P_2$ to begin with, there would of course have been no surplus at all. Next, let Figure 2–7 show the meaning of a shortage. Suppose the amount offered for sale is $OA$, and that the price is $P_2B$. Hence buyers try to buy the amount $OB$, with the result that a shortage equal to $AB$ exists. The shortage can take different forms. Retailers might have the commodity in stock only part of the time. If dealers establish waiting lists, the length of the waiting period becomes another measure of the size of the shortage.

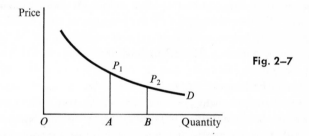

Fig. 2–7

Prices are often said to perform a rationing function. A large crop sells at a low price, a small one at a high price. The idea of the demand curve shows at once why and how this is so.

### Demand and "Need"

The demand concept is often ignored or overlooked by those who should know better, with the result that some great issues of public policy become beclouded and confused. Take the example of water. Water shortages have occurred in many communities, and from time to time, forecasts of a future water shortage for the whole nation are made. Population is growing, so are the urban communities, and so is industrial production. At present rates of consumption — per household, per ton of steel, per acre of irrigated land, etc. — the future "needs" for water will exceed the physical amounts available. Such is the common pattern of thought, which operates with the idea of the need for water as if the need were a fixed (or almost a fixed) number of gallons of water, per household, per ton of steel, etc. The common view looks to the need for water, not to the demand for it.

That there is a need for water is beyond dispute, but for how much? Does the suburbanite need enough so that he can let the garden hose run for a few more hours because it's too much trouble to go out and turn it off? Do the owners of an industrial plant need so much that they can always draw fresh amounts and not have to install equipment to re-use water?

Obviously, if the price of water were higher, less of it would be used in households, in industry, and in agriculture. When the price of water is adjusted so that the amount available is equal to the demand *at that price,* there can be no shortage. The future might hold the prospect of more expensive water, but proper pricing policies will prevent "shortages."

## Summary

The *demand function* for a commodity is the relation between the various amounts of the commodity that might be bought and (1) the possible prices of the commodity, (2) the incomes of the buyers, (3) their tastes, and (4) the prices of closely related commodities. A *commodity* can be broadly or narrowly defined; how to do so depends on the purpose of analysis. Similarly, *markets* can be broadly or narrowly defined and *time periods* can be long or short.

When buyers' incomes and tastes as well as the prices of closely related commodities are held constant, attention centers on the relation between demand and price. A *demand schedule* is a list of possible prices and of quantities that would be bought at each possible price in a market in a period of time. A *demand curve* portrays the demand-price relation. The *law of demand* causes a demand curve to have a *negative slope;* exceptions are rare and unimportant. An *increase in demand* means that the entire demand curve shifts to the right; a decrease in demand is a shift to the left. Demand curves shift or change because of changes in consumer desires, in consumer incomes, and in the prices of substitutes and complements.

The concept of the demand curve has wide application. The concept contributes to clear thinking on issues that are often in a state of confusion.

## SELECTED REFERENCES

Alfred Marshall, *Principles of Economics,* 8th ed. (London: Macmillan, 1920), Book III, Chaps. 1, 2, 3. A good interpretation is to be found in

Milton Friedman, "The Marshallian Demand Curve," *Journal of Political Economy,* Vol. LVII, December, 1949, pp. 463–495; reprinted in Milton Friedman, *Essays in Positive Economics* (Chicago: University of Chicago Press, 1953). Demand analysis for the business firm is presented by Joel Dean, *Managerial Economics* (New York: Prentice-Hall, 1951), Chap. 4. The classic work on empirical demand study is Henry Schultz, *The Theory and Measurement of Demand* (Chicago: University of Chicago Press, 1938).

## EXERCISES AND PROBLEMS

1. Exercises in the definition of commodities: Divide each of the following commodities into its groups and subgroups, and describe the characteristics of demand as the process of subdivision is carried on: Books, furniture, pens, recreation, soft drinks, trucks.

2. The demand for a commodity is affected by other prices. Describe the relevant *other* prices for the following commodities: Air transportation, bricks, fresh orange juice, high-test gasoline, natural gas.

3. Practice drawing demand curves. For example, take the nationwide annual demand for new automobiles. Start a demand curve with 6 million cars at $2500. Then, with price assumed to be the only variable affecting purchases, make guesses as to other points on the demand curve. Practice reading a demand curve from both axes: How many cars would be bought at $2800? What would the price have to be if 8 million cars are to be bought?

4. Construct a hypothetical demand curve for pay television. Suppose there are 100,000 television sets in private homes in a metropolitan area and that all of the sets are equipped to receive special programs on payment of a fee. Suppose too that pay television has been in existence long enough for its novelty to wear off. Let the "commodity" be high-quality first-run movies, one being broadcast each week. Let the possible fees for seeing any one of these movies on pay television be 25¢, or 50¢, or 75¢, or $1.00, etc. Make up a plausible demand schedule — the number of thousands of sets turned on to pay TV in an average week.

5. People need medical care. Of that, there can be no doubt. But what about demand? For simplicity and convenience, let a unit of medical care be defined as one consultation with a physician. Would people buy the same number of units of medical care at $10 each as they would at $2 each? As many at $25 each as at $10? Construct a hypothetical demand schedule for medical care in a community of 10,000 families. In your demand schedule, include a fee of $0, i.e., free medical care. Write a short statement in explanation of your hypothetical estimate.

6. Draw a diagram to show the position of a retailer who at the end of a season announces reduced prices to clear his stocks. In your diagram show a relation between the price reduction and the stocks the dealer wants to get rid of.

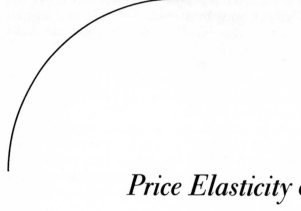

# Price Elasticity of Demand

## 3

So far, demand has been described as the inverse relation between price and quantity. At lower prices, more is bought. But how much more? A great deal or just a little? To answer questions like these is to make use of the concept of price elasticity of demand. Broadly, demand is elastic if quantity is highly responsive to price, and inelastic if it is not.

### The Meaning of Elasticity

Price elasticity of demand is one of a family of concepts of elasticity. In economics, elasticity always means a ratio of the relative changes in two quantities. Alfred Marshall was the first economist to give a clear formulation of price elasticity as the ratio of a relative change in quantity to a relative change in price. Let $E$ stand for elasticity. Then

$$E = \frac{\text{relative change in quantity}}{\text{relative change in price}} .$$

Equivalently, elasticity is the percentage change in quantity divided by the percentage change in price. If the percentages are known — they can often be estimated — then the numerical size of $E$ can be calculated. Suppose the percentages are 2 for quantity and 1 for price, and that the price falls. Since it falls, price changes by minus 1 per cent. Then

$$E = \frac{2\%}{-1\%} = -2.$$

If, instead, price goes up, the *quantity* change is minus 2 per cent. Therefore $E$ is always negative; because it is, the minus sign can henceforth be disregarded. To do so is common practice.

Other elasticity concepts occurring in demand analysis are income elasticity and cross elasticity, and the elasticity of price expectations. They are discussed in Chapters 6 and 7. In what now follows, price elasticity will simply be called elasticity. To do this accords with the custom of economists; the several elasticity concepts can hardly be confused and are easily distinguished when the context calls for it.

Why does the definition of elasticity express the changes in quantity and price as *relative* changes? The reason is that a given absolute change can be relatively large or relatively small. Suppose a price goes up by five cents. This is a relatively large increase for chewing gum or for a newspaper. But a five-cent price increase is relatively small if it applies to an electric appliance or to a suit of clothes. Similarly, a change in quantity of a thousand bushels is relatively large if it applies to a rare herb and is extremely small if it applies to wheat.

### The Coefficient of Elasticity

$E$ is also called the coefficient of elasticity of demand. It is a pure number, that is, it stands by itself, being independent of units of measurement. When numerical estimates are possible, the coefficients of elasticity of different commodities can be directly compared. Another common way to state the coefficient of elasticity of demand is as follows:

$$E = \frac{\Delta Q}{Q} \div \frac{\Delta P}{P} = \frac{\Delta Q}{Q} \times \frac{P}{\Delta P} = \frac{P}{Q} \frac{\Delta Q}{\Delta P}.$$

Here, $Q$ is quantity, $P$ is price, and $\Delta$ (delta) is the symbol meaning "a change in." Thus, $\frac{\Delta Q}{Q}$ is a relative change in quantity, and $\frac{\Delta P}{P}$ is a relative change in price.

To continue with definitions: If the coefficient $E$ is greater than 1, demand is said to be elastic. If $E$ equals 1, demand has unit elasticity. If $E$ is less than 1, but more than 0, demand is inelastic. If the coefficient is zero, demand is said to be perfectly inelastic. A zero coefficient means that a change in price is accompanied by no change — at all — in the quantity bought. Hence $\Delta Q$ is zero, making the whole fraction zero.

If a change in price causes an infinitely large change in quantity, then $\Delta Q$ in the fraction is infinitely large. This gives the coefficient the value of infinity. When the coefficient is infinity, demand is said to be infinitely, or perfectly, elastic. Because he sells so small a part of the total, the demand for the wheat of any *one* wheat farmer is perfectly elastic at the prevailing price. This means that the farmer can sell all he has at that price without causing the price to change. He could sell no more at less than the prevailing price, and nothing at all at any higher price.

### Elasticity and Expenditure

If demand is elastic, a given fall in price causes a relatively larger increase in the amount bought. From this it follows that a drop in price causes consumers to make a larger money expenditure on a commodity whose demand is elastic. If demand is inelastic, a fall in price causes consumers to spend less money on the commodity. And if demand has unit elasticity, a fall in price causes no change in expenditures.

These relations can be illustrated with simple hypothetical demand schedules. This is done in Table 3–1, which contains three demand schedules. Each has the same prices, but the quantities are different, being so chosen as to make the demand schedules elastic, unit-elastic, and inelastic.

#### TABLE 3–1

#### Demand Schedules with Different Elasticities

| Elastic Demand | | | Unit-Elastic Demand | | | Inelastic Demand | | |
|---|---|---|---|---|---|---|---|---|
| *P* | *Q* | *PQ* | *P* | *Q* | *PQ* | *P* | *Q* | *PQ* |
| $10 | 1,000 units | $10,000 | $10 | 900 units | $9,000 | $10 | 1,000 units | $10,000 |
| 9 | 2,000 units | 18,000 | 9 | 1,000 units | 9,000 | 9 | 1,050 units | 9,450 |
| 8 | 3,000 units | 24,000 | 8 | 1,125 units | 9,000 | 8 | 1,100 units | 8,800 |

Note: *PQ* is price multiplied by quantity, and is therefore the total dollar expenditure by consumers, at each price.

Table 3–1 has one flaw, though an unavoidable one. In the unit-elastic demand schedule, the relative changes in price and in quantity are close, but are not exactly identical. A change in price from $10 to $9 is a drop of 10 per cent, but the corresponding increase in quantity bought is 11-1/9 per cent. The discrepancy results from the choice of discrete numbers — after all, 9 and 10 are far apart, farther apart than 9.9 and 10, which are farther apart than 9.99 and 10, and so on. Often popping up in arithmetical illustrations of economic relations, such discrepancies are not serious, but they cause arithmetic to be an awkward servant.

The relations between elasticity and expenditure are stated in more general form in Table 3–2.

**TABLE 3–2**

### Elasticity and Expenditure

|  | Elastic | Unit Elasticity | Inelastic | Perfectly Inelastic |
|---|---|---|---|---|
| Value of coefficient | $>1$ | $1$ | $<1>0$ | $0$ |
| Effect of fall in price | $\dfrac{\Delta Q}{Q}>\dfrac{\Delta P}{P}$ <br> larger expenditure | $\dfrac{\Delta Q}{Q}=\dfrac{\Delta P}{P}$ <br> constant expenditure | $\dfrac{\Delta Q}{Q}<\dfrac{\Delta P}{P}$ <br> smaller expenditure | $\Delta Q=0$ <br> fall in expenditure is proportional to fall in price |
| Effect of rise in price | $\dfrac{\Delta Q}{Q}>\dfrac{\Delta P}{P}$ <br> smaller expenditure | $\dfrac{\Delta Q}{Q}=\dfrac{\Delta P}{P}$ <br> constant expenditure | $\dfrac{\Delta Q}{Q}<\dfrac{\Delta P}{P}$ <br> larger expenditure | $\Delta Q=0$ <br> rise in expenditure is proportional to rise in price |

Notes: The symbol $>$ means "greater than," and the symbol $<$ means "less than." Thus in the first row above, under inelastic, $<1>0$ means less than 1 but greater than 0. For example, the coefficient can be anywhere between 0.9 and 0.1.

### Elastic and Inelastic Demand Curves

Elasticity and inelasticity of demand can be easily portrayed through demand curves. Figure 3–1 shows five demand curves of differing elasticities. Elastic demand is drawn as a curve that is relatively flat, whereas

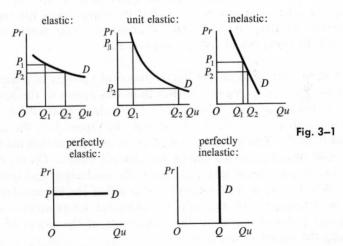

Differing Elasticities of Demand

Fig. 3–1

the curve for an inelastic demand is relatively steep. Price changes are shown in the upper part of Figure 3–1. Suppose that price falls from $P_1$ to $P_2$. Then quantity increases from $Q_1$ to $Q_2$. Total dollar expenditures of the buyers are the *rectangles* — prices multiplied by quantities. In the elastic demand, the rectangle $P_2Q_2$ is bigger than the rectangle $P_1Q_1$, signifying a larger total expenditure at the lower price. The opposite is true of the inelastic demand. When demand is unit elastic at all prices, the rectangles have exactly the same areas. A demand curve with unit elasticity is called a *rectangular hyperbola*. The lower part of Figure 3–1 shows a perfectly elastic demand curve which is a horizontal line, and a perfectly inelastic demand curve which is a vertical line.

Four warnings must now be uttered. The first is that to portray elastic demand as a relatively flat curve and inelastic demand as a relatively steep curve is a convention accurate enough for some purposes, but not for others. If, as is often true, it matters in an economic problem only whether demand is elastic or inelastic, a flat curve or a steep curve will do. But if a problem makes it important to take a close look at elasticity, slope turns out to be a poor or even a wrong measure.[1] After all, the slope of a demand curve is $\dfrac{\Delta P}{\Delta Q}$, whereas elasticity is $\dfrac{P\,\Delta Q}{Q\,\Delta P}$. These reminders lead to the idea of varying elasticities on the same demand curve, an idea that will be discussed shortly.

The second warning is about the scales on the axes of the diagram. If elastic demand is to be represented by a flat curve, the scales have to be in order. If the price axis has the scale 10, 9, 8, etc., and if the quantity axis has the scale 1, 2, 3, etc., then the curve is relatively flat — over that range of prices and quantities. But if the same prices are coupled with quantities of 101, 102, 103, etc., demand of course would be inelastic, though the curve would still be relatively flat.

A third warning is on the interpretation of changes in prices. Suppose that the price of a commodity rises from one month to the next and that less is bought at the higher price. From these facts alone, no certain inference about elasticity can be drawn. In Figure 3–2, the price rise is from $P_1$ to $P_2$. This could be caused by an *increase* in demand from $D_1$ to $D_2$; both of these demand curves are relatively elastic. On the other hand, the rise in price could take place along the unchanged and inelastic curve $D_3$. Whether the demand remains unchanged or has increased is something to be estimated with the help of additional information — on buyers' incomes and tastes, and on the movements of the prices of substitutes during the month in question.

---

[1] When a demand curve is plotted on double logarithmic paper, slope does become an exact measure of elasticity, because double log scales compare percentage changes. See Note 5 in the Appendix to Part Two.

The fourth warning is about another kind of misinterpretation, namely, drawing wrong conclusions from reflection on personal experience. Suppose, for example, that the bus fare goes up 10 cents and that despite this, you keep on riding the bus just as often as before. It is wrong to leap to the conclusion that the demand for bus service is *therefore* perfectly or highly inelastic. The demand for bus service comes from thousands of people in the city. Their mass response to the change in fare is the demand behavior under examination here. The theory of the behavior of the individual consumer is in Chapter 4 and 6. One of the differences between the behavior of people en masse and as individuals is in the response to changes in price. The mass, or market, demand for a commodity can be elastic, even though the demands of many of the buyers are inelastic. Part of the explanation for this can be found in the concept of "petty goods."[2] These are commodities so cheap that consumers do not try to economize in buying them; demands for them are highly inelastic. But what is a petty good for you is not necessarily petty for me. People differ in temperament, incomes, and social patterns of behavior.

### Arc and Point Elasticity

So far, the terms "elastic" and "inelastic" have been applied to the whole demand for a commodity. This is accurate enough for some purposes, but not for others, because the demand for a commodity can be elastic in one price range and inelastic in another. The degree of elasticity or of inelasticity — as indicated by the size of the coefficient — can also vary from one price range to another.

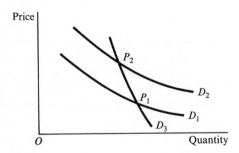

**Fig. 3–2**

[2] Ruby Turner Norris, *The Theory of Consumer's Demand,* rev. ed. (New Haven: Yale University Press, 1952), pp. 69–72.

Figures 3–3 and 3–4 show two demand curves. Notice that the demand curve in Figure 3–3 is elastic at high prices and inelastic at low prices. The demand curve in Figure 3–4 is just the opposite. Both kinds of demand curves are possible.

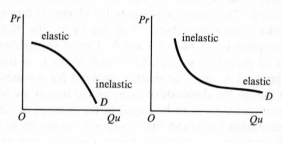

Elasticities and Price Ranges

**Fig. 3–3**          **Fig. 3–4**

But by itself, price range is not a precise expression. Suppose it is something definite, as it often is in practical problems. For example, what is the elasticity of demand for gasoline in the price range of 34 to 36 cents per gallon? To ask this kind of question is to ask about arc elasticity. An arc is a portion of a curved line, hence a portion or segment of a demand curve. Arc elasticity is the elasticity at the mid-point of an arc of a demand curve. If numerical estimates of the demand for a commodity are available, then the arc elasticity between two prices can be estimated. The usual formula for arc elasticity is $\dfrac{Q_1 - Q_2}{Q_1 + Q_2} \div \dfrac{P_1 - P_2}{P_1 + P_2}$. In this formula, $P_1$ and $P_2$ are two prices, and $Q_1$ and $Q_2$ are the corresponding quantities.[3]

---

[3] This formula is needed because the formula $\dfrac{\Delta Q}{Q} \div \dfrac{\Delta P}{P}$ gives different results depending on whether the price is raised or lowered. Suppose the prices are 10 and 8 and the quantities 1 and 3. A price reduction is a drop of 20 per cent, but a price rise is 25 per cent. And an increase in quantity is 200 per cent, whereas a decline in quantity is 66-2/3 per cent. With the formula $\dfrac{\Delta Q}{Q} \div \dfrac{\Delta P}{P}$, the price reduction results in a coefficient of $\frac{2}{1} \div \frac{2}{10} = 2 \times \frac{10}{2} = 10$. A price increase results in a coefficient of $\frac{2}{3} \div \frac{2}{8} = \frac{2}{3} \times \frac{8}{2} = 2\frac{2}{3}$. But the formula $\dfrac{Q_1 - Q_2}{Q_1 + Q_2} \div \dfrac{P_1 - P_2}{P_1 + P_2}$, by taking an average of prices and quantities, gives a better result, namely,

$$\frac{1 - 3}{1 + 3} \div \frac{10 - 8}{10 + 8} = \frac{2}{4} \div \frac{2}{18} = 4\frac{1}{2}.$$

The closer the numbers, the more accurate the coefficient when calculated from this formula. It is not the only one, but the circumstances and particular facts of a practical problem help to dictate the choice of a formula for calculating arc elasticity.

The arc elasticity formula can also be written as

$$\frac{\Delta Q}{Q_1 + Q_2} \div \frac{\Delta P}{P_1 + P_2}$$

This is easier to remember. The two formulas are equivalent because $\Delta Q$ is a difference (a change) in quantities $(Q_1 - Q_2)$ and $\Delta P$ is a difference in price $(P_1 - P_2)$.

If a gasoline pricing problem has to do with the range from 34 to 36 cents per gallon, why not between 34 and 35 cents? Or between 34 and 34-5/10 cents, or between 34 and 34-1/10 cents? Price ranges can indeed be narrowed; in business transactions, prices are occasionally quoted to one ten-thousandth of a cent. Suppose an arc of a demand curve is made smaller and smaller. How small can it be made? Logically, it can be shrunk until it becomes a point on a demand curve. When elasticity is measured at a point on a demand curve, it is called point elasticity of demand.

Point Elasticity of Demand

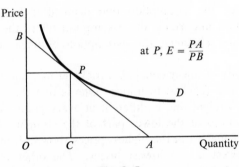

Fig. 3–5

Figure 3–5 shows how to find the elasticity at a point on a demand curve. On the demand curve $D$, take any point, such as $P$. Draw a tangent to the demand curve at point $P$. Then the ratio $\dfrac{PA}{PB}$ is an exact measure of elasticity at point $P$.[4] In Figure 3–5, demand at $P$ is elastic because $PA$ is longer than $PB$. It is about twice as long, so that the coefficient is about 2.

---

[4] Proof: $E = \dfrac{P}{Q} \dfrac{\Delta Q}{\Delta P}$. The term $\dfrac{\Delta Q}{\Delta P}$ is the reciprocal of the slope. The slope of the line $BA$ in Figure 3–5 is $\dfrac{PC}{CA}$. In Figure 3–5, $P$ is $PC$, $Q$ is $OC$, and $\dfrac{\Delta Q}{\Delta P}$ is $\dfrac{CA}{PC}$. Therefore, $E = \dfrac{PC}{OC} \times \dfrac{CA}{PC} = \dfrac{CA}{OC}$. And since the triangles $PCA$ and $BOA$ are similar, $\dfrac{CA}{OC} = \dfrac{PA}{PB}$.

Point elasticity can also be defined as the ratio of an infinitesimally small relative change in quantity to an infinitesimally small change in price. If an arc is made as small as possible, i.e., shrunk to a point, then the relative changes must be made as small as possible — infinitesimally small. Though the logic of point elasticity is exact, the concept might not at first seem useful. In fact, however, it is useful and has been used many times. In the statistical measurement of demand, quantitative data are fed into mathematical formulas that often contain the point elasticity idea. (See Notes 3 and 4 in the Appendix to Part Two.) If the formulas do a good job of describing the demand for a commodity, they can be used for prediction.

### Elasticity When Demand is Linear

The law of demand requires only that a demand curve slope downward to the right. When discussion is abstract, describing "the" demand for "a" commodity, it is legitimate to take the simplest form of a demand curve. This is the straight line. Demand is then said to be linear. Empirical studies have sometimes found that demands for some actual commodities are linear. Hence the assumption that demand is linear is sometimes realistic. But more important, the assumption offers the convenience of simplicity. In later chapters, the assumption of linear demand will be used frequently.

But the elasticity of linear demand is tricky at first and has to be looked into. There are two features to notice. One is that the (point) elasticity of demand on a straight line is different at every point. Elasticity at any one point is the ratio of the lower part of the straight line to the upper part. Elasticity is highest at the highest prices shown, declines as prices go down, and is lowest at the lowest prices. The other feature, which is important in some applications to be taken up in later chapters, is this: If a linear demand moves to the right, shifting parallel to itself, elasticity at any given price diminishes as demand increases.

Figure 3–6 shows the differing elasticities of a linear demand curve. Elasticity is unity at the mid-point between the axes, because the two parts of the line are of course equal in length, with a ratio of unity. Above the mid-point, demand is elastic, because the lower part is longer than the upper part. Below the mid-point, demand is inelastic, the lower part being shorter than the upper. Another way to prove this, and to reinforce the notion of elasticity as a ratio of relative changes, is as follows: Take a price change from $P_1$ to $P_2$ and another from $P_3$ to $P_4$. The price changes are equal *absolutely* and so are the corresponding quantity changes. But they are *not* equal *relatively*. The first price change, $P_1P_2$, has to be measured against $OP_1$; the second change, $P_3P_4$, against $OP_3$. Similarly with the quantity changes: $Q_1Q_2$ against $OQ_1$, and $Q_3Q_4$ against $OQ_3$.

Another glance at Figure 3–6 shows that the first price change is relatively smaller than the corresponding quantity change. Hence, demand here is elastic. The second price change, $P_3P_4$, is relatively larger than the corresponding change in quantity; therefore, demand is inelastic.

Figure 3–6 has four rectangles, showing consumer expenditures at each of the four prices. The second expenditure rectangle is larger than the first, but the fourth is smaller than the third. The sizes of the rectangles therefore also show the differences in elasticities.

Elasticity of Linear Demand

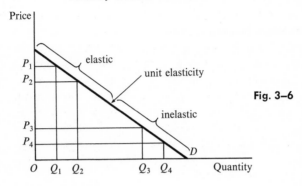

**Fig. 3–6**

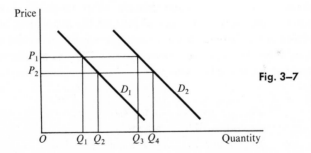

Elasticity and Change
in Linear Demand

**Fig. 3–7**

Figure 3–7 shows an increase in a linear demand from $D_1$ to $D_2$. The two demand curves are parallel, signifying that the quantity increases at each price are equal. But at any price or range of prices, $D_2$ is less elastic (or more inelastic) than $D_1$. Here is the proof: The quantity change $Q_1Q_2$ is relatively larger than $Q_3Q_4$ although their absolute sizes are the same, because $Q_1Q_2$ is larger, measured against $OQ_1$, than $Q_3Q_4$ measured against $OQ_3$. To generalize: Increases in demand cause the elasticities at a price to become steadily smaller. So expressed, the generalization holds for curved as well as for straight lines.

### The Determinants of Elasticity

What makes the demand for one commodity elastic and the demand for another inelastic? The determinants of the price elasticity of demand for a commodity can be put under three headings: (1) the number and kinds of its substitutes, (2) the commodity's position in buyers' budgets, and (3) the number of its uses.

Of the three determinants, a commodity's substitutes are the most important. If a commodity has many close substitutes, its demand is almost certain to be elastic, perhaps highly so. If price goes up, consumers buy less of the commodity and buy more of its substitutes. If its price goes down, consumers desert the substitutes and buy the commodity in (relatively) much larger quantities. So far, so good. But again, the real question is the definition of a commodity. The more narrowly and the more specifically a commodity is defined, the more close substitutes it has and the more elastic is the demand for it. The demand for a particular brand of mentholated toothpaste is more elastic than the demand for mentholated toothpaste, which is more elastic than the demand for toothpaste in general, which is more elastic than the demand for dentifrices (pastes, powders, and liquids). The pattern is similar throughout the entire range of commodities.

If a commodity is so defined that it has perfect substitutes, then its elasticity of demand is perfect, or infinite. Suppose the commodity is the wheat produced by one wheat farmer. This particular wheat does have perfect substitutes, namely, the wheat produced by other wheat farmers. If the one wheat grower tried to sell his wheat above the going price at any one time, he could sell none at all. The coefficient of elasticity of demand for *his* wheat is infinity.

The position of a commodity in buyers' budgets also influences its elasticity. Budget position means the fraction of total expenditures devoted to a single commodity. The demands for soap, salt, matches, ink, and for many other similar commodities are highly inelastic, because the typical household spends only a few cents a week on each of them. The percentages of family budgets devoted to such commodities are exceedingly small. Observe, however, that the demands for such commodities are inelastic, not perfectly inelastic.

The more uses a commodity can be put to, the more elastic its demand. If a commodity has only a few uses, its demand is likely to be inelastic. The various uses of any commodity can be imagined as standing in a hierarchy. If the price of a commodity is very high, consumers will put the few units they buy only to the most important use of the commodity. At successively lower prices, more of the commodity is bought, to be devoted to the less important uses. Any cookbook shows a multitude of uses for eggs, a fact tending to make the demand for them elastic.

Any judgment of the elasticity of the demand for a commodity must take all three determinants into account. They can reinforce one another, or work in opposite directions. A commodity can have several uses, but no close substitutes. Another commodity with many substitutes can have a low position in consumers' budgets.

### Time and Elasticity

The demand for a commodity always exists in some period of time, which can be a day, a week, a month, a season, a year, or a period of several years. Elasticity of demand varies with the length of time periods. In general, demand is more elastic (or less inelastic) the longer the period of time. The longer the period of time, the greater is the ease of substitution for both consumers and business firms. If, for example, the price of fuel oil should rise but not the prices of other fuels, it is likely that the consumption of fuel oil in the month after the price increase would diminish very little. The demand for fuel oil in any one month, then, is probably highly inelastic. But the demand over a year is certain to be less inelastic or perhaps slightly elastic, because a year is long enough for people building new houses and renovating old houses to change their plans about the kinds of furnaces to install. Over a period of, say, five years or more, the demand for fuel oil is probably highly elastic, because such a period is long enough to permit full substitution.

Another illustration of the importance of time as an influence on elasticity comes from a statistical study of the demand for meat.[5] The study shows that the retail demand for meat is slightly inelastic in the short run. The short run here means the year-to-year demand.[6] But the long-run retail demand for meat is elastic. One of the meanings of these findings is this: Suppose something happened to cause the amount of meat produced to be curtailed and held at a lower level for several years. If the demand for meat were stable, the price would first rise and would then eventually fall, relatively less than the decline in the amount. Consumers would spend less on meat (because the demand in the long run is elastic), and therefore of course the meat industry would have smaller receipts. These matters are

[5] Elmer J. Working, *Demand for Meat* (Chicago: Institute of Meat Packing, 1954), pp. xi, 79, 87. This study was a result of a cooperative research project of the Institute of Meat Packing, the University of Chicago, and the University of Illinois.

[6] In later chapters the expressions short run and long run will be assigned somewhat different meanings.

illustrated in Figure 3–8. The year-to-year demand is $D_S$ and the long-run demand is $D_L$. Let the initial price and quantity be $P_1$ and $OQ_1$. Then the quantity falls to $OQ_2$, remaining there a long time. The price first rises from $P_1$ to $P_2$. But over the course of time, the demand curve swings to its long-run position and the price falls to $P_3$.

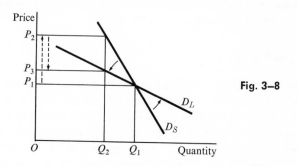

Fig. 3–8

## Applications

Many of the applications of the concept of price elasticity of demand have to do with pricing decisions of business firms or of government agencies that directly or indirectly regulate prices. All too often decisions on prices fail to take elasticity into account, or give it insufficient attention. Changes in costs usually dominate decisions on prices; costs can be calculated, and higher costs usually seem to be a valid justification for higher prices. Even if demand and its elasticity cannot always be calculated, they should not be ignored or taken for granted.

### Estimating Elasticities

If a decision to raise or lower a price is going to be based in part on the elasticity of demand for the commodity or service, then of course the decision-maker has to have some idea of the size of the coefficient. He need not think of elasticity quite in this way, but he does have to have an estimate of how a change in price affects the expenditures of the buyers. These expenditures of course are the same amounts as the total revenues of the seller (or sellers).

Quantitative estimates of coefficients of elasticity can be made if there are enough data on past prices and quantities, and if there are no obstacles to interpretation. Hundreds of such estimates have been made. Some of them are the fruits of sophisticated statistical analyses that yield precise numerical values of coefficients of elasticity. Others are simple direct tests to see merely if a demand is elastic or inelastic. Occasionally, experiments are possible. Bottles of ink can be sold at 15 cents retail in some cities and at 25 cents in other cities during the same period of time. The differences in sales show if the demand is elastic or inelastic in this range of prices. The main analytical task is to isolate the effects of price changes on quantities bought. These effects must be isolated from those of the other influences — changes in income, changes in the prices of related goods, and changes in taste.

### Economic Policy

The farm policies of the federal government include the objective of raising farm prices. Higher prices result in higher gross incomes for farmers because the demands for most farm products are inelastic, as is well known from empirical studies. If government keeps part of a crop off the market, the ensuing rise in gross income to the farmers depends on just *how* inelastic the demand that year actually is. Inelasticity of demand is also the explanation of "the paradox of plenty," namely, that a bountiful crop brings a *smaller* total revenue to its growers. Suppose for the moment that the demand for a particular farm product were elastic. To raise the gross incomes of these farmers, would the federal government try to raise the price of this product by keeping some of it off the market? No, because to do this with an elastic demand would be to lower gross incomes.

Economic policies directed to increasing exports must also take account of elasticities of demand. Suppose that a country expands the physical volume of its exports by lowering their prices, e.g., by devaluation of its currency. If the country is unlucky, the demands for its exports are inelastic. If they are, the money receipts from more physical exports become smaller, not larger.

In the middle 1930's, the Interstate Commerce Commission ordered the railroads in the eastern part of the country to lower their passenger coach fares. The railroads resisted the order, believing that they would suffer a loss of gross revenue. But the ICC insisted, and proved to be right. In that period, the demand for coach service was indeed elastic, the coefficient being approximately 2.0. Hence the eastern railroads enjoyed a larger, not a smaller, gross revenue from the cut in fares they were at first reluctant to make. Another example from the 1930's was the dispute over the elasticity of demand for electricity in the Tennessee Valley and neighboring regions. The Tennessee Valley Authority thought that the demand was elastic and proceeded to set its prices low. The neighboring private power companies at first disagreed, but later they too found advantage in reducing their rates. True enough the demand was growing, but it was also elastic. Like anyone else, however, government agencies can make wrong estimates of elasticity. In 1960, the Commonwealth of Virginia raised the prices of alcoholic beverages sold in its stores by 10 per cent. In the first year, total revenue fell off, the demand evidently being elastic.

### Business

Businessmen seem to think that demand is inelastic. Such, at least, is the impression conveyed by many public and private statements by businessmen on their pricing policies. The common experience has been to see price increases followed by larger gross revenues and to see price decreases associated with smaller gross revenues. But price increases often occur when demand curves shift to the right, just as price decreases are often made when demand curves shift to the left. It was shown earlier with the help of Figure 3–2 on page 35 that people can easily misinterpret experience, confuse shifts of demand curves with differences in position on a demand curve, and therefore fall into the belief that demand is inelastic.

Empirical studies have often showed that demand is elastic where a rough guess would lead to the opposite conclusion. The demand for subway transportation in New York City, for example, is elastic.

A business firm producing and selling many different products usually finds marked differences in elasticities from one product to another. The products sell in different markets and face different kinds of substitutes in each. For example, take three steel products. There is no close substitute for steel rails. Hence the demand for them is highly inelastic, but it is not perfectly inelastic because a response to high prices could be to make old rails last longer. Stainless steel, on the other hand, does have close substitutes in some of its uses. Tin plate faces close competition from plastics, glass, and other materials employed to package beer, oils, paint, and some food products. A principle of profit maximization is that if a firm prices its products by adding a percentage markup to costs, the markup should vary from one product to another in accordance with the elasticities of demand for the separate products.[7]

Just as businessmen sometimes err in their beliefs about elasticity, so do the critics of business. The prices and price policies of the key industries, particularly those dominated by large corporations, are under constant public scrutiny. From time to time, public criticism hits on elasticity, though of course the word elasticity is seldom heard. The critics urge that this or that industry or large corporation should, in its own interest, lower its prices, because to do so would much expand consumption with benefits to both consumers and employees. In short, demand is believed to be elastic. In the late 1930's, the steel industry came under a barrage of

---

[7] This principle is explained at greater length in Chapter 19.

criticism for failing to price its products so as to stabilize production and employment. But careful statistical investigations showed that the demand for "steel" — all the thousands of steel products considered as if they were one commodity — is probably fairly inelastic. In 1957, Walter Reuther of the United Automobile Workers publicly urged the automobile industry to reduce prices by $100 per car, adding that a million more cars would therefore be sold. This amounted to saying that the coefficient of the elasticity of demand for automobiles is about 4.0 ($100 was a price cut of about 4 per cent, and one million more cars was an increase in sales of about 16 per cent). Statistical studies of the demand for automobiles show, however, that elasticity varies from year to year, with the coefficient ranging from about 0.5 to about 1.5. The coefficient has been more often above 1.0 than below it.

### Summary

Price elasticity of demand is the ratio of a relative change in quantity to a relative change in price. The *coefficient of elasticity, E,* is found by dividing the relative change in quantity by the corresponding relative change in price. If $E > 1$, demand is *elastic.* If $E = 1$, demand has *unit elasticity.* If $E < 1$, demand is *inelastic.* If $E$ equals infinity, demand is *perfectly elastic.* And if $E$ equals zero, demand is *perfectly inelastic.* Elasticity is related to expenditure: If a decline in price causes an increase in expenditure, demand is elastic; if a decrease, demand is inelastic.

A demand curve can have different elasticities. *Arc elasticity* measures elasticity at the mid-point of an arc of a demand curve. *Point elasticity* is a measure at a point on a demand curve; the ratio of the lower to the upper part of a tangent to a demand curve is the elasticity at the point of tangency. A *linear demand curve* has a different elasticity at every point.

Whether the demand for a commodity is elastic or inelastic depends on the number and closeness of its *substitutes.* A commodity's *position in consumers' budgets* and the *number of its uses* also influence its elasticity. *Time* is another determinant; the longer the period of time, the more elastic (or the less inelastic) is the demand for a commodity.

Knowledge of elasticity is important in business pricing decisions and in the execution, as well as the appraisal, of economic policies affecting prices.

### SELECTED REFERENCES

Alfred Marshall, *Principles of Economics,* 8th ed. (London: Macmillan, 1920), Book III, Chap. 4. A. C. Pigou, *Alfred Marshall and Current*

*Thought* (London: Macmillan, 1953), Part I, Lecture III. Joel Dean, *Managerial Economics* (New York: Prentice-Hall, 1951), Chap. 4. Milton H. Spencer and Louis Siegelman, *Managerial Economics* (Homewood: Irwin, 1959), Chap. 5. Ruby Turner Norris, *The Theory of Consumer's Demand,* rev. ed. (New Haven: Yale University Press: 1952), Chap. 9.

## EXERCISES AND PROBLEMS

1. Water is essential to life. But the demand for it at prices now prevailing is probably highly elastic. Why?

2. The demand for salt in some countries has been found to be elastic. Explain how this could be so.

3. Suppose that in year 1 the federal excise tax on cigarettes is doubled, and that in year 3 the total revenue from the cigarette tax is twice as high as in year 1. What conclusions about the demand for cigarettes can be drawn?

4. A useful exercise: Take the demand schedule where prices are 10¢, 9¢, 8¢, etc. and quantities are 1, 2, 3, etc. units. Imagine that the price falls. Use the arc elasticity formula to work out the elasticities for each drop in price from 10¢ to 9¢, etc. all the way down to 2¢ to 1¢.

5. Consider this demand schedule:

| P | Q |
|------|-----|
| 4.00 | 7.0 |
| 3.75 | 8.0 |
| 3.50 | 9.0 |
| 3.25 | 9.5 |

Imagine that this is the demand for bus transportation in an area. The prices are the average fares in cents per passenger mile; the quantities are millions of passenger miles per month. Suppose the practical problem is one of lowering fares. What is the coefficient of elasticity of demand at 3.75 cents? At 3.50 cents? What could cause the difference in the values of the coefficients?

# Neoclassical Utility

# and Consumer Demand

4

THE MEANING OF UTILITY · TOTAL UTILITY AND MARGINAL UTILITY
· THE EQUIMARGINAL PRINCIPLE · THE MARGINAL UTILITY OF
MONEY INCOME · EQUILIBRIUM OF THE CONSUMER · INTER-
PERSONAL COMPARISONS OF UTILITY · APPLICATIONS ·

The demand curves for consumer goods described in Chapters 2 and 3
are market, or aggregate, demand curves. They are composed of the
demand curves of many individual consumers. The behavior of the individual consumer is the subject of this chapter and of the next two. This
one confines itself to the neoclassical utility analysis of consumer demand.
The concept of utility, which will be defined shortly, was employed by the
classical economists of the late eighteenth and nineteenth centuries. The
twentieth-century version of the concept is the neoclassical.

The words "consumer" and "individual," need a brief explanation.
These words will be used here to mean a consuming (or spending) unit
with a budget. The unit can consist of one person or of the two or more
persons in a family. The one budget for the unit is the essential thing for
the purposes of the theory of consumer demand or "theory of consumption" as it is also called. How the members of a family come to their
joint decisions on the family budget is, fortunately, a matter that does not
have to be gone into here. Consuming units are also referred to as households. Simple models of an enterprise economy can be built on the assump-

tion that the economy consists of households and firms — consuming units and producing units. Just as the household is imagined as having one decision-maker, who is *the* consumer, so the firm is imagined as being guided by one decision-maker, the entrepreneur. Another point: The consumer will be referred to as "he" for the sake of convenience, even though most retail purchases are said to be made by women.

### The Meaning of Utility

With given prices of commodities and services, and with a given income, a consumer makes his purchases according to his tastes (or desires, or preferences, or wants — these words are synonyms in this context). A consumer desires a unit of commodity $A$ more than he desires a unit of commodity $B$ because commodity $A$ has more utility to him. Utility means want-satisfying power. It is some property common to all commodities wanted by a person. Utility resides in the mind of the consumer. The consumer knows it by introspection. Utility is subjective, not objective. A commodity does not have to be useful in the ordinary sense of that word; the commodity might satisfy a frivolous desire or even one that some people would consider immoral. The concept is ethically neutral.

Neoclassical utility is descended from the long obsolete pain-and-pleasure psychology of the nineteenth century. Utility also had associations with the social philosophy of utilitarianism and its slogan, "the greatest happiness of the greatest number." For these and other reasons to be mentioned later, the concept was under heavy attack for several decades. But utility is a sturdy idea. Its simplicity and common-sense appeal cause it not just to survive, but to thrive. In its neoclassical version, utility has lost all but the faintest vestiges of pretense as a premise taken over from psychology. Unlike their classical forebears, modern economic theorists are not amateur psychologists. Modern theorists do not profess to *know* why people buy things. Theorists now make only the modest *assumption* that people buy things because of utility.

### Cardinal and Ordinal Utility

Neoclassical utility and the ideas treated in Chapter 5 are concepts of *cardinal* utility, whereas Chapter 6 discusses *ordinal* utility. The terms cardinal and ordinal are borrowed from the vocabulary of mathematics. The numbers 1, 2, 3, etc. are cardinal numbers. The number 2, for example, is twice the size of number 1. In contrast, the numbers 1st, 2nd, 3rd, etc. are ordinal numbers. Such numbers are ordered, or ranked, and there is no way of knowing, just from the ranking, what is the size relation of the numbers. The second one might or might not be twice as big as the first one. The ordinal numbers 1st, 2nd, and 3rd *could* be 10, 20, and 30, or they *could* be 1, 1,000, and 1,000,000.

To use the concept of cardinal utility is to assume that quantities of utility are meaningful, that it makes sense to say, for example, that you get twice as much satisfaction from a cup of coffee as from a glass of milk. On the other hand, the concept of ordinal utility permits you to say only that you *prefer* a cup of coffee to a glass of milk. But ordinal utility does not let you compare quantities of satisfaction or utility.

Why not? Economists who insist on using the concept of ordinal utility maintain that quantities of utility are inherently immeasurable, theoretically and conceptually, as well as practically. The same economists also maintain that many aspects of the theory of consumer behavior can be explained without the idea of measurable utility.

Neoclassical cardinal utility carries with it the assumption of measurability. The units of measurement are imaginary; they are called "utils." Thus, under some given conditions, someone thinks of one apple as having 4 utils and an orange as having 2 utils. This is just another way of saying that one apple has twice as much utility as one orange.

### Rational Behavior

When he behaves rationally, the consumer calculates deliberately, chooses consistently, and maximizes utility. Deliberate choice sets aside the role of habit. Of course, we all do buy many things every week out of sheer habit. Habit is the great economizer of mental energy. But to take habit into account is to begin to look at an enormous variety of patterns of human behavior. The assumption of deliberate calculations — the thoughts of exceedingly thrifty persons — avoids a formidable difficulty. Consistent choice rules out vacillating and erratic behavior. If a person prefers $A$ to $B$, and $B$ to $C$, then consistency compels him to prefer $A$ to $C$. The maximization of utility means that the consumer makes those choices that will result in his having the greatest possible amount of utility — given his circumstances.

True enough, the consumer is often ignorant about the best way to satisfy his own wants. More important than that is the insufficient and imperfect knowledge that most consumers have about many of the products they buy. Then too, it is a common experience to be disappointed by a purchase — to find that the utility enjoyed is less than the utility that had been anticipated. But ignorance, imperfect knowledge, and the gap between expectations and fulfillment are also set aside in the theory of consumer behavior, again for the sake of simplicity. The concept of utility carries with it the further assumption that wants and the subjective utilities of commodities are not influenced by prices, in the sense that the prices of commodities are assumed not to influence evaluations of their desirabilities. This assumption puts a heavy strain on the imagination. Who can be sure that he could draw up a list of his wants and of the commodities to satisfy them, a list that would not be affected in the least by his knowledge of prices? Wants are influenced by reflection on experience, and such reflection can hardly be free of knowledge of the relative prices of commodities.

### Total Utility and Marginal Utility

The next step is to examine the relation between utility and quantity. Consider a consumer and one of the commodities he wants. Imagine that the consumer contemplates 1, 2, 3, etc. units of the commodity. He does not do this in a time sequence, but instead, the consumer thinks what it would be like to have 1 unit, *or* 2, *or* 3, *or* etc. Hence the different quantities are simultaneously existing possibilities.

One unit of the commodity possesses some amount of utility to the consumer. Two units possess more, 3 units still more, and so on. As quantity increases, total utility increases. But total utility increases at a *diminishing* rate. Why this is so will be demonstrated shortly. To increase at diminishing rate means that the successive increases, or increments, become smaller and smaller. Thus, 3 units have more utility than 2, and 4 have more than 3; but the gain in utility from acquiring the fourth unit is less than the gain from acquiring the third. The *marginal utility*[1] of 3 units is the utility of any one of the 3 units — it is the gain or increment from having 3 units instead of 2. To generalize: The marginal utility ($MU$) of any number $n$ is the total utility ($TU$) of that number minus the total utility of one less. Thus: $MU$ of $n = TU$ of $n - TU$ of $(n - 1)$.

Figure 4–1 shows the relations between total utility and marginal utility. In the upper part of the figure, the three bars show increasing total utility. Then the curve takes over and indicates how total utility continues to grow as more units are added. The lower part of the figure displays only the *increases* in total utility, i.e., the marginal utilities of different quantities of the commodity. The marginal utility of any quantity can also be stated as the *slope* of the total utility curve for the same quantity. The slope of the total curve at a point is the gain of utility at that point and is equal to the height of the marginal utility curve at the corresponding quantity.

When the total utility curve reaches the maximum, its slope becomes zero, as shown by the horizontal line that is tangent at the maximum point. Marginal utility is zero when total utility is a maximum; when the total is

---

[1] A note on the word "marginal": This word has been used in economic theory for many decades, always with the same meaning, which is the rate of change of a total. The total can be utility, as above, or cost, revenue, product, etc. Quite another meaning of "marginal" has come into common usage, i.e., marginal as signifying inferior or poor or doubtful. Even economists sometimes use the word in this other sense in ordinary conversation.

a maximum it is neither increasing nor decreasing, and since marginal utility is the increase or decrease, it has to be zero. Finally, when total utility is declining, its increases are negative, which is the same thing as saying that marginal utility is negative.

The economic meaning of zero marginal utility is that you have all you want of the commodity in question. You don't want another unit or two of it because you have enough, nor do you care if you lose a unit because you have so many. Negative marginal utility means that you have so many units of something that you'd rather have fewer; cats, for example.

Total Utility and  Marginal Utility

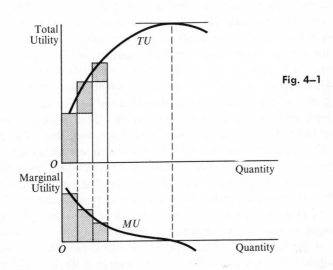

Fig. 4–1

Total utility and marginal utility are just one pair of total-marginal relations. Others will come along in later chapters. The relations between any total and its marginal are the same. The relations are summarized in Table 4–1.

**TABLE  4–1**

*change*

Relations Between Total Quantities and Marginal Quantities

| *When Total Is* | *Then Marginal Is* |
|---|---|
| increasing at a constant rate | constant |
| increasing at an increasing rate | increasing |
| increasing at a decreasing rate | decreasing |
| at a maximum | zero |
| decreasing | negative |

### Diminishing Marginal Utility

Imagine the consumer contemplating all of the commodities he wants and thinking of different quantities of each. For each commodity, diminishing marginal utility prevails. The more you have of anything, the less important to you is any *one* unit of it. So certain is this generalization, because it expresses a universal human experience, that it too is often referred to as a law, the law of diminishing marginal utility.

(The author once asked the students in a class if they could think of any exceptions to the law of diminishing marginal utility. A coed in the front row responded by asking in a quiet and earnest voice, "What about things you can't get enough of, such as love?" This question of course rendered the author speechless. Subsequent reflection, however, has convinced him that economic theory does have something to say, namely, that the marginal utility of a kiss ought never be negative.)

For the law of diminishing marginal utility to hold, certain conditions must exist. The units of the commodity must be relevantly defined. The law holds for pairs of shoes, but not for a single shoe. If the units of a vacation are defined as days, it might be that the second day of a vacation would have more utility than the first. Hence there would be increasing marginal utility for the second and perhaps the third day. But from the fourth day on, additional days would be less and less satisfying. The law holds for individual commodities desired by individual consumers with given tastes. If a consumer's tastes change, so that he likes a commodity more, then the marginal utility of any quantity of that commodity rises. The utilities of commodities are also interdependent. The marginal utility of six oranges a week to a consumer is conditioned by the availability of grapefruit, frozen orange juice, and other citrus products. If they were not available, the marginal utility of six oranges a week would doubtless be higher.

### Indivisible Goods

The diminishing marginal utility of larger quantities of a commodity is clear when the commodity is bought in small units, such as oranges per week, pounds of steak per month, and so on. Such commodities are said to be divisible. But what about the commodities that are bought one at a time at long intervals? Such commodities are indivisible goods — automobiles, television sets, overcoats, etc. And what of the commodities that are bought once (usually) in a lifetime, such as wedding cakes?[2] Most

---

[2] Someone, however, is bound to insist that the law of diminishing marginal utility does indeed apply to a wedding cake, because the bride-to-be and her mother have to decide, among other things, how big the cake should be. The bigger the cake, the more pieces can be served; the more pieces, at least after some number, the less the utility per piece.

indivisible commodities are, however, durable consumer goods, which yield units of service over periods of time — the miles of an automobile, the hours of a radio or television set, the degrees of warmth of a furnace, and so on. The mind of the rationally behaving consumer concentrates on the marginal utilities of the miles per year, of the hours per year, etc., of the so-called indivisible goods. Besides, such goods are typically paid for in installments; the payments stretch out over time, just as do the units of service. Then too, cars and TV sets, to mention just two examples, can be rented by persons who want just a few units of service. Two generations ago, the English economist Philip Wicksteed described with eloquent detail the rules of "economical administration," i.e., rational consumer behavior. With clarity not since surpassed, Wicksteed shows how the thrifty man looks upon the marginal utilities of the services from his watch, his coat, and his piano.

Why does marginal utility diminish? Several kinds of explanations are possible. Some of these are physiological and psychological — too many units of a commodity bring physical satiation, or, the response to a repeated stimulus diminishes. Even though they have been relied on by economists, such explanations lack generality, and anyway are not needed. Another explanation is this: If a consumer could have everything he wants without having to pay anything, he would choose those quantities of each good that would make the marginal utility of each one zero; i.e., he would maximize total utility for each good. Marginal utility would therefore have to diminish to get to zero. If this were not so, the consumer who could have everything free would take infinite quantities of everything. The best explanation, however, is to visualize each commodity as having several uses and to assume that each consumer ranks the uses in his mind. One unit of a commodity is put to its most important use. If the consumer has two units, he devotes one of them to the next most important use, and so on. Marginal utility diminishes because of the successively less important uses of additional quantities of a commodity.

## The Equimarginal Principle

Usually, more than one unit of a commodity can be put to each of its uses. If a consumer possesses some quantity of a commodity, he allocates the units among the several uses of the commodity in such a way as to contribute most to his well-being. The best, or the optimum, allocation is one that causes the marginal utilities in *each* use to be equal. For if this were not so, the consumer could improve his well-being by cutting back in one use and expanding in another. Suppose that a drought causes a farmer's well to yield him very little water and that he has to give careful thought on how to use what he has. In the farmhouse, water is used for drinking, cooking, washing, and for other purposes; elsewhere on the farm, water is given to the animals and is used for cleaning. With very little water, the farmer must be careful with each pint. His final decisions on the allocation of water are such that he could not improve matters by switching a pint from one use to another. The utility of the last pint in each use is equal.

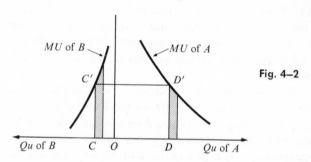

The Equimarginal Principle

Fig. 4–2

A simple illustration of the equimarginal principle is given in Figure 4–2. Here are only two uses for a commodity, $A$ and $B$. The Figure is a Janus diagram; it has two faces that look in opposite directions. Use $A$ is on the right side, and use $B$ is on the left. The curves of marginal utility for each use are shown. The $A$ curve is farther from the vertical axis than the $B$ curve. Thus the desire for use $A$ is stronger — the marginal utility of any quantity of the commodity in use $A$ is greater than that of the same quantity in use $B$. In Figure 4–2, the quantity of the commodity available to the consumer is assumed to be $CD$. The optimum allocation is to put $OD$ units to use $A$; and $OC$ units to use $B$. The equal marginal utilities are $D'D$ and $C'C$. If more of the commodity were devoted to $A$, less would have to be devoted to $B$, and the gain in utility would be less than the loss. The gain in utility is the shaded area to the right of $D'D$; the loss of utility is the shaded area to the right of $C'C$.[3]

## The Marginal Utility of Money Income

The law of diminishing marginal utility applies to money income as well as to goods and services. It is better of course to have $10,000 a year than $5,000. But is *one* dollar as important when a consumer has $10,000 as when he has $5,000? The marginal utility of money is the utility of

[3] The amount of utility is always the area under the marginal utility curve.

one dollar; for some purposes, however, it is convenient to think of money in larger units, such as one hundred dollars. Because a consumer with given tastes in a given period of time applies any *additional* dollars he gets to less and less important uses, the law must hold. Still, the concept of the marginal utility of money is surrounded with difficulties. They will be discussed later; meanwhile, let the diminution be assumed.

Thus far, the consumer's wants have been discussed. Now his income is brought in. If he has $5,000 a year, the marginal utility of money is higher than if instead, and in the same time period, he had $10,000 a year. With $5,000, he is more careful with a dollar and therefore might take a taxi only in a heavy rain, whereas with $10,000, he might use taxis several times a month. In other words, one dollar yields more utility or satisfaction if income is low than if it is high.

## Equilibrium of the Consumer

The consumer's desire for different quantities of the commodity is represented by the diminishing marginal utility of the commodity to him. The size of his money income determines the utility of a dollar. Therefore, the utility of units of the commodity can be measured in money, and the dollar importance to him of 1 unit, 2 units, 3 units, etc., can be stated. With this information, the demand curve of a consumer for a commodity can be constructed.

### The Demand Curve of the Consumer

A consumer's demand curve looks like those described in Chapters 2 and 3. The quantity bought, at any price, by one consumer is of course relatively small. Diminishing marginal utility is the cause of the downward slope of the demand curve of a consumer.

The market demand curve described in Chapter 2 is simply the sum of the demand curves of the individuals who are actual or potential consumers in a market. The individual demand curves are added horizontally, that is, the amounts bought in the market at each possible price are the sums of the amounts the consumers buy at that price. At high prices, some consumers do not buy at all because the high prices lie above any points on *their* individual demand curves. At successively lower prices, more and more is bought for two reasons. One is that each consumer buys more at lower prices because of diminishing marginal utility; the other is that each lower price brings in new buyers whose tastes or incomes did not permit them to buy at higher prices.

The law of demand, therefore, rests firmly upon the principle of diminishing marginal utility as well as upon differences in tastes among consumers and upon differences in their incomes.

Figure 4–3 shows the demand curve of a consumer for, say, shirts. The price of a shirt is $3.00. The horizontal line from $3.00 signifies that the price to the consumer is the same no matter how many units he buys. The consumer buys 5 shirts. Why this number? If he bought 6, he would be buying a quantity whose marginal utility is less than the price he has to pay. Or, to put it loosely, the 6th shirt is not worth what it costs. The best alternative purchase he could make with that $3.00 would yield him more utility than does the 6th shirt. On the other hand, if he bought only 4 shirts, he would be giving up an opportunity to buy something worth its price to him.

Equilibrium of the Consumer

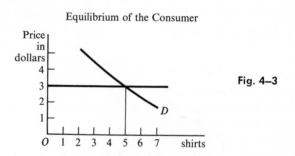

Fig. 4–3

The equilibrium of the consumer is the first of many equilibrium concepts in the theory of relative prices. The consumer is in equilibrium when he buys the quantity whose marginal utility is equal to the marginal utility of the dollars represented by the price.[4] The shorthand statement of consumer equilibrium is: Marginal utility equals price. Equilibrium means that the consumer does not want to buy any other quantity. The quantity he buys is the equilibrium quantity. If the consumer were by some chance to buy a different quantity, he would want to change.

Equilibrium has the general meaning of a balance of opposing forces. The consumer's force is his desire, which is limited by his income. The opposing force is price, the sign and condition of the availability of a commodity. If price rises, the consumer buys less; if it falls, he buys more. If his desire becomes stronger, he buys more; if weaker, less. If both price and desire change, the new equilibrium reflects the strengths of the two forces.

Equilibrium of the consumer has still another aspect. When he buys the equilibrium quantity, the consumer maximizes his utility or satisfaction.

[4] A logically complete statement of the equilibrium of the consumer must repeat that marginal utility is diminishing. For, if marginal utility were increasing, as it could over some range of quantity and under unusual circumstances, it would still be equal to price. And if $MU = P$, with $MU$ increasing, there is no equilibrium, because the consumer would want to buy more.

Maximization is not a state of bliss; maximization means only the most satisfaction under the circumstances.

### The Optimum Budget

The optimum budget for a consumer is the budget containing plans for the purchases of commodities in such quantities that the marginal utility of each commodity is equal to the marginal utility represented by its price. When he makes up his personal or family budget, the consumer knows the size of his income, and of course his income is the decisive limit, or constraint, upon his budget. With a given income, a dollar has a certain meaning to the consumer, i.e., its utility is the marginal utility of money to him. This means that the significance of each price the consumer has to pay is modified by the marginal utility of money. Take two of the commodities the consumer buys, $A$ and $B$. Let $P_A$ and $P_B$ stand for their prices, $MU_A$ and $MU_B$ for their marginal utilities, and let $m$ be the marginal utility of money to the consumer. Then $P_A \times m = MU_A$ and $P_B \times m = MU_B$. This means that the price of $A$ multiplied by the marginal utility of money equals the marginal utility of $A$. Similarly for $B$. Next, let the two equations be divided in this way:

$$\frac{P_A \times m}{P_B \times m} = \frac{MU_A}{MU_B}.$$

The $m$'s cancel out, so that

$$\frac{P_A}{P_B} = \frac{MU_A}{MU_B}.$$

Therefore,

$$\frac{MU_A}{P_A} = \frac{MU_B}{P_B}.$$

This means that the ratio of the prices of two commodities is equal to the ratio of their marginal utilities, and that the marginal utility of one commodity divided by its price equals the marginal utility of the other commodity divided by its price. The same thing holds for commodities $C$, $D$, $E$, etc. Therefore, the optimum budget of the consumer can be written as $\frac{MU_A}{P_A} = \frac{MU_B}{P_B} = \frac{MU_C}{P_C} =$ etc. This is true of the rational — the carefully and coldly calculating — consumer with a given money income. If his income changes, the significances of the $P$'s change, a new $m$ coming in to do this. But in the budget for a new income, $m$ once more cancels out.[5]

---

[5] This discussion ignores the income effect, i.e., the effect of a change in the price of a commodity upon the consumer's real income. The income effect is discussed in Chapter 6. When the consumer spends a small proportion of his income on any one commodity, it is permissible to ignore, as Marshall does, the income effect of a change in price.

The optimum budget of the consumer can also be stated in another way. In his budget, the consumer allocates dollars to food, to clothing, to recreation, to dental care, and so on. He does so in accordance with the utilities of the commodities and their prices. When the budget is optimum, the utility or satisfaction received from the *last* dollar spent on each commodity is equal. Here is the equimarginal principle again. It does not mean that the consumer spends equal amounts of money on each commodity. Not at all. He spends different amounts, but the *last* dollar spent on each commodity yields the same increment of satisfaction.

### Consumer's Surplus

In modern societies, a consumer is able to buy a multitude of commodities for any one of which, taken by itself, he would be willing to pay much more than he does in fact have to pay. The difference between the amount a consumer *would* pay for the quantity of a commodity he buys and the amount he *does* pay is called "consumer's surplus."

The doctrine of consumer's surplus has had much attention from economic theorists, with the inevitable result that thought stimulated by controversy has caused the doctrine to assume several highly complicated forms. But the original and simple form of the doctrine, as first stated by Alfred Marshall, will be presented here. Marshall's doctrine remains sturdy, mainly because of its simplicity and because, in some analyses, it is hard to get along without it.

As an example, consider the consumer's surplus that a consumer gets from his purchases of coffee. Table 4–2 gives hypothetical data. Suppose that the price of coffee is 75 cents a pound and that the consumer buys 5 pounds, paying $3.75 a month for coffee. Assume that as in the Table its total utility to him is $7.75. Therefore, his consumer's surplus from coffee is $4.00. For further clarification, the information in the first two columns of Table 4–2 should be spelled out: If the price of coffee were

#### TABLE 4–2

#### The Calculation of Consumer's Surplus

| Price | Quantity Bought | Total Expenditure | Total Utility[a] | Consumer's Surplus[b] |
|-------|-----------------|-------------------|------------------|------------------------|
| (1) | (2) | (3) | (4) | (5) |
| $3.00 | 1 lb. | $3.00 | $3.00 | — |
| 2.00 | 2 | 4.00 | 5.00 | $1.00 |
| 1.00 | 4 | 4.00 | 7.00 | 3.00 |
| 0.75 | 5 | 3.75 | 7.75 | 4.00 |

[a] Total utility is measurable in dollars under the assumption that the marginal utility of money ($m$) is constant.
[b] Column (4) minus column (3).

$3.00, he would buy one pound a month. Perhaps he would pay more, even much more if he had to, to buy one pound a month. Anyway, let his highest price for one pound be $3.00. He will not buy two pounds unless the price is $2.00, owing of course to diminishing marginal utility. But if he buys two pounds, he pays $2.00 for each, a total of $4.00. But one pound alone is worth at least $3.00 to him, and the second pound is worth $2.00 to him; hence the total utility of two pounds is $5.00. Thus the consumer's surplus for two pounds is $1.00. And so on, down the schedule.

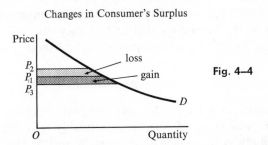

Changes in Consumer's Surplus

Fig. 4–4

If the price of a commodity goes up, the consumer is worse off, and if the price goes down, he is better off. The effects of price changes on the well-being, or welfare, of a consumer can be conceived as changes in consumers' surplus. In Figure 4–4, an initial price is $P_1$. Higher and lower prices are $P_2$ and $P_3$. The loss of consumer's surplus from a higher price is shown by the area indicated in the figure. Similarly, the lower price brings a gain in consumer's surplus. The sizes of the gains and losses depend on how great are the price changes, as well as upon the elasticity of demand. (Note 6 in the Appendix to Part Two is on consumer's surplus.)

### Interpersonal Comparisons of Utility

Any application of the utility analysis in theoretical solution of problems of economic policy faces an obstacle that many economists refuse to pass. The obstacle is the validity of interpersonal comparisons of utility. Suppose that Jones and Smith have the same income, the same background, do similar kinds of work, and live in the same community. Do they get the same pleasure from spending a hundred dollars, from driving their cars, from playing golf? Many theorists now say that this question, or any other like it, is simply unanswerable. No one can peek into the minds of Jones and Smith; no one can compare the satisfactions they derive from consumption. If one man's utilities cannot be compared with another's, the utilities cannot be added. Therefore, nothing can be said about the sum total of the utilities enjoyed by the people who buy a commodity. It follows that consumers' surpluses of the many buyers of a commodity cannot be totalled, even conceptually.

But this view is too strict. Anyone who would try to adhere to it would simply have to shut his brain to serious thought about great political, social, and economic issues. It is impossible to think about such issues without assuming that, for the purpose at hand, people are pretty much alike, and alike too, in their capacities for receiving satisfactions from consumption. Certainly the neoclassical cardinal utility concept implies comparison and addition. The lesson taught by doubts of the validity of interpersonal comparisons is that when they are made, such comparisons should be made carefully in the knowledge that at best they can only be rough. Even if people are for many purposes pretty much alike, they are not identical.

## Applications

The concepts of total utility and marginal utility are aids to clear thinking. The total utility of water is incalculably high, yet its marginal utility — the utility of one gallon — is normally so low that most people cheerfully "waste" many gallons a day. The total utility of a bridge can also be high; but if there is no toll, people cross it as much as they please, the utility of a crossing being zero $(MU = P = O)$. On the other hand, the marginal utility of champagne, for example, is high, whereas its total utility to most people who buy it is probably low.

Ever since the early 1930's, surplus foodstuffs have been distributed under various programs to needy families. On one occasion when the surplus food was oranges, the good citizens in a community were shocked and indignant to see children of destitute families playing ball with some of the oranges. The indignation was, however, misdirected. It should have gone to the administrators who apparently gave "too many" oranges to families in the one community, so many in fact that marginal utility approached zero. What could be more rational than to allocate the last oranges to their last use — as makeshift balls?

### The Redistribution of Income

In the United States, government imposes progressive income taxes and provides social services. Income is thus transferred from the high-income groups to low-income groups. Does the transfer of income from rich to poor increase the nation's economic welfare?

Let it be assumed, for the purpose of this discussion, that the transfer of income has no effect on incentives to produce. The question, then, is the effect of transfer upon economic welfare as the satisfactions from con-

sumption. Assume next that all persons have the same capacity for enjoying consumer goods and services, and therefore that the *same* curve of
the diminishing marginal utility of income can be drawn for every person.

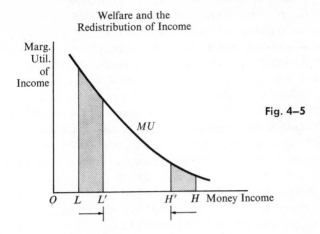

Welfare and the
Redistribution of Income

**Fig. 4–5**

Figure 4–5 shows such a curve. In the figure, *OL* is a poor man's income and *OH* is a rich man's income. Let the rich man's income be reduced by *HH'*, and let the same amount of money income be transferred
to the poor man, so that his income rises by *LL'*. It is clear from the figure
that the gain in utility — the shaded area above *LL'* — to the poor man
exceeds the loss to the rich man — the shaded area above *HH'*. Hence the
total utility — economic welfare — of both together is larger. With reasoning like this, some economists have actually advocated that government
redistribute income.

Is the reasoning correct? Most economists hotly say that it is not, because even if interpersonal comparisons of utility are admissible, people
differ, and no one knows the shapes of the curves. Nevertheless, remember
that income is in fact redistributed. What is the effect on economic welfare? The question remains open.[6]

### Progressive Income Taxation

Continuous controversy has long surrounded the subject of progressive
income taxation. Apart from the disputes over the soundness of actual
tax systems such as the existing federal personal income tax in the United

---

[6] Some theorists, however, evade the prohibition of interpersonal comparisons of
utilities by pretending that "policy makers" assign different "distributional weights"
to different classes of persons. With a transfer of income, the "weight" assigned to
the rich man's loss is smaller than the "weight" of the poor man's gain. Here, then,
is another way of justifying some redistribution of income.

States, controversy and honest doubt still attach to the *principle* of progressive income taxation. The principle can be explained and justified because of the need for revenue, because the income tax is one of the stabilizers of national income, because the tax reduces the inequalities of personal income, and because it achieves an equitable distribution of the burden of taxation. Discussion here will confine itself to the last point — equity — and its connection with the concepts of utility and marginal utility. Is the income tax, in principle, the fairest of all taxes?

It has long since been generally agreed that equity in taxation means taxing according to ability to pay and that ability to pay is a function of income. The development of utility theory in the second half of the nineteenth century led to agreement that, ideally, taxpayers should make equal sacrifices in paying taxes out of their incomes. Now what does equal sacrifice mean? It does not mean the payment of equal amounts of money to government. No, equal sacrifice means equal *subjective* sacrifice, i.e., equal losses of utility by taxpayers. But equal sacrifice, by itself, is not a clear concept and has to be divided into three concepts: (1) Equal *marginal* sacrifice means that the sacrifice accompanying the surrender of the last dollar in taxes is equal for each taxpayer. When marginal sacrifices are equal, aggregate sacrifice by all taxpayers together is a minimum. Here is still another application of the equimarginal principle. But marginal sacrifices can be made equal only if incomes after taxes are equal (assuming the same marginal utility of income for all persons). Hence, as a proposal, equal marginal sacrifice deserves at the very least to be called radical. (2) Equal *absolute* sacrifice means that the total utilities given up in taxes by each taxpayer are equal. The poor man makes as big a subjective sacrifice as the rich man. (3) Equal *proportional* sacrifice means that poor and rich give up the same percentage of the total utilities they get from their incomes.

What about progression? Do the doctrines of equal absolute sacrifice and of equal proportional sacrifice call for progressive rates of taxation on personal incomes? No, they do not necessarily, for the answer depends on how fast the marginal utility of income diminishes. Since no one knows or can probably ever know just how fast this is, utility theory comes out with a negative answer. But negative answers are important too, because they often, as here, show sloppy thinking for what it is. It should not be blandly taken for granted that progressive income taxation mean fairness or equity in sharing the burden of taxes, if equity means equality (or an attempt at it) of absolute or proportional sacrifice.

There is more to be said. Proportional taxation would be called for if marginal utility declined in accordance with Bernoulli's hypothesis. Daniel Bernoulli (1700–1782), the Swiss mathematician, said approximately that after some minimum income is attained, the marginal utility of income declines by a rate equal to the relative (i.e., percentage) increase in income.[7] Such a curve of the diminishing marginal utility of income is like curve *A* in Figure 4–6. Curve *A* is a rectangular hyperbola; it has the same properties as a demand curve with unitary elasticity throughout.

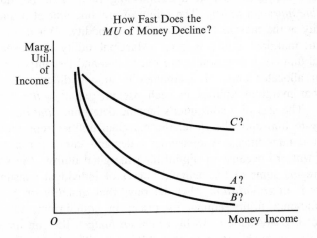

How Fast Does the
*MU* of Money Decline?

**Fig. 4–6**

Under this hypothesis, a man with an income of $20,000 who pays a $4,000 tax makes the same sacrifice as a man with $10,000 who pays $2,000. The subjective sacrifice is the same (both absolutely and proportionally) because the marginal utility of a $20,000 income is half that of a $10,000 income. That is, $4,000 times one-half equals $2,000 times one. It is only if the marginal utility of income declines *faster* than in Bernoulli's hypothesis that progressive taxation is justified on grounds of equity. The curve has to look like curve *B* in Figure 4–6. With the faster decline, the $20,000 income would have less than half the marginal utility of the $10,000 income, and the tax would therefore have to be more than $4,000 to match, subjectively, the $10,000-a-year man's $2,000 tax sacrifice. And if marginal utility should decline as in curve *C,* equity would call for regressive, not progressive, rates of personal income taxation. It follows that the progressive income tax rests upon an uncertain foundation of logic, at least so far as equality of sacrifice is concerned.

## Summary

The neoclassical theory of consumer behavior rests on the concept of utility, which is subjective want-satisfying power, a property common to

[7] See Note 7 in the Appendix to Part Two.

commodities. *Cardinal utility* is utility assumed to be measurable in principle. *Rational behavior* by consumers is the making of deliberate, calculating, and consistent choices aimed at maximizing utility. As a consumer acquires, in fact or in contemplation, more units of a commodity, their *total utility* increases, but at a diminishing rate. This is equivalent to *diminishing marginal utility*. The utility of any one unit of a quantity of a commodity is the marginal utility of the commodity. When total utility is maximum, marginal utility is zero. Marginal utility diminishes because additional units of a commodity are put to less and less important uses. A consumer allocates units of a commodity among different uses in such a way that marginal utilities in each use are equal — *the equimarginal principle*. The size of a consumer's income determines *the marginal utility of money* to him and, therefore, the marginal utilities represented by the prices of commodities. A consumer's demand curve for a commodity slopes downward because of diminishing marginal utility. Market demand curves are the sums of the demand curves of individual consumers. The consumer is in *equilibrium* when he buys that quantity of a commodity whose marginal utility equals its price; in equilibrium, the consumer maximizes his satisfaction. In his *optimum budget*, the consumer buys *all* commodities in such amounts that $MU = P$. The last dollar spent on each commodity yields the same increment of satisfaction. Consumer's *surplus* is the excess of total utility measured in dollars over the expenditure for a commodity. Some economists have advocated the redistribution of income by government because, they argue, dollars of income transferred from the rich to the poor would increase the *economic welfare* enjoyed by both together, owing to the diminishing marginal utility of money income. Other economists disagree, either because they deny the validity of *interpersonal comparisons of utility* or because they contend that the marginal utility of income diminishes in different unknown ways for different persons. Because no one knows how fast the marginal utility of money income diminishes, *the equity of the principle of progressive income taxation* rests on an uncertain logical foundation.

## SELECTED REFERENCES

Alfred Marshall, *Principles of Economics,* 8th ed. (London: Macmillan, 1930), Book III. An advanced discussion is in J. R. Hicks, *A Revision of Demand Theory* (London: Oxford, 1956).

On the utilities of indivisible goods: Philip H. Wicksteed, *The Common Sense of Political Economy* (London: 1910. Reprinted and edited by Lionel Robbins, London: Routledge, 1933), Chap. 3.

On the redistribution of income: A. C. Pigou, *The Economics of Welfare,* 4th ed. (London: Macmillan, 1932). Part I, Chap. VIII, Part IV. Appendix XI in the reprint of 1952 contains Pigou's defense of the validity of the comparability of utilities. An extreme position is taken by Abba P. Lerner, *The Economics of Control* (New York: Macmillan, 1944), Chap. 3. A clear exposition is in Howard R. Bowen, *Toward Social Economy* (New York: Rinehart, 1948), Chap. 19.

On progressive income taxation: Richard A. Musgrave, *The Theory of Public Finance* (New York: McGraw-Hill, 1959), Chap. 5. A less technical but fuller discussion is contained in Walter J. Blum and Harry Kalven Jr., *The Uneasy Case for Progressive Taxation* (Chicago: University of Chicago Press, 1953).

## EXERCISES AND PROBLEMS

1. For a rich man and a poor man, draw curves of the marginal utility of income in such a way as to increase their joint welfare by a transfer of income from the poor man to the rich man.

2. In the eighteenth century, the "diamonds and water paradox" was discussed. The paradox was this: Why are diamonds, which are useless baubles, so valuable when water, which is essential to life, is so cheap? Resolve the paradox with the concept of marginal utility.

3. Draw diagrams to show different positions of equilibrium of a consumer in his purchases of one commodity. For example, show him buying *more* at a higher price because a change in desire more than offsets the higher price.

4. What is the marginal utility of the services of a public library to an avid reader who lives nearby? The total utility? The consumer's surplus?

5. Suppose that 100 thrifty housewives go to the same supermarket on the same day. Those who buy the same items have the same marginal utilities for each of these items. Why? Do the housewives therefore have identical tastes? Do they therefore buy equal amounts of each item? Why?

6. Show how a sensible ("rational") student would allocate 20 hours of time to preparation for three examinations in accordance with the equimarginal principle.

# Modern Utility Theory

## 5

THE ST. PETERSBURG PARADOX • CHOICES UNDER RISK • THE
NEUMANN-MORGENSTERN METHOD OF MEASURING UTILITY • THE
FRIEDMAN-SAVAGE HYPOTHESIS • APPLICATIONS •

This chapter surveys the simpler forms of some of the main ideas of modern utility theory. Though it is a product of the postwar period, the theory is also called *Bernoullian utility theory,* after Daniel Bernoulli, the eighteenth century Swiss mathematician mentioned in the last chapter. The modern theory establishes a method of measuring utility under certain conditions, shows the possibility of the *increasing* marginal utility of money, and creates a logical foundation for making certain kinds of rational decisions.

The neoclassical theory of utility reviewed in Chapter 4 stands firmly on the principle of diminishing marginal utility and on the rule that consumers maximize their total utilities. The neoclassical theory can also be called one of consumer behavior where all of the choices are made among *riskless* alternatives. Here stands the consumer in the supermarket: These and those goods are available; all have price tags; the consumer has such-and-such an income; and he is a person with some given kind of tastes. The consumer faces no uncertainties as to the availabilities of commodities and no uncertainties as to their prices. Nor is he uncertain about the size of his income. Knowing these things exactly, the consumer of the neoclassical theory calmly makes his choices, maximizing his utility by equating the marginal utility of each commodity to its price.

The marginal utility of money income also diminishes for the consumer of the neoclassical theory. For this reason, the rational consumer would never buy a lottery ticket or take part in any other kind of gambling, even fair gambling. Why not?

### The St. Petersburg Paradox

At one point in his career, Bernoulli became interested in a problem called the "St. Petersburg paradox." The problem is why people are unwilling to make bets at better than 50–50 odds when their mathematical expectations of winning money, in a particular kind of gamble, are greater the more money they bet. (See Note 7 in the Appendix to Part Two.) Bernoulli's solution to the paradox was to say in effect that the marginal utility of money diminishes as money income increases. If you have $1,000 and can make a fair (i.e., no crooked dice, marked cards, etc.) bet at even odds of winning or losing $100, you will not do it if you make a rational decision. If you win, you will have $1,100 and the gain of utility from $100 added to $1,000. If you lose, you will have $900 and the loss of utility from $100 subtracted from $1,000. Diminishing marginal utility means that the gain of utility is smaller than the loss, even though the amounts of money are equal.

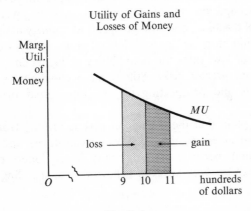

Utility of Gains and
Losses of Money

**Fig. 5–1**

This proposition is demonstrated in Figure 5–1. The horizontal axis is marked in hundreds of dollars. The distances between 9 and 10 and between 10 and 11 are equal. The loss and the gain in utility are shown as the areas under the curve of marginal utility. The loss of utility is always greater than the gain; how much greater of course depends on how fast or how slowly marginal utility diminishes.

The proposition ignores of course the pleasures of gambling, such as they are. Among the many who have censured these pleasures is Alfred Marshall, who said that they are likely to make people restless and feverish and to develop personalities as incapable of steady work as they are of enjoying the higher and more solid things of life. However this might be, the utility flowing from the excitement of gambling will be set aside in this discussion. So too will the house percentage, when it might be relevant.[1]

## Choices under Risk

Gambling has just been mentioned and will be returned to a little later. Gambling gets attention from economic theorists and from mathematicians not for its own sake, but because in most gambling the odds, or probabilities, are exact and can, therefore, be put to exact analysis. The importance of the analysis of gambling is the light it throws upon choices that are accompanied by risk.[2]

Any person must make a wide range of choices subject to varying degrees of risk. Many kinds of insurance are available. The individual decides which kinds to buy and the amounts of each kind. He must choose what to do with his liquid assets — to hold them in the form of money or to convert them into a savings account, or government bonds, or blue chip stocks, or into some highly speculative investment. Here are degrees of risk. The individual must also choose an occupation; perhaps he decides to change his occupation. Some occupations, such as government employment and school teaching, offer the prospects of security along with incomes that remain within more or less well-defined limits. Other occupations such as the practice of law, offer the possibilities of higher incomes along with less security, i.e., greater risk. Still other occupations, such as playing professional golf and prospecting for oil, offer great prizes along with extreme risks.

It should be plain that the discussion here is drifting from the behavior of people as consumers to their behavior as investors and workers. The drift is intentional, because modern utility theory offers explanations of choices under risk for *both* kinds of behavior — in spending income and in earning it.

## The Neumann-Morgenstern Method of Measuring Utility

One of the great accomplishments of modern utility theory is a method of measuring utility. The measurement is theoretical or conceptual. It does

---

[1] In Nevada, for example, roulette wheels have 38 numbers. The payoff is 36 to 1. The gambling house lives on the extra 2 numbers.

[2] In this chapter, risk and uncertainty are not distinguished. They are, however, in Chapter 8.

not make possible an instrument that will allow you to find out how much the bride *really* enjoyed the present you gave her. In the modern theory, measurement is confined to the *expected* utilities that determine choices when there are risks. The measurement is also practical in the sense that it can be tested by controlled experiments of behavior and in the further sense that it can be built into a way of thinking about how to make rational decisions where there are measurable risks.

Although others had tackled the problem before, the credit for the method of measuring utility goes to John von Neumann and Oskar Morgenstern who developed it in their well-known *Theory of Games and Economic Behavior.*[3] Many others have extended and refined the method which amounts to an extension of Bernoulli's idea that in taking risks, people look to expected utility, not expected money.

When put in the simplest way, the essence of the method is to convert the betting odds a rational individual would insist on having into an index of the utility of money to him. Take again the example of the man who has $1,000 and is offered bets or lottery tickets where he can win or lose $100. Remember that the individual wants not the maximum expected payoff in money, but the maximum expected *utility*. What the money means to him, rather than its amount, is what counts.

(To reinforce Bernoulli's point: Suppose you have right now, this month, just enough money to carry you through the school year, and that you cannot get any more from any source. Would you toss a coin for your money, double or nothing? If you did, you'd be a strange person, because the loss of your money would mean a great loss of utility; you would have to quit college. If you would win, you would have a gain in utility, but could the gain possibly be as great as the loss?)

The Neumann-Morgenstern method can be illustrated with three hypothetical examples:

(1) A person is asked to take a 50–50 chance of winning or losing $100. He refuses. Then he is offered odds of 55–45. This could be done, for example, by letting him pick at random a ball from an urn containing 55 white balls and 45 black balls. He wins if he picks a white ball. He refuses again. The offer then becomes 60–40.[4] This one he accepts, though he is just barely induced to do so. How can this information be converted into knowledge of the utility of money to the individual? In this way: Let the loss of utility from losing $100 be *arbitrarily* set at 15 units of utility or "utils." He has a 40-per cent chance of losing, so that

---

[3] 2nd ed. (Princeton: Princeton University Press, 1947).

[4] The standard actuarial, or expected money, value of a bet is $WP - L(1 - P)$, where $W$ is the win, $L$ is the loss, and $P \, (= 1)$ is probability. A $100 bet at 50-50 odds has an expected money value of $0.5 \times \$100 - (1 - 0.5) \times \$100 = \$0$. At 60–40 odds, the value is $0.6 \times \$100 - (1 - 0.6) \times \$100 = \$20$.

his probable or expected loss of utility is 0.4 times 15 utils, or 6 utils. Because he is just barely willing to accept the 60–40 odds, his probable or expected gain of utility must also be 6 utils. It follows that the utility of another $100 to him is 10 utils, because 0.6 times 10 utils is 6 utils, the probable or expected gain at 60–40 odds.

For further clarification, what was just said can be restated this way:

$$\text{expected gain in utility} = \text{expected loss of utility}$$

$$\text{probability of gain} \times \text{utils of gain} = \text{probability of loss} \times \text{utils of loss}$$

$$0.6 \times \text{utils of gain} = 0.4 \times 15$$

therefore

$$\text{utils of gain} = \frac{6}{0.6}$$
$$= 10$$

The result here is that the acceptance of the 60–40 odds shows that the utility of $100 added to $1,000 is less than the utility of $100 taken away from $1,000. To assign 10 utils to the gain and 15 utils to the loss is arbitrary; any other pair of numbers would do provided they have the same relative sizes.

If this same person wins his bet and accepts another bet at the same odds, the utility to him of $100 added to $1,100 is 6-2/3 utils by the same line of reasoning. So then, by starting at $900 and adding increments of $100, and by assigning 15 utils to the first $100 after $900, he shows by the odds he demands that his index of marginal utility is 15, 10, 6-2/3, etc. utils. For the sake of emphasis, it should be repeated that the numbers are arbitrary; they can be multiplied by any one number, and any one number can be added to them. If such numbers are put on a diagram, such as Figure 5–1 on page 67, the curve can be located only arbitrarily. The curve can be high or low in the diagram, and there is no way to find its starting point. Despite these limitations, the Neumann-Morgenstern method does indeed establish a set of numbers measuring utility. The limitations are not peculiar to the problem of measuring utility, for, in fact, the choice of the size of the unit of measurement is always arbitrary. Remember the Fahrenheit and Centigrade scales for temperature.

(2) If another rational person would accept a bet with 50–50 odds, it can be concluded for him that the gain in utility equals the loss, and that for him, the marginal utility of money is *constant,* at least in the range $900 – $1,100.

(3) If a third rational person has a positive preference for risk and is willing to accept bets at *unfavorable* odds, the marginal utility of money for him must be *increasing.*

The Neumann-Morgenstern method, therefore, yields measures of cardinal utility, either conceptually or as the outcomes of actual experiments. The method has indeed been substantiated by controlled experiments. The Neumann-Morgenstern cardinal utility is not, however, identical with the older neoclassical cardinal utility. The Neumann-Morgenstern method does not measure the strength of feelings toward goods and services. All that the N-M method can do is to illumine the actions of persons making choices in the face of risk. But by opening up new possibilities of measurement, Neumann and Morgenstern have given new strength to the older idea of neoclassical cardinal utility.

## The Friedman-Savage Hypothesis

Does the marginal utility of money always diminish? If it does, how can the widespread practice of gambling be explained? More than that, why do some persons actually prefer to make choices among alternatives with high degrees of risk? To point to the entertainment and pleasure that many people find in gambling is not enough, nor does it suffice to dismiss gambling and other decisions under risk as "irrational." Though the world abounds with people who are thoughtless and scatterbrained in their decisions, much gambling is done with cold and careful calculations. Remember, too, that gambling has flourished for centuries and in many cultures. Whatever its morals and legality might be, gambling is not an aberration in the behavior of a part of the population.

Anyone who buys ordinary insurance behaves as if the marginal utility of income were diminishing. The payment of insurance premiums is a sacrifice of money and thus a loss of utility. Though this loss is certain, it is also relatively small and is much less than the expected loss of utility in the uncertain event that the house would burn down, the jewelry be stolen, etc.[5] To buy insurance is therefore to *avoid* risk.

In a well-known article published in 1948, Milton Friedman and L. J. Savage advance a hypothesis that explains why the same groups of people both buy insurance and engage in gambling, why they both avoid and choose risks. Stated briefly and without regard for its refinements, the Friedman-Savage hypothesis is that for most people, the marginal utility of income diminishes when incomes are below some level, increases for incomes between that level and some higher level, and diminishes again when incomes are above the high level.

---

[5] Suppose that the probability of loss of a piece of property worth $500 is 1/5. Then the expected monetary value of the loss is $100. If a rational person pays an insurance premium of, say, $125 to avoid the risk of loss, his action demonstrates diminishing marginal utility, because the utility of the $500 that might be lost is more than 5 times the utility of the certain loss of $125.

The Friedman-Savage hypothesis is illustrated in Figure 5–2. The roller-coaster curve[6] has three segments indicating from left to right, diminishing, increasing, and then again diminishing marginal utility of income. The dashed vertical lines in Figure 5–2 separate the three segments. Suppose a person has an income $OA$ which is still in the first diminishing segment. He buys insurance because the payment is small when compared with the large loss of utility, even though the probability is low that he would suffer the loss without insurance. The loss of utility is large because he looks up the curve to the left where $L$ is. The same person also buys long-shot lottery tickets or makes similar gambles. Here though the payment is small, the probability of winning is also small. The expected utility of the gamble would be negative were it not for the rising marginal utility of the possible gain in income shown on the rising part of the curve where $M$ is.

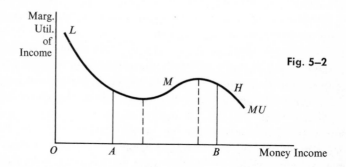

A person with an income $OB$ in Figure 5–2 has a high income; because of this, he has no preference for risk and is unwilling to gamble or to undertake risky investments except, of course, at odds favorable to him.

Friedman and Savage tentatively believe that the three segments of the curve in Figure 5–2 are descriptive of the attitudes of people in different socioeconomic groups. They recognize the multitude of differences from one person to another even in the same socioeconomic group; some persons are inveterate gamblers, others avoid all possible risks. Still, Friedman and Savage think that the curve describes the propensities of broad classes. The middle group with the increasing marginal utility of money are those, they argue, who are eager to take risks to improve themselves. The expectation of more money means much to this group of persons; if their efforts succeed, they lift themselves into the next socioeconomic class.

---

[6] Friedman and Savage draw total utility curves, like the one in the upper part of Figure 4–1 on page 51 of this book. The curve in Figure 5–2 is consistent with their curves.

These persons want not just more consumer goods; they look up in the social scale. They want to rise, to change the patterns of their lives. No wonder that marginal utility increases for them.

### Applications

Since the end of World War II, much work has gone into expanding and refining the concepts of modern utility theory. Part of the research effort has devoted itself to the task of finding formal techniques for making rational decisions.

The thrifty housewife needs no advice derived from the formal theory of economic behavior. Rather, her problem is technical — the accuracy and completeness of the information on, for example, new fabrics. Over the centuries, gamblers have often run for help to mathematicians who then found new stimulus to advance knowledge. Apart from this, superstition seems to dominate gambling. But to many kinds of business decisions, formal theory is being increasingly applied.

To make a rational decision on a risky investment, for example, two pieces of information must be obtained or estimated as well as possible. One is the numerical probabilities of successes or failures, of probable money gains and probable money losses. The other is the utility function of the decision-maker.

An index of the utility function can be constructed after the method of von Neumann and Morgenstern by careful and deliberate introspection. To do this is perhaps like making your own thermometer without instruments or external guides, relying solely on your own feelings of hot and cold. Still, careful introspection is better than a hasty guess. So constructed, an index tells, for example, whether or not $100,000 has twice the utility of $50,000 (i.e., whether marginal utility rises or falls in that range). Such an index also measures how serious is a loss, whether it means a purely temporary embarrassment or poses a threat of bankruptcy.

In the rational decision, the probabilities of success and failure are joined with the index of utility: Go ahead with the investment or project if the expected gain in utility exceeds the expected loss; decline, if it is the other way around.

Does this apply to a corporation, which certainly has no soul and not always a definite collective mind? The *neoclassical* cardinal utility concept never did have any meaning for a corporation, which can hardly be said to have subjective feelings toward individual goods and services. Though the literature on utility as a basis for decision-making refers mainly to individual businessmen, it should be possible to construct an index of the utility of money for a corporation when certain conditions are taken into account. The conditions are the ease or difficulty of financing. If a corporation can acquire new funds in any amount at any time and at the same cost, then the marginal utility of money is constant. This being so, utility can be disregarded, because expected money and expected utility are then identical. If, however, a corporation faces difficulty or perhaps an impossibility of acquiring new funds, a loss on a risky venture might be a grave matter. The utility index would show a decline in marginal utility. The odds favoring the risky venture would have to be high to justify it. Just how high is to be determined by calculations which include the construction of a numerical index of utility. The index might adequately, if crudely, reflect the consensus of the executives who make the decision.

### Summary

Modern utility theory deals with *choices subject to risk*. Rational decisions look to *expected utility,* not expected money value, when risks are present. The *Neumann-Morgenstern method* of measuring the utility of money to a person is to find the odds, or probabilities, the person will accept in deciding whether to put a sum of money to risk, as in a gamble. If the person insists on favorable odds, then for him the marginal utility of money diminishes. If he accepts even odds, the marginal utility of money is constant, at least over some range. And if a person willingly accepts unfavorable odds, the marginal utility of money increases, over some range. The *Friedman-Savage hypothesis* holds that the marginal utility of money to many persons does indeed increase over some range of income, for otherwise much behavior could not be explained. Modern utility theory is being increasingly applied in methods of formal decision-making for use by business enterprises.

## SELECTED REFERENCES

An excellent treatment with a full bibliography is contained in Ernest W. Adams, "Survey of Bernoullian Utility Theory," in Herbert Solomon (ed.), *Mathematical Thinking in the Measurement of Behavior* (Glencoe: Free Press, 1960). A rigorous but nonmathematical discussion is by Armen A. Alchian, "The Meaning of Utility Measurement," *American Economic Review,* Vol. XLIII, No. 1, March, 1953, pp. 26–50. A good exposition is contained in William J. Baumol, *Economic Theory and Operations Analysis* (Englewood Cliffs: Prentice-Hall, 1961), Chap. 17.

Milton Friedman and L. J. Savage, "The Utility Analysis of Choices Involving Risk," *Journal of Political Economy,* Vol. LVI, 1948, pp. 279–304. Reprinted in George J. Stigler and Kenneth E. Boulding, eds., American Economic Association, *Readings in Price Theory* (Homewood: Irwin, 1952), Chap. 3.

A simple discussion of the uses of modern utility theory for decision-making is contained in Harold Bierman, Jr., Lawrence E. Fouraker, and Robert K. Jaedicke, *Quantitative Analysis for Business Decisions* (Homewood: Irwin, 1961), Chap. 7.

## EXERCISES AND PROBLEMS

1. After making appropriate assumptions, construct utility indexes for (a) a college student, (b) a retired man with property and securities, (c) a speculator in oil lands, and (d) a young man with his own business.

2. The curve in Figure 5–2 has three segments, one for each of three socioeconomic classes. Draw a curve with five segments and give it a socioeconomic interpretation.

3. Suppose a successful businessman is thinking of going into politics. He knows that he will have to spend much money in political life. Speculate on the marginal utility of money to him.

# Indifference-Curve Analysis

# of Consumer Demand

# 6

PREFERENCE AND INDIFFERENCE • INDIFFERENCE SCHEDULES •
INDIFFERENCE CURVES • EQUILIBRIUM OF THE CONSUMER •
EFFECTS OF CHANGES IN INCOME • EFFECTS OF CHANGES
IN PRICES • APPLICATIONS •

The attacks on the neoclassical cardinal utility concept early in the twentieth century were skirmishes on the outposts. But in the 1930's, heavy artillery was brought up and fired with apparently devastating results. The wreckage was swept away and ordinal utility was set on a throne consisting of a box of tools containing indifference curves.

The indifference curve, to be explained shortly, was not new. Invented late in the nineteenth century by the English economist, F. Y. Edgeworth, the indifference curve was carried to the continent of Europe where it stayed for several decades. The Italian economist, Vilfredo Pareto, put the indifference curve to extensive use. Not until the 1930's did it return to the English-speaking world. Two English economists, R. G. D. Allen and J. R. Hicks, fired the heavy shells at cardinal utility. They urged that the theory of consumer behavior be built anew on the basis of ordinal utility. Their views prevailed. The indifference curve replaced the curve of diminishing marginal utility.

So it seemed for a while. But as Chapter 4 shows, neoclassical utility survives and has gained the new ally of Neumann-Morgenstern measurable utility. The ordinal attack turned out to have no more effect than to tone down some of the claims for cardinal utility. It has also been found that ordinal utility has its own shortcomings. Thus, both kinds of utility coexist in economic theory, and peacefully at that.

## Preference and Indifference

Ordinal utility means that the consumer is assumed to order, or rank, the subjective utilities of goods. That is all. There is no need to assume that the consumer knows quantities of utilities. Suppose the consumer prefers a unit of commodity $A$ to a unit of commodity $B$, and that he also prefers $A$ to $C$. But suppose also that he has no preference between $B$ and $C$. If offered a choice between a unit of $B$ and one of $C$, he is indifferent, not caring which one he gets.

The tastes of the consumer can therefore be described with the ideas of preference and indifference. If he can choose between two goods or collections of goods, he always prefers one to the other or else he is indifferent. This statement presupposes either that he can have one of the collections of goods as a gift or else that their prices are the same. Prices will be brought into the discussion later. Observe that the only assumption is *that* the consumer prefers or is indifferent. *Why* he prefers can be left out of it. And so can *by how much* the consumer prefers. This last is the assumption omitted in the indifference-curve analysis of consumer demand; the assumption is not needed. The neoclassical cardinal utility analysis of Chapter 4 says that $A$ is preferred to $B$ because $A$ has more utility.[1]

## Indifference Schedules

The ordinal utility analysis of demand is usually called the indifference-curve analysis because indifference curves are its main analytical tool. To understand indifference curves, it is best to begin with indifference schedules.

An indifference schedule is a list of combinations of two commodities, the list being so arranged that a consumer is indifferent to the combinations, preferring none of them to any of the others. Table 6–1 contains two indifference schedules. Consider Schedule $A$. There are two commodities, which are $X$ and $Y$. The reason for having two commodities is that the

[1] In the 1930's, Hicks and others made much of the difference between ordinal and cardinal utility. Postwar thinking narrows the gap. For example, consumers often experience difficulty in making choices. Suppose that the consumer prefers $A$ to $B$ and $B$ to $C$, but that it is harder to make the choice of $A$ over $B$ than of $B$ over $C$. It then can be hypothesized that the difference of (cardinal) utility between $A$ and $B$ is less than between $B$ and $C$. Consumers are also sometimes inconsistent. Suppose a consumer chooses $A$ over $B$ 70 per cent of the time, and $B$ over $C$ 90 per cent of the time. Here again it can be argued that the difference of (cardinal) utility between $A$ and $B$ is less than between $B$ and $C$.

analysis is two-variable and, hence, can be put on a two-dimensional diagram; the analysis of more than two commodities requires advanced mathematics. The consumer is imagined as contemplating various combinations of units of $X$ and of $Y$. In Schedule $A$, these combinations are 10 units of $X$ and 0 units of $Y$, 7 of $X$ and 1 of $Y$, and so on. The consumer desires both commodities, but the question here is the relation between his desires and the *quantities* of the commodities. In Schedule $A$, the quantities of $X$ and $Y$ are so arranged that the consumer is indifferent among the combinations. Each one is equally desirable; he considers himself equally well off in having any one of the combinations as in having any other.

### TABLE 6–1
#### Two Indifference Schedules

| A | | | B | |
|---|---|---|---|---|
| X | Y | | X | Y |
| 10 | 0 | | 12 | 0 |
| 7 | 1 | | 10 | 1 |
| 5 | 2 | | 8 | 2 |
| 4 | 4 | | 6 | 4 |

Similarly, each one of the combinations in Schedule $B$ is as desirable as any of the others in the same schedule. But Schedule $B$ begins with 12 of $X$ and none of $Y$. On the assumption that more of a commodity is preferable to less, *any* combination in $B$ is preferred to *any* combination in $A$.

To extend all this: Imagine a consumer who likes two commodities. Take at random a combination of so many units of the one commodity and so many units of the other. Given this combination, there must be others to which the consumer is indifferent. Given the combination, there are others less and others more desirable. Look again at Table 6–1. The table has only two indifference schedules. Imagine it as having many more, stretching far to the right — Schedules $C$, $D$, $E$, $F$, etc. Moreover, the schedules in the table show only four combinations of $X$ and $Y$. Imagine them stretching farther down until the $X$ columns show the number zero.

### Indifference Curves

The next step is to go from indifference schedules to indifference curves. Here too is another move from arithmetic to geometry, a move that achieves the convenience of smooth curves and leaves behind the awkwardness of jumping from one number to another. Here too the smooth curve means that the commodities in question are assumed to be divisible into very small units.

Figure 6–1 is an indifference diagram; on it is an indifference curve. The diagram itself is unlike those appearing in earlier chapters; those diagrams have quantity on the horizontal axis and either price or utility on the vertical axis. But the indifference diagram has quantity on *both* axes. The horizontal axis measures physical units of a commodity *X,* and the vertical axis measures physical units of a commodity *Y.* Any point in the field, therefore, represents one combination of quantities of *X* and of *Y.* Take any point such as *A* in Figure 6–1. At the point *A,* the number of units of *X* and of *Y* is shown by the lengths of the lines *x* and *y.* Through point *A* an indifference curve is drawn and drawn in such a way that any other point on the curve shows quantities of *X* and of *Y* that are equally desirable to the consumer. If he could choose among all the combinations of *X* and *Y* on the curve, he would be indifferent because, to repeat, all of the combinations leave him on the same level of satisfaction. Think of the consumer as sliding up and down the indifference curve; there being no law of gravity here, he can slide up as easily as he can slide down. No matter where he is, he is equally well off — as an actual or potential consumer of *X* and *Y.*

An Indifference Curve

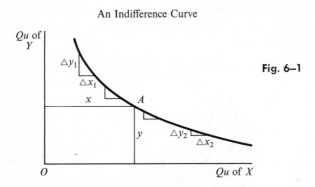

Fig. 6–1

Why is the indifference curve shaped the way it is in Figure 6–1? The curve is bent so that it is relatively steep at the top and relatively flat at the bottom; the curve is *convex* to the origin. The explanation is this: Imagine the consumer sliding down the curve in Figure 6–1. As he does so, the consumer is substituting[2] — only in his mind, of course — *Y* for *X.* As

[2] A note on word usage: In this book, which follows the convention of the literature on price theory, "to substitute *y* for *x*" means to give up *y* and to acquire *x.* This usage is likely to be confusing at first, because it is the opposite of ordinary usage, where, for example, to substitute eggs for meat means to put eggs in the place of meat. In price theory, however, to substitute means to give up, to trade off, to get rid of.

he moves down the curve, the consumer is trading off units of $Y$ for units of $X$, subject always to the condition that each new combination is subjectively no better and no worse.

At the top of the curve, the consumer substitutes $\Delta y_1$ of $Y$ for $\Delta x_1$ of $X$ as he slides down the curve. Here the consumer has lots of $Y$ and not much of $X$; thus the marginal utility of $Y$ is low and that of $X$ is high. Hence, he is willing to trade $\Delta y_1$ units of $Y$ to get $\Delta x_1$ of $X$. Thus the length $\Delta y_1$ is greater than the length $\Delta x_1$ — at the top of the curve. But as the consumer slides down the curve, the marginal utilities of $X$ and $Y$ change. In Figure 6–1, the length $\Delta x$ is uniform. Therefore, the lengths of the lines $\Delta y$ become shorter and shorter as the consumer slides down the curve. This signifies that when he has lots of $X$ and not much $Y$, the consumer is willing to trade off just a little of $Y$ to get the same number of units of $X$. Notice how short is the length of $\Delta y_2$ at the bottom of the curve.

The rate at which the consumer trades off $Y$ for $X$ is called the *marginal rate of substitution*. As he slides down the curve, the consumer substitutes $Y$ for $X$. And because, as was just explained, he is willing to give up less and less $Y$ for a given gain in $X$, the marginal rate of substitution diminishes. It diminishes in the other direction too, because if the consumer slides *up* the curve, he is willing to trade off diminishing amounts of $X$ for given gains in $Y$.

An Indifference Map

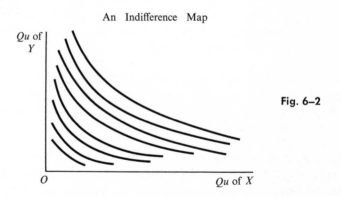

*Qu* of
$Y$

Fig. 6–2

$O$                                   *Qu* of $X$

So far, only one indifference curve has been described. A complete description of a consumer's tastes for two commodities is provided by the *indifference map* which corresponds to an entire system of indifference schedules. Since the field in the diagram contains an infinite number of points and since an indifference curve passes through every point, it follows that the number of indifference curves is infinite. Figure 6–2 shows several indifference curves. Taken together, they comprise the indifference map of the consumer. Each curve shows $X$ and $Y$ combinations that are equally good to the consumer. Any curve that lies to the right of another is said to be higher. Any one of the combinations on a higher indifference curve is preferable to any of those on a lower curve. Indifference, therefore, means sliding back and forth on any one curve, and preference means moving northeast on the map.

### The Shapes of Indifference Curves

If nothing more is said about it, the only requirement for the shape of a demand curve is that it slope downward to the right. Similarly, the only requirement for an indifference curve is that it be convex to the origin. The diminishing marginal rate of substitution of $Y$ for $X$ and of $X$ for $Y$ makes the curve convex. Within this limitation, however, many variations of shapes are possible. The variations reflect differences in taste. The tastes of any one consumer for pairs of different commodities vary from one pair to another; for the same two commodities, each consumer has different tastes.

Take two commodities that are very close substitutes. An example is nickels and dimes. For many purposes, they are perfect substitutes at the constant ratio of two to one. But consider a person who frequently uses parking meters that take dimes and who, therefore, wants to be sure that his small change always includes a dime or two. For such a person, nickels and dimes are not perfect substitutes. His indifference curves for nickels and dimes would have a slope of roughly two to one, and would be bent just slightly.

If two commodities have a rigid one-to-one complementary relation in the mind of the consumer, the indifference curves are right angles. An example is right shoes and left shoes; the consumer is no better off in having two or more right shoes if he has only one left shoe; and vice versa. But he is better off if he has more pairs of shoes, that is, he moves due northeast on his indifference map.

Provided that they are convex to the origin, indifference curves can take any shape between the extremes of the straight line and the right angle. Indifference maps are often drawn so that the curves appear to be parallel to one another. Parallelism, however, is almost devoid of economic significance.[3] An indifference curve can change its general shape in different regions of the field. A move to the northeast is a move to combinations successively preferred. It is also a move to larger quantities of both commodities. Larger quantities of anything are put to more and more uses.

---

[3] Except that, if indifference curves are parallel in a due north-south direction, the income effect is exactly zero. See below.

If $X$ and $Y$ are, say, apples and pears, larger quantities of both mean that the extra apples are turned into applesauce and the extra pears into gifts. Hence, the apple-pear relation can be different for large quantities than for small.[4]

### Prices and Budgets

The next step is to introduce the prices of commodities and the consumer's budget. A consumer's purchases can be determined once prices, his budget, and his tastes are known. An advantage of the indifference-curve diagram is that all three variables can be represented at once.

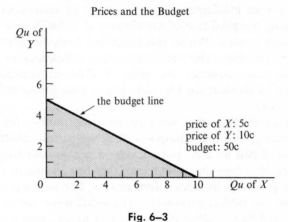

Prices and the Budget

**Fig. 6–3**

Figure 6–3 shows how prices and the consumer's budget are put on the diagram. Let the price of $X$ be 5 cents a unit and the price of $Y$ 10 cents. Let the consumer's budget be 50 cents a time period. Then the consumer could buy 10 units of $X$ if he spent his whole budget on $X$, and he could buy 5 units of $Y$ if he spent the 50 cents on it. A straight line between $10X$ and $5Y$ shows every possibility of spending the budget on the two commodities at their given prices. The straight line is the budget line.[5] A glance at Figure 6–3 shows this: The consumer can buy $10X$ and $0Y$, or $8X$ and $1Y$, or $4X$ and $3Y$, etc. And for that matter, he can also buy any quantity *inside* the shaded area; but if he does this, he is not spending all of his 50 cents. Remember that the diagram shows only physical quantities

[4] A consumer can have so much of a commodity that it is a nuisance, i.e., its marginal utility is negative. This can be shown on an indifference diagram by making an indifference curve curl around and go in the opposite direction.

[5] Terminology for this line is not standardized. Other names in the literature for the budget line are: budget restraint, consumption possibility line, expenditure line, outlay line, price line, and price-income line.

of $X$ and $Y$. Prices and the budget are represented indirectly by the physical quantities. The budget line can be thought of as the limiting boundary on the consumer's opportunities for acquiring $X$ and $Y$.

The *slope* of the budget line shows the ratio of the prices of the two commodities. The slope is one to two, because one unit of $Y$ can be bought with the same amount of money that buys two units of $X$. If both prices were equal, the budget line would have a 45° angle. The *position* of the budget line depends on the size of the budget. If the budget were larger (or smaller), the line would be farther to the right (or left). Changes in prices and in the budget are shown by changing the slope and position of the budget line.

For many purposes, it is convenient to let the horizontal axis represent amounts of a commodity and the vertical axis an amount of money income per time period. Then $X$ is a commodity, and $Y$ is money income. To do this is really to say that $Y$ stands for all other commodities. One commodity, $X$, is then compared with all other commodities which are represented by money income.

### Equilibrium of the Consumer

How much of $X$ and of $Y$ does the consumer buy? He buys those amounts of the two commodities that make him most satisfied according to his own notions of being well off. He has no reason to change his purchases, and is, therefore, in equilibrium.

Equilibrium of the Consumer

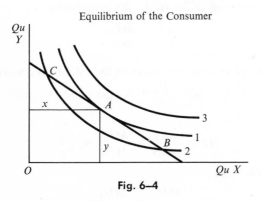

**Fig. 6–4**

In Figure 6–4, the straight line is the budget line, its slope showing the ratio of the prices and its position the size of the consumer's budget. The three curves are three of the indifference curves selected from those comprising the consumer's indifference map. He is in equilibrium at point $A$, which is on the budget line, and also on indifference curve *1*, which just touches — is tangent to — the budget line. The opportunities open to the consumer are those anywhere on the budget line or, for that matter, any-where below it. The consumer wants to be on the highest attainable indifference curve. This is curve *1*, tangent to the budget line. The combination of *x* and *y* at *A* is thus preferred to all others attainable. If the consumer were to buy less *X* and more *Y*, moving up to *C*, he would be on a lower indifference curve, curve *2*. If he did the opposite and moved down to *B*, he would also be on the lower curve *2*. The consumer of course would like to be on a still higher indifference curve such as *3*. But he cannot get there because his budget is too low, or the prices are too high, or because of some combination of these.

When the consumer is in equilibrium, his highest attainable indifference curve is tangent to the budget line. The slopes of the curve and of the line are therefore equal. Has this equality of slopes any economic meaning?

Yes it has. The slope of the indifference curve is $\frac{\Delta Y}{\Delta X}$, which means a change in *Y* divided by a change in *X*. This is the marginal rate of sub-stitution — *MRS.* Suppose the change is a small movement *down* the indifference curve. Then $\frac{\Delta Y}{\Delta X}$, or *MRS*, means a small loss of *Y* divided by a small gain in *X*. But the *utility* of the loss is equal to that of the gain by definition of the indifference curve. Therefore

$$\Delta Y \times MU_Y = \Delta X \times MU_X.$$

That is, the loss of *Y* times the marginal utility of *Y* is equal to the gain of *X* times the marginal utility of *X*. By transposing,

$$\frac{\Delta Y}{\Delta X} = \frac{MU_X}{MU_Y}.$$

That is, the slope of the curve is equal to the ratio of the marginal utilities. The slope of the budget line is $\frac{P_X}{P_Y}$.[6] At the point of equilibrium, accordingly,

$$MRS = \frac{\Delta Y}{\Delta X} = \frac{MU_X}{MU_Y} = \frac{P_X}{P_Y}.$$

It therefore follows that

$$\frac{MU_X}{P_X} = \frac{MU_Y}{P_Y}.$$

All of which means that when the consumer is in equilibrium, the marginal rate of substitution is equal to the ratio of the prices of the two com-

---

[6] Because slope $= \dfrac{\text{amount of } Y}{\text{amount of } X} = \dfrac{\text{budget}}{P_Y} \div \dfrac{\text{budget}}{P_X} = \dfrac{P_X}{P_Y}.$

modities. Equivalently, the last equation says that the marginal utilities derived from the last dollar spent on each good are equal. (See Note 8 in the Appendix to Part Two.) This last statement is of course identical with one of the propositions or theorems of neoclassical cardinal analysis (see pages 57 and 58).

### Effects of Changes in Income

Consider next what happens with a change in the income of the consumer, with prices and his tastes remaining constant.

In general, the higher his income, the more of a commodity a consumer will buy. This is shown in Figure 6–5. In this diagram, $X$ is a commodity and $Y$ is income in dollars per month, for example. The budget line, from left to right, begins on the $Y$-axis with dollars of monthly income; it goes to a point on the $X$-axis that indicates the amount of $X$ the consumer could buy if he spent his whole income on $X$. Of course he doesn't, but this is the way to bring in the *price* of $X$. The budget line is moved to the right to indicate larger incomes; it is moved parallel to itself because the constant slope means constancy of prices.

At higher incomes, higher indifference curves become tangent to the budget lines. Through the successive points of tangency a line is drawn. This line is the *income-consumption curve;* the heavy line with the arrowhead traces out the path of the changes in the consumption of the commodity $X$ as income varies.

Effects of Changes in Income

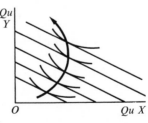

a normal commodity:                    an inferior good:

Fig. 6–5                    Fig. 6–6

In Figure 6–6, the income-consumption curve first moves northeast, then curls around and moves northwest, signifying that after the consumer's income reaches a certain level, he consumes *less* of $X$. Commodities of which this is true are called *inferior goods.* Standard examples are margarine and potatoes.

Though this technical definition of "inferior good" is well established in economic literature, some of the connotations of the expression "inferior good" might be misleading. One connotation is that in the long list of the commodities produced in a modern society, a few can be found that are inferior, that is, deficient in some respect. Another connotation seems to be that inferior goods are poor people's goods. When income rises and poverty is left behind, consumption of the inferior goods declines. Actually, however, to consume less of a commodity at higher incomes is a form of behavior much more common than might at first be supposed. If their social environment causes movie actors to buy Cadillacs when their incomes are high, and to buy Rolls Royces when their incomes are still higher, then for these people, Cadillacs are an inferior good. They are not inferior automobiles, let it be noted, but are an inferior good to *some* buyers. To generalize: When commodities are defined as specific grades or qualities of goods and services, and if there are several grades or qualities, then almost any commodity so defined can be an inferior good for somebody or some class of persons.

### Income Elasticity

The relation between changes in income and changes in consumption can be expressed through the concept of income elasticity of demand. Just as price elasticity of demand means the ratio of the percentage change in the quantity demanded to the percentage change in price, so the income elasticity of demand means the ratio of the percentage change in the quantity demanded to the percentage change in income. In the expression

$$E_y = \frac{\Delta Q}{Q} \div \frac{\Delta Y}{Y} = \frac{Y}{Q} \frac{\Delta Q}{\Delta Y}$$

$E_y$ stands for the coefficient of income elasticity and $Y$ for income. If the value of the coefficient is greater than unity, income elasticity is said to be high; if it is less than unity, income elasticity is said to be low. For all except inferior goods, the sign of the coefficient is positive, because both income and quantity purchased change in the same direction.

The slope of the income-consumption curve gives an indication of income elasticity. If the curve is relatively flat, $E_y$ is high; if it has an angle of $45°$, $E_y$ is unity; if the curve is steep, $E_y$ is low; if the curve is a vertical line, $E_y$ is zero; and if the curve has a negative slope, $E_y$ is negative.[7]

---

[7] The observations about slope and elasticity on page 34 also apply here. The slope of the income-consumption curve is $\frac{\Delta Y}{\Delta Q}$, whereas its elasticity is $\frac{\Delta Q}{\Delta Y} \frac{Y}{Q}$. Though the statements above are not fully accurate, they can hardly be misleading.

**Effects of Changes in Prices**

The indifference-curve analysis has, to repeat, three explicit variables. Two can be held constant while the third is made to change. When the price of a commodity changes, the consumer alters his purchases, provided of course that his tastes and income remain constant.

Effects of Changes in Prices

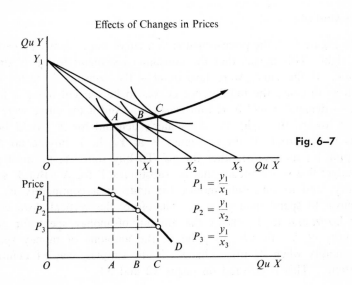

Fig. 6–7

The effects of changes in price are shown in the upper part of Figure 6–7. In this Figure, $X$ is a commodity and $Y$ is money income. First of all, let the consumer be in equilibrium at $A$. His budget line is $Y_1X_1$, which is touched at $A$ by the indifference curve shown in the diagram. Suppose the price of $X$ falls. To represent this, the foot of the budget line is moved to the *right* by a distance proportionate to the fall in price. The amount $OX_1$ is the quantity of $X$ that could be bought at the initial price if the entire budget were spent on $X$. With a fall in price, the consumer could buy more with his entire budget, namely, the amount $OX_2$. With another reduction in price, he could buy still more, say, $OX_3$. Each fall in price establishes a new budget line — $Y_1X_2$, $Y_1X_3$, etc. To each, an indifference curve is tangent — at point $B$, point $C$, etc. The line drawn through the points of tangency is the *price-consumption curve*. The line shows how the consumption, or purchase, of $X$ varies as its price varies.

The price-consumption curve represents sets of prices of $X$ and the quantities of $X$ the consumer buys at each price. The curve, therefore, contains the information from which the consumer's demand curve can be constructed. The lower part of Figure 6–7 shows how this can be done.

In the lower diagram, the horizontal axis is quantity. The quantities $A$, $B$, and $C$ are marked off. The vertical axis is price. The prices are found from the upper part by dividing money income by the maximum quantity of $X$ that can be bought. This gives the three prices $P_1$, $P_2$, and $P_3$ in the lower diagram. The three prices and the three quantities $A$, $B$, and $C$ give three points on the demand curve $D$.

### Price Elasticity

In Figure 6–7, the price-consumption curve slopes gently upward toward the right. This means that the consumer's demand for $X$ is slightly inelastic. If the curve were horizontal — the consumer's tastes could be such as to cause the indifference curves to be tangent along a horizontal line — demand would have unit elasticity. And if the curve were to slope down toward the right, the consumer's demand for $X$ would be elastic. This is the proof: If the consumer is at $Y_1$, he is buying no $X$ and is keeping his money for other things. To buy some $X$, he must go down a budget line which means that he substitutes $Y$ for $X$. But $Y$ stands for money, and to substitute money for units of a commodity is, in plain English, to spend money on it. Therefore, the vertical distance from a line horizontal to $Y_1$ shows the amount of money spent for any given quantity of $X$. Finally, to point to the amounts of money spent on a commodity when its price changes is the simplest way of defining price elasticity. This is covered on pages 32 and 33.

### The Income Effect and the Substitution Effect

Suppose that you live in an apartment and that your landlord suddenly announces that he is cutting all monthly rents in half and that he will keep maintenance and other services at the same level. The effect of this action is as if your income were increased. Your response is to move from a three-room to a four-room apartment in the same building because now that rooms are much cheaper, you rent more rooms. You have two reasons to do so. One — the income effect — is that you are better off. The other — the substitution effect — is that each room is now less expensive.

The income effect and the substitution effect are the names for the two effects of a change in price to the consumer. The expression "substitution effect" means nothing more than that the consumer buys a larger quantity of a commodity whose price falls, quite independently of the gain in his real income. In the upper part of Figure 6–8, the consumer is in initial equilibrium at point $A$, where indifference curve $1$ is tangent to the budget line $Y_1X_1$. Let the price of $X$ fall, so that the new budget line is $Y_1X_2$. Indifference curve $2$ is tangent to the new budget line at point $B$. Indifference curve *2* is of course higher than curve *1*. The consumer *could have* got to point *C* on curve *2* by an increase of his money income (assuming no change in price). This is shown by the line $Y_2X_3$, which is parallel to the original budget line $Y_1X_1$. The consumer's actual *money* income does not increase, but the fall in price has an effect *as if* his income had increased, because his *real* income rises. The increase in the consumption of *X* is divided into two parts: In Figure 6–8, the income effect is the increase in quantity from $OA_1$ to $OC_1$. The substitution effect is the increase in quantity from $OC_1$ to $OB_1$.

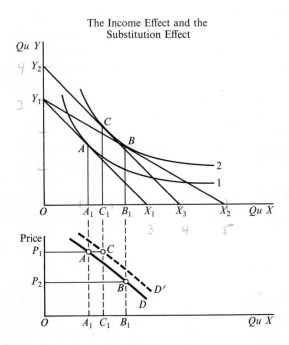

The Income Effect and the
Substitution Effect

Fig. 6–8

The lower part of Figure 6–8 translates the upper part into a demand diagram, with price and quantity on the axes. The initial price is $P_1$ (equal to $Y_1 \div X_1$). The demand curve *D* shows the increase in quantity demanded from $OA_1$ to $OB_1$. The dashed curve *D'* shows the hypothetical gain in income, with the accompanying increase in quantity demanded from $OA_1$ to $OC_1$. Here too, $A_1C_1$ is the income effect and $C_1B_1$ is the substitution effect.

The significance of the income effect is that a fall in the price of a commodity can make the consumer better off, just as if he had more money, as in the hypothetical rent example above.

Generally the two effects work in the same direction; with a fall in price, both lead to increases in consumption, i.e., in the quantity demanded. The income effect, however, can be negligible. If the price of a bottle of ink drops by 5 cents, you are not going to jump for joy and revise your entire budget. This is the same thing as saying that price changes have no effect on the marginal utility of income for the consumer. For the income effect to be zero, the indifference curves have to be exactly parallel in the north-south direction.

### The Giffen Effect

The income effect can also be negative. If it is, the indifference curves are so shaped that point $C$ in Figure 6–8 lies northwest of point $A$. But again, the substitution effect is positive and outweighs a negative effect, so that a fall in price still causes the consumer to buy more. Theorists like to speculate, however, on the possibility of a negative income effect so strong that it swamps the substitution effect, causing the consumer to buy *less* when price falls. Point $B$ in Figure 6–8 would then, owing to the shapes of the indifference curves, lie northwest of point $A$. This is called the Giffen effect, which is also mentioned in Chapter 2 (page 24). Could this ever happen? It could, perhaps, in circumstances where the consumer is so poor that he lives on a diet mainly of bread (the commodity $X$). A big fall in the price of bread frees income to buy other foods such as meat, thus causing the consumer to buy less bread.

### Importance of the Income Effect

The income effects of changes in prices are normally so small that for most purposes they can be disregarded. The usual indifference curve diagrams, those in this chapter being no exception, contain a gross exaggeration. They show, as J. R. Hicks himself says,[8] the consumer spending a preposterously large part of his income on the one commodity $X$. It was explained earlier that the amount spent is the distance down from the left end of the budget line. This amount is made large in the diagrams for no other reason than to make them clear. The same reason also calls for large changes in price in the diagrams. The two exaggerations in the diagrams make the income effect look much more important than it is.

With the exception of housing, the commodities bought by consumers in the United States account each for a tiny fraction of income. Then too, during any time period in which tastes can be imagined as constant, price changes are always small.

[8] *A Revision of Demand Theory* (London: Oxford, 1956), p. 60n.

## Applications

The indifference curves of consumers cannot be measured and portrayed in actual numbers. A few attempts to derive numbers from experiments have been fruitless.[9] Nevertheless, the indifference-curve technique of analysis is a means of clear thinking on problems with important practical aspects.

### The Income Tax Versus the Excise Tax

Consider the welfare implications of income taxation as compared with excise taxation, i.e., the taxation of particular commodities. When a legislature deliberates the choice of imposing higher taxes on incomes or on commodities, it must take many things into account — administrative matters, effects on the distribution of income, upon the industries affected, on incentives, on the stability of the economy. In addition, a legislature might ask itself: Which imposes the greater burden, a higher income tax or a higher excise tax? Which hurts more?

This question can be answered for a single taxpayer, who can be thought of as representative of a group of taxpayers with the same income. To make the problem clear-cut, let it be assumed that the additional income tax is equal in dollar amount to the additional tax on a commodity consumed by the taxpayer. Assume further that the taxpayer will not stop buying the commodity because of its higher price which is due to the tax. The dollar amount could be something like, say, one hundred dollars. To repeat, which is worse? To have to pay one hundred dollars a year more in income tax or one hundred dollars more in indirect taxes on a commodity? Or does it make any difference?

The problem is solved in Figure 6–9. The taxpayer has an income $OY_1$ and is a consumer of commodity $X$. The initial price of $X$ is indicated indirectly by $OX_1$ (if he spent all his income on $X$, he could buy $OX_1$ units of it). Thus the initial budget line is $Y_1X_1$. Let the consumer be in equilibrium at point $A$, which is on indifference curve $1$. The imposition of a tax on commodity $X$ raises its price. The higher price of $X$ results in a new budget line, $Y_1X_2$. As indicated in Figure 6–9, the price of $X$ more than doubles, i.e., $OX_2$ is less than half $OX_1$. This, of course, is an exag-

[9] Perhaps observation of the higher apes, so it has been ruefully hoped, could throw "some light" on human tastes and preferences. This is (or was) the opinion of W. Allen Wallis and Milton Friedman, "The Empirical Derivation of Indifference Functions," in Oscar Lange, Francis McIntyre, and Theodore O. Yntema (eds.), *Studies in Mathematical Economics and Econometrics* (Chicago: University of Chicago Press, 1942), p. 181.

geration because excise taxes hardly ever have so strong an effect. But this exaggeration too makes for a better diagram and does not affect the conclusion. On the budget line $Y_1X_2$, the taxpayer is in equilibrium at

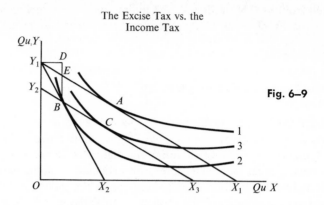

The Excise Tax vs. the
Income Tax

Fig. 6–9

point $B$ on indifference curve 2. He now buys less of $X$, because B lies left of $A$. The next step is to measure the indirect tax bill. To buy the amount of $X$ indicated by $B$, the consumer spends an amount of money equal to $DB$. If he bought no $X$ at all, he would be at $D$ $(= Y_1)$. If he had bought the same quantity of $X$ at the former lower price, he would have spent $DE$. Hence $EB$ is the amount of the tax. (An arithmetical example: Suppose the consumer formerly bought 10 units @ $4 and now buys 8 units @ $6. He now spends $48. But if he had bought 8 units @ $4, he would have spent $32. Therefore $16 of the $48 are his indirect tax bill.) Next, take an income tax of the same amount as $EB$. Measure down from $Y_1$ the distance $Y_1Y_2 = EB$. That is, his income after income tax is $Y_2O$. Draw the new budget line $Y_2X_3$ parallel to the first one. In-difference curve 3 touches $Y_2X_3$ at $C$. Since indifference curve 2 is lower than 3, it follows that the excise tax hurts more than the income tax of the same amount.

The indifference-curve analysis always yields this conclusion no matter what is the shape of the indifference curves, provided only that they are convex. But notice that the analysis says only *that* an excise tax puts a taxpayer on a lower curve than does an income tax of equal amount. The analysis does not say *how much* worse is the subjective burden of the excise tax.

The common sense of the conclusion is that the excise tax is worse be-cause it distorts the budget of the consumer, who has to adjust around the higher price of *one* commodity and cannot spread the decrease in his pur-chasing power as advantageously over many commodities as would be pos-sible if he paid the income tax instead of the excise tax.

## Subsidies to Consumers

Another application of the indifference-curve analysis is to the effects of subsidies to persons with low incomes. Suppose that the government makes certain commodities available at lower prices to certain low-income groups. To do this is a normal activity of the modern social-service state. As an illustration, take public housing. Assume that the tenants in public housing projects pay about half the rent that would be charged for similar accommodations and that the other half of the rent is a subsidy. (This assumption, by the way, is quite realistic.) Is the benefit to the tenants as great as the cost of the subsidy?

Subsidies to Consumers

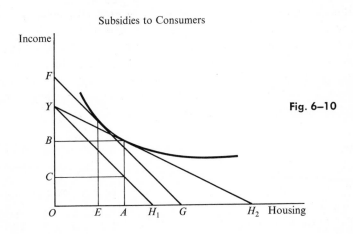

Fig. 6–10

Figure 6–10 furnishes the answer to this question. In the figure, the position of one consumer (and his family) is portrayed. Income is on the vertical axis and housing — measured in square feet of floor space — is on the horizontal. Let the consumer's income be $YO$. If he rented unsubsidized housing and spent all of his income on it, he could rent $OH_1$ square feet. Hence $YH_1$ is the budget line without subsidy. The subsidy is given by reducing rents one half. So the budget line with subsidy is $YH_2$; this is the same as a reduction in price by one half, i.e., $OH_2$ is twice $OH_1$. The consumer is in equilibrium when he rents $OA$ of housing; this is the amount indicated by the tangency of the indifference curve to the budget line with subsidy. Now the next step: The amount of the subsidy is $BC$ dollars. This is explained as follows: In equilibrium, the consumer spends $YB$ on housing. Without subsidy and renting the same amount, he would have to spend $YC$. Hence the cost to the government of the subsidy is $BC$, the vertical distance between the two budget lines. But to the consumer, the subsidy is not cash but more housing. What is the money equivalent of the subsidy to the consumer? In Figure 6–10, it is *FY* dollars. The budget line without subsidy is moved to the right just far enough to become tangent to the indifference curve. This is the line *FG,* whose meaning is the increase in *money* income that makes the consumer just as well off as the subsidy. Clearly, *FY* is less than *BC.* In fact it will always be, whatever the subsidy and whatever the preferences of consumers, so long as only the indifference curves remain convex and smooth. Thus the cost of giving subsidies to consumers is always greater than the money equivalent of the subjective gain to the consumers. Here, of course, is a special case of the general principle that, apart from considerations of etiquette and sentiment, you can make someone happier if you give him cash instead of a commodity, even if the commodity is something he wants.

But the validity of the principle does not by itself condemn public housing programs. They must be judged by criteria going beyond the subjective benefits to the tenants. Another glance at Figure 6–10 shows that with the subsidy, the consumer chooses *OA* of housing. But if he got the equivalent cash subsidy, he would choose *OE* housing, which is less. Accordingly, the subsidy induces him to rent more (square feet of) housing. This, too, is one of the goals of a public housing program.

### Summary

The indifference-curve analysis of consumer demand is based on the concept of *ordinal utility*. Having a choice between two combinations of goods, the consumer either prefers one combination or he is indifferent. The *indifference curve* shows all combinations of two commodities that give the same satisfaction to a consumer. The indifference curve is convex because of the *diminishing marginal rate of substitution* between the two commodities. A complete description of a consumer's tastes for two commodities is provided by the *indifference map*. The consumer's budget and the prices of the two commodities are represented by the *budget line*. The slope of the budget line is the ratio of the price of *X* to the price of *Y*. The position of the line reflects the size of the budget. The consumer is in *equilibrium* when he buys the two commodities in the quantities defined by the tangency of an indifference curve to the budget line. In equilibrium, the ratio of the prices is equal to the marginal rate of substitution.

If income increases, the budget line moves to the right. The *income-consumption curve* goes through the points of tangency of indifference curves with parallel budget lines. If the income-consumption curve has a positive slope, the commodity is normal. But if the curve has a negative slope, the commodity is called an *inferior good*. When the *Y*-axis measures money income and the *X*-axis physical quantities of a commodity, the slope of the income-consumption curve gives an indication of *income elas-*

*ticity of demand,* which is the percentage change in quantity demanded divided by the percentage change in income.

If the price of commodity $X$ changes, the budget line changes its slope. The *price-consumption curve* goes through the points of tangency of indifference curves with budget lines of different slopes. The *income effect* of a change in price is the change in quantity demanded attributable to the ensuing change in real income, whereas the *substitution effect* is the change in quantity demanded that is independent of the change in real income. Generally, the income and the substitution effects of a fall in price work together in leading to an increase in the quantity demanded. In the *Giffen effect,* however, the income effect is negative and strong enough to offset the substitution effect. The income effect, however, is nearly always very small.

Indifference-curve analysis is a means of clear thinking on problems concerning the behavior and economic welfare of consumers.

## SELECTED REFERENCES

J. R. Hicks, *Value and Capital,* 2d ed. (London: Oxford, 1946). Also by Hicks, *A Revision of Demand Theory* (London: Oxford, 1956).

A good commentary on the cardinal-ordinal controversy is in D. H. (Sir Dennis) Robertson, *Utility and All That* (New York: Macmillan, 1952), Chap. 1.

Some good applications of indifference curve analysis are in George J. Stigler, *The Theory of Price,* rev. ed. (New York: Macmillan, 1952), Chap. 5.

The tax application has had its own little controversy. See Milton Friedman, "The 'Welfare' Effects of an Income Tax and an Excise Tax," *Journal of Political Economy,* LX, February, 1952, pp. 25–33. Reprinted in Milton Friedman, *Essays in Positive Economics* (Chicago: University of Chicago Press, 1953).

The housing application is adapted and modified from a food-stamp application in Tibor Scitovsky, *Welfare and Competition* (Homewood: Irwin, 1951), pp. 65–67.

## EXERCISES AND PROBLEMS

1. Draw a diagram like Figure 6–1 on page 79, but make the increments in $Y$ constant. Explain your diagram.

2. Draw indifference curves to show commodity $Y$ as a nuisance over some range of quantity. Do the same for $X$.

3. Draw a budget line with $P_X = 25¢$, $P_Y = 10¢$, and a budget of $1.00.

4. Draw a diagram with the consumer in equilibrium. Then change both income and $P_X$ by moving and changing the slope of the budget line. Show the new equilibrium.

5. Show that if indifference curves were straight lines or were concave, the consumer would always buy one of the commodities, not both.

6. In Figure 6–6 on page 85, $X$ is the inferior good. Draw a diagram that makes $Y$ the inferior good.

7. Draw diagrams with different shapes of price-consumption curves.

8. Draw diagrams with various prices of $Y$, holding the price of $X$ constant.

9. Draw diagrams like Figure 6–8, but with a zero income effect and a negative income effect.

10. Draw a diagram for the Giffen effect.

# More Topics in the Theory
# of Demand

7

Several more topics in the theory of demand are still to be covered. The earlier chapters place most of their emphasis on price. This chapter goes farther into the roles played by consumer incomes, by the prices of other commodities, and by time. The last section of this chapter will also analyze demand from the points of view of the sellers of commodities.

## Income Elasticity

His income is, of course, one of the determinants of a consumer's purchases of a commodity. The concept of income elasticity of demand, as applied to the individual consumer, has already been described (page 86). Consider now the income elasticity of the demand for a commodity when there are many buyers. To repeat the definition of the coefficient of income elasticity: $E_y$ is the relative change in quantity bought divided by the corresponding relative change in the incomes of the buyers.[1]

[1] In this book, the symbol $E$ stands for price elasticity of demand. The symbols for the other elasticity concepts have subscripts, to distinguish them. Note 4 in the Appendix to Part Two gives the simple mathematics of income elasticity of demand.

When other determinants of the demand for a commodity are held constant while consumers' incomes vary, the relationship is sometimes called income demand. The idea of demand as a function of income is portrayed in Figure 7–1. Here are five income-demand curves. The curve marked *high* $(E_y > 1)$ shows increases in income accompanied by relatively large increases in amounts bought. The *unit* $(E_y = 1)$ curve is drawn at a 45° angle (the axes would have to be calibrated so that equal absolute changes in each would signify the same percentage changes). The curve marked *low* $(E_y < 1)$ shows quantity increasing relatively less than income. The curve marked *zero* $(E_y = 0)$ shows that quantity bought is constant regardless of changes in income. The curve marked *neg.*, i.e., *negative* $(E_y < 0)$ says that less is bought at higher incomes and that more is bought at lower incomes.

Income Elasticities

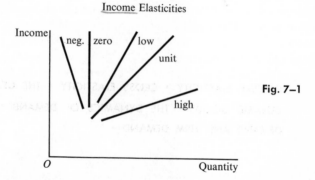

Fig. 7–1

Notice the difference in terminology here. If the coefficient is greater than one, income elasticity is "high;" if the coefficient is less than one, income elasticity is "low." In contrast, demand is "elastic" if the coefficient of *price* elasticity is greater than one and "inelastic" if it is less than one.

Commodities differ widely in their income elasticities. Furs, jewelry, the better grades of steak, and automobiles are examples of commodities whose income elasticities tend to be high. In contrast, soap, salt, matches, newspapers, etc. have low income elasticities of demand. The proportion of income spent on a commodity is a major determinant of how high or how low is its income elasticity. An exception to this statement is probably housing, which takes a sizable part of anyone's income; housing seems to have a coefficient close to unity. But commodities that people regard as expensive, as luxuries, generally have high income elasticities. Indeed the simplest and best way to define luxuries is to say that they are commodities with high income elasticities of demand. Similarly, necessities can be defined as commodities with low income elasticities; cigarettes, for example. These definitions are analytical — they bypass the moral connotations that hover over the everyday ideas of luxuries and necessities.

### Income Sensitivity

A rough and ready but practical companion to the concept of income elasticity is the income sensitivity of consumption expenditures. Income elasticity has to do with changes in *physical units* purchased, whereas income sensitivity deals with changes in *dollar expenditures*. The income sensitivity of a commodity in a period of time is measured by calculating the percentage change in dollar expenditures associated with a one-per cent change in disposable income in the same period. Income sensitivity therefore also has a coefficient. In the calculations made by the United States Department of Commerce, the effects of long-term growth or decline in consumption are eliminated by statistical procedures. But the coefficients of income sensitivity are still rough and ready, because there is no way to disentangle the effects of changes in income from the effects of changes in prices and in tastes. The many data on income sensitivity have, however, some modest use in business forecasting.

The Department of Commerce has found that the following commodities and services have high income sensitivities (coefficients equal to 1.5 or more): telephone service, automobiles, air transportation, television repair, and foreign travel. These are just a few examples. Commodities and services with low income sensitivities (coefficients less than 0.5) are exemplified by shoes, clothing, local bus transportation, and dental care.

### Cross Elasticity

Consider some simple relations between demands and prices. Suppose the price of commodity $A$ goes up. Hence less of $A$ is bought. Some of the consumers shift to a substitute, commodity $B$. Hence the demand for $B$ rises, and if the price of $B$ remains the same, more of $B$ is bought. Next, suppose that commodity $C$ is complementary with $A$. After $A$'s price rise and the consequent decline in the purchase of $A$, less of $C$ is wanted. Thus the demand for $C$ diminishes. In general, therefore, a rise in the price of a commodity increases the demand for its substitutes and diminishes the demand for its complements.

In practical problems of demand analysis, commodities stand in more or less definite clusters of substitutes and complements. The concept of cross elasticity of demand is useful in handling intercommodity relations. Once more, take two commodities, $A$ and $B$. Let $A$'s price go up. What is the effect on the quantity of $B$ that is bought? The expression for cross elasticity of demand is

$$E_{BP_A} = \frac{\Delta Q_B}{Q_B} \div \frac{\Delta P_A}{P_A}$$

The coefficient $E_{BP_A}$ is therefore the relative (percentage) change in the quantity demanded of commodity $B$ divided by the relative (percentage) change in the price of commodity $A$. The coefficient is positive if $A$ and $B$ are substitutes because the price change and the quantity change are in the same direction. If the price of $A$ goes up, so does the quantity of $B$, and vice versa. But if $A$ and $B$ are complements, the coefficient is negative because changes in the price of one commodity cause opposite changes in the quantity demanded of the other.

Suppose that the two commodities are oleomargarine and butter. The cross-elasticity formula shows the relative (e.g., percentage) gain in pounds of butter purchased for a rise in the price of oleo. Other things of course are held constant; they are consumer tastes for both oleo and butter, consumer incomes, and the price of butter. In some time period, the coefficient has a value, say, 0.4, which means that a 10-per cent rise in the price of oleo causes consumers to buy 4 per cent more butter. If, however, the relationship is reversed — if oleo consumption is made to depend on the price of butter — does the coefficient have the same numerical value? No, the coefficient is likely to be lower, say, 0.2, which would mean that a 10-per cent change in the price of butter causes a 2-per cent change in the consumption of oleo. Why the difference? Some households buy both; some buy only one. The households buying both oleo and butter probably put the two fats to different uses. Thus, substitution is a complex process; it does not work the same way in both directions. (See Note 4 in the Appendix to Part Two.)

### The Relevant Market

The closer two commodities are as substitutes for each other, the greater is the size of the cross-elasticity coefficient. Close substitutes have high cross elasticities of demand. Two commodities are poor substitutes for each other, if the cross elasticities are low.

These ideas find important application in the enforcement of the antitrust laws. It is unlawful to monopolize, with intent to do so, the production and (interstate) sale of a commodity. But what is a commodity? Remember that a commodity can be defined broadly or narrowly, generally or specifically. So, too, in the antitrust field, the "relevant market" presents a problem of definition. Is the product of a particular business firm a monopolized product, that is, are buyers so restricted in choice that they must buy from the one business firm and have no alternatives? For *any* product, there are substitutes of one kind or another. If, however, they are poor substitutes, their cross elasticities of demand with the product are low. Here, then, is one way of defining a monopolized product. Similarly, a business firm charged with violating the laws against monopolization will try to prove that cross elasticities between its product and other similar ones are high, that therefore substitutes are close, and that buyers do indeed have effective choices. Unfortunately, no one has been able to show, either conceptually or practically, just how to draw a clear line between high and low cross elasticities of demand.

A good illustration is given by the well-known *Cellophane* decision by the federal courts in 1953. In 1947, the Department of Justice brought suit against the du Pont Company for having illegally monopolized the production and sale of cellophane. The legal proceedings were long and complicated; in the end, the courts held that the government could not prove its charges. In the eyes of the law, du Pont was not a monopolist in marketing cellophane. The relevant market, the courts decided, was the market for "flexible packaging materials," of which cellophane is only one, along with waxed paper, aluminum foil, pliofilm, polyethylene, and many others. In other words, the courts accepted the argument that the cross elasticities of demand between cellophane and other flexible packaging materials are high, that therefore they are all close substitutes, and that therefore du Pont had no monopoly. The government argued in vain that in some of its important uses the cross elasticities of demand between cellophane and its substitutes are low, that therefore they are poor or unacceptable substitutes, and that therefore du Pont really did have a monopoly.

Defining the relevant market in an antitrust case, accordingly, is much the same problem as defining a commodity. The cross-elasticity concept helps a little: If it is clear that several things have high cross elasticities among themselves, then they can be lumped together as one commodity, bought and sold in one "relevant" market. If, however, it is clear that their cross elasticities are low, then they are all separate commodities, just as are the markets they are sold in.

## The Demand for Durable Goods

Durable goods are those yielding a series of services to their owners over periods of time. Automobiles yield miles of service, television sets yield hours of viewing, washing machines yield loads of clean laundry, and so on. Most durable goods are bought one at a time, with the obvious exception of the large business firm that acquires several trucks in one purchase. In general, it is not meaningful to think of the demand of the individual consumer or firm as a schedule of quantities and possible prices. But when individual demands are aggregated, schedules then emerge.

The demands for most durable consumer goods fluctuate widely during the course of the business cycle. One cause is that the bulk of consumer durables seem to have coefficients of income elasticity larger than unity. Many durables are relatively expensive when their prices are measured against consumer incomes; hence incomes are important determinants of quantities bought. (This is not true, of course, of such consumer durables as ashtrays, combs, fountain pens, and many other similar commodities.)

Great interest attaches to the demands for housing, automobiles, and the major household appliances. These demands play an important and visible role in the general expansions and contractions of the entire economy. The fluctuations in the demands for durables come not alone from variations in consumer incomes, but also from the relations between commodity stocks and flows.

At any one time, a stock of a durable good exists. Over a period of time, such as a year, some units in the stock become worn out and are scrapped, or disappear from the stock for other reasons. The new units bought in such quantities as to maintain the stock at a given size are called the _replacement demand_. Additional units whose purchase increases the total size of the stock constitute the _expansion demand_. If the total stock shrinks in size, the expansion demand is a negative quantity, i.e., a subtraction from replacement demand. Accordingly, consumers can be visualized as wanting to hold, over a period of several years, a stock of a durable good. This is their _stock demand_. Their demand during a year is their _flow demand_, i.e., replacement plus expansion demand. Suppose that stock demand increases. Then flow demand is likely to increase relatively much more. To illustrate: Say that 20 million units of an appliance are in use and that replacement demand is 10 per cent, or 2 million units. Suppose now that because of a change in tastes and in incomes, consumers decide to hold 22 million units; their stock demand increases 10 per cent. Then, in the year in question, flow demand jumps up by 100 per cent — the 2 million replacement units plus the 2 million additional new units.

The demand for consumer durables contains other complications. Replacements are hardly ever made on an exact time schedule. Consumers can and do exercise much choice in deciding when to replace. The old car can nearly always be made to last longer. On the other hand, dramatic style changes may make the early purchase of a new one seem desirable. Financing arrangements are also important; down payments, interest rates, lengths of loans, and methods of payment have a powerful influence on quantities bought. It follows that although the demand for consumer durable goods is affected by price, the influence of price is obscured or seemingly outweighed by changes in income, by the interactions between stock demand and flow demand, and by financing arrangements.

## The Dynamics of Demand

The word "dynamics" is used here to mean simply change over time. If the demand for a commodity is a function of price, of tastes, of incomes, and of the prices of substitutes and complements, it is also a function of time. For the most part, however, price theory specifies that demand holds for some one given period of time. To do this makes it possible to draw a demand curve, whose properties and consequences can then be analyzed.

So too in practical work. To lay the foundation for a business pricing decision, the analyst must expend considerable ingenuity in making an estimate of *the* demand for a product for the next six months or some such period of time.

Yet it is well to bear in mind that demand curves are much more likely to be in constant motion than to be standing still. Consumer tastes change, so do incomes, and so do the other prices. These matters have been mentioned and emphasized before. Chapter 3 stresses the influence of time upon price elasticity — the longer the time, the greater the possibilities of substitution and therefore the larger the coefficient of price elasticity.

The demand curves for many commodities steadily shift to the right over long periods of time simply because of the growth of the economy which, among other things, results in ever larger numbers of consumers. Secular gains in productivity mean that consumers have higher incomes. Some demand curves move faster to the right than others, owing to structural changes in tastes. The postwar period has seen, for example, strong increases in the demand for air transportation, automobile insurance, and electricity. The process of innovation brings wholly new products. Demands for them spring out of nowhere, expand rapidly, and sooner or later take on a more or less stable shape. Yet it is not fully accurate to say that the demands for new products come from nowhere. Once again, the meaning of "commodity" has to be put into play. The sudden and powerful demand for a new drug is really a part of the general demand for medical care; the new drug displaces an old one whose demand drops way off. The postwar demand for television sets accompanied a decline in the demand for admissions to motion-picture theaters; the demands for TV, radio, high fi, etc. are parts of the general demand for commercially provided entertainment. Accordingly, though the demands for broad classes of commodities expand fairly steadily over longer periods of time, the demands for specific products can undergo strong shifts.

The cyclical swings in the demands for commodities with high-income elasticities have already been mentioned. One more type of change in demand remains for brief mention. The demands for some commodities have seasonal patterns. The demand curves can be imagined as moving back and fourth between the seasonal lows and highs. So, too, some services have demands subject to weekly and daily rhythms. Business firms sometimes lower their prices for the periods when seasonal, or weekly, or daily demands are at their farthermost left positions. Examples are lower prices at resorts in the "off" season, lower fares on airlines on certain days of the week, and lower admission charges at movies in the afternoon.[2]

---

[2] These are also examples of "price discrimination," which is the subject of Chapter 20.

### Price Expectations

So far the price expectations of consumers have not been taken into account. Consumers have been described as facing given prices of the commodity in question and of its substitutes and complements. Suppose now that consumers make definite plans for their purchases of commodities in successive periods of time stretching into the future. For the sake of simplicity, let the discussion be confined at first to one consumer. The consumer looks into the future and makes plans on how much of each commodity to buy in each period. His plans for future purchases depend on his estimates of the prices he expects to prevail in future periods. Let it also be assumed that the consumer's expectations are of definite prices, not probable prices or ranges of prices. He might expect seasonal variations in prices and accordingly will plan to buy more when prices are low and less when they are high. When he does this, the consumer is making substitutions over time. To these substitutions there are certain limits, which are set by the consumer's tastes and by the varying durabilities and storabilities of commodities. Suppose, for example, that you expect that the net retail price of a new car you are interested in will be lower at the end of the model year. So you plan to buy one then, meanwhile continuing to drive your old car. Suppose also that you are sure that a gasoline price war will break out in your area three months from now. As a rational manager of your finances, you will plan to use your car more during the price war so as to enjoy the lower price of gasoline. But obviously, the possibilities of substituting the consumption of gasoline over time are quite small.

Suppose now that the consumer believes, rightly or wrongly, that the price of some one commodity will rise steadily in the periods ahead. Acting on this belief, he will buy more now, within the limits of substitution over time. Therefore, the expectation of higher prices in the future increases demand now.

### Elasticity of Price Expectations

Just how much demand is affected by price expectations depends in good part upon the elasticity of price expectations. Here is another elasticity concept, devised by the English economist J. R. Hicks in 1939. People's price expectations are influenced by many things — by political news, by current and recent economic events, by the prevailing climate of opinion, and by experience with changes in prices. Hicks's concept ties together price experience with expectations of future prices.

The elasticity of price expectations is the ratio of the relative change in expected future prices to the relative change in current prices. Suppose that a consumer or a businessman sees that the price of a commodity has just gone up by 10 per cent. (Here, too, "relative change" can be expressed as a percentage). If, therefore, the consumer or businessman takes his original estimate of a future price of that commodity and raises the estimate by 20 per cent, he then has an elasticity of price expectations of 2.

Table 7–1 shows the possible ranges of elasticities of price expectations of buyers in a market.

A rise in the prices currently being paid will cause the demand curve to shift to the right, if buyers have elasticities of price expectations that are greater than unity. Demand increases because buyers want to buy more now to avoid the even higher prices they expect to prevail in the future. On the other hand, if elasticities are low or negative, a rise in price now

**TABLE 7–1**

### Elasticity of Price Expectations
#### (Attitudes of Buyers toward a Rise in a Current Price)

| Elasticity | Coefficient[a] | Remarks[b] |
|---|---|---|
| High | $>1$ | Buyers expect that future prices will keep on rising. |
| Unit | $1$ | Buyers expect current rise will be permanent. |
| Low | $<1 >0$ | Buyers expect current rise will be temporary. |
| Zero | $0$ | Buyers expect current rise to have no effect on future prices. |
| Negative | $<0$ | Buyers expect that current rise will be followed by a *fall* in future prices. |

[a] Let future prices be $F$, and current prices be $C$. Then the coefficient of the elasticity of price expectations is $\dfrac{\Delta F}{F} \div \dfrac{\Delta C}{C}$.

[b] Buyers normally have different elasticities of price expectations. The remarks are all based on the simplifying assumption that the buyers in a market have the same elasticities.

causes demand to diminish. The demand curve shifts to the left as buyers wait for the price to come down in the future. And if elasticity is unity, a change in the prices being currently paid has no effect at all on the current demand. If, for example, a rise of 10 per cent in the current price causes buyers to revise their original estimates of future price by plus 10 per cent, the ratio of current and future prices remains constant. Thus there is no reason to alter purchase plans.

## Industry Demand and Firm Demand

Up to now, the whole subject of demand has been discussed from the point of view of consumers and their behavior in spending money on commodities. But buyers' expenditures are the same amounts of money as sellers' receipts. A jump to the other side of the market permits a view of demand as seen by the sellers of commodities.

First of all, the demand for the output of an industry must be distinguished from the demand for the output of a single firm in the industry. The distinction is tied to the classification of market structures, which will now be given a brief introduction. Later chapters will describe and analyze them more closely.

### Market Structures

The standard classification of market structures is simple, being based on just two ideas — the number of firms in an industry and the homogeneity or differentiation of the firms' products.

*Pure competition* in an industry means many firms producing homogeneous products. How many is "many"? It is any number such that each firm sells so small a part of the total output of the industry that the firm cannot see the effects of its actions on price. Hence the firm ignores these effects. A firm in an industry with pure competition is a price-taker, not a price-maker. Homogeneity of product means that each firm's product is, to the buyers, a perfect substitute for the product of any other firm in the industry. Usually this means uniform grades and standards specifying the physical characteristics of a commodity. British economists and some American economists use the expression perfect competition instead of pure competition. Nearly always the context is clear enough to prevent possible confusion. But competition can also be pure *and* perfect, and when it is, the word perfect is not a synonym for pure. In *pure and perfect competition,* the number of firms is large, their products are homogeneous; in addition, the firms have perfect (i.e., full) knowledge of the market, and resources are perfectly (i.e., instantaneously and frictionlessly) mobile. Perfection of competition in this sense is not something real, nor has anyone ever pretended that it is. Instead, perfection of competition is a simplifying assumption to use in handling complicated problems.

Pure competition among firms exists in the markets for most farm products and in the markets for some mineral and forest products. Pure competition is not remote. It is, indeed, a fact of everyday experience, for pure competition also prevails among consumers. They too are price-takers. They too, as individuals, buy so little of any one commodity that each act of purchase has no appreciable influence on price. The consumer is a price maker only when he can bargain effectively and sway a price decision in his favor.

Since the word "impure" can possibly suggest irrelevant connotations, competition that is not pure is called *imperfect competition.* It has two forms, monopolistic competition and oligopoly. *Monopolistic competition* in an industry means that there are many firms, each producing and selling differentiated products. The products of the firms are close but imperfect substitutes for one another. The products of different firms within the industry are not identical, as they are in pure competition. *Oligopoly* means a few sellers. Few means a number small enough that each firm knows that its actions visibly affect the whole industry. Rivalry among oligopolistic firms is open and conscious. The products of oligopolistic firms can be physically homogeneous or they can be differentiated. Oligopoly prevails in many American manufacturing industries as well as in many financial and transportation markets.

The literal meaning of *monopoly* is one seller. One definition of monopoly is to identify the firm with the industry. This definition, which is adequate for present purposes, easily applies to industries such as electric power where, in any one market, only one firm is the producer.[3]

### Industry and Firm Demand in Pure Competition

The demand for the output of an industry is the demand for a commodity. Such a demand can be elastic or inelastic. The demand for the product of any one firm in an industry of pure competition is, however,

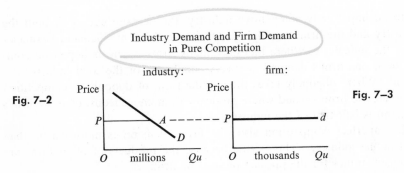

Industry Demand and Firm Demand
in Pure Competition

industry:                 firm:

**Fig. 7–2**                                                      **Fig. 7–3**

perfectly elastic. Figures 7–2 and 7–3 show the relations between the two demands. On the left is the industry demand curve whose quantities are marked in millions of, say, bushels. On the right is the demand curve of a firm. Demand is perfectly elastic at price *OP*. Notice that the quantity axis for the firm is marked in thousands. Though the one curve is horizontal and the other slopes, the two are wholly compatible. The amount *PA* is some thousands of times greater than the amount *Pd*. The horizontality of the firm's demand curve means that if it were to sell more, the firm would not have to accept a lower price. The slope of the industry demand

---

[3] Chapter 19 goes farther into the problem of defining monopoly.

curve means that if all firms together would offer substantially more for sale, they would notice an obvious fall in price.

The firm in pure competition can sell any amount, within the range of its own capacity to produce, without perceptibly affecting price. To the firm, the price is given. The firm is a price-taker. But the industry's demand is limited, which is only another way of saying that the industry faces a downward sloping demand curve.

## Marginal Revenue

The concept of marginal revenue will appear frequently in the chapters to come. It can be introduced briefly now. The marginal revenue of a seller is the addition to total revenue when he sells one unit more. Or, it is the loss of total revenue when he sells one unit less.

For the firm under pure competition, marginal revenue $(MR)$ is identical with price. That is, $MR = P$. If a farmer sells 10,000 bushels at $2 a bushel, he could also sell 10,001 bushels at the same price. The extra $2 for the extra bushel is his marginal revenue, and $2 is also the price.

### Industry and Firm Demand in Imperfect Competition

In an imperfectly competitive industry, the demand curves of both the industry and the firm are sloping. Of course the firm's demand is smaller than the industry's. Where there are many firms, as in monopolistic competition, one firm's demand is a very small part of the total industry demand. Where oligopoly takes the specific form of duopoly — competition between two firms — and where products are homogeneous, then the firm's demand is half that of the industry.

In imperfect competition also, the firm's demand is more elastic than that of the industry. This is true because the products of other firms are close substitutes for the product of any one firm.

Marginal revenue does *not* equal price for firms that are monopolies or are in industries with imperfect competition. All such firms have sloping demand curves, which means that if they sell more than any given amount, they must accept lower prices. If a firm is selling 3 units at $8 each and then sells 4 units at $7, its marginal revenue is $4. That is, total revenue for 4 units is $28, whereas total revenue for 3 units is $24. Observe that the reduction in price from $8 to $7 results in a marginal revenue which is less than price. Except for firms in pure competition, marginal revenue is always less than price.

The full logic of the relations between price, marginal revenue, and elasticity will not be needed until Chapter 19, on monopoly pricing. Further explanation of those relations is therefore postponed. For the chapters immediately to follow, it suffices to know that the expression for the extra revenue from an extra unit of sales is marginal revenue and that marginal revenue equals price for firms in pure competition.

### Summary

*Income elasticity* differs much from one commodity to another. *Income sensitivity* of demand is a rough measure of the relation between percentage changes in expenditures on a commodity and percentage changes in disposable income. *Cross elasticity* of demand relates percentage changes in the quantity demanded of one commodity to percentage changes in the price of another commodity. Low cross elasticities of demand between a commodity and its substitutes could be an indication that the commodity is monopolized. Consumers have a *stock demand* for durable goods, the amounts they want to hold over periods of time. Consumers' annual purchases are *flow demand,* which can fluctuate widely. The demands for commodities undergo continual changes. The *elasticity of price expectations* can have a strong influence on current demands.

In pure competition, the *industry demand* curve slopes, but the curve for *firm demand* is horizontal. In monopoly and imperfect competition, all firms have sloping demand curves. *Marginal revenue* is the extra revenue from selling an extra unit. Marginal revenue equals price to the firm in pure competition; to all other firms, marginal revenue is less than price.

## SELECTED REFERENCES

General references on the topics covered in this chapter are George J. Stigler, *The Theory of Price,* rev. ed. (New York: Macmillan, 1952), Chap. 4; Joel Dean, *Managerial Economics* (New York: Prentice-Hall, 1951), Chap. 4, especially pp. 191–210; Milton H. Spencer and Louis Siegelman, *Managerial Economics* (Homewood: Irwin, 1959), Chap. 5.

On the use of the cross elasticity concept in antitrust analysis: George W. Stocking and Willard F. Mueller, "The Cellophane Case and the New Competition," *American Economic Review,* Vol. XLV, No. 1, March, 1955, pp. 29–63; reprinted in American Economic Association, *Readings in Industrial Organization and Public Policy* (Homewood: Irwin, 1958).

On the demand for durable goods: Spencer and Siegelman, cited above; Arnold C. Harberger, ed., *The Demand for Durable Goods* (Chicago: University of Chicago Press, 1960).

On the elasticity of price expectations: J. R. Hicks, *Value and Capital,* 2d ed. (London: Oxford, 1946), pp. 203–206.

On shifts in demand over time: Henry Schultz, *The Theory and Measurement of Demand* (Chicago: University of Chicago Press, 1938).

## EXERCISES AND PROBLEMS

1. The lines in Figure 7–1 on page 98 are straight. Shouldn't they be curved? Why?

2. If a commodity has a low price elasticity, why is it also likely to have a low income elasticity?

3. Speculate on the cross elasticities of demand between rail coach and bus transportation, gas and electric stoves, ham and eggs, coffee and tea.

4. Work out the relation between stock demand and flow demand, using pianos as the example.

5. Describe the effect on the current demand for a commodity when its future prices are expected to *fall*. Do this for different elasticities of expectations.

6. Show that the marginal cost of a commodity to a consumer is the same as its price.

# PART TWO

## MATHEMATICAL NOTES

This Appendix and the others in this book contain brief mathematical notes whose purpose is to extend and to give greater precision to some of the ideas contained in the text. Because they are incomplete and elementary, the notes are not extracts from the corpus of mathematical economics. Perhaps, however, the notes will convey a little of the flavor of mathematical economics to readers who remember some algebra and the elements of the calculus.

The symbols used in this Appendix are the following:

$p$ = price

$q$ = quantity

$y$ = income

$p_r$ = price of related goods

$w$ = wants or tastes

$E$ = price elasticity

$E_y$ = income elasticity

$E_r$ = cross elasticity with respect to price of related good

$U$ = utility

$MU$ = marginal utility

$P$ = probability

$\Delta p$ = change in p

$\Delta q$ = change in q

$f(p,q)$ = function of p and q

The letters $a, b, c$, etc. are used as coefficients or exponents of economic variables to denote the parameters of a function. A parameter is the value required to cause a function to assume the characteristics that describe an actual relationship.

### Note 1. Slope and the Derivative

The slope of a function is the rate of change of the function per unit change in one or more of the variables that determine the function. General expressions can be obtained that describe the slope for all relevant values of the independent variables. Then a specific value for the slope at any given point can be found by substitution of the coordinate value of that point in the general expression. Sometimes the slope is obtained from a graph of the function by noting the direction of a tangent to the curve of a function at a given point. In mathematics, slope is change in vertical direction relative to change in horizontal direction only when the horizontal axis represents the independent variable and the vertical axis the functional value. If $p$ is a function of $q$, then the slope of $f(q)$ is the reciprocal of the slope of $f(p)$ when $q$ is defined as a function of $p$. This accounts for some of the references to "slope" and the "reciprocal of slope" in economic literature in which the axes are reversed.

The derivative of a function is the function that describes the behavior of slope as the independent variable moves over its range of possible values. By substituting the independent variable value for any given point in the derivative function, the slope, or rate of change, of the function is obtained for that point on the curve. Here is an illustration:

> If $y$ is a function of $x$, say, $y = f(x) = 4x^3 + 4x - 2$, then the derivative of $y$ with respect to $x$ is $12x^2 + 4$ (general expression). When $x = 1$, $f(x) = 6$, and the slope or rate of change of $y$ with respect to $x$ at point $(1,6)$ is $12(1)^2 + 4 = 16$. This means that momentarily at the given point, $y$ is changing value at a rate 16 times that of $x$. For the point $(-1,-10)$ the slope is also 16, but at point $(0,-2)$ the slope is 4.

The derivative of a function is represented by a symbol, e.g., $\dfrac{dy}{dx} = \dfrac{df(x)}{dx}$, when $y = f(x)$. This expression is not to be interpreted as the ratio of two products; but simply taken altogether as one symbol, it represents the rate of change of $f(x)$, or $y$, per one unit change in $x$, at any given point on the function as $x$ changes in value. More specifically,

$$\frac{df(x)}{dx} = \operatorname*{Limit\ of}_{\Delta x \to 0} \frac{\Delta f(x)}{\Delta x} = \operatorname*{Limit\ of}_{\Delta x \to 0} \frac{f(x + \Delta x) - f(x)}{\Delta x}$$

This means that as $\Delta x$ approaches zero, the limit of $\dfrac{\Delta f(x)}{\Delta x}$ is $\dfrac{df(x)}{dx}$, just as point elasticity is the limit of arc elasticity as the arc approaches zero, i.e., becomes a point.

The rules of differentiation, i.e., the process of finding the derivatives of a function, needed in these mathematical notes are the following:

1. Derivative of a constant is zero.

2. If $y = f(x) = ax^n$, then $\dfrac{dy}{dx} = anx^{n-1}$

3. If $y = ax^n + bx^k + \cdots$, then $\dfrac{dy}{dx} = anx^{n-1} + bkx^{k-1} + \cdots$

4. If $y = a[f(x)]^n$, then $\dfrac{dy}{dx} = an[f(x)]^{n-1}\dfrac{df(x)}{dx}$.

5. If $y = uv$, $u = f_1(x)$, $v = f_2(x)$, then $\dfrac{dy}{dx} = u\dfrac{dv}{dx} + v\dfrac{du}{dx}$.

6. If $y = a^v$, $v = f(x)$, then $\dfrac{dy}{dx} = a^v\dfrac{dv}{dx}\log_e a$, and when $a = e$,

    $y = e^v$, then $\dfrac{dy}{dx} = e^v\dfrac{dv}{dx}$

### Note 2.    The Demand Function

In general, the demand function for a commodity can be written as

$$q = f(p, y, p_r, w).$$

The exact form of such a function depends on how consumers respond to changes in the value of each of the determinants — price, income, price of related commodities, and taste. When changes in demand are proportional to changes in the other determinants, the demand function is linear; when nonproportional, the form is curvilinear.

If income, the prices of related commodities, and taste are all assumed to be constant, the function reduces to the simple form, $q = f(p)$. But when the other determinants are not constant or when structural changes occur in time, a dynamic function must be used to allow for all changes. *Econometrics* is the discipline that combines economic and statistical theory for the purpose of measuring actual economic relations. Mathematical models are established on the basis of economic theory. Statistical procedures are utilized to estimate the values of model parameters from empirical data.

The following examples show three model forms used in actual studies of demand:

1. $q = a + bp + cp_r + dy$ This linear form was used by Henry L. Schultz in a study of the demand for beef, 1922–33. Pork is the related commodity used in this function.

2. $q = ap^b p_r^c y^d w^e$ This nonlinear form was used by R. Stone to estimate demand for beer in the United Kingdom, 1920–38. In this function $p_r$ represents the price of all other commodities, $w$ is an index of strength of beer and may be construed as an index of taste.

3. $q = ap^b y^c 10^{f(t)}$, where $f(t) = dt + et^2 + gt^3$ is a function of time. Beatrice Aitchison used this form in a 1941 study of "Demand for Rail Passenger Travel" prepared for the Interstate Commerce Commission.

Notice that the three functions are all different both in form and in the combinations of determinants used to account for changes in demand.

### Note 3.    Demand and Price

When income, price of related goods, tastes, and other determinants are held constant, the demand function takes the simple form, $q = f(p)$. The form of the function can vary considerably as long as the curve is monotonic (i.e., always moving in the same direction) with quantity varying inversely with price. The curve of $q = ap^{-b}$ is convex to the origin whereas that of $q = a - b^{(p-c)}$ is concave. For the former, elasticity is constant throughout the range of relevant values and for the latter, elasticity is relatively high at higher levels of price and relatively low at lower levels of price.

In this book, the linear demand function plays a prominent role. Its behavior is described by the function

$$q = a - bp \qquad b > 0$$

The value of $a$ is the quantity corresponding to zero price, i.e., the intercept on the quantity axis. For a fixed value of $b$, the entire curve shifts parallel to an initial position with a change in the value of $a$. The value of $b$ is the change in quantity associated with a change of one unit in $p$. When taken with the minus sign $(-b)$, this value represents the slope of the function relative to the price axis. (In the text of this book, as in economic literature generally, the term "slope" is used for the vertical change on the price-quantity diagram. This "slope" is the reciprocal of that defined above.)

The most commonly used curvilinear form is one with constant elasticity: $q = ap^{-b}$. Here, $a$ is the locational value just as for the straight line and represents the quantity associated with a price of 1. The value of $b$ determines the curvature of the function, and as shown below, $(-b)$ is the coefficient of elasticity.

## Note 4.    Elasticity of Demand

The coefficient of price elasticity of demand, when $q = f(p)$, is defined as follows:

$$E = \frac{dq}{dp}\frac{p}{q}.$$

For the straight-line demand curve $(q = a - bp)$, the derivative $\frac{dq}{dp}$ is equal to $-b$ and the value of the coefficient of elasticity becomes

$$E = -b\frac{p}{q}.$$

Since $\frac{dq}{dp} = \frac{\Delta q}{\Delta p}$ when the relationship between $q$ and $p$ is linear, the definition of coefficient of elasticity can also be stated as the ratio of the percentage change in quantity to the percentage change in price:

$$E = \frac{\Delta q}{\Delta p}\frac{p}{q} = \frac{\Delta q}{q}\bigg/\frac{\Delta p}{p}.$$

This last definition is correct only for the straight line.

For the constant elastic curve $q = ap^{-b}$, the derivative $\dfrac{dq}{dp}$ becomes $-abp^{-b-1}$. Then

$$E = -abp^{-b-1}\,\frac{p}{q} = \frac{-abp^{-b}}{q} = -b \quad \text{since} \quad q = ap^{-b}.$$

The exponent of the price variable in a nonlinear demand function is therefore the coefficient of price elasticity of demand.

*Income elasticity of demand* is the rate of change of quantity with respect to changes in income, other determinants remaining constant. With constant price and variable income, the linear income-demand function can be written

$$q = a + cy \qquad c > 0.$$

Then since the derivative $\dfrac{dq}{dy}$ is equal to $c$, the coefficient of elasticity can be written

$$E_y = c\,\frac{y}{q}.$$

The curvilinear income-demand function with constant elasticity can be written $q = ay^c$. The value of $E_y$ is then $c$.

*Cross elasticity of demand* is the rate of change in quantity associated with changes in the price of a related good. The coefficient of cross elasticity, $E_r$, is defined as $\dfrac{dq}{dp_r}\,\dfrac{p_r}{q}$.

Consider two commodities $A$ and $B$. If commodity $A$ is under examination, $B$ is the related commodity and $p_B$ is its price. The opposite holds for $B$. Then two linear demand schedules can be functionally described as

$$q_A = a_1 + b_1 p_A + c_1 p_B,$$
$$q_B = a_2 + b_2 p_A + c_2 p_B.$$

These functions show that the quantity demanded of each commodity depends on that commodity's price and also on the price of the other commodity. For these functions, the derivatives with respect to related price are

$$\frac{dq_A}{dp_B} = b_1\,\frac{dp_A}{dp_B} + c_1 = c_1 \qquad \text{when } p_A \text{ is constant,}$$

$$\frac{dq_B}{dp_A} = b_2 + c_2\,\frac{dp_B}{dp_A} = b_2 \qquad \text{when } p_B \text{ is constant.}$$

Then

$$E_r = E_{p_B} = c_1\,\frac{p_B}{q_A},$$
$$E_r = E_{p_A} = b_2\,\frac{p_A}{q_B}.$$

In general, these two coefficients are not expected to be equal. For equality, it is necessary that the ratio of slopes $c_1/b_2$ be equal to the ratio of expenditures at the initial point $(p_A, q_A, p_B, q_B)$.

If

$$E_{p_B} = E_{p_A}$$

then

$$c_1 \frac{p_B}{q_A} = b_2 \frac{p_A}{q_B}$$

or $\dfrac{c_1}{b_2} = \dfrac{p_A q_A}{p_B q_B}$ = ratio of initial expenditures.

With all other factors constant, a positive value of $E_r$ implies that $A$ and $B$ are substitute commodities, a negative value that they are complements.

### Note 5.    Log Scale for Constant Elasticity

If $q = ap^{-b}$, then $\log q = \log a - b \log p$. In this form, the logarithms follow a straight-line pattern and the slope $(-b)$ of the logarithmic equation is the coefficient of elasticity of the original function. Therefore, if price and quantity are plotted on graph paper with both scales logarithmic, the slope of the resulting line is the coefficient of elasticity for that function possessing constant elasticity. If the line slopes downward to the right at a 45-degree angle, the curve is unit elastic; if less steep than 45 degrees, it is elastic; otherwise, it is inelastic.

### Note 6.    Consumer's Surplus

Consumer's surplus is the difference between the total area under a demand curve and the area representing expenditure by the consumer. Thus for any given price $(p_1)$ and its associated quantity $(q_1)$,

$$\text{Consumer's surplus} = \int_0^{q_1} f(q) \, dq - p_1 q_1$$

where the integral sign $(\int)$ represents the process of summation — in this case from zero quantity to given quantity $(q_1)$.

The difference in consumer's surplus $(\Delta c)$ for two different prices $(p_1$ and $p_2)$ is

$$\Delta c = \int_{p_1}^{p_2} f(p) \, dp.$$

When $p_2$ is greater than $p_1$, $\Delta c$ is negative, and when $p_2$ is less than $p_1$, it is positive. Another way of expressing $\Delta c$ is in terms of the quantity change, which becomes

$$\Delta c = \int_{q_2}^{q_1} f(q)\, dq - (p_1 q_1 - p_2 q_2)$$

$$= \int_{q_2}^{q_1} f(q)\, dq - \text{(change in expenditure)}.$$

### Note 7.   The St. Petersburg Paradox

Bernoulli thought that the marginal utility of money declines in a particular way as additional increments of money are received. His hypothesis states that the marginal utility of money is inversely proportional to the amount already possessed. With $U$ standing for utility and $M$ the initial amount of money, the hypothesis can be stated as

$$\frac{dU}{dM} = \frac{k}{M} \text{ where } k \text{ is some positive constant.}$$

Then

$$U = k(\log M + \log C) = \log (CM)^k, \text{ where } C \text{ is another constant.}$$

It was Bernoulli's contention that rational decisions under circumstances of risk would be made on the basis of expected utility rather than expected monetary value. The game in the St. Petersburg paradox is one that calls for the tossing of a coin until it falls heads up; then a payment equal to $2^x$ is made — where $x$ is the number of tosses required to obtain a head. Since mathematical expectation, i.e., expected monetary value, is equal to the sum of the products formed by multiplying a given sum of money by its probability of payment, the mathematical expectation for this game is

$$Exp\ (M) = \tfrac{1}{2}(2) + \tfrac{1}{4}(4) + \tfrac{1}{8}(8) + \cdots$$
$$= 1 + 1 + 1 + \cdots = \text{infinite sum.}$$

Although the expected monetary value is infinite, no rational person would want to play the game. This was the St. Petersburg paradox, which is resolved by the concept of the diminishing marginal utility of money.

The expected gain in *utility* is $\sum_{1}^{\infty} \frac{k}{2^x} \{\log (M + 2^x) - \log M\}$.

Without loss in generality, $M$ may be assumed to equal $2^n$. Then it can be shown that the expected gain in utility $E(\Delta U)$ decreases as the value of $M$ increases and approaches zero as the initial amount of money approaches infinity.

With $M = 2^x$, $E(\Delta U) = \sum\limits_{1}^{\infty} \dfrac{k}{2^x} \{\log (2^n + 2^x) - \log 2^n\}$. The sum indi-

cated here is less than $\dfrac{k}{3 \cdot 2^n} (3 \log_e 2 + 3n + 1)$.

Since $k$ is a positive constant, it is obvious that this function of $n$ decreases rapidly as $n$ increases. When $n = 3$, the value is $.5k$ and when $n = 10$ it is approximately $.01k$. Consequently, the ratio of the utility of the expected winnings to the utility of the initial amount of money decreases still more rapidly as $M$ is increased.

### Note 8.    The Indifference Curve Analysis of Demand

The indifference map of a consumer's preferences for two goods is a system of curves, having the property that one and only one curve of the system passes through each point in the positive quadrant of the $xy$ plane, when $x$ and $y$ represent quantities of the two goods. Indifference curves are generally somewhat similar to hyperbolic functions and are negatively inclined to each axis. Symbolically, the equation for any given indifference curve which possesses constant utility can be written

$$U = \phi(x, y).$$

If $U$ is allowed to vary, this function then describes the utility surface with each indifference curve being the intersection of that surface and a plane parallel to and $U$ units from the $xy$-plane. Changes in a consumer's relative tastes for the two goods alter the function $\phi$.

Many functional relations might be used to describe the relative tastes of a consumer. One such relation is

$$U = x + y + \sqrt{2xy}.$$

Now with the consumer's income represented by $M$, and the prices of $x$ and $y$ by $p_x$ and $p_y$, respectively, the maximum consumer's budget for (or expenditure on) these two commodities is represented by the following relationship:

$$M = xp_x + yp_y.$$

Hence, the basic problem is to find values for $x$ and $y$ that will maximize $U$ and that can be purchased with $M$.

One method for determining the maximum value of a function of two or more variables subject to functional constraints employs the LaGrange multiplier technique. Assume that $U = \phi(x,y)$ is to be maximized subject to a constraint relationship, $f(x,y) = 0$. From these two functions, form a third function

$G(x,y) = \phi(x,y) + \lambda f(x,y)$ where $\lambda$ is the LaGrange multiplier.

Conditions necessary for maximizing $U$ are

$$\frac{\partial G}{\partial x} = \frac{\partial \phi}{\partial x} + \lambda \frac{\partial f}{\partial x} = 0$$

$$\frac{\partial G}{\partial y} = \frac{\partial \phi}{\partial y} + \lambda \frac{\partial f}{\partial y} = 0.$$

Then

$$\frac{\partial \phi}{\partial x} = -\lambda \frac{\partial f}{\partial x}$$

$$\frac{\partial \phi}{\partial y} = -\lambda \frac{\partial f}{\partial y}.$$

And if $f(x,y) = xp_x + yp_y - M = 0$

$$\frac{\partial f}{\partial x} = p_x, \quad \frac{\partial f}{\partial y} = p_y.$$

And

$$\frac{\frac{\partial \phi}{\partial x}}{\frac{\partial \phi}{\partial y}} = \frac{-\lambda p_x}{-\lambda p_y} = \frac{p_x}{p_y}.$$

This demonstrates that total utility is maximized when the ratio of the marginal utilities is equal to the ratio of the prices.

# PART THREE

*The Theory*

*of the Firm*

# The Firm and Its Decisions

## 8

In the market economy, the units are households and firms whose activities as consumers and as producers are linked together by the network of prices. This chapter and the four to follow contain the essentials of the theory of the firm. Many million firms produce commodities and services in the United States. The word "firm" is broader than the expression "business enterprise," because firms also include farming enterprises as well as professional, technical, and service activities operated as independent income-producing units. Hence, to speak of *the* firm is to use the same kind of abstraction as *the* consumer. The many differences among firms are ignored so that the characteristics common to all of them can be described.

### The Firm and the Entrepreneur

The firm is a unit engaged in production for a sale at a profit and with the objective of maximizing the profit. Though it can be an individual proprietorship, or a partnership, or a corporation, the form of organization of a firm is not important in price theory. The essence of the idea of the firm is the profit-maximizing unit. If the several divisions or branches of a large corporation are required by top management to earn profits, each independently of the others and subject only to broad policy direction from on high, then each of the divisions or branches can be regarded as a separate firm.

The firm is personified in the entrepreneur, who exercises ultimate and decisive control over the activities of the firm. The entrepreneur brings the firm into existence and takes it out, should he find a need to do so. The entrepreneur decides to expand or to contract output. If he can, he sets prices. As a pure type, the entrepreneur performs no work in the firm; others do it for him. But he makes the decisions. The entrepreneur need own only enough of the firm to have control of it. In the United States, of course, millions of small businessmen and farmers combine in their own persons the roles of owners, managers, and entrepreneurs. In many contexts, management and the entrepreneurial function are nearly synonymous terms. If, however, management connotes day-by-day supervision and the execution of delegated tasks, then managers are not entrepreneurs. They are hired men, not the makers of the decisions that are analyzed in price theory. In principle, and sometimes in fact, the entrepreneur need never visit his firm; a few phone calls a year are enough.

In large corporations, however, it is often difficult to identify the entrepreneur or even to be sure who performs his function. Final decisions in the large corporation are often made by the group of men usually called the top management. Multiple goals are likely to be more important in large firms than in small firms. The possible kinds of compromises among multiple goals in large corporations managed by committees defy simple analysis. This matter will be returned to later.

### The Firm's Costs

The firm always acts so as to maximize its profits, which are its revenues minus its costs. The assumption of profit maximization for firms is symmetrical with the assumption of utility maximization for consumers. Some of the problems surrounding the assumption of profit maximization will be discussed later in this chapter. It is necessary first of all to assign clear meanings to the terms "costs" and "profits." The word "revenue" poses no difficulties. The revenue of a firm is simply its selling price multiplied by the number of units it sells; alternative expressions are gross receipts and gross income. Sometimes sales are not final, with the result that firms have to cope with the problem of goods that are returned by customers; matters of this kind are ignored in economic analysis.

### Cost Concepts

The fundamental concept of cost is *alternative cost,* which means that the cost of anything is the value of the alternative, or the opportunity, that is sacrificed. Another name for alternative cost is _opportunity cost._ The alternative cost of producing fuel oil in a refinery is the value of the gasoline that could have been produced from the same crude oil. The alternative cost of being in business for yourself is the sacrifice of the income you could eàrn by working for somebody else and by investing your capital in other ways. The alternative-cost concept has a wide range of applications. Two business examples have just been mentioned. The concept can also be applied to the consumer: Fundamentally, the cost of a vacation in Europe is not so much the money as the foregoing of the enjoyment of the new automobile that could have been bought with the same money. So too, discussion of national problems often looks beyond the budgeted billions of dollars and says that the real cost of putting more resources into mobilization is the sacrifice of civilian goods. This, of course, is the familiar guns-and-butter problem. Conversely, it can be said that the alternative cost of public-works projects constructed during a depression is zero, or close to it. True enough, money has to be spent for the projects, but if the resources going into them would be otherwise unused, they are not diverted. For the nation as a whole, no alternative benefits from the resources are sacrificed.

Thus to use the concept of alternative cost is to compare benefits, those anticipated and those foregone.

Modern theorists do not attempt to push the cost concept back to the subjective pain, toil, and sacrifice of the producer. But in the nineteenth century, theorists did make the attempt, and set up the subjective disutility suffered by producers as counterforce to the subjective utility enjoyed by consumers. Alfred Marshall had a parable about a boy picking black-berries for his own eating.[1] The trouble of picking them is disutility; the pleasure of eating the berries is utility. The boy stops when he has had enough — he is in equilibrium, he maximizes, having equated the marginal disutility of picking with the marginal utility of eating. Marshall intended the seemingly artless example to stand as a microcosm of the whole economic process — the balancing of fundamental forces in an equilibrium. But the concept of cost as the disutility borne by producers became ex- posed to the ridicule of critics who doubted that a millionaire capitalist suffers much when he makes his entrepreneurial decisions. (Such criticism notwithstanding, decision-making can be a painful process for _anyone._)

Modern economics, however, does explain the behavior of people as suppliers of labor services and as entrepreneurs in terms of subjective preferences for leisure and income. This point will be taken up later in this chapter and in Chapter 13.

[1] Alfred Marshall, _Principles of Economics,_ 8th ed. (London: Macmillan, 1920), p. 331.

### Business Costs and Full Costs

A firm's *business costs* are its total money expenses as computed by ordinary accounting methods. These expenses include all payments and contractual obligations made by the firm together with the book cost of depreciation on plant and equipment. To define the *full costs* of a firm, two additions to business expenses must be made. They are the alternative or opportunity costs of the firm and *normal profits.* The opportunity costs of the firm include interest on the funds invested in the firm by its owners and the value of the labor services of the entrepreneur, if he works in the firm and if he receives no salary as a business expense. Normal profits are an additional amount, sufficient, but just sufficient, to induce the entrepreneur to continue to produce the same product. Why are normal profits a "cost"? They are a cost of a commodity because, unless the entrepreneur expects to receive in the long run a revenue that will cover his business expenses, his opportunity costs, and some minimum in addition (i.e., normal profits), he will not plan to produce the commodity in question. Another way to see normal profits as a cost is from the perspective of the consumer. If the consumer is to have some commodity available over a long period of time, he must expect to pay prices that cover full costs. Part of those full costs is a minimum inducement to producers. The minimum inducement includes normal profits.

The full costs of a firm are conventionally divided into *variable costs* and *fixed costs.* Variable costs vary with output and are the payments for labor, materials, fuel and power, etc. Fixed costs are those that continue even if, in the short run, the firm stops producing. Fixed costs include interest payments, depreciation, certain insurance, certain taxes, some salaries, etc. Although economic theorists are rarely explicit about it, fixed costs also include opportunity costs and normal profits. Fixed costs so defined include, therefore, more than the everyday business notion of overhead expense.

Variable costs are relevant for the short-run decisions of a firm. In the short run, the firm has given plant and equipment, which it cannot alter. Full costs are relevant for the long run when the firm can vary the size of its plant and equipment.

### Cost Concepts and Rational Decisions

By their very nature, decisions are made for the future. Whether it is a few minutes away or fifty years away, the future lies ahead. Economic decisions are to buy or to sell, to borrow or to lend, to expand or contract production, to work more or less, etc. — in the future. Like many others, economic decisions often mean choosing one of several possible courses of action — which size of plant to build, which product to produce, which machine to buy, etc. Each possible course of action has its future revenue and its future cost. Rational decisions mean choosing the optimum combinations of revenue and of cost.

Hence the only costs to be taken into account in rational decision-making are future costs. Past costs are bygones, interesting perhaps, but still only bygones. There would be no need to emphasize this point if the truth in it were not so widely ignored. Most people have a mania for loading all they can into a cost calculation for fear of leaving something out.

A simple everyday example of costs and a decision is this: You are going to make a trip; you can drive your own car or ride on a bus, or a plane, or a train. To decide which way to go, you consider comfort and convenience, length of time, and cost. How do you figure the cost of making the trip in your own car? The variable costs are for gas and oil, and for a long trip, the cost of an extra grease job. The overhead costs are depreciation, insurance, annual taxes, and other expenses such as membership in an automobile club. The rational way to calculate the cost of one trip is to look *only* at the variable costs. The overhead costs are ignored. Not that they don't exist; they are real enough, and are normally much larger than the variable costs. The overhead costs are there whether or not you make that trip. The trip by car is cheaper than by plane, if the gas and oil cost less than the plane ticket. On the other hand, if you are thinking of buying a car to make many long trips in the next two or three years, you will then calculate the total of the overhead and variable costs.

When the future is the short run, therefore, only the variable costs should be counted. When the future is the long run, full costs should be counted.

### Net Profits and Net Revenue

In this book, profits will be the general term. Its meaning should be clear in each context. Profits always mean revenue minus costs. Different contexts require different cost concepts. Revenue minus full costs will be called *net profits*. Full costs belong to the long run, and so do net profits. Some economists refer to net profits as pure profits or economic profits. Revenue minus business expenses can be called *business profits* because this is the profit concept of the accountant and of the businessman. It must be evident that business profits are always larger than net profits, because business expenses are always less than full costs.

Revenue minus variable costs will be called *net revenue*.[2] Net revenue is the profit concept applicable to the short run.

---

[2] In Marshall's terminology, net revenue is quasi-rent. Though the term quasi-rent is still used, it seems preferable to employ the simpler and more direct expression.

Table 8–1 presents the definitions of costs and profits in summary form.

**TABLE 8–1**

### Revenues, Costs, and Profits

| | |
|---|---|
| Revenue *minus* business costs | = business profits |
| Revenue *minus* variable costs | = net revenue |
| Revenue *minus* full costs | = net profits |
| Business costs + alternative costs + normal profit | = full costs |
| Fixed costs + variable costs | = full costs |

### The Profit-Maximizing Assumption

The assumption that entrepreneurs try to make the biggest profits they can is, by and large, a good assumption. It is good, though not perfect. In general, an assumption has to stand one or both of two tests. One test is realism. The profit-maximizing assumption passes this test fairly well, because there would be much agreement that most businessmen most of the time appear to be striving hard for high profits. And if they do not in fact attain literal maximization, it is not for lack of desire or effort, but because businessmen must make their plans and decisions in the midst of constant change and uncertainty. The second test of an assumption is its usefulness in predicting the effects flowing from given causes. Then the question to ask is: Realistic or not, does the assumption work, does it give good results? Most economic theorists argue here that, considering its simplicity, the profit-maximizing assumption scores even better.

Still, the assumption continues to be questioned and debated. Almost anyone knows or can observe businessmen who quite patently do not try to squeeze out the last dollar of profits from their operations. And when they make public statements, businessmen hardly ever seem to want more than fair or reasonable profits.

### Marginalism

Another expression for profit-maximizing behavior is marginalism or marginal behavior. Marginal behavior is maximizing behavior, both of the consumer and the entrepreneur. The consumer maximizes his satisfaction from his purchase of a commodity by adjusting the quantity so that marginal utility equals price. This can be restated by saying that the consumer adjusts quantity so that marginal gain equals marginal cost (the price he pays for the last unit bought is, of course, its cost to him, and the extra cost of the last unit is marginal cost). So, too, the firm maximizes profits by adjusting the quantity produced and sold so that marginal gain, i.e., marginal revenue, equals marginal cost.

Much controversy, most of it unnecessary, has surrounded the idea of marginalism. Because businessmen are usually unacquainted with the terms "marginal revenues" and "marginal costs," critics have asked how anyone in his right mind can maintain that businessmen equate the two quantities. In fact, however, marginalism requires businessmen to do nothing more than to maximize their profits. If they do so, they are behaving marginally whether they know it or not. A hundred businessmen might give one hundred different kinds of explanations of how they maximize profits. Marginalism is the one general explanation blanketing them all.

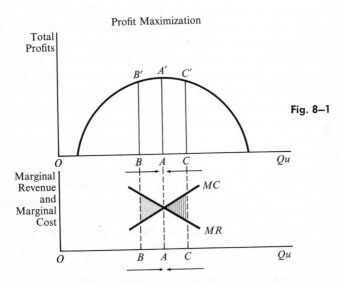

Profit Maximization

Fig. 8–1

Marginal behavior in maximizing profits is illustrated in Figure 8–1. It makes no difference here whether the profits are net profits or net revenue; the same analysis applies to both. The upper part of the figure shows a hypothetical profits curve, the amount of profits being measured as the height of the curve. The vertical axis is total profits in thousands of dollars, not a rate of profit per unit of output. The horizontal axis is quantity of output in physical units. The profits curve says that below some output there are no profits. When output is increased past that point, profits rise to a maximum, which is $AA'$. If output continues to be increased past $OA$, profits begin to fall, becoming zero at some (too) large output.

In the lower part of Figure 8–1, the horizontal axis is the same. The vertical axis measures not total cost and total revenue, but the dollar cost and dollar revenue associated with each single unit of output. The line $MC$ is marginal cost, the extra cost of an extra unit. The line $MR$ is marginal revenue, the extra revenue from an extra unit. Take the output $OB$. This output is profitable, but the firm can earn more profits by expanding to output $OA$. The additional output $BA$ adds to profits. This is evident from the upper part of the figure because $AA'$ is longer than $BB'$. The shaded area in the lower part of the figure is the excess of extra revenue over extra cost for the output $BA$. When $MR = MC$, profits are not being added to, nor are they being subtracted from. Therefore, profits must be at a maximum.[3]

Suppose the firm were to produce the output $OC$. Profits here are good, let it be imagined, but they are not maximum. If the firm cuts back from $OC$ to $OA$, it adds to profits. The striped area in the lower figure is the reduction of profit by producing $OC$ instead of $OA$.

Marginalism also means that adjustments are made with pinpoint precision. Usually, however, entrepreneurs have to make their output adjustments in great lumps or chunks. When there are discontinuities, adjustments are said to be incremental. Because they are approximations of marginal adjustments, incremental adjustments differ only in degree, not in kind. Marginal adjustments mean smooth curves; incremental adjustments mean jagged, or kinked, or discontinuous lines.

### Satisficing Behavior

If maximizing were to be denied as a valid premise of business behavior, something else would have to be put in its place. One possibility is the assumption of "satisficing"[4] behavior. Business firms would be thought of as striving for profits that are satisfactory, rather than maximum. A justification for the satisficing assumption would be that motives to action come from drives, and that actions are completed when drives are satisfied. But a major trouble with a satisficing assumption would be to find a single clear definition of satisfactory profits. Several "standards" of profits can be mentioned. A company could aim for profits *high* enough to attract outside capital, or to provide for expansion, or to equal the profits of other companies. On the other hand, a company could aim for profits *low* enough to thwart potential competition, to stave off possible government regulation, or to frustrate pressures from the union for higher wages.

Standards such as these can be meaningful in the analysis of one company or industry in one period of time. But they have no use at all in a broad inquiry into the operation of the economy because such standards are vague and shifting. In the theory of oligopoly (Chapters 22, 23, and 24), however, there is some need to allow for profit behavior other than the maximizing kind.

---

[3] See Note 1 in the Appendix to Part Three.

[4] You will have to look hard for a dictionary containing this word; it does, however, seem to fill a need.

## Uncertainty

The idea of profit maximization implies that the entrepreneur can choose among several sizes of profits. One of them is the maximum; this one of course is his choice. Thus the entrepreneur knows exactly what his costs and revenues are and what they will be. He makes his decisions under the condition of certainty.

Decisions have to be made for the future; knowledge of the future is necessarily imperfect. Will a fire destroy his buildings this year? The entrepreneur cannot be sure about this, but against the possibility of fire, he can buy insurance and dismiss the matter from his mind. Will his employees steal from him? This worry too can be set aside by buying insurance. All such possible future events can be lumped together as "risks." For present purposes, it suffices to say that anything insurable is a risk. In contrast, those future events that are inherently not insurable and that cannot be foreseen exactly are uncertainties. The American economist, Frank H. Knight, drew the distinction between risk and uncertainty, building a theory of net profits on the concept of uncertainty.

Since revenues are to be received and costs are to be incurred in the future, their amounts are uncertain, even if only to a small degree. In general, the longer the planning period, the more uncertain are the quantities that go into the making of decisions. Rational decision-making under conditions of uncertainty must rest on calculated *probabilities* of future prices and costs and, therefore, on the probabilities of future profits. There are theories of such decision-making; in part, they incorporate the concept of cardinal utility explained in Chapter 5. But these theories are exceedingly complicated and are themselves in a state of flux. For simplicity's sake, they will be bypassed here. Let the fog of uncertainty be lifted, and let the entrepreneur make his decisions in the clear if artificial light of certainty.

## Multiple Objectives

Still another of the problems surrounding the assumption of profit maximization is whether maximum profits are the sole objective of a firm. Spokesmen for business draw attention to several other objectives, especially those of large corporations. Here is a partial list: maintaining or increasing market share, growing for the sake of growing, creating or maintaining a desirable public "image," fulfilling social responsibilities, maintaining a desirable financial position, achieving good labor relations, and so on.

The real question is whether such other objectives are distinctly separate from profits or whether they are direct or indirect means of increasing profits, now or in the future. Once more the need for simplicity imposes the further assumption that other objectives of the firm are ancillary to profits.

It seems worthwhile, however, to make a short digression from the theme of profit maximization as the sole objective and to show how an entrepreneur behaves when he compromises maximum profits with one other objective.

### Profits and One Other Objective

If the entrepreneur seeks the best combination of profits and one other goal, it is possible to show his decision on an indifference diagram. The analysis here was first developed by Tibor Scitovsky of the University of California at Berkeley.

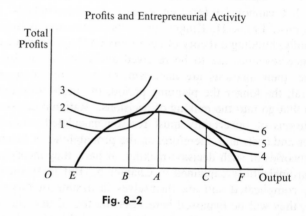

Profits and Entrepreneurial Activity

**Fig. 8–2**

In Figure 8–2, the vertical axis measures profits and the horizontal axis measures output. The curve *EF* is another profits curve. For any output less than *OE* and greater than *OF,* there are no profits. Profits are a maximum when output is *OA.* Clearly, a curve such as *EF* could have many shapes. In the figure, the curve resembles a semicircle simply for convenience. Next, let the horizontal axis also measure both entrepreneurial activity and a subjective attitude toward it. More output requires more activity, more effort. Less output means more leisure. In the figure, the indifference curves *1, 2,* and *3* show the attitude of one type of businessman. He always wants more profits and thus wants to be on the highest indifference curve attainable. But he is unwilling after some point to put forth more effort unless profits rise sharply; hence his indifference curves turn up, to the right. But they first slope down, meaning that this businessman prefers some range of activity; he would rather accept a little less profits than be idle. Thus these indifference curves are U-shaped, signifying that the businessman has a preferred range of output and of activity. Indifference curve *2* is tangent to the profits curve; therefore this entrepreneur would choose to produce the output *OB,* which is less than the profit-maximizing output *OA.* The other indifference curves — those marked *4, 5,* and *6* — apply to a different kind of entrepreneurial behavior. This second businessman likes activity for its own sake. He prefers a bigger to a smaller operation and is willing to sacrifice some profits to have a big operation. His indifference curves slope downward to the right. Curve *5* is his highest attainable. And so he chooses the output *OC,* which of course is larger than *OA.* An entrepreneur who would care about profits *only* would have *horizontal* indifference curves one of which would be tangent to the profits curve at its top, meaning the choice of the profit-maximizing output *OA.*

### Applications

As Oscar Wilde said, nature imitates art. The theory of the profit-maximizing firm is a theory of rational business behavior. The postwar period has seen the growth and proliferation of systematic applications of marginalism to actual business decisions. Though the rough guess and the rule of thumb still prevail, they are beginning to yield to the precision of marginalism. Many new applied disciplines now flourish — managerial economics, operations research, management science, linear programming (Chapter 12). Much of the hard work done in these fields consists of getting quantitative information and of beating and pounding it into the shapes required by theory so that business executives can be provided with the bases for making rational decisions. Much of the applied theory, some of it wholly new, is the extension and complication of the ideas described in this book.

### Summary

In the market economy, the producing unit is the *firm,* which is personified in the *entrepreneur* who makes the ultimate decisions. The goal of the firm is to maximize its profits, which are revenues minus costs. The fundamental cost concept is *alternative,* or *opportunity,* cost, defined as the value of the alternative sacrificed. A firm's *business costs* are its total money expenses as computed by ordinary accounting methods. A firm's *full costs* are its business costs plus alternative costs plus *normal profits.* Full costs are divided into *variable costs* and *fixed costs.* Rational decisions look only to future costs. Short-run decisions count only variable costs, whereas long-run decisions count full costs. Revenue minus full costs gives *net profits;* revenue minus business costs gives *business profits;* and revenue minus variable costs is *net revenue.* Profit-maximizing behavior is *marginal behavior* because profits are maximum when marginal revenue equals marginal cost. The usefulness of the profit-maximizing assumption has been subject to much debate. Attempts to put in its place an assumption of satisficing behavior have not succeeded. Business goals other than profits can be treated as ancillary to profits. The new applied disciplines contribute to the actual spread of marginal behavior in the business world.

## SELECTED REFERENCES

General: Frank H. Knight, *Risk, Uncertainty and Profit* (Boston: Houghton Mifflin, 1921). Neil W. Chamberlain, *The Firm: Micro-Economic Planning and Action* (New York: McGraw-Hill, 1962).

On profit maximization: Herbert A. Simon, "Theories of Decision-Making in Economics and Behavioral Science," *American Economic Review,* Vol. XLIX, No. 3, June, 1959, pp. 253–283. Tibor Scitovsky, "A Note on Profit Maximisation and Its Implications," *Review of Economic Studies,* Vol. XI, 1943. Reprinted in George J. Stigler and Kenneth E. Boulding (eds.), *Readings in Price Theory* (Homewood: Irwin, 1952), Chap. 17.

Business applications: Joel Dean, *Managerial Economics* (New York: Prentice-Hall, 1951). Milton H. Spencer and Louis Siegelman, *Managerial Economics* (Homewood: Irwin, 1959).

## EXERCISES AND PROBLEMS

1. Make up a set of plausible numbers to fit the definitions of net profits, business profits, and net revenue.

2. Suppose you are going to sell your car. In deciding whether to accept an offer, how much weight should you give to the cost of the car to you, i.e., the price you paid for it?

3. What is the alternative cost to a college of a football team?

4. Draw and explain a diagram like Figure 8–2 showing a businessman who accepts very low profits if he can have a big operation.

# The Theory of Production

## 9

The theory of production plays two roles in the theory of relative prices. One is to provide a base for the analysis of the relations between costs and volumes of output. Costs influence supplies which, together with demands, determine prices. The other role for the theory of production is to serve as a base for the theory of the demand of firms for factors of production.

Production means the transformation of inputs — the things bought by a firm — into outputs — the things it sells. The word "production" of course is not limited to physical changes in matter; the word embraces the rendering of services, such as transporting, financing, wholesaling, and retailing.

A note on terminology: The words "inputs" and "factors of production" are near synonyms and in many contexts are used interchangeably. In general, however, the connotation of inputs is broader. Inputs are *all* the things that firms buy. When the expression "factors of production" takes on a narrower meaning, then factors are labor and capital. (In this book, land is treated as a form of capital.) A synonym for factors of production is "productive services." The words "output," "product," and "production" are exact synonyms in this book; these words will appear in the contexts where customary usage prescribes them.

## The Production Function

The production function is the name for the relation between the physical inputs and the physical outputs of a firm. If a small factory produces 100 wooden chairs per eight-hour shift, then its production function consists of the *minimum* quantities of wood, glue, varnish, labor time, machine time, floor space, electricity, etc. that are required to produce the 100 chairs. Or to put it the other way around: The production function of the same factory consists of the *maximum* number of chairs that can be produced with given quantities of wood, glue, varnish, etc. Like a demand curve, i.e., a demand function, a production function must be specified for a period of time. It is a flow of inputs resulting in a flow of outputs during some period of time. (See Note 2 in the Appendix to Part Three.)

Each firm has a production function whose form is determined by the state of technology. When technology improves, a new production function comes into being. The new one has a greater flow of outputs from the same inputs, or smaller quantities of inputs for the same output. Conversely, a new production function can have less output for given inputs if, for example, they include soil which has suffered physical deterioration.

Economists have examined many actual production functions and have employed statistical analyses to measure relations between changes in physical inputs and physical outputs. A famous statistical production function is the Cobb-Douglas[1] production function. In its original form, it applied not to a firm, but to the whole of manufacturing in the United States. In the Cobb-Douglas function, output is manufacturing production. The inputs are labor and capital. Roughly speaking, the Cobb-Douglas formula says that labor contributes about three-quarters of increases in manufacturing production and capital the remaining one quarter. In the postwar period, economists have shown a heightened interest in the Cobb-Douglas production function because it exhibits constant returns to scale — an idea that will be taken up shortly.

Knowledge of the details of production functions is necessarily technical or engineering knowledge and is as broad and as complex as the whole of technology. For the most part, economic theory deals with the properties

---

[1] Senator Paul H. Douglas, a distinguished economist, and C. W. Cobb, his collaborator. Note 3 in the Appendix to Part Three shows the mathematical form of the Cobb-Douglas production function.

or features shared by all production functions without regard for the multitudinous differences among them.

Economic theory looks to two kinds of input-output relations in production functions. One is the relation where quantities of some inputs are fixed while quantities of other inputs vary. In the other relation, all of the inputs are variable.

This chapter discusses only the relations between physical inputs and outputs. The prices that firms pay for their inputs and receive for their outputs are not brought in until the next chapter.

### Variable Proportions and Diminishing Returns

Assume now that a firm's production function consists of fixed quantities of all inputs except one; this one is the variable input. Like a commodity, an input can be defined broadly or narrowly. An input can be one grade of labor or it can be units or crews of men and equipment. In any event, the problem now is this: The firm can increase output by varying the quantities of just one input. What is the input-output relation?

Suppose that the inputs fixed in amount are plant, equipment, and land, and that the variable input is labor. When the firm expands output by employing more labor, it alters the *proportions* between the fixed and the variable inputs. The law of variable proportions, also known as the law of diminishing returns, can be stated as follows: When total output, or production, of a commodity is increased by adding units of a variable input while the quantities of other inputs are held constant, the increases in total production become, after some point, smaller and smaller.

Observe that total production increases — it does not diminish. What does diminish is the size of the increases. The law of diminishing (marginal) returns is exactly symmetrical with the law of diminishing (marginal) utility. Both totals increase, but at a diminishing rate. (In everyday conversation, the expression "diminishing returns" usually has a different meaning, namely, that something or other gets worse and worse or becomes fruitless.)

Imagine a farmer who is making his plans for the next growing season. He has land comprising so many acres, with buildings, fences, and equipment of various sorts. Among the decisions the farmer makes is how many men to hire for the season. In coming to this decision, the farmer must reflect on the physical productivity of labor on his farm. Table 9–1 contains hypothetical data.

The data in Table 9–1 are to be read as statements of alternatives. *If* the farmer would hire 3 men for the season, *then* the total product from the farm would be 270 units. If instead he would hire 4 men, the total product would be 300 units. And so on. The basic data in the first two columns are the production function. The third and fourth columns are derived from the first two. The average product per man is obtained by dividing, whereas the numbers in the column headed "marginal product" are obtained by subtracting. With 3 men, 270 units are produced, i.e., 50 units *more* are produced. Thus the marginal product of 3 men is 50 units and of 4 men, 30 units. As farm hands, the men are assumed to have equal efficiencies, so that there is nothing peculiar about the fourth man that causes the marginal product of 4 men to be less than that of 3.

**TABLE 9–1**

**A Production Function with One Variable Input**

| Number of Men | Total Product | Average Product | Marginal Product |
|:---:|:---:|:---:|:---:|
| | (*In physical units*) | | |
| 1 | 100 | 100 | 100 |
| 2 | 220 | 110 | 120 |
| 3 | 270 | 90 | 50 |
| 4 | 300 | 75 | 30 |
| 5 | 320 | 64 | 20 |
| 6 | 330 | 55 | 10 |
| 7 | 330 | 47 | 0 |
| 8 | 320 | 40 | −10 |

Another note on terminology: In the discussion here, the expression is "marginal product" rather than "marginal physical product." In this book, the two expressions have exactly the same meaning. The shorter one is used when, as here, the context deals with physical products only. The longer expression is used for emphasis and clarity, especially to distinguish physical products in tons, yards, bushels, etc. from their dollar values.

There is still more in Table 9–1. Both the average and the marginal products increase at first, and then decline. The marginal product drops off faster than the average. When 6 men are employed, total product is a maximum. No more is produced with 7 men; the marginal product of 7 men is zero. And the marginal product of 8 men is *minus* 10 units — by getting in each other's way, the 8 men actually produce less than 6 or 7.

The marginal product of any quantity of the variable input depends on the state of technology and on the amounts and qualities of the fixed inputs. With improved knowledge of methods of production, the numbers in the schedule of marginal product would increase. So they would also if the enterprise had more and better equipment among its fixed inputs. Even with such changes, however, the revised schedules in Table 9–1 would still convey the same message, namely, that after some point, total product would grow at a slower rate, and marginal product would diminish.

Input-output relations are given general expression in the smooth curves of Figure 9–1. The curve of total product rises first at an increasing rate and then at a decreasing rate to its maximum. The curves of average product (*AP*) and of marginal product (*MP*) are derived from the curve for total product. The *MP* curve represents the slope of the total product curve at each point. When this slope is zero, at point *M, MP* is zero as the lower part of the figure shows.

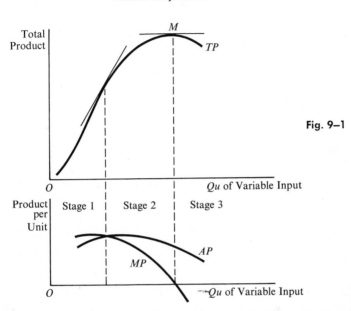

Variable Proportions

Fig. 9–1

Curves such as those shown in Figure 9–1 are general representations of production functions with fixed and variable inputs. To illustrate particular instances, many thousands of them would be drawn, each different from the others in some way. The stage of increasing marginal product can be absent, or brief, or long. When it diminishes, marginal product can do so rapidly or slowly. Diminishing marginal product has been demonstrated over and over again in such applications as putting different quantities of fertilizer on otherwise identical plots of land.

### The Three Stages

When one input is variable, the relations between the input and product are conventionally divided into three "Stages." They are marked on Figure 9–1.

In *Stage 1,* total product increases at an increasing rate. Two men produce more than twice as much as one man. Marginal product and average product are both rising. Because marginal product is greater than the average, marginal product pulls up the average. When marginal product begins to fall, it still exceeds the average and so continues to exert an upward pull on the average. Where marginal and average products are equal, the marginal neither pulls the average up nor pushes it down; thus average product is momentarily constant at a maximum value. Here is the boundary of Stage 1.

In *Stage 2,* total product continues to increase, but at a diminishing rate. The right-hand boundary of Stage 2 is at maximum total product and zero marginal product. In Stage 2 also, both average and marginal products are declining. Marginal product, being below the average product, pulls the average down.

In *Stage 3,* total product is declining.

### Rational Decisions in Stage 2

There is nothing "wrong" about diminishing returns — the diminishing but still positive marginal products of Stage 2. Nor do diminishing returns mean "inefficiency." Rational producers always choose a volume of production in Stage 2; just which volume cannot be said until prices are introduced, which is done in the next chapter. It must be clear that a rational producer never operates in Stage 3, because he would be producing less, and would be using more units of the variable input. In Stage 3, there is too much labor, in an absolute sense. Even if the labor costs nothing, there is still too much. The boundary between Stages 2 and 3, therefore, marks one limit of the range of rational production decisions. If the labor costs nothing and if production is at all profitable, then the volume of production is maximized at the right-hand boundary of Stage 2.

The other boundary is between Stages 1 and 2. Here, average product is a maximum. Suppose the firm is producing in Stage 1 and that production is profitable. If it is, profits can be increased by expansion, because more units of input increase production in greater proportion. Thus the firm always has an incentive to expand through Stage 1 and, in fact, to expand all the way out of it.[2]

### Returns to Scale

The assumption that some inputs are fixed in amount can now be set aside for the time being. The firm, therefore, expands production by using

---

[2] This statement applies to the purely competitive firm, which sells its product and buys its inputs at fixed prices. In monopoly and imperfect competition, the firm might find its most profitable level of output in Stage 1.

more of *all* inputs — more labor, more equipment, more space. If the increase in output is proportional to the increase in the quantities of the inputs, returns to scale are said to be constant. A doubling or quadrupling of inputs causes a doubling or quadrupling of output. If instead the increase in output is more than proportional, returns to scale are increasing. And if the increase in output is less than proportional, returns to scale are decreasing.

Some words of caution: Everyone is familiar with such phrases as "the economies of large-scale production," or "the advantages of mass production," and others like them. The trouble is that such phrases carry several meanings, some of which are irrelevant here and are therefore possible sources of confusion. The often observably greater efficiency of large producing units, in contrast to small ones, is frequently caused by the fact that the large units use newer and better techniques of production than the older and smaller units. However important they may be, improvements in technology are *not* part of the concept of returns to scale. The concept deals with a given technology.

It is now assumed that in expanding its scale, any firm first passes through a phase of increasing returns to scale, then a phase of constant returns, and then a phase of decreasing returns to scale. Expansion can take much time; during a period of time, technological improvements can be embodied in larger scales of operation. To set technological changes apart, varying returns to scale can be conceived as elements in the *plan* of the firm. Think of the firm as making a decision now on expansion. Though many things enter into the decision, only one is under discussion here — the relation between size and efficiency, the meaning of efficiency here being the ratio of output to input.

### Increasing Returns to Scale

Among the causes of increasing returns to scale are purely dimensional relations. If the diameter of a pipe is doubled, the flow through it is more than doubled. A wooden box that is a 3-foot cube can contain 27 times as much as a box that is a 1-foot cube, but only 9 times as much wood is needed for the larger box. If the labor and materials in a motor are doubled, its horsepower is more than doubled. The carrying capacity of a truck increases faster than its weight. After some point, however, such increases in dimensional efficiency come to an end. When they become larger, the pipe and the box have to be made out of thicker and stronger materials. The heavier a motor, the more likely it is to need a special foundation. The size of a truck is limited by the widths of streets, the heights of overpasses, the capacities of bridges, etc.

A closely related cause of increasing returns to scale is indivisibility. In general, indivisibility means that equipment is available only in minimum sizes or in definite ranges of sizes. As a firm's scale of operations increases, it can use the minimum sizes and then the larger sizes of more efficient equipment. But indivisibility is a matter of degree. Though there cannot be half a typewriter, a typewriter can be rented half time. Though there cannot be half an accountant, part-time accounting services can be employed. Indivisibility therefore quickly exhausts itself as a cause of increasing returns to scale.

Still another cause of increasing returns to scale comes from higher degrees of specialization, as Adam Smith pointed out nearly two centuries ago. With more labor, the firm can subdivide tasks, with gains in the efficiency of labor. With more machinery, the firm can buy special types and also assign special jobs even to standardized kinds of machinery.

Specialization, however, nearly always means some alteration in proportions. A change in proportions is not consistent with the strict and literal meaning of scale — changes in inputs in equal proportions. But again, the seeming inconsistency can be removed by using broad rather than narrow definitions of inputs. A firm can double both its labor and its capital and still alter the proportions in which some of its labor is employed with some of its equipment. And what does doubling of capital mean? The literal meaning is twice as many of each kind of equipment. A looser and more useful meaning is double the dollar outlay on equipment. Then too, to make labor and capital commensurate, dollar outlays have to be used.[3]

### Constant Returns to Scale

The phase of increasing returns to scale cannot go on indefinitely. The firm then enters the phase of constant returns to scale; doubling all the inputs now simply doubles the output.

The phase of constant returns to scale can be brief, before decreasing returns to scale set in. Though some theorists are inclined to look upon constant returns with jaundiced eyes, empirical evidence suggests that the phase of constant returns is long, that it typically covers a wide range of output. And if after overcoming the inefficiencies of too small a scale, a firm has returns that increase only by the tiniest degrees and if the decreases in decreasing returns are exceedingly small, then it can be *assumed* that returns to scale are constant. Such an assumption has great practical convenience, and it introduces a welcome simplification of theoretical analysis.

---

[3] But then the term "returns to scale" ceases to describe a purely technological relationship. The expressions "constant," "increasing," and "decreasing returns to scale" simply become synonyms for "constant," "decreasing," and "increasing average *costs*."

Economists often use the language of mathematics in referring to constant returns. A production function exhibiting constant returns to scale is said to be "linear and homogeneous," or "homogeneous of the first degree." The Cobb-Douglas production function referred to earlier is linear and homogeneous.

### Decreasing Returns to Scale

Can a firm keep on indefinitely doubling its inputs and hence always doubling its output? Everyone seems to agree that the answer is no, that eventually there must be decreasing returns to scale. The real problem is to find the clear cause or causes. On this point there is no agreement, even on the theoretical issue. Some economists hold that the entrepreneur himself is actually a fixed factor — though all other inputs can be increased, he cannot be. He and his decision-making are indivisible and incapable of augmentation. In this view, decreasing returns to scale is actually a special case of variable proportions. Other economists believe that decreasing returns to scale arise from the mounting difficulties of coordination and control as scale increases.

### Two Variable Inputs

So far, the firm has been imagined as increasing output either by using more of one input or more of all inputs. Attention is now turned to a firm's expanding its production by using more of two inputs that are substitutes for each other.

In Chapter 4, the behavior of a consumer is illustrated by a curve of diminishing marginal utility, and in Chapter 6 by a set of indifference curves. The theory of production is symmetrical, because the input-output relation can also be portrayed with a single curve of diminishing marginal productivity as well as by a set of curves that look like indifference curves.

The production function can now be conceived as consisting of certain fixed inputs and of two variable inputs. First comes the arithmetical and then the geometrical illustration.

The simple numbers in Table 9–2 illustrate some aspects of the substitution and combination of two variable inputs. The table is to be read from the lower lefthand corner, to be read up and to the right. The machines can be imagined as, say, power saws and the outputs as cords of wood. Two men and 2 saws produce 10 cords a day, 4 men and 4 saws produce 20 cords a day, and so on. Thus the numbers in the table exhibit constant returns to scale — if *both* inputs are doubled, then output is doubled. (Perhaps the reader may wonder how, say, 2 men can use 4 or more saws, or how 2 saws can be used by 4 or more men. But there is more to cutting wood than just using saws; underbrush must be got out of the way, the cut wood has to be piled, the saws have to be tended to and their teeth kept sharp, etc.) If, however, any column is read up or any row read across, it is clear that the increase in output is less than proportional to the increase in input. Except for the diagonal from lower left to upper right, therefore, any other reading of the table discloses diminishing marginal physical productivity. The table, then, gives an illustration of the coexistence of constant returns to scale and diminishing marginal returns in the same production function.

### Substitution Between Inputs

**TABLE 9–2**

Outputs from Different Combinations of Two Inputs

| *Number of Machines* | *Outputs* | | | |
|:---:|:---:|:---:|:---:|:---:|
| 8 | 25 | 30 | 35 | 40 |
| 6 | 20 | 25 | 30 | 35 |
| 4 | 15 | 20 | 25 | 30 |
| 2 | 10 | 15 | 20 | 25 |
| | 2 | 4 | 6 | 8 |
| | *Number of Men* | | | |

Table 9–2 shows something else: 2 more (fewer) men and 2 fewer (more) machines result in the same output. This means a rate of substitution of 2 for 2. And since 2:2 is the same as 1:1, the numbers in the table can be interpreted as if they say that a saw is a perfect substitute for a man, and vice versa. Though this is not impossible, it does seem unlikely. It is more realistic to suppose that if a crew of men is going to have a saw (or a man) taken away from it, output can be maintained only by adding more than one man (or a saw). To illustrate imperfect substitution would require a much more intricate set of numbers than those in Table 9–2.

### Isoquants

A production function with two variable inputs can be represented by a family of isoquants. The word "isoquants" simply means equal quantities; another expression is "isoproduct curves." Figure 9–2 shows one family of isoquants. The curves in the figure look like indifference curves, which they are not, although still another name sometimes given them is "production indifference curves." Take the isoquant labeled "100." The number 100 here means 100 units of output. The curve shows the different combinations of units of labor and capital that can be used to produce 100 units of output. Point $A$ on the curve shows that 100 units of output can be produced by $l$ units of labor and $c$ of capital; point $B$ shows that the same output can be produced with $l'$ and $c'$ units. The curves labeled "200," "300," and "400" show the different possible combinations of labor and

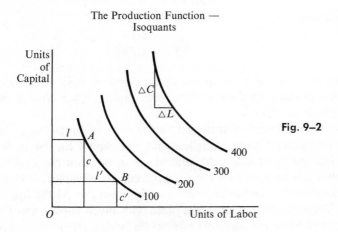

The Production Function —
Isoquants

Fig. 9–2

capital that can produce 200, 300, and 400 units of output. The reader's imagination can easily see other isoquants for other quantities of output. The shape of the isoquants displays the substitutability of the two inputs. If the inputs were perfect substitutes, the isoquants would be straight lines. If they are good substitutes, the isoquants are slightly convex, as in Figure 9–2. If the inputs are poor substitutes, the isoquants would be highly convex.[4]

### The Slope of an Isoquant

The slope of an isoquant at a point is the marginal rate of technical substitution ($MRTS$) at that point. Consider a small movement down an isoquant, where a small amount of capital is traded off — substituted — for a small amount of labor. By definition of an isoquant, output is constant,

[4] Sometimes isoquants are drawn so as to be bent around like hairpins. Toward the $y$-axis, such isoquants curl up and away from the axis; and at the other end, they curl up and away from the $x$-axis. This means that, for example, "too much" labor would have to be accompanied by more, not less, capital to hold output at a given level.

the gain in output from a little more labor being equal to the loss of output from a little less capital. The gain in output is the extra product of labor, i.e., the marginal physical product of the additional units of labor ($MPP_L \times \Delta L$). The loss of output is the foregone marginal physical product of the subtracted units of capital ($MPP_C \times \Delta C$).

Accordingly,

$$\text{slope} = MRTS = \frac{\Delta C}{\Delta L}$$

$$\text{loss of output} = \text{gain in output}$$

$$\Delta C \times MPP_C = \Delta L \times MPP_L.$$

Therefore,

$$\frac{\Delta C}{\Delta L} = \frac{MPP_L}{MPP_C}.$$

Thus the slope of an isoquant, at any point, is equal to the ratio of the marginal physical products of labor and capital. (See Note 4 in the Appendix to Part Three.)

The marginal rate of technical substitution is diminishing. Movement down an isoquant means that less and less capital can be traded off for given increments of labor. Movement up an isoquant means that less and less labor can be traded off for given increments of capital. These relations are equivalent to diminishing returns. To illustrate: At the upper left end of an isoquant, production takes place with much capital and little labor. If a unit of labor is added and production held constant, then several units of capital can be sacrificed or traded off. But as still more labor is added, it becomes harder and harder to maintain output by sacrificing capital. Therefore, less and less capital can be given up in moving down the curve.

### Proportion and Scale

Isoquant diagrams can also be used to exhibit and distinguish between proportion and scale. True enough, proportion and scale were distinguished earlier in this chapter. Since they are easily and often confused, it is well to reinforce understanding by using the isoquant technique of analysis.

In Figure 9–2, the isoquants are equidistant along any straight line drawn from the origin. This means that if both labor and capital are increased in equal proportion, output expands by the same proportion. If labor and capital are the *only* inputs, then the isoquants of Figure 9–2 show constant returns to *scale*. But if there are other *fixed* inputs, such as floor space, then the same isoquants show *constant proportional returns*. This is equivalent to constant and equal average and marginal products when just one input is variable.

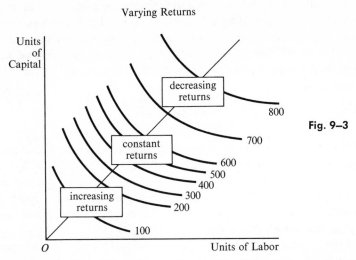

Varying Returns

Fig. 9–3

In Figure 9–3, varying returns are illustrated. They too can be either varying returns to scale or varying proportional returns, depending on the absence or presence of fixed factors. In Figure 9–3, the straight line from the origin is first crossed by the isoquants at smaller, then at equal, and finally at increasing intervals.

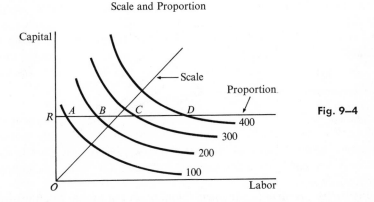

Scale and Proportion

Fig. 9–4

Figure 9–4 can be made to illustrate scale and proportion and the difference between them. Let labor and capital be the only inputs. The isoquants are drawn to show constant returns to scale. Take point $R$ in the figure. Point $R$ is chosen more or less at random, and represents $OR$ units of capital. Let this amount be held constant. When it is, production can be expanded by adding more units of labor, along line $RD$. If production is at 100 units, it can be increased to 200 units by adding *AB* units of labor, and to 300 units by adding *BC* units of labor. But *BC* is longer than *AB,* which means that it takes more additional labor to increase production from 200 to 300 units than it does from 100 to 200. Hence there is a diminishing marginal product for labor when the amount of capital is fixed.

### An Application

The classical economists of the early nineteenth century saw the growth of population as a force dooming mankind to a perpetually low material level of existence. But the steady advance of technology showed how false was the prediction. Per capita real incomes in Western Europe and North America are much higher than they were a century and a half ago. Productivity has grown faster than population.

At the present time, however, the fear of too rapidly growing population has emerged again. In many parts of Africa and Asia, the population explosion threatens, so some observers believe, to wipe out the gains from the new technology being introduced in these areas.

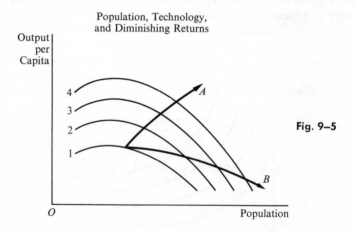

Fig. 9–5

Figure 9–5 contributes to clear thinking on the logical relations between population, technology, and diminishing returns. Imagine a country with given resources and institutions, and with a labor force of given aptitudes and skills. Let the ratio of the labor force to the population be constant, so that population can stand for labor force. In Figure 9–5, curve *1* is a curve of average physical output per capita. The average curve is used here, because average physical output and average real income are the same thing. At the left the curve rises, signifying that when population is very small, more people working on given resources have an increasing average product per capita. This is one way of defining "underpopulation." Similarly, the number of people corresponding to the highest point on curve *1* (or any of the other curves) can be, and has been, called the "optimum" population. The declining part of the curve is the region of diminishing average returns, of "overpopulation."

Curves *1, 2, 3,* and *4* in Figure 9–5 stand for successively higher productivities in, say, four successive decades. Improved technology raises the curves, which still, however, decline to the right. Gains in technology and diminishing returns are not logical contradictions, though sometimes they have been viewed as if they somehow are. Suppose now that population grows while technology advances, as indicated by line *A*. Here technology races ahead of population, with the result that output per capita rises decade by decade. The rising levels of living are indicated by the points of intersection of line *A* with the four successive productivity curves. If, however, population outstrips technology, as shown by line *B,* the country is doomed to a steadily *lower* average income per capita.

### Summary

The *production function* of a firm states the relation between its physical inputs and its physical output. When a firm increases output by holding all inputs constant but one, the gains in output are subject to the law of *variable proportions* or of *diminishing returns.* After some point, *marginal product* diminishes. The relations between total product and quantities of a variable input are divided into three stages. Relevant is *Stage 2,* which begins where marginal and average products are equal and ends where marginal product is zero. When a firm increases output by using more of all inputs, the input-output relation is one of scale. *Returns to scale* can be increasing, constant, and decreasing.

A firm can also increase output by using more of one or both of two inputs that are substitutes. The production function can then be represented by a family of *isoquants.* The slope of an isoquant is the *marginal rate of technical substitution* between the inputs and is also the ratio of their marginal physical productivities. An isoquant diagram can show both proportion and scale.

### SELECTED REFERENCES

A standard advanced work: Sune Carlson, *A Study on the Pure Theory of Production,* Stockholm Economic Studies No. 9 (London: P. S. King, 1939).

John M. Cassels, "On the Law of Variable Proportions," in *Explorations in Economics* (New York: McGraw-Hill, 1936); reprinted in American Economic Association, *Readings in the Theory of Income Distribution* (Philadelphia: Blakiston, 1946). Edward H. Chamberlin, *The Theory of Monopolistic Competition,* 7th ed. (Cambridge: Harvard University Press, 1956), Appendix B. George J. Stigler, *The Theory of Price,* rev. ed. (New York: Macmillan, 1952), Chap. 6 and 7. William J. Baumol, *Economic Theory and Operations Analysis* (Englewood Cliffs, N.J.: Prentice-Hall, 1961), Chap. 9.

Some empirical production functions are discussed in Milton H. Spencer and Louis Siegelman, *Managerial Economics* (Homewood: Irwin, 1959), Chap. 6.

On the Cobb-Douglas production function: Paul H. Douglas, "Are There Laws of Production?" *American Economic Review,* Vol. XXXVIII, No. 1, March, 1948. This was Douglas's presidential address to the American Economic Association in 1947.

## EXERCISES AND PROBLEMS

1. What happens to the curve of the marginal physical product of labor if the weather turns out to be better than the farmer had expected? If the insects are worse?

2. On an isoquant diagram, draw new isoquants to show the effects (a) of a labor-saving innovation, (b) of a capital-saving innovation, and (c) of a technological change improving the efficiencies of both labor and capital.

3. On an isoquant diagram, show the diminishing marginal product of capital when the amount of labor is fixed.

4. Apply the concepts of variable proportions, constant proportions, and scale to a filling station, a supermarket, and a restaurant.

# Choices of Inputs

# and Outputs

# 10

ONE VARIABLE INPUT • TWO VARIABLE INPUTS • MANY INPUTS •

TWO OUTPUTS • AN APPLICATION •

Consider the decisions the firm must make in buying its inputs. The firm buys or leases machinery, hires many kinds of labor, buys raw or semi-finished materials, buys electrical energy, fuel, and water, buys supplies of many kinds, etc. The physical combination of the firm's inputs has already been described under the name of the production function. The possible physical combinations of the inputs in the production function are determined by technology; they change as technology changes. Each input has a price that the firm must pay. The prices of the inputs, along with the roles of the inputs in the production function, influence the firm's decisions as to how much of each to buy.

Assume that the firm wants to minimize the cost of any output it produces. Given the total revenue of a volume of output, the minimization of cost is, of course, the same thing as the maximization of profits. The cost curves of the firm, which will be described in Chapter 11, are drawn on the assumption that *each* point on a cost curve represents the least cost of the corresponding output. The theory of the firm's choices of inputs states the conditions that achieve cost minimization. The theory also develops the basis for the demand of a firm for inputs and, in so doing, creates the demand side of the theory of the determination of incomes (Chapter 25).

In this chapter, it will be assumed that the production function of the firm permits the substitution of one input for another by very small degrees. Chapter 12 will drop this assumption and, instead, will show how the firm makes its decisions on inputs when they are not substitutable or when they are substitutable only within fixed limits. In other words, this chapter assumes, for example, that in employing machine-hours and man-hours, the firm can produce with more of one and less of the other, and that it is meaningful to substitute one machine-hour for one man-hour, and vice versa. Chapter 12 will take up the complementary relation between machines and men, where, for example, the one-machine-one-operator relation is fixed. The two theories do not oppose, but rather supplement, one another. Easy substitution in the production function is the simpler assumption, and being more general, can explain more. This assumption, too, fits the long run, where all is variable. The assumption of rigid input proportions and of limited substitution is appropriate for the short run where much is fixed, and for certain kinds of practical problems.

### One Variable Input

Consider first the simplest case. Here the firm can produce more or it can produce less by varying the amount of one input. Suppose the input is a certain grade of labor. To solve for the optimum amount of this labor to hire, the firm must fit together three pieces of information — the price to be paid for the labor, the productivity of the labor, and the price of the product sold by the firm.

To maintain simplicity, let it also be assumed for the time being that the firm has no control at all over the price it must pay for the labor and over the price the firm gets for its product. Under these assumptions, the optimum amount of a variable input is the amount whose marginal physical product has a value equal to the price of the input. The last man hired just pays for himself.

The meaning of marginal physical product was explained in Chapter 9. The product is measured in such units as bushels, or yards, or tons. The value of marginal physical product is the marginal physical unit multiplied by the price received by the firm. Suppose the marginal physical product of 20 men is 4 tons a day; this means that 20 men, as opposed to 19, cause output to be 4 tons *larger*. Suppose next that the firm gets $7.50 a ton. The value of the marginal product of 20 men is then $30.00. If the daily wage (i.e., the total labor cost, including social security taxes, fringe benefits, etc. to the employer) is $30.00, then it will just pay the firm to hire 20 men. It would not pay to hire more than 20, because the value of the marginal physical product declines, becoming less than the wage. Nor would it pay to hire fewer than 20 men, because then the firm would not avail itself of the opportunity of buying units of an input that bring in more money than they cost.

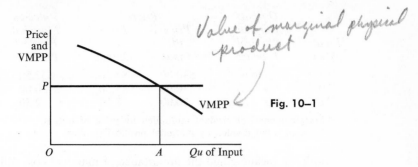

Fig. 10–1

Figure 10–1 shows the determination of the optimum quantity of a variable input. The horizontal axis measures quantities of a variable input. The vertical axis measures dollars — the price of the variable input and the dollar value of the marginal physical product. Let the price of the input be *OP* and the value of the marginal physical product be the curve *VMPP.* The optimum quantity of the variable input is *OA,* the quantity whose *VMPP* equals its price. Any larger quantity has a *VMPP* less than price, and any smaller quantity a *VMPP* greater than price, signifying therefore a missed opportunity. The quantity *OA* can also be called an equilibrium quantity. In the neighborhood of the equilibrium, *VMPP* must be declining, for if it were rising or if it were constant and above price, the firm would expand without limit, which is absurd. If the *VMPP* curve were everywhere below the price line, the firm would not use this input at all.

Remember that there are three variables here — two prices and physical productivity. If the firm should receive a higher price for its product, the *VMPP* curve shifts to the right. So it does too with an improvement in technology. If the price of the input changes, the horizontal price line shifts up or down. Any of these changes, or a combination of them, results in a new equilibrium, a new optimum quantity of input.

The main points of the foregoing discussion are summed up in Table 10–1. The numbers in this table can be imagined as part of a larger set; only those in the region of equilibrium — the region of rational decision-making — are included. The last column in Table 10–1 gives the marginal cost, i.e., the cost of an additional unit of output. When 20 men are employed instead of 19, the extra man costs $30.00 and the extra output is 4 tons. Hence the extra cost of one ton at this level of output is $7.50. Notice that marginal cost equals the price of the output for the equilibrium quantity of input.

**TABLE 10–1**

### Optimum Quantity of One Variable Input

| Input: Men | Output: Marginal Physical Product | Prices | | Value of Marginal Physical Product[a] | Marginal Cost[b] |
|---|---|---|---|---|---|
| | | Price of Input | Price of Output | | |
| 19 | 5 tons | $30.00 | $7.50 | $37.50 | $ 6.00 |
| 20 | 4 | 30.00 | 7.50 | 30.00 | 7.50 |
| 21 | 3 | 30.00 | 7.50 | 22.50 | 10.00 |

[a] Marginal physical product multiplied by price of output.
[b] Price of input divided by marginal physical product.

Both the meaning and the importance of marginal cost will be gone into more fully in the next and in later chapters. At this point, it suffices to show the relation between the marginal cost of output and the marginal physical product of a single variable input.

The relations under examination here can be restated this way:

$$\frac{\text{price of input}}{\text{marginal physical product}} = \text{marginal cost} = \text{price of output}.$$

### Two Variable Inputs

Suppose next that the firm has two variable inputs, that the firm can expand or contract output by using more or less of one or both of them. The isoquants described in the last chapter can now be put to further use.

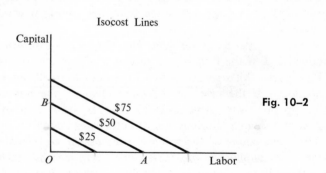

Isocost Lines

Fig. 10–2

### Isocost Lines

To choose optimum quantities of two inputs, the firm must take their physical productivities and their prices into account. Productivities are shown by isoquants. The prices of the inputs are represented on the same diagram by isocost lines. Figure 10–2 shows three of them. Take the line *BA:* So many units (e.g., hours) of labor, shown by the length *OA,* cost the firm $50. For $50, the firm can also buy OB of capital — e.g., machine-hours. In the figure, the length *OA* is twice the length *OB,* which means that the price of a unit of labor is half that of a unit of capital. Thus the slope of the line shows the ratio of the prices. Any point on the line *BA* represents an expenditure of $50 for the corresponding number of units of labor and of capital. The $75 line lies proportionately farther to the right, signifying that more of either or both of labor and capital can be bought at the same prices. The isocost lines are straight, which means that the firm has no control over the prices of the inputs, and that the prices are the same no matter how many units the firm buys.

### The Optimum Combination of Inputs

The firm wants to produce any volume of output at least cost. The least cost of any output, when it is shown on an isoquant, is given by the point of tangency of the isoquant to an isocost curve. This can be seen in Figure 10–3. Here are two isoquants, each tangent to an isocost line. Any

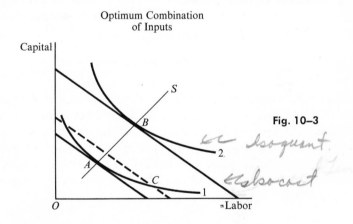

Optimum Combination
of Inputs

Fig. 10–3

Isoquant

Isocost

other point on either isoquant would be on an isocost line farther to the right. That is, any other point on an isoquant would represent the same amount of output, but at a higher cost. For example, take the point *C* on isoquant *1.* The labor and capital represented by *C* produce the same quantity of output as the labor and capital represented by *A;* but the isocost line for *C* — the dashed line — lies farther to the right than the isocost line shown for *A.* Tangency therefore means minimum cost.

The line *S* in Figure 10–3 connects the points of tangency, i.e., points *A* and *B,* and others not shown. The firm expands output along the line *S.*

The condition for minimum cost is that the firm choose those quantities of the two inputs that correspond to the tangencies of isocost lines and isoquants. At the points of tangency, slopes are equal. The slope of the isocost lines is the ratio of the prices of the inputs. The slope of the isoquants is the ratio of the marginal physical products of the inputs. The slope is also the marginal rate of technical substitution between the inputs; this was shown on page 146. Let $C$ stand for capital and $L$ for labor. Therefore,

$$\frac{P_L}{P_C} = \frac{MPP_L}{MPP_C} \quad \text{And} \quad \frac{MPP_C}{P_C} = \frac{MPP_L}{P_L}$$

That is to say, if a machine-hour costs twice as much as a labor hour, the marginal physical product of a machine hour is twice that of a labor hour. To put it another way, a dollar's worth of machine-hours yields the same addition to total product as a dollar's worth of labor-hours.

It is plain that the firm's behavior in making its optimum purchases of variable inputs is exactly symmetrical with the behavior of the consumer. Both the firm and the consumer buy things in such quantities as to equate marginal importance with price. Just as the consumer adjusts his budget so as to equate satisfaction from the last dollar spent on each commodity, so the firm adjusts its expenditures so as to get equal amounts of its product from the last dollar spent on each input.

## Many Inputs

The next step is to generalize the results of the one- and two-variable analyses. To handle three inputs, a three-dimensional diagram would have to be drawn. For four and more inputs, exact analysis requires calculus. But the purchase of many inputs does not cause the behavior of the firm to differ in any important way. The optimum choices of quantities of many inputs can be indicated by extending the two-variable analysis.

Let the firm's inputs be $A, B, \ldots N$. By extension of previous results, it is true that

$$\frac{MPP_A}{P_A} = \frac{MPP_B}{P_B} = \cdots = \frac{MPP_N}{P_N}.$$

It is also true that

$$\frac{P_A}{MPP_A} = \frac{P_B}{MPP_B} = \cdots = \frac{P_N}{MPP_N} = MC.$$

And since $MC = P_O$, where $P_O$ is the price of the firm's output, it follows that

$$\frac{P_A}{MPP_A} = \frac{P_B}{MPP_B} = \cdots = \frac{P_N}{MPP_N} = P_O.$$

This last set of equations says that the value of the marginal physical product of *each* input (e.g., $MPP_A \times P_O = P_A$) is equal to the price paid for the input. Accordingly, when the firm minimizes costs and maximizes profits, it buys *all* of its inputs in such quantities that the values of their marginal physical products are equal to their prices.

## Changes in Input Prices

Suppose that there is a fall in the price of one of the firm's inputs. Then the firm buys more of this input, equating the value of the lower marginal physical product of a larger quantity with the lower price. But the effects of a fall in the price of an input go farther than this. Suppose the input is one kind of fertilizer. More is used at the lower price. The larger quantity of the one kind of fertilizer lowers the marginal physical productivity of another kind of fertilizer which is a close substitute. Hence less of the substitute fertilizer is used, the quantity being cut back so that its *VMPP* again equals its price. Other inputs, such as labor and gasoline, may be complements to the kind of fertilizer whose price falls. More fertilizer may require more labor and gasoline. *Their MPP's* also change, and in so doing change the *MPP,* and thus the *VMPP,* of the fertilizer.

Thus the effect of a change in the price of one input is to cause a ripple through the equations relating input productivities, prices, and costs. Several adjustments in inputs have to be made because the price of just one of them has changed. Of course, the farmer does not have to go to the nearest research center and ask to have a mathematical economist solve his problem on a computer. The farmer's experience and knowledge tell him what to do. And if he does keep his costs as low as possible, given his output, the farmer does act as if a computer had presented him with the solution.

A change in the price of a consumer good has a substitution and an income effect for the consumer. This was described on pages 88 and 89. Similar effects prevail for the firm. A fall in the price of an input causes more of it to be used, even if the total output of the firm remains constant. This is the substitution effect. But a cheaper input lowers costs, which causes the firm to expand total output, which in turn increases still more the use of the cheaper input. This is the output or expansion effect.

## Two Outputs

So far, the firm has been described as having one output, or product. Nearly all firms, however, produce more than one product. Consider now a firm with two products. How does the firm choose the proportions in which to produce its two products?

The formal answer to this question is symmetrical with the statement of the choice of input proportions. As with two inputs, so with two outputs.

The firm produces two outputs, or products, in such proportions that the marginal rate of substitution (or transformation) between the products is equal to the ratio of their prices.

### The Production Possibility Curve

In Figure 10–4, the curve $Y_1X_1$ is a production possibility curve. It shows the different quantities of the two products, $X$ and $Y$, that can be produced with some given amount of the firm's resources. With these

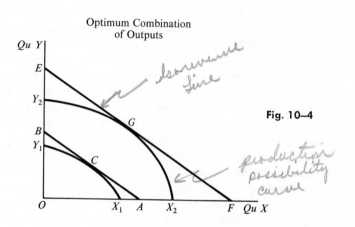

Fig. 10–4

resources, the firm can produce $OY_1$ of $Y$, or $OX_1$ of $X$, or any combination of $X$ and $Y$ as shown by the curve. With more resources, the firm can produce more, as shown for example by the curve $Y_2X_2$. Similarly shaped curves are often drawn to show the guns-and-butter problem of a nation at war; if more armaments are produced, then fewer civilian goods can be produced. The curve $Y_1X_1$ is *concave* to the origin, which means that if the output of $X$ is increased by equal amounts, the sacrifices of $Y$ become larger and larger; and if the output of $Y$ is increased by equal amounts, the sacrifices of $X$ become larger.

### Isorevenue Lines

The firm wants of course to maximize the revenue it gets from selling its products. In Figure 10–4, the lines $BA$ and $EF$ are isorevenue lines. The line $BA$ is constructed in this way: The quantity $OB$ of $Y$ multiplied by the price of $Y$ would bring in a certain amount of revenue. The same revenue could be obtained by selling $OA$ of $X$. Because $OA$ is more than $OB$, the price of $X$ is lower than the price of $Y$. The slope of the line is the ratio of the price of $X$ to the price of $Y$.[1] The line $AB$ happens to be drawn so that the price ratio is 2/3; the price of $X$ is, say, 50 cents and the price of $Y$ is 75 cents. Any point on the line $BA$ shows the different quantities of $X$ and $Y$ whose sale brings in the same revenue. The line $EF$, which is parallel to $BA$, shows more revenue from the sale of larger quantities at the same prices.

### The Optimum Combination of Outputs

When the firm is on the production possibility curve $Y_1X_1$, it maximizes its revenue by producing $X$ and $Y$ in the proportions indicated by point $C$. This point is on the highest attainable isorevenue line. Any other combination of $X$ and $Y$ would be produced at the same total cost, of the given resources, but it would be on a lower isorevenue line, i.e., one with less revenue. Tangency here means maximum revenue for a given total outlay.

The optimum combination is therefore represented by the tangency of the production possibility curve to an isorevenue line. With tangency, slopes are equal, signifying the equality of the marginal rate of substitution of the outputs and the ratio of their prices.

With the production possibility curve $Y_2X_2$, the optimum combination is at point $G$, by the same line of reasoning. As the firm expands its outputs, it does so along a path marked out by points $C$ and $G$.

It should now be evident why the production-possibility curve must be concave. If the curve were convex or were a straight line, the firm would produce only one product, not two, because to do so would put the firm on the highest isorevenue line.

### An Application

The ideas discussed in this chapter can be applied to decision-making in national defense.[2] Suppose there are two major weapons and that the problem of defense policy is how to use them together. Their effectiveness — their valuable output — is measured in one dimension, the expected number of targets they can destroy. For the potential destruction of some given number of targets, say, 100 targets, the two weapons can be employed in different combinations. Within limits, the two weapons are substitutes.

Therefore, isoquants for the two weapons can be plotted. This is done in Figure 10–5. Here are four isoquants, one each for the expected destruc-

---

[1] Since $YP_Y = XP_X$, and since slope $= \dfrac{Y}{X}$, it follows that slope $= \dfrac{P_X}{P_Y}$.

[2] Charles J. Hitch and Roland N. McKean, *The Economics of Defense in the Nuclear Age* (Cambridge: Harvard University Press, 1960). The application above is adapted from pp. 114–118 of Hitch and McKean.

tion of 50, 100, 200, and 300 targets. Assume that each point on each isoquant represents the best tactical employment of and support for that particular combination of the two weapons. How to decide which of the points is best? The answer is to bring in costs. Figure 10–5 has one isocost line, joining the points for 1,000 of weapon *A* and 500 of weapon *B*. Imagine that the budget is such that *x* billion dollars, but no more, can be spent on *A* and *B*. If the whole budget goes for *A*, 1000 units of it can be available; if the whole budget is spent on *B*, 500 units can be procured. Or, the budget can be divided between *A* and *B*, with results shown by the line *CD*. The straightness of line *CD* means that both weapons are produced under conditions of constant unit cost.

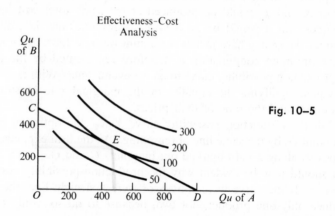

Effectiveness–Cost Analysis

Fig. 10–5

The correct decision, of course, is to plan to use the two weapons in the proportions shown by point *E*. Given the budget, the only possible proportions are those on the isocost line *CD*; in this context, the line is often called an "exchange curve." Any proportions other than *E* would mean the potential destruction of fewer targets. The point *E* shows how to get the most for the money.

Clearly, modifications in the weapons will change the shapes and positions of the isoquants. Similarly, a different budget alters the isocost line. Hence the optimum point *E* will shift.

This example is simple — only two inputs and only one output. Geometry cannot handle more complicated models; they require advanced mathematical analysis.

One more remark about this application. It may be distasteful to those who think that such decisions should not have to be made. Yet swords can be turned into plowshares in more senses than one: Some of the military research in the postwar period has been directed to better utilization of resources for defense. Part of this research is applied economic theory. The new knowledge gained can also be put to work for the better utilization of government's civilian resources.

## Summary

A firm buys inputs in quantities determined by the production function and the prices of the inputs. This chapter deals only with firms having no control over the prices they pay and receive. A firm buys one variable input in such a quantity that *the value of the marginal physical product of the input is equal to the price of the input.* The price of the input divided by marginal physical product is equal to the price of the output. The prices of two variable inputs are represented by *isocost lines.* The firm buys two variable inputs in such proportions that the ratio of their marginal physical products is equal to the ratio of their prices. Minimum costs mean that isoquants are tangent to isocost lines. A firm with many inputs buys them all in quantities whose *VMPP's* equal their prices. A firm with two outputs produces and sells them in such proportions that the ratio of the prices equals the marginal rate of substitution. To maximize revenues, *isorevenue lines* are tangent to *production possibility curves.*

## SELECTED REFERENCES

J. R. Hicks, *Value and Capital,* 2nd ed. (London: Oxford, 1946), Chap. VI. Tibor Scitovsky, *Welfare and Competition* (Homewood: Irwin, 1951), Chap. VII. William J. Baumol, *Economic Theory and Operations Analysis* (Englewood Cliffs, N.J.: Prentice-Hall, 1961), Chaps. 9 and 10.

Applications: To forest farming: William A. Duerr, *Fundamentals of Forestry Economics* (New York: McGraw-Hill, 1960), Chap. 7 on Combining Multiple Labor Inputs and Chap. 12 on Multiple-Product Management. To the national defense: Charles J. Hitch and Roland N. McKean, *The Economics of Defense in the Nuclear Age* (Cambridge: Harvard University Press, 1960), Chap. 7.

## EXERCISES AND PROBLEMS

1. Suppose a firm can obtain a valuable input without having to pay for it (e.g., apprentices who receive no pay, or free water or electricity from a municipality eager to encourage new industry). How does the firm decide how much of the free input to take?

2. After making different assumptions, draw diagrams that are variations of Figure 10–1 on page 153. For example, assume a technological improvement.

3. For two inputs, draw and explain a diagram showing much more use of one input than of the other. Do this by varying both the isoquants and the prices.

4. Draw diagrams to prove that a firm would produce one product, not two, if the production possibility curve were convex. Do this for both X and Y.

5. Suppose the production possibility curve were a straight line with the same slope as the isorevenue line. What then?

# Cost-Output Relations

## 11

The relations between changes in the costs of a firm and changes in its output will now be examined. The firm's decisions on profit-maximizing outputs depend on the behavior of its costs as well as upon the behavior of its revenue.

### Cost Functions

The general name for the relation between costs and output is "cost function." The production function of a firm and the prices it pays for its inputs determine the firm's cost function. Since a production function can take different forms, with either one or some or all of the inputs variable, cost functions can take different forms. Price theory gives most of its attention, however, to two cost functions — the short-run cost function and the long-run cost function. On diagrams, these are of course the short-run and the long-run cost curves of the firm.

### The Short Run and the Long Run

In the short run, some inputs are fixed in amount; a firm can expand or contract its output only by varying the amounts of other inputs. Output can range from zero, if the firm shuts down altogether, to some maximum permitted by the fixed factors. In the long run, all inputs are variable in amount; a firm's output can range from zero to an indefinitely large quantity.

The short run and the long are not definite periods of calendar time. Strictly speaking, they are sets of conditions, not periods of time at all. Still, it is almost impossible to keep the idea of time out of analyses of the short run and the long. Even if it is never mentioned, calendar time lurks in the background, and as an idea might just as well be faced. The fixed factors of the firm in the short run are its plant and equipment, and in some industries, unique kinds of skilled labor. Where plant and equipment are large and complicated, requiring heavy investments and actual construction times of two years or more, the short run can be many years in length. But the short run can also be just a few weeks long, if firms can easily procure additional equipment and skilled labor, and if their needs for buildings are modest or minimal. Trucking is probably an example here. Similarly, as a length of time, the long run can vary from a period of two or three decades to just a few weeks. An example of a long run of short calendar duration might be the public-relations industry, which needs only ordinary office furnishings and machines as its equipment, and rented space as its plant, and which uses nonspecialized labor, mostly newspapermen. In any large city, this industry should be able to expand and contract with the greatest of speed and ease.

Between the short run and the long run, there can be no sharp or exact distinction. Whether conceived as sets of conditions or as periods of time, the two merge into each other.

### Short-Run Cost Curves

In the short run, the costs of the firm are divided into fixed costs and variable costs. The fixed costs are mainly those of the fixed plant and equipment of the firm. The clearest way to define fixed costs is to say that they are the costs that continue if the firm is temporarily shut down, producing nothing at all. Fixed costs include such items as interest on the investment in plant and equipment, most kinds of insurance, property taxes, depreciation and maintenance, etc., and the salaries and wages of those people who would continue to be employed even in a temporary shut-down. The fixed costs of a firm also include, as Chapter 8 explains, the opportunity costs of the owners of the firm, as well as normal profits. The variable costs are those that vary with the volume of output. These costs include wages, payments for raw materials and other goods bought by the firm, payments for fuel, excise taxes (if any), interest on short-term loans, etc.

Many systems of classifying costs have been devised, and in practice it is sometimes not easy to decide whether a particular cost belongs in the group of fixed or variable costs. But economic analysis sets all such difficulties aside, building its explanations on the simple twofold division.

### Constant Average Variable Cost

The simplest cost-output relation for the firm in the short run carries the assumption that average variable cost, i.e., variable cost per unit, is constant — that it is the same whatever the volume of output. This means a production function with variable inputs — labor and materials — combined under conditions of constant proportional returns. Suppose that the fixed cost of a firm is $1,000, and that the cost of labor and materials is 50 cents for each unit produced. With this information, a cost schedule can be built, as in Table 11–1.

### TABLE 11–1

#### A Simple Short-Run Cost Schedule

| Output in Physical Units | Total Fixed Cost | Average Variable Cost | Total Variable Cost | Total Cost | Average Cost |
|---|---|---|---|---|---|
| 0 | $1,000 | $ 0 | $ 0 | $1,000 | . . . . |
| 1,000 | 1,000 | 0.50 | 500 | 1,500 | $1.50 |
| 2,000 | 1,000 | 0.50 | 1,000 | 2,000 | 1.00 |
| 3,000 | 1,000 | 0.50 | 1,500 | 2,500 | 0.83 |

Because average variable cost in the table is constant, total variable cost increases proportionately with output. The fixed cost is $1,000 at zero output, and remains at this level at any output. The larger the output, the smaller is the fixed cost per unit because it is spread over more units. The last column of Table 11–2 shows the decline in average cost. Average cost means the total cost per unit. Average cost equals average fixed cost plus average variable cost, i.e., $AC = AFC + AVC$.

Notice that with the constant average variable cost, the extra cost of an extra unit, i.e., marginal cost, is the same amount of money. In other words, when it is constant, average variable cost is equal to marginal cost.

### The Break-even Chart

Though simple, Table 11–1 is far from unrealistic. Much business thinking and decision-making are based on relations no more complicated. The common device of the break-even chart is constructed from the same relations. The only additional piece of information needed for a break-even chart is selling price. Suppose that the same firm can sell its product at $1 a unit and that the firm gets this price no matter how many units it sells (i.e., the demand for the firm's product is perfectly elastic).

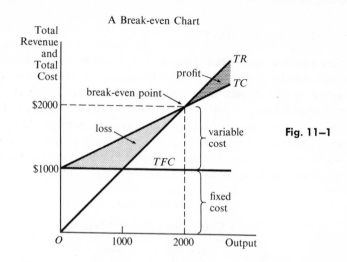

A Break-even Chart

**Fig. 11–1**

Figure 11–1 shows a break-even chart based on the data of Table 11–1 and the $1 selling price. The *TR* line shows the total revenue at any output — $1 multiplied by the number of units of output. The *TFC* line is horizontal at the $1,000 level. The *TC* line shows total costs, fixed plus variable; the line is drawn to start at $1,000, which means that the total variable cost is added to the fixed cost. The *break-even point* is the intersection of *TR* and *TC*. With 2,000 units of output, total revenue is $2,000 and total cost is $2,000. A larger output yields a profit, a smaller one a loss.

The break-even chart shown in Figure 11–1 is only one form of this analytical device.[1] It is presumably useful in practice because the chart makes the position of a firm visible with one quick glance. In practice, too, cost figures are often hard to compute, and some doubt and uncertainty may accompany choices as to which items to put into the group of fixed costs and which into the variable. Thus, if a firm finds itself operating near the break-even point, the executives might want to see if costs can be reduced, or even if they should be recalculated, or what if anything can be done to increase sales.

---

[1] When a firm has many products, dollars are plotted on both axes of the chart. The total revenue curve is then a straight line at a 45° angle. Total costs are then plotted against sales revenues, to find the sales volume in dollars that is the break-even point.

Break-even charts are usually drawn with straight lines, though they need not be. The straight-lines mean the linear assumption that changes in total costs are proportional to changes in output. For small changes in output above or below the break-even point, the assumption is often correct or so close to the true relation that it can be justified. A firm is not likely to be much interested in cost-output relations for very small or very large outputs when they lie outside the realms of experience and expectation. Why not then draw straight lines over the whole range? For this reason, no importance should be attached to what is obviously an absurdity: The profit area grows and grows without limit as output rises above the break-even level.

### The Conventional Cost Curves

Economic analysis goes beyond the remembered experiences of business firms and considers the whole range of cost-output relations for the firm in the short run. With zero output, the firm has its fixed inputs, employing no variable ones. To produce a small output, the firm adds units of its variable inputs. Because proportions are out of whack when output is small, the average and marginal physical products of the variable inputs increase. As output expands, proportions continue to alter. For some range of output, the average and marginal products can be constant, and therefore equal to each other. But as output expands still more, it becomes circumscribed and ultimately limited by the sizes of the fixed inputs. For large outputs, the marginal and average products of the variable inputs must diminish.

All this means that, over the whole range of possible short-run output from zero to the physical maximum,[2] total cost increases at a decreasing rate, then at a constant rate, and then at an increasing rate. This means too that marginal cost first declines, then becomes constant, and then rises.

Figure 11–2 presents a view of the relations between total cost, marginal cost, and the marginal (physical) product of the variable inputs.

Chapter 10 shows how the firm combines its variable inputs, buying each one in such quantities that the value of its marginal contribution is equal to its cost to the firm. Doing this, the firm minimizes its costs, the costs of *any* volume of output. *Each* point on the *TC* curve in Figure 11–2 is as low as possible.

Figure 11–3 is the standard or conventional diagram of the short-run cost curves of the firm, when cost is calculated as cost per unit of output.

---

[2] The maximum physical output from a fixed plant is rarely a precise amount. Much depends on the time period and on whether equipment is utilized at normal rates. A piece of machinery can nearly always be run at a rate well past its rated capacity for a short period of time.

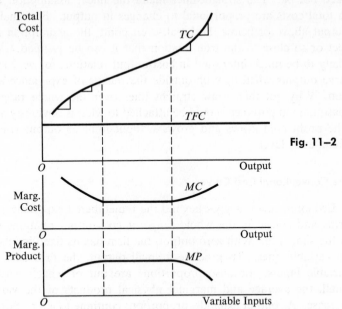

Total Cost, Marginal Cost,
and Marginal Product

Fig. 11–2

Other cost curves, including simpler ones, will be presented shortly. If there is one set of related curves for the firm, any firm, Figure 11–3 has it, because this figure embraces all that can be put in one set of integrated

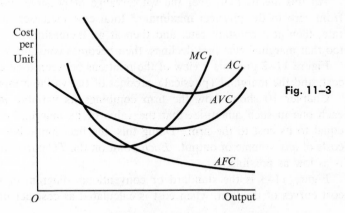

Short-Run Cost Curves

Fig. 11–3

generalizations. Here are the definitions and constructions: The *AFC* curve is *average fixed cost* per unit. This curve is a rectangular hyperbola asymptotic to the axes, which means that the curve approaches the vertical and the horizontal at each end. For very small outputs, fixed cost per unit is high, and for large outputs it is low. To call the *AFC* curve a rectangular hyperbola is only to say that the fixed cost is fixed — as a total amount — and that the average fixed cost multiplied by output is always exactly the same amount. The *AVC* curve is *average variable cost*. This curve declines at first, reaches a minimum, and then rises, for reasons already indicated. The *AC* curve is *average total cost* per unit; it is the sum of *AFC* and *AVC* for each output. The minimum of the *AC* is at a higher volume of output than the minimum point of the *AVC* curve, because the *AFC* curve always declines as output increases. The *MC* curve is the curve of *marginal cost*. The marginal cost of any output is the addition to total cost because that output is produced instead of an output one unit less. The *MC* curve declines faster than the *AVC* and the *AC* curves, and rises faster than they do. The *MC* curve also goes through the minimum points of the *AVC* and *AC* curves. Why these things are so will be explained shortly. Notice that all the curves are smooth and continuous. Of course, the *AFC* curve has to be, by its very nature. But the other curves in Figure 11–3 do not have the kinks or bumps that would reflect discontinuities in the production function. *Each* point on the *AVC, AC,* and *MC* curves is a minimum for its particular level of output. This also follows from the firm's choices of inputs. By minimizing the cost of *any* volume of output, the firm keeps the three cost curves in their lowest positions.

### The Importance of Marginal Cost

Marginal cost has already been formally defined. But for clarity of understanding, it is desirable to elaborate and restate the definition. What is the marginal cost of 1,000 units a week? It is the extra cost of producing 1,000 units instead of 999 units a week. Any output, whether it is 1,000 or 10,000, or any other number, has its marginal cost — the change in total cost by producing that number instead of one unit less. The fundamental notion is that of the rate of change in total cost associated with the smallest possible change in output, which is one unit.

Marginal cost is independent of the fixed cost. It makes no difference what the fixed cost is, whether it is a thousand dollars or ten million dollars; marginal cost is unaffected. Remember that marginal cost is the *addition* to total cost when another unit of output is produced. One more unit causes nothing to be added to the fixed cost. Marginal cost is associated only with the variable costs.[3]

[3] A more formal proof of the independence of marginal cost from fixed cost is this ($n$ stands for any volume of output):

$$MC(n) = TC(n) - TC(n-1)$$
$$= [TVC(n) + TFC] - [TVC(n-1) + TFC]$$
$$= TVC(n) - TVC(n-1)$$

When $MC$ is less than $AVC$ and $AC$, it pulls them down; when $MC$ is greater than $AVC$ and $AC$, it pulls them up. When $MC$ equals $AVC$ or $AC$, they are neither being pulled down nor up, but are at a minimum. Therefore, $MC = AVC$ and $MC = AC$ when $AVC$ and $AC$ are minimum. This point has much economic significance, which is explained in Chapter 15. A formal proof of these equalities is in Note 5 in the Appendix to Part Three.

A useful thing to know about a marginal-cost curve is that the area under it is equal to the total variable cost of the same output. Take any output, $n$. A line drawn from the $MC$ curve to $n$ is the marginal cost of $n$. The line can be imagined as a very thin bar. Next to it on the left is another thin bar, the $MC$ of $n - 1$ units. Next to this one is another, the $MC$ of $n - 2$ units. And so on. All the thin bars merge into an area which is the total variable cost of the output $n$.

Marginal cost is important because it is the cost concept relevant in rational decision-making. Rational decisions are those that lead not just to good profits, but to maximum profits; if losses are unavoidable, rational decisions lead to minimum losses.

### Other Types of Short-Run Cost Curves

It was said before that if only one cost curve for the firm in the short run is to be studied, it is the cost curve (i.e., the related group of them) shown in Figure 11–3 on page 168. The different cost curves of millions of different firms can be thought of as almost endless variants of the one generalization. But the cost curve of Figure 11–3 can also be viewed as one of three main types, rather than as the one general type.

The average cost of a firm in the short run always declines to a minimum; then it rises. How much it declines depends on the proportion of fixed to total costs. If the proportion of fixed costs is high, the decline in average cost is rapid. The output whose average cost is the minimum can be called the "capacity output."[4] Capacity here does not mean maximum output, but rather the designed output. A plant is designed, perhaps by engineers, to produce so many units a week or a month at a minimum cost per unit. In the short run, the plant may be operated below or above the designed output. If a plant is operated at 80 per cent of the designed output, then 80 per cent is its "rate of capacity utilization." Average cost is higher for outputs below, and higher for outputs above, the designed or capacity output. Thus the average cost curve is always $U$-shaped. The two sides of the $U$ can be steep, or so nearly flat that the curve looks more like the

---

[4] Some theorists call it optimum output. But to do so can be misleading, because of the implication that the firm always wants to produce this output. The firm wants to produce this output, however, only when it happens to coincide with the profit-maximizing output.

profile of a shallow saucer. If the capacity output, i.e., the minimum-cost output, happens also to be a physical limit that cannot be exceeded, then the *AVC* and *MC* curves rise vertically at the capacity output.

But the curves of average variable cost and of marginal cost need not have a smooth *U*-shape, as they do in Figure 11–3. In fact, both curves can be horizontal over a wide range of output.

Plants can be indivisible or divisible. An indivisible plant is exemplified by blast furnaces, refineries, and distilleries. Such a plant has a single complex of equipment, the whole being designed to produce one small range of output. Indivisibility is a matter of degree, the extreme being perfect indivisibility, meaning that a plant could produce one exact output only. In contrast, a divisible plant consists of several complexes of more or less identical equipment. Examples are textile mills and hydro-electric plants with several units of turbines and generators. Divisibility, which is also called segmentation, means that output can be increased by putting another machine (or group of them) into operation, then another, then another, and so on. Divisibility also means that output can often be expanded by working a second shift, and a third. It can also mean, in some industries, that machines can be operated at faster or slower rates.

## TABLE 11–2

### Cost-Output Relations in Three Types of Plants

| Cost Behavior | Indivisible Plant with Varying Input Proportions | Divisible Plant with Constant Variable Input Proportions | Imperfectly Divisible Plant with Constant Variable Input Proportions |
|---|---|---|---|
| Average Cost: | U-shaped. The sides of the U can be steep | U-shaped | U-shaped, but with discontinuities |
| Average Variable Cost: | U-shaped | Constant over a wide range of output. Equal to marginal cost. | Discontinuous, but otherwise constant over a wide range of output. When constant, equal to marginal cost. |
| Marginal Cost: | U-shaped | Constant over a wide range of output. Equal to average variable cost. | Discontinuous, but otherwise constant over a wide range of output. When constant, equal to average variable cost. |

The firm's plant and equipment and the variable inputs can be combined in varying or in constant proportions. Up to this point, the assumption has been that the proportions are variable, as indeed they often are. But now the constant proportion — e.g., one man to operate one machine — has to be recognized as a fact of life too and built into the analysis.

The ideas just mentioned are now combined to furnish the basis for three types of plants and hence three types of short-run cost curves. For convenient comparison, they are shown in Table 11–2.

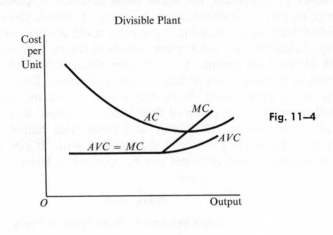

Divisible Plant

Fig. 11–4

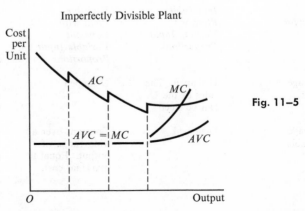

Imperfectly Divisible Plant

Fig. 11–5

The cost curve for the indivisible plant in Table 11–2 is the conventional set of curves displayed in Figure 11–3. The curves for the perfectly divisible plant with constant proportional returns for the variable inputs are shown in Figure 11–4. The curves for the imperfectly divisible plant are contained in Figure 11–5. The $AC$ curve in Figure 11–5 is jagged, and the $AVC$ and $MC$ curves are discontinuous where the jags occur. When output is expanded, another group of machines is put into operation, to the accompaniment of the cost of making them ready. The readiness cost accounts for the short vertical portions of the $AC$ curve. The gaps in the $AVC$ and $MC$ curves just below the jags really mean that it is not worthwhile to modify the $AVC$ and $MC$ curves to allow for the readiness cost.

The $AVC$ and $MC$ curves in Figures 11–4 and 11–5 turn up at the right, to signify that more machines and labor would have to be crowded into the same floor space, with lower productivities and higher costs per unit of output.

### Cost Curves for New Products

The rapid pace of technology since the end of World War II, together with the cultivation of sophisticated arts of management, have caused close attention to be given to the costs of new products. One result of this attention is the emergence of the idea of "the learning curve." The expression itself is borrowed from psychology, which has found that any creature, a rat or a man, learns something at some rate by repeated trials. The learning curve states the relation between achievement and the number of trials, or time. Analogously, a business firm producing a new product can learn, with experience, how to reduce costs to the attainable minimum.

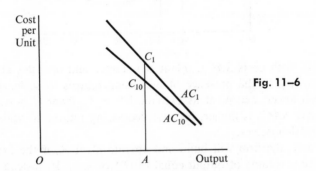

Fig. 11–6

In Figure 11–6, the curve $AC$ is the cost curve of a new product produced in a given plant. Suppose the firm produces the amount $OA$ per month. The unit cost of $OA$ in the *first* month is $C_1A$. But as the months go by, everyone becomes more familiar with the new job, coordination is improved, procedures and tools are modified, etc., all with the result that by, say, the tenth month, costs have been reduced as far as possible. Hence, $AC_{10}$ is the final cost curve. The amount $OA$ can now be produced at the cost $C_{10}A$. Between the first and the tenth month, costs steadily fall; the intermediate cost curves are not shown in Figure 11–6. The initial and final curves in the figure are drawn so that the final one $(AC_{10})$ is 80 per cent of the initial. A cost reduction of 20 per cent is not uncommon with new products.

### Long-Run Cost Curves

In the long run, all is variable. The firm's production function has no fixed inputs; the firm has no fixed costs. The firm expands its output by building and operating a wholly new and larger plant. Input-output relations in the production function are those of returns to scale.

Figure 11–7 has three short-run cost curves. The curves for the full average cost of the firm are now labeled $SAC$, i.e., short-run average cost. The curves in Figure, 11–7 are for three sizes of plant. Plant $A$ is the

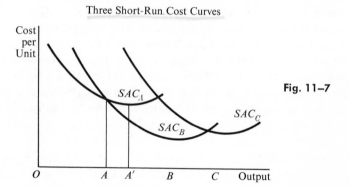

Three Short-Run. Cost Curves

Fig. 11–7

smallest, with costs $SAC_A$. Plant $B$ is larger and operates at much lower costs, owing to the presence of increasing returns to scale. Curve $SAC_B$ is much lower, except at its extreme left end. Plant $C$ is still larger, but the curve $SAC_C$ is higher, because decreasing returns to scale have begun to show themselves.

Clearly, the firm will build and operate plant $A$, if the firm expects to produce a volume of output equal to $OA$ or less. If, instead, output is to be in the range of $OB$ or $OC$, the firm will decide on plant $B$ or plant $C$. Notice that if the firm is to produce an output a little larger than $OA$, it would choose plant $B$, because costs are lower. Take the output $OA'$. This output is the capacity of plant $A$ and is the minimum cost from operating plant $A$. Obviously it is better, in producing the amount $OA'$, to run plant $B$ at *less* than its capacity. This proposition can be generalized: When there are increasing returns to scale, the minimum cost of any output can be obtained by operating, at less than its capacity, a plant that is larger than the plant whose own minimum cost corresponds to the output in question.

Imagine next that the firm can build many plants, each one just a little larger. The several curves in Figure 11–8 are the *SAC* curves for successively larger plants. The curve *LAC,* long-run average cost, is tangent to the lower portions of the *SAC* curves. Geometrically, the *LAC* curve is the "envelope" of the *SAC* curves.

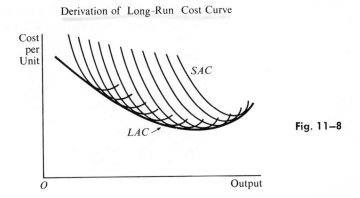

Derivation of Long-Run Cost Curve

Fig. 11–8

Like other people, economic theorists can make mistakes. A famous mistake in the literature of price theory was the one committed by Jacob Viner in his well-known article of 1931 in which he developed the modern theory of the cost curves of a firm. Viner instructed his draftsman, though in vain, to draw the charts for the article so that the *LAC* curve would be tangent to the *SAC* curves at their minimum points. This is possible, however, only if the *LAC* curve is a horizontal line. When the *LAC* curve is declining, it is tangent to the *SAC* curves necessarily to the left of their minimum points. And when the *LAC* curve is rising, it has to touch the *SAC* curves to the right of their minimum points. Viner later acknowledged his mistake with good grace. In reprints of his article, he allowed the error to stand uncorrected so that others can have the pleasure of enjoying a knowledge of geometry superior to his of 1932.

Of course, a firm does not build dozens of plants, just to see what happens to costs. But a firm does have to decide how big its plant should be. In making the decision, the firm surveys the range of minimum costs. The firm knows the range either from experience or from engineering studies. For this reason, the *LAC* curve is often referred to as "the planning curve" of the firm.

It is quite plain that the short-run cost curve of the firm has to be *U*-shaped; the presence of the fixed inputs sees to that. What of the shape of the long-run cost curve? Everyone agrees that the long-run curve first turns down, because of initial economies of scale. But must there be a unique minimum-cost point and an upturn after that?

The conventional shape of the long-run cost curve is shown in Figure 11–9. Here the long-run marginal cost curve is also shown; this curve shows the change in total cost when output is expanded with the construction of successively larger plants. Suppose the firm is producing at the minimum point on *LAC*. Figure 11–9 also displays the short-run average and marginal cost curves for the same output. If it expands output with the same plant, the firm moves along the *SMC* curve. But if it expands output by building a bigger plant, the firm moves along the lower *LMC* curve.

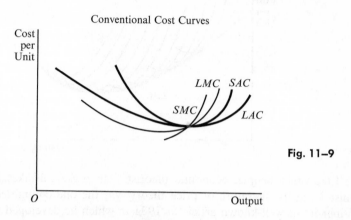

Conventional Cost Curves

**Fig. 11–9**

Chapter 15 will show that the logic of profit maximization in the long run and in pure competition requires the *LAC* curve to turn up at the right. The discussion of decreasing returns to scale in Chapter 9 shows that though there is agreement that returns to scale eventually decrease, there is little agreement as to just why this must be so. Decreasing returns and a rising *LAC* curve are of course the opposite sides of the same coin.

Actually, it is probable that the shape of the curve in Figure 11–10 is typical. Much postwar thinking and empirical research support this version.

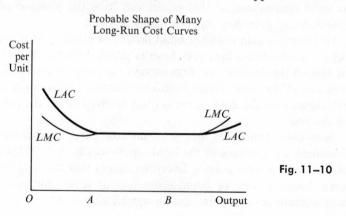

Probable Shape of Many
Long-Run Cost Curves

**Fig. 11–10**

Observe that between outputs $OA$ and $OB$ the curve is perfectly flat. Over this range, all sizes of plants have the same minimum costs. In many industries, in fact, different sizes of plants do coexist and apparently have about the same costs. The length of the initial declining portion of the curve must, however, differ much from one industry to the other.

In brief, the long-run curve is more likely to be $L$-shaped than $U$-shaped.

### Applications

The chief applications of the cost-output analyses presented in this chapter are as aids to clear thinking. An apparently universal belief is that higher volumes bring lower costs. This is the everyday doctrine of spreading the overhead over more units so as to cut cost per unit. The doctrine is true — in the short run and over some range of output. But it is not true for outputs beyond the capacity output. Furthermore, how fast unit cost falls with volume depends on how large the fixed costs are. If they are a small part of total costs, and if the average variable and marginal costs are constant, then the decline in unit cost with larger volumes of output is not much. At the other extreme, if fixed costs are a large fraction of the total, and if average variable and marginal costs fall over a wide range of output, then unit cost declines rapidly with more output.

Then too, the long-run cost-output relation should never be confused with the short-run relation.

#### Allocation of Output between Two Plants

Suppose a firm has two plants and that the firm's market is in a temporarily depressed condition. The output the firm can sell is well below the combined capacities of the two plants. How should the firm allocate output between the two plants so as to minimize cost? The cost to be minimized is the total variable cost. There is no sense in talking about minimizing the fixed cost, in a problem like this, because it is a short-run problem. The fixed cost is fixed and cannot be minimized.

To minimize its variable cost, the firm allocates output between its two plants so that the two marginal costs are equal. This statement is illustrated in Figure 11–11. The figure is so constructed that $OD$ is the total output to be allocated. This output is given because this is the amount that consumers take at the price charged by the firm. This output can be produced by *either* one of the firm's two plants — plant $A$ or plant $B$. The marginal cost of plant $A$ is given by the curve $MC_A$, which goes from left to right. Plant $B$'s marginal cost curve — $MC_B$ — goes from right to left. The two curves intersect at point $C$. When plant $A$ produces the amount $OQ$, and when plant $B$ produces the amount $DQ$, cost is minimized. If plant $A$

produced more and plant $B$ less, cost would be higher, because the $MC_A$ curve lies above the $MC_B$ curve to the right of point $C$. Similarly, cost would be higher if plant $B$ produced more and plant $A$ less. Another way of stating that point $C$ gives minimum cost is this: Total variable cost is the area under the marginal cost curves (page 170). Another look at Figure 11–11 shows that the area for the combined output is least when point $C$ defines the allocation of output.

Notice that the curves in Figure 11–11 are drawn so that plant $B$ has a lower marginal cost for any given output. Nevertheless, it is rational to have some output from plant $A$. Notice too that both curves are rising

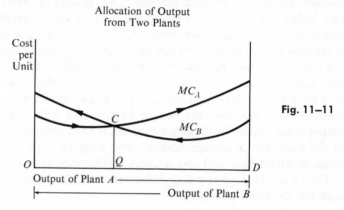

Allocation of Output
from Two Plants

Fig. 11–11

at point $C$. This condition is necessary for the solution. Rising marginal cost apparently does, in fact, exist in the industry from which this application is taken. The industry is the production of electric energy; marginal cost consists mainly in the cost of fuel per kilowatt hour.[5]

### Marginal Cost and Incremental Cost

Marginal cost holds the attention of the rational decision-maker. Suppose, however, that he cannot even in his imagination, vary his output by one unit more or less. For many different kinds of practical reasons, outputs are often variable only in batches, or in more or less definite increments of some size. Incremental cost, the cost of an extra batch, is therefore often the closest practical approximation to marginal cost. Rational business decisions, accordingly, can be made on the basis of incremental cost which is compared with incremental revenue, the extra revenue from the same-sized batch of output.

[5] Fred M. Westfield, "Marginal Analysis, Multi-Plant Firms, and Business Practice: An Example," *Quarterly Journal of Economics,* 1955. Reprinted in Edward H. Bowman and Robert B. Fetter (eds.), *Analyses of Industrial Operations* (Homewood: Irwin, 1959).

## Shape of the Long-Run Cost Curve

It is not much of an exaggeration to say that a good part of the economic foundation of the antitrust laws depends on the shape of the long-run curve of a firm. The antitrust laws maintain competition. Among other things, competition means the existence of many firms in an industry rather than one or a few. If long-run cost curves would decline and keep on declining indefinitely, then costs would be at a minimum if only one firm produced each commodity. If this were so, the policy of maintaining competition would stand condemned on the ground that it would keep costs up; it would result in economic inefficiency. The shape of the long-run cost curve, as shown in Figure 11–10 on page 176, is probably typical of cost curves in much of American industry.

One of the justifications of the government regulation of the public utility industries also has to do with the shape of the long-run cost curve. Some of these industries, e.g., electric power, are natural monopolies, which can be defined as industries where competition would result in wasteful duplication of facilities. The same idea can be expressed this way: A natural monopoly enjoys such great economies of scale that it produces on the declining part of its long-run cost curve. If two companies were to do business in the same area, each one would produce less. Each would therefore be farther up and to the left on its cost curve. The total costs of the two together would be thus higher than if there were only one firm.

## Summary

Price theory devotes its attention to two cost-output relations: the short run and the long. The simplest short-run relation contains the assumption that average variable cost is constant. Then marginal cost and average variable cost are equal. Average fixed cost plus average variable cost equals average cost. The *break-even chart* shows the output whose total cost equals its total revenue, as well as the outputs where profits and losses exist. The family of the conventional *short-run cost curves* consists of the curves for *average fixed cost, average variable cost, average cost,* and *marginal cost.* The *AVC, AC,* and *MC* curves are U-shaped because of variable proportions in the production function, which has some fixed inputs in the short run. The *MC* curve intersects both the *AVC* and the *AC* curves at their minimum points. The *MC* curve is the key curve because rational decisions are based on marginal costs. In *divisible plants, AVC = MC* over some range of output. Cost curves for new products typically drop down as the firm gains experience. The *long-run cost curve* of a firm is derived by drawing a curve tangent to a succession of *SAC* curves for ever larger plants. The *LAC* curve shows the minimum cost of any output. The *LAC* curve can be horizontal over some range of output; it is more likely to be *L*-shaped than *U*-shaped. The theory of the cost-output relations of the firm has numerous applications, both in business decision-making and as a foundation for economic policy in the antitrust and public utility fields.

## SELECTED REFERENCES

On the theory: Jacob Viner, "Cost Curves and Supply Curves," *Zeitschrift für Nationalökonomie,* 1931. Reprinted in George J. Stigler and Kenneth E. Boulding, (eds.), *Readings in Price Theory* (Homewood: Irwin, 1952). George J. Stigler, *The Theory of Price,* rev. ed. (New York: Macmillan, 1952), Chap. 6, 7, and 8. George J. Stigler, "Production and Distribution in the Short Run," *Journal of Political Economy,* 1939. Reprinted in American Economic Association, *Readings in the Theory of Income Distribution* (Philadelphia: Blakiston, 1946). Edward H. Chamberlin, *The Theory of Monopolistic Competition,* 7th ed. (Cambridge: Harvard University Press, 1956), Appendix B.

Empirical and statistical investigations of the theory: Joel Dean, *Managerial Economics* (New York: Prentice-Hall, 1951), Chap. 5. J. Johnston, *Statistical Cost Analysis* (New York: McGraw-Hill, 1960). George J. Stigler, "The Economies of Scale," *Journal of Law and Economics,* Vol. I, October, 1958, pp. 54–71.

## EXERCISES AND PROBLEMS

1. Construct a break-even chart with cost curves like those in Figure 11–2 and with a total revenue curve corresponding to the sloping demand curve for a firm.

2. Show that where *LAC* is rising, the firm is operating at an output in excess of the level where *SAC* is a minimum.

3. Why does *SAC* descend faster than *LAC*?

4. Suppose you publish paperback books which sell at retail for 50¢; of this, you receive 35¢. Suppose that before you can print a single copy of a book, you have to spend $4500 — mainly for typesetting and for the metal plates from which the book is printed. Assume that paper and binding for each copy cost you 20¢. For this one book, what is the fixed cost, the variable cost, the marginal cost? What is the break-even point? Make a cost schedule like that in Table 11–1. Draw a break-even chart for the book.

5. Imagine that the executives of a business firm complain about the rising costs of labor and materials during the last year. Examination of the firm's cost records reveals, however, that average (business) cost has *not* gone up during the year. How can this be?

6. When is it appropriate to talk about *the* cost of production — as a single number — and when is it not appropriate to do so?

# Linear Programming

# 12

From time immemorial, men have made their decisions on how to produce their commodities. Throughout most of history, the decisions were made in the same way year after year in conformity with the patterns dictated by custom and culture. Under the capitalism of the last two centuries, decisions on production began to be increasingly rational, becoming conscious and deliberate choices of the best means to attain clearly defined ends. Price theory is the generalized description of rational decisions in production, as well as in exchange and consumption.

But the theory of the firm, as presented in the last three chapters, shows the businessman as making decisions about one variable at a time or, at the most, about two at a time. Suppose that, as is so often true, the businessman must take dozens or hundreds of variables into account all at once. What then? Economic theory can still give the answer, can still point to the cost-minimizing or profit-maximizing decision. Theory's answers here are not in the simple geometry of the last three chapters; the answers are couched in the language of higher mathematics. Generally speaking, however, the form of the mathematics is such that the answers cannot be put to specific practical use.

Alfred Marshall handled the problem of production decisions with his "principle of substitution." He saw the businessman as always studying his production function and his input prices. As they change, the businessman is continually substituting one input for another, thus keeping his costs as low as possible. The businessman, said Marshall, works not so much with formal calculation as by trained instinct.

A method of formal calculation is now available, however. The method can be regarded as an extension and a special case of price theory. At the same time, the method which is called "linear programming" can be applied in the solution of a wide range of practical business problems.

### Linear Programming

Linear programming[1] is a technique that uses sophisticated mathematics to solve certain kinds of problems, especially production problems. *Linear* means that the relationships handled are the same as those represented by straight lines. *Programming* simply means systematic planning or decision-making. Also called "mathematical programming" and "activity analysis," the technique was developed in 1947 by the mathematician George B. Dantzig for the purpose of scheduling the complicated procurement activities of the United States Air Force.[2]

Since 1947, linear programming has advanced far both in its theory and in its applications to practical problems in industry. The postwar development of computers has contributed to the growth of linear programming, which in practice usually requires extensive numerical computations. Linear programming has become a set of special cases of the economic theory of the firm. As presented in Chapters 8–11, the conventional theory, as it can now be called, is more general; it covers the short run and the long, linear and curvilinear relations, and cost-output relations over any range of output.

Because some of its leading ideas are mathematical, a complete description of linear programming cannot be given here. But its economic content can be surveyed, along with some of the modifications it makes in the theory of the firm.

### Some Basic Concepts of Linear Programming

Apart from those that are purely mathematical, the main ideas of linear programming are essentially simple. Both the theory and its applications

---

[1] A formal definition: Linear programming is the maximization (or minimization) of a linear function of variables subject to a constraint of linear inequalities.

[2] Actually, the Russian mathematician L. V. Kantorovich first formulated linear programming. But Dantzig invented a superior technique of computation.

have concentrated on the short-run decisions as to output by firms with given prices for both their inputs and their outputs.

## Optimization and Choice

The central feature of linear programming is that it gives actual numerical solutions to problems of making optimum choices when the problems have to be solved within definite bounds or constraints.

## Linearity

Linearity is both a simplifying assumption and a useful statement about the input-output relations that often prevail. The linear assumption makes the complicated mathematics of programming simpler than they would otherwise have to be. The economic meanings of linearity are constant returns (marginal products and average products are equal) and, again, the given prices of inputs and outputs (which can be shown on price-quantity diagrams by horizontal lines). Though the American economy did not suddenly become linear after 1947, the existence of constant returns over some range of output is common. This of course means that costs per unit are constant over that range and that average variable costs and marginal costs are equal. Linear programming techniques, accordingly, can be applied when cost curves resemble those in Figure 11–4 on page 172. Then too, even if the returns and costs of a firm are not exactly linear, they might be so close to it that the linear assumption is warranted for all practical purposes.

Linear assumptions are frequently employed in this book for the sake of simplicity and owing to the influence of linear programming itself.

Occasionally, however, the linear assumption leads to ludicrous results. Baumol mentions a linear-programming problem of prescribing the optimum number of warehouses a company ought to have.[3] A possible solution was — one warehouse for each customer. The computer did not blow a tube on this one; no, the computer faithfully followed the linear instruction that, no matter what the size of a warehouse, the cost of a unit of warehousing service is always the same. The instruction should have been to keep the linearity within a definite range of warehouse sizes.

Not all mathematical programming is linear. Nonlinear, or curvilinear, programming techniques set up problems like those in conventional theory, where curves instead of straight lines show the relations. But nonlinear programming raises such formidable mathematical difficulties that not

[3] William J. Baumol, *Economic Theory and Operations Analysis* (Englewood Cliffs, N.J.: Prentice-Hall, 1961), p. 109.

much has been done with it. Still another variant is integer programming. Here the problems are set up so that the solutions come out in integers, i.e., whole numbers. No fractions are allowed. The solution to a transportation problem is, say, 8 jet planes, not 7¾ or 8½.

## Processes

A process is another basic concept in linear programming. A process, also called an activity, is a way of doing things. A process is a combination of particular inputs to produce a particular output. A truck driver and his truck are a process — they can carry so many tons so many miles in a week. The *level* of a process means how many trucks with one driver each are used. The linear assumption means that two trucks carry twice as much as one, four trucks twice as much as two, etc.

The notion of a process is essentially technological. A process is a complex, large or small, of men and equipment. Each process uses factors — labor and capital — in fixed ratios. Thus there is no substitution within a process. In contrast, conventional theory assumes easy substitution among inputs — along a smooth isoquant.

The firm has several processes, each of which can be carried on at several levels to produce the firm's product. One process can be substituted for another. When two or more processes are used together, they do not interfere with one another or enhance one another. This last is another simplifying assumption. A typical linear programming problem is to find the optimum combination of processes, i.e., the combination that minimizes costs when there are constraints. A simple example will be given below.

## The Objective Function

Linear programming has fashioned its own language. Simple economic ideas are dressed in new terminology. A good example is "the objective function."

The objective function, also called the criterion function, states the determinants of the quantity to be maximized or to be minimized. Profits, or revenues, are the objective function when they are to be maximized. Costs are the objective function when the problem calls for them to be minimized. Cost minimization is the "dual" of profit maximization, and vice versa. The significance of the dual is that the solution to a firm's problem of minimizing costs can be converted mathematically into the solution for maximizing profits, without having to start the whole analysis from the very beginning. Much deep thought and hard work have to go into just setting up a problem in linear programming.

### Constraints

Constraints, also called restraints, are limitations. They are things you can't do and things you have to do. The budget of a consumer is a constraint. If a firm is maximizing revenue, then it is limited or constrained by the facts that it has, for example, only 10 machines, only so many square feet of floor space, etc. Also, machine $A$ has to have one operator, machine $B$ has to have at least two, etc. Constraints are also known as inequalities. That is to say, 10 or fewer ($\leqq 10$) machines are available and two or more ($\geqq 2$) men are needed to operate machine $B$, and so on.

### Feasible Solutions    *Positive solutions*

Feasible solutions can be explored after the constraints are established. Feasible solutions for the consumer are all of the possible combinations of commodities he can possibly, i.e., feasibly, buy, given his income and the prices of the commodities. With two commodities, feasible solutions for the consumer are all those combinations of the two goods that are on and to the left of the budget line; for a reminder, see Figure 6–3 on page 82. Similarly, one kind of feasible solution for the firm consists of all the combinations of two inputs that lie on or to the right of an isocost line; see Figure 10–3 on page 155.

### Optimum Solutions

The optimum solution, of course, is the best of the feasible solutions. Sometimes linear programming results in finding several feasible solutions, all equally good and all better than any others. Then there is no single optimum. Simple examples of this will be given below.

The simplex method of solution is not simple but is the name of a commonly used mathematical and computational procedure for finding the optimum solution. In essence, the simplex method, which itself is a kind of marginal calculation, consists of successively testing feasible solutions, successively eliminating the poorer ones, until finally the optimum solution emerges.

With geometrical techniques resembling those employed in the preceding chapters, three specimens of linear-programming analysis will now follow. Two show how a firm minimizes its costs and one how a firm maximizes its revenue.

### Minimizing Costs

In conventional theory, the firm minimizes the costs of using two inputs by buying them in such proportions that the isoquants are tangent to the isocost lines. The constraints that are central to linear-programming techniques have the effect of modifying the shapes of isoquants.

### A Simplified Diet Problem

The diet problem was one of the first to be tackled by the linear programming techniques. The problem is to minimize the cost of a diet that has to meet minimum nutritional requirements, which are the constraints. Happily, the diets in question are for animals. Several feedstuffs are purchasable. All have different prices per unit; all possess different amounts per pound of nutrients — vitamins, minerals, proteins, calories, etc. Which combination is cheapest for the purpose?

Consider a highly simplified example. A farmer feeds animals with two varieties of grain. The diet for the animals must give them each day certain minimum amounts of three nutrients. The objective function is the minimization of the cost of the diet. There are two variables, each with a price. There are three constraints. What are feasible solutions? What is the optimum solution?

In Figure 12–1, the horizontal axis shows pounds of grain $A$ and the vertical axis measures pounds of grain $B$. The minimum daily requirement per animal of nutrient I is met by $OF$ pounds of grain $A$, or by $OE$ pounds

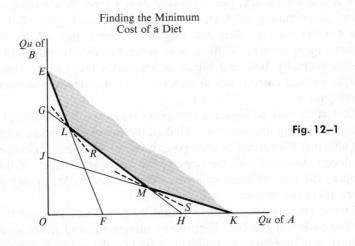

Finding the Minimum
Cost of a Diet

Fig. 12–1

of grain $B$. Thus the line $EF$ shows how to combine grains $A$ and $B$ to provide nutrient I. Clearly, grain $A$ is much richer in this nutrient, because fewer pounds of it are needed. Similarly, lines $GH$ and $JK$ show how the two grains can be combined to provide the minimum daily requirement of nutrients II and III.

The heavy line segments *ELMK* show how to combine the two grains to meet all three of the nutritional constraints. Any point on the heavy line meets one of the requirements and exceeds the other two. Notice too that the heavy line does look like an isoquant. The line is not, however, a smooth curve; it consists of *linear* segments.

Feasible solutions are points on the heavy line or to the right of it. The stippled area is a zone of feasible solutions. *Any* point in it is feasible, showing that the animals can be fed as they should. But the animals are not pets. Because they are being raised to be sold at a profit, the farmer wants minimum costs.

To solve for the optimum, prices have to be brought in. They come in as isocost lines, showing ratios of the prices of grain *A* and grain *B*. In Figure 12–1, the dashed lines *R* and *S* are two possible isocost lines. To minimize costs, the farmer wants to get to the lowest attainable isocost line. Take first the isocost line *R*. In the figure, line *R* occupies its lowest position, touching the point *L*. The point *L* is the optimum when the price ratio is indicated by the line *R*. Here grain *B* has the lower price per pound, the optimum solution being to feed more pounds of *B* than of *A*. Suppose, however, that prices are indicated by the isocost line *S*. Then the optimum would be at *M,* because here *A* is the cheaper grain.

Assume that the price ratio is in fact given by the slope of the line *R*. Then, as was just shown, *L* is the optimum solution. Notice that the solution is not a tangency, but a *corner*. When there is a unique optimum, linear programming solutions are always corners. Figure 12–1 has only two corners because there are only three constraints. With more constraints, more corners. If there were several feedstuffs instead of just two grains, geometry fails and higher mathematics takes over. But still the unique solution corresponds to a corner; the computers are instructed to go hunting for it.

One more look at Figure 12–1 shows this: The line *R* can pivot a bit while still hitting the corner *L*. That is, the prices can change a little without affecting *L's* optimality. Suppose, however, that line *R* changes so that its slope is identical with the slope of the line segment *LM*. If this should happen, the one optimum vanishes. Then *either L, M,* or *any* point between them is optimum.

Linear programming is in fact used by companies that sell feed mixes for livestock and poultry. With many ingredients and many separate nutritional requirements, the problem of finding the actual minimum cost of a feed mix is formidable. It cannot be solved on the back of an envelope. Feed companies employ research organizations, whose inputs of labor and capital — mathematicians and computers — provide linear-programming solutions. The prices of some of the ingredients in feed mixes are constantly changing. The feed companies telephone the price changes to the research organizations. In a short time, the feed companies get the instructions they seek — whether and how to alter their feed mixes so as to keep their costs always as low as possible. It is just as if, in Figure 12–1, prices would change from R to S, moving the corner optimum from L to M.

Only one more point needs to be made about feeding the animals. How many pounds of the correctly proportioned feed should they get? No linear programming is required here because this is a straightforward problem in diminishing returns. The more pounds per day, the greater the gain in weight (or the more milk or eggs, or whatever it might be). The abundant empirical evidence on this kind of input-output relation always shows diminishing marginal physical returns. Clearly the solution depends upon the (minimized) cost of the feed mix, the price of the output, and on how fast the marginal returns diminish. The analysis to be applied here is described on pages 152 and 153.

Note 6 in the Appendix to Part Three gives a very simple numerical example of the minimization of costs subject to constraints.

### Choice of Processes

A firm's labor and equipment are organized in complexes, i.e., processes or activities. One of the firm's problems is how best to combine its processes, how to divide its output among them. A simplified example will now be presented.

First comes the concept of the process ray. Figure 12–2 contains three process rays. Consider first the line OB which is a process ray. The horizontal axis measures labor hours; the vertical axis measures machine hours. The line OB is scaled in units of the firm's output. The marks on the line can be taken to represent, successively, 10, 20, 30, etc. units of output per period, or 100, 200, 300, etc. units. The line OB is drawn at an angle of 45°, signifying a process with equal numbers of labor hours and machine hours at any level. The line OB therefore stands for a one-man, one-machine process. In contrast, the line OA stands for one man and two machines; the number of machine hours is always double the corresponding number of labor hours on line OA. Notice that OA is scaled a little differently; process A is, say, older and physically less efficient. The line OC stands for still a different man-machine process; here the machine needs two operators.

The kinked line EFG in Figure 12–2 is an isoquant or, at least, a portion of one. Any point on the line EFG represents a process or a combination of two processes that produces the same quantity of output. An output of 40 (or 400, etc.) units can be produced with process A (point E), or with a combination of A and B (points between E and F), or with process B, or with a combination of B and C (points between F and G), or with process C.

In other words: At point $E$ in Figure 12–2, the firm is using process $A$ exclusively and has an output of 40 units. At point $E$, the firm is on the

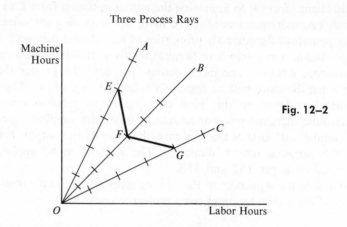

Three Process Rays

Machine Hours

$O$                    Labor Hours

**Fig. 12–2**

process ray $A$. If instead the firm is at a point on the line $EF$, the firm is using two processes — both $A$ and $B$. Then the firm is part way up the process ray $A$ and part way up the process ray $B$. The *combined* output from the two processes is also 40 units, i.e., the same as using either process $A$ or process $B$. Similarly, if the firm is at a point between $F$ and $G$, the firm is part way up both the process rays $B$ and $C$. Here too the combined output is 40 units.[4]

Figure 12–3 is constructed similarly. For the time being, let the lines $L_M$ and $L_L$ and the stippled area be ignored. Here are the same three processes and the isoquants *1*, *2*, and *3;* other isoquants can be visualized. Each one shows processes and combinations that produce the same output. Isoquants farther northeast signify larger amounts of output. The vertical and horizontal portions of the isoquants have no particular meaning; they are shown to display the similarity between these isoquants and those presented in Chapters 9 and 10.

Figure 12–3 also has one isocost line, the dashed line. The isocost line hits isoquant *2* at a corner. If the line is moved parallel to itself, it will always hit an isoquant at the corner on process ray $B$. Therefore, process $B$ is optimal, being the cheapest one to use when costs are as reflected in the slope of the dashed line. Observe that here too there is no tangency as in conventional theory. Minimum costs are at corners. If the isocost line were nearly flat, it would hit the corner on process $C$. If it were nearly

---

[4] Rigorous proof here is fairly complicated. It is to be found on pp. 805–806 of the Dorfman article cited at the end of this chapter.

vertical, the isocost line would hit the corner on process $A$. In Figure 12–3 also, an isocost line could conceivably have a slope equal to that of one of the line segments. If this were so, there would be no single optimum.

The upshot, so far, is that process $B$ is used because it is the cheapest. This is hardly a surprising result.

Now, let two constraints be brought in.

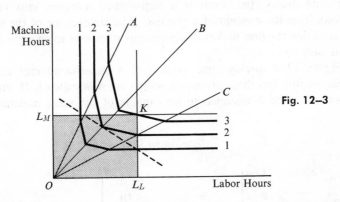

Choosing the Best Combination
of Processes

Fig. 12–3

In Figure 12–3, the lines $L_L$ and $L_M$ express the fact that the firm cannot use more than $OL_L$ of labor hours or more than $OL_M$ of machine hours owing, say, to limitations of floor space. These limitations are the constraints. The zone of feasible solutions is the shaded area. The firm wants to produce as much as possible within its constraints.[5] The highest attainable output is shown by point $K$, at the northeast corner of the rectangle of feasible solutions. Point $K$ is on isoquant 3 and represents a combination of processes $B$ and $C$. The price ratio is the same, but it no longer plays the same role when constraints are introduced.

With two constraints, two processes are used. Which two depends on what the constraints are. Another look at Figure 12–3 will show that if the labor-hour constraint line were moved to the left far enough, the optimum solution would be a combination of processes $A$ and $B$.

One of the principles, or theorems, of linear programming is that when there are several processes and several constraints, the optimum solution is to combine as many processes as there are constraints. The two-constraint, two-process case was just illustrated. With 10 constraints, 10 processes are combined in an optimum solution.

[5] The analysis here runs in physical quantities. Physical output is to be maximized subject to constraints. The analysis can be converted to values, by making each point on a process ray correspond to a certain value of output.

## Step-Shaped Cost Curves

The cost curves of firms in conventional theory are smooth, continuous, and *U-shaped*. The general shape of these curves is shown in Figure 11–3 on page 168. Even when average variable cost curves and marginal cost curves are flat over some range, conventional theory requires them to turn upward after some volume of output is reached. See Figure 11–4 on page 172.

When linear-programming analysis is converted into the form of conventional theory, the result is a step-shaped marginal cost curve. This follows from the concept of a process. The significance of the step-shaped curve is that the firm makes discontinuous responses to changes in the price of its output.

Figure 12–4 displays one version of a step-shaped cost curve. Here again the firm has three processes, which are now called I, II, and III. For simplicity, each is assumed to be capable of the same maximum output.

Step-Shaped Cost Curve

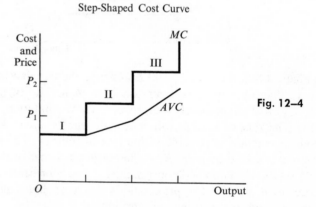

Fig. 12–4

Cost of output with process I is lower than with II, and lower with II than with III. The step-shaped curve is the firm's marginal cost curve. The horizontal segments reflect the linear assumption and the vertical segments the constraints. The average variable cost curve averages the variable costs when two or more processes are used.

If the price the firm gets for its output is $P_1$, then it operates process I only. If instead the price is $P_2$, the firm operates processes I and II. But notice that $P_1$ or $P_2$ can move up or down within the range of the vertical segments of the cost curve without any change in the firm's output. The firm is therefore insensitive to certain changes in the price of its output. This statement accords with the finding, earlier in this chapter, that certain changes in input prices do not alter the optimum.

A firm with distinct processes, therefore, responds discontinuously to variations in price.

## Maximizing Revenue

With production possibility curves and isorevenue lines, the conventional theory shows how the firm chooses the proportions in which it produces two products. The production-possibility curves are smooth and continuous, signifying that the firm's resources permit it to substitute one output for another by infinitesimally small amounts.

In the typical linear programming problem, the firm has to decide on its product mix, i.e., its output proportions within the bounds imposed by constraints. They, of course, can take on many forms. Suppose, for example, that the firm's products have to be assembled, painted, and packaged. Assembling, painting, and packaging are done in departments, each of which has — in the short run — a fixed physical capacity. These fixed or limited capacities are constraints.

Optimum Combination
of Two Products

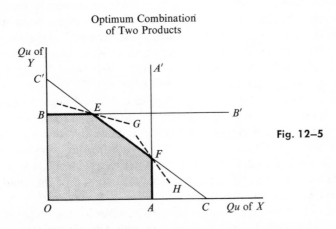

Fig. 12–5

Figure 12–5 gives a simple illustration of maximizing the revenue from two products subject to the constraints of limited capacities. In Figure 12–5, the firm has two products, $X$ and $Y$. The production of $X$ and $Y$ is subject to constraints $A$, $B$, and $C$. Constraint $A$ limits the production of $X$; no more than $OA$ of $X$ can be produced. Constraint $B$ limits the production of $Y$; no more than $OB$ of $Y$ can be produced. The rectangle formed by the lines $AA'$ and $BB'$ accordingly shows the combined effects of the two constraints. In addition, constraint $C$ limits the production of *both* $X$ and $Y$. Therefore, the shaded area in Figure 12–5 is the zone of feasible production. The three straight lines $BE$, $EF$, and $FA$ join to form the linear-programming version of the production possibility curve. Any combination of $X$ and $Y$ inside the lines inside the zone can be produced, but it is not possible or feasible to produce any combination represented by a point lying outside the zone.

The prices of $X$ and $Y$ also have to be taken into account. They can be indicated by the slopes of isorevenue lines.[6] The dashed line $G$ in Figure 12–5 is an isorevenue line, the highest of the lines with the same slope the firm can reach, given its zone of feasible production. Observe again the corner solution. Here the corner is at Point $E$. At this point, the firm produces much more of $Y$ than of $X$, partly because the slope of the line $G$ shows that the price of $Y$ is much higher than the price of $X$.[7] On the other hand, suppose the prices of $X$ and $Y$ are different, as indicated by the slope of the isorevenue line $H$. With this isorevenue line, the firm goes to the corner $F$, producing much more of $X$ than of $Y$.

Another look at Figure 12–5 will show that each of the isorevenue lines could have different slopes while still hitting the same corners. This too means that within some ranges the price ratios can vary, but the firm still holds to the same optimum choice of outputs. But if the prices of the outputs change enough, the firm hops from one corner to the other.

Even a diagram as simple as Figure 12–5 contains a complication. Suppose the slope of the isorevenue line is exactly equal to the slope of the line $EF$. What then? If this should be so, there is no corner to go to. There is no single optimum, no unique solution. *Any* point between $E$ and $F$ is just as good as any other; *any* such point signifies the same total revenue. This kind of thing indeed often happens in actual linear programming applications. When it does, the firm has to bring in some other criterion of decision to help it choose a particular combination of its products to produce and sell. Other criteria could be drawn from estimates of the future markets for $X$ and $Y$, or from the firm's plans for altering its production facilities. So far as the linear programming goes, the firm could just as well draw lots in making its decision.

Note 6 in the Appendix to Part Three gives a very simple numerical example of the maximization of revenue subject to constraints.

### Applications

In its full-blown mathematical form, not in the simplified version presented here, linear programming is applied to a wide range of practical

---

[6] Instead of prices, profits can also be used. This can be done by determining the incremental profit for $X$ and for $Y$, i.e., the difference between price and cost per unit. Then isoprofit lines instead of isorevenue lines are constructed.

[7] If the line $G$ is extended to both axes, it can be seen that the firm has to sell nearly three times as many units of $X$ to get the same revenue from selling any given number of units of $Y$.

business problems. One class of problems is known as the transportation problem. Here a firm owns several plants from which it ships its product to several destinations. The plants have different capacities, shipping costs per ton vary from one route (from a plant to a destination) to another, and the markets at the destinations have different sizes. With such variables, an exact solution to the minimization of total shipping costs cannot be figured out with everyday methods of calculation. But linear programmers can and do solve such problems. Another class of problems exists in petroleum refining. For example, a type of automotive gasoline must meet definite specifications as to knock rating, etc. The gasoline is produced from several distinct kinds of semirefined oil, called blending stocks. Linear programming shows how to achieve the minimum cost blend for the specified gasoline.

Several of the many applications are discussed in some of the references cited at the end of this chapter.

Frequently, linear-programming solutions to practical problems give results that are close to the solutions practical men arrive at by trial and error. Linear-programming analyses often come up with plans that will, for example, reduce costs by no more than 3 or 5 per cent. Trained instinct, indeed, usually leads to results as good as those yielded by formal calculation. A trial-and-error solution might be good, but how can anyone be sure it actually is optimum? Here is one of the great achievements of linear programming: Even if it comes forth with the same answer produced by trained instinct, the logic of linear programming can prove that the answer is, in fact, optimum. Business firms, of course, continually face wholly new problem in whose solution the mathematician faces little rivalry from the practical man.

Business executives sometimes decline to act on linear-programming solutions. A firm might be told, for example, to eliminate hundreds of items from its line of products if the firm really wants to maximize its profits. The executives of the firm prefer not to do so, for complicated reasons of their own. They might look farther into the future than the analyst and see a long-run advantage in maintaining a full line of products. Another linear programmer might tell a company to cut down on the number of its warehouses to minimize costs. After thanking him for his labors, the executives of this company add that they had forgotten to tell him that keeping the company's reputation for promptness of deliveries is more important than saving a few thousand dollars on warehousing costs.

Like conventional theory, linear programming can produce clear results only by adherence to the idea of maximizing or minimizing a clearly specified variable. Nor can the solutions be better than the accuracy and completeness of the information fed into the calculations.

## Summary

Linear programming is a method of mathematical analysis for the solution of problems of maximization and minimization of variables subject to constraints. Created in the postwar period, linear programming has been applied to a wide range of practical business problems and can be regarded as a special case of the theory of the firm. Input-output, cost-output, and price-output relations are treated as *linear relations*. In producing its outputs, a firm combines *processes,* which are fixed combinations of particular inputs. The minimization of costs or the maximization of profits is the *objective function,* which is subject to *constraints.* Of several *feasible solutions,* one is the *optimum solution,* although sometimes there can be no unique optimum. Simple linear-programming analyses can be presented geometrically. Isoquants then become linear-segmented lines instead of smooth curves. Costs are minimized when isocost lines touch *corners.* Revenues are maximized when isorevenue lines touch the corners of linear-segmented production possibility curves. Marginal cost curves are linear and can be step-shaped. Linear programming has limitations similar to those of conventional theory.

## SELECTED REFERENCES

No mathematics (except for geometry): William Fellner, *Emergence and Content of Modern Economic Analysis* (New York: McGraw-Hill, 1960), pp. 266–274. Robert Dorfman, "Mathematical, or 'Linear,' Programming," *American Economic Review,* Vol. XLIII, No. 5, Part I, December, 1953, pp. 797–825.

Simple mathematics (elementary algebra): Joseph McKenna, *Intermediate Economic Theory* (New York: Dryden, 1958), Chap. 4. John F. Due and Robert W. Clower, *Intermediate Economic Analysis,* 4th ed. (Homewood: Irwin, 1961), Chap. 21. William J. Baumol, "Activity Analysis in One Lesson," *American Economic Review,* Vol. XLVIII, No. 5, December, 1958, pp. 837–87.

More advanced: William J. Baumol, *Economic Theory and Operations Analysis* (Englewood Cliffs, N.J.: Prentice-Hall, 1961), Chap. 5. Kenneth E. Boulding and W. Allen Spivey, *Linear Programming and the Theory of the Firm* (New York: Macmillan, 1960).

A classic: T. C. Koopmans, ed., *Activity Analysis of Production and Allocation,* Cowles Commission Monograph No. 13 (New York: Wiley, 1951).

A standard work: Robert Dorfman, Paul A. Samuelson, and Robert M. Solow, *Linear Programming and Economic Analysis* (New York: McGraw-Hill, 1958).

Business applications: Edward H. Bowman and Robert B. Fetter (eds.), *Analyses of Industrial Operations* (Homewood: Irwin, 1959), Chap. 1–8. Alan S. Manne, *Economic Analysis for Business Decisions* (New York: McGraw-Hill, 1961). Harold Bierman, Jr., Lawrence E. Fouraker, and Robert K. Jaedicke, *Quantitative Analysis for Business Decisions* (Homewood: Irwin, 1961), Chap. 14–17.

## EXERCISES AND PROBLEMS

1. Besides your income, name some of the constraints that affect you as a consumer.

2. Construct a diagram like Figure 12–1 on page 187, but with two restraints. Make an assumption about prices, and find a solution. Do the same thing with five restraints.

3. Construct a diagram like Figure 12–2 on page 190, but mark the successive outputs in a different way. Then draw in an isoquant.

4. Construct a diagram like Figure 12–3 on page 191, but modify the constraints so as to show that the optimum is a combination of processes *A* and *B*.

5. Suppose the steps in Figure 12–4 on page 192 are made smaller and smaller. What ultimately happens?

6. Draw a step-shaped cost curve to represent this: A firm has a new plant and an old one which it uses for standby purposes. Both plants can be operated on regular shifts and on overtime.

7. Construct a diagram like Figure 12–5, but with five constraints instead of three. Assume some prices and find the optimum product mix.

# PART THREE

## MATHEMATICAL NOTES

### Note 1. The Maximization of Profits

The profits of a firm depend on the size of its output. At some volume of output, profits are at a maximum; this book always assumes the existence of a unique maximum.

Let $\pi$ be profits, $q$ the output of the firm, $R$ the firm's revenue, and $C$ the firm's total costs. $\pi$, $R$, and $C$ are all functions of $q$.

$$\pi = R - C$$

When profits are a maximum, the first derivative of $\pi$ with respect to $q$ is equal to zero. Therefore

$$\frac{d\pi}{dq} = \frac{dR}{dq} - \frac{dC}{dq} = 0,$$

or,

$$\frac{dR}{dq} = \frac{dC}{dq}.$$

The first derivative of $R$ with respect to $q$, $\frac{dR}{dq}$, is marginal revenue. Similarly, $\frac{dC}{dq}$ is marginal cost. Therefore, profits are maximized when

marginal revenue = marginal cost.

### Note 2. The Production Function

The production function is the relation between physical quantities of a firm's inputs and the physical quantity of its output. Let $q$ be output, and $a, b, c,$ etc. be inputs. In general,

$$q = f(a, b, c, \ldots)$$

In econometric studies, the problem is to select the relevant inputs and the mathematical form of the equation. A statistical production function for an auto laundry gave good results with two inputs — the plant and the number of workers. Statistical production functions for Iowa farms required 5 inputs — land, labor, the improvements on the farms, the farmers' liquid assets, and their cash operating expenses.

For many purposes, no more than two variables are needed to display the properties of production functions. Now let

$$q = f(a, b)$$

and suppose that $a$ is units of labor and $b$ is units of land. If land is held constant and labor is varied in amount, the marginal productivity of labor is given by the partial derivative. Thus,

$$\frac{\partial q}{\partial a} = f_a(a, b).$$

Suppose that the production function is

$$q = 10a - a^2 + ab.$$

Then the marginal productivity of $a$ is

$$\frac{\partial q}{\partial a} = 10 - 2a + b.$$

If $a = 3$ and $b = 6$, the marginal productivity of $a$ is 10. Thus if $b$ is held constant, the limit of the ratio between the increment in output $q$ and the increment in the amount of labor tends to 10 at the indicated level of inputs.

### Note 3. The Cobb-Douglas Production Function

The Cobb-Douglas production function can be applied to a sector of the economy, such as manufacturing, or to the whole economy. This production function is an empirical hypothesis that has given good statistical results.

The function takes the form

$$Q = kL^a C^{(1-a)}$$

where $Q$ is output, $L$ is the quantity of labor, $C$ is the quantity of capital employed, and $k$ and $a$ ($a < 1$) are positive constants. The function is linear and homogeneous. Suppose that the quantities of labor and capital are increased in equal proportions. Let $L$ become $gL$ and let $C$ become $gC$. (If $g$ is 1.10, there is an increase of 10 per cent in each factor of production.) Then

$$k(gL)^a(gC)^{1-a} = g^a g^{(1-a)} kL^a C^{1-a},$$
$$= gkL^a C^{1-a} = gQ.$$

Thus output increases in the same proportion. Returns to scale are constant.

**Note 4.   Isoquants**

Figure 9–2 on page ·145 shows the production function as a family of isoquants. So that the language of this note will be consistent with that of Chapter 9, the two inputs are now labor, $L$, and capital, $C$. For a given level of output $q_1$, the isoquant is given by the equation

$$q_1 = f(L, C).$$

The slope of the tangent to any point on the isoquant is negative. The slope is the marginal rate of technical substitution ($MRTS$):

$$MRTS = -\frac{dC}{dL}.$$

The production function is the whole family of isoquants,

$$q = f(L, C).$$

The total differential of the production function is

$$dq = f_L\, dL + f_C\, dC.$$

Here, $f_L$ and $f_C$, the partial derivatives of $q$ with respect to $L$ and $C$, are the marginal productivities of labor and capital, as shown in Note 2 above. But $dq = 0$ for movements along an isoquant. Therefore

$$0 = f_L\, dL + f_C\, dC,$$

and

$$f_L\, dL = -f_C\, dC,$$

and

$$\frac{f_L}{f_C} = -\frac{dC}{dL}.$$

Thus the marginal rate of technical substitution between labor and capital is equal to the ratio of their marginal productivities.

**Note 5.   Short-Run Cost Functions**

The general form of the short-run cost function of a firm is

$$TC = f(q) + b.$$

That is, total cost $TC$ is some function of output $f(q)$ plus the fixed cost $b$. This equation and the deductions from it are useful in reinforcing the definitions in Chapter 11 and in explaining the relation between average and marginal cost.

Costs per unit — average cost ($AC$), average variable cost ($AVC$), and average fixed cost ($AFC$) — are defined as follows:

$$AC = \frac{f(q) + b}{q} = \frac{TC}{q},$$

$$AVC = \frac{f(q)}{q},$$

$$AFC = \frac{b}{q}.$$

Marginal cost is the derivative of total cost with respect to output:

$$MC = \frac{dTC}{dq} = TC'.$$

Although there are two average cost curves — $AC$ and $AVC$ — there is only one $MC$ curve. The derivatives of total cost and total variable cost are identical, because $b$, the fixed-cost term, disappears upon differentiation.

$MC = AC$, when $AC$ is a minimum. For $AC$ to be a minimum, its derivative is set equal to zero:

$$AC' = \frac{qTC' - TC}{q^2} = 0,$$

$$= \frac{TC'}{q} - \frac{TC}{q^2} = 0,$$

and

$$TC' = \frac{TC}{q}.$$

Similarly, $MC = AVC$, when $AVC$ is a minimum.

The conventional $U$-shaped cost curve of the firm, as shown in Figure 11–3 on page 168, can be represented by making total cost a cubic function of output. For example,

$$TC = aq^3 - bq^2 + cq + d.$$

Here the parameters are $a$, $b$, $c$, and $d$. The fixed cost is $d$. A change in $d$ would shift the position of the cost curve without changing its shape. Changes in $a$, $b$, and $c$ would, however, alter both the shape and the position of the curve.

### Note 6.   Linear Programming

*Minimization of cost:* Assume that a product is to be produced by mixing two ingredients ($A$ and $B$) which weigh 5 and 10 pounds per unit, respectively. The final product is to weigh 150 pounds. Costs per unit are $2 and $8 for $A$ and $B$, respectively. What is the mix that will minimize the unit cost of production if not more than 20 units of $A$ and not less than

14 units of $B$ can be used? These last are the constraints, along with the weight of 150 pounds.

This information can be written in mathematical language as follows:

$$C = \$2A + \$8B, \quad \text{the cost function to be minimized}$$

$$\left.\begin{array}{l} 5A + 10B = 150 \\ A \le 20, \ B \ge 14 \end{array}\right\} \text{constraints}$$

From the equation controlling weight, it follows that

$$B = 15 - \frac{A}{2}.$$

Then, since $B \ge 14$

$$15 - \frac{A}{2} \ge 14,$$

or

$$1 \le \frac{A}{2}.$$

Hence $A = 0$ or $2$ and $B = 15$ or $14$.

For $A = 0$, $B = 15$, $C = \$120$

$A = 2$, $B = 14$, $C = \$116$, the minimum cost of producing the product that meets all specifications.

*Maximization of revenue:* Assume that a drug manufacturer desires to obtain a production schedule to maximize the total revenue from sale of two drugs ($A$ and $B$) whose unit prices are 60 cents and 40 cents, respectively. Production is limited by the capacity to produce the drugs, the capacity to produce containers, and by the amount of labor available for processing and handling. The limitations, or constraints, on production are these:

1. Capacity to produce drugs is 1000 units of $A$ or $B$, or a proportionate linear mix of $A$ and $B$.
2. Capacity to produce containers is 1600 units of $A$, or 800 units of $B$, or a proportionate linear mix of $A$ and $B$.
3. Labor is available for 800 units of $A$, or 1600 units of $B$, or a proportionate linear mix of $A$ and $B$.

By taking into account the fraction of total capacity needed to produce one unit of each drug and container, the following inequalities indicate values for $A$ and $B$ that are permissible:

(1) $\dfrac{A}{1000} + \dfrac{B}{1000} \le 1$ or $A + B \le 1000$

(2) $\dfrac{A}{1600} + \dfrac{B}{800} \le 1$ or $A + 2B \le 1600$

(3) $\dfrac{A}{800} + \dfrac{B}{1600} \le 1$ or $2A + B \le 1600$

If the inequality signs are ignored, the resulting equalities describe the upper contour which bounds the convex set of all feasible values (i.e., the linear-segmented production possibility curve). Then by solving these equations in pairs, the intersection (or corner) values of $A$ and $B$ are obtained. These values are:

(1 & 2) $A = 400,\quad B = 600$

(1 & 3) $A = 600,\quad B = 400$

(2 & 3) $A = \dfrac{1600}{3},\quad B = \dfrac{1600}{3}$.

The revenue function to be maximized is:

$$R = \$.60A + \$.40B$$

For (1 & 2)  $R = \$.60(400) + \$.40(600) = \$480$

  (1 & 3)  $R = \$.60(600) + \$.40(400) = \$520.$

Since the intersection of (2 & 3) falls outside the limitation on drug production, i.e., $\dfrac{1600}{3} + \dfrac{1600}{3} > 1000$, which is impossible, the maximum revenue is $520 from sale of 600 units of $A$ and 400 units of $B$.

Both of these problems could be solved by the graphic method or by the more complicated simplex method.

# PART FOUR

*Competitive Pricing*

# The Supply of Commodities

# and Services

## 13

THE MEANING OF SUPPLY • ELASTICITY OF SUPPLY • THE SUPPLY OF SERVICES FROM HOUSEHOLDS • APPLICATIONS •

The theory of demand and the theory of the firm combine to give the theory of the determination of prices and outputs. This theory will be surveyed in the three chapters following this one. The present chapter adds to the kit of analytical tools needed to examine the formation of prices and outputs.

The concept of supply has really been implicit all along, in the descriptions of the prices paid by consumers for commodities and by business firms for inputs. When consumers and firms are unable to influence the prices they must pay, the supplies of the commodities and inputs are, to the buyers individually, perfectly elastic. This will be explained shortly.

### The Meaning of Supply

The meaning of supply is symmetrical with the meaning of demand; thus there is no need to go into the definition of supply at length. In economics, the word "supply" always means a schedule — a schedule of possible prices and of amounts that would be sold at each price. A supply function is the relation between different quantities sold and the determinants of the quantities. In ordinary conversation, however, the word "supply" often signifies some one definite amount, such as the number of bushels of wheat produced last year.

## Supply Schedules

Like a demand schedule, a supply schedule is a relation between prices and quantities for a given commodity, in a given market, and in a given period of time. Quantity is made to depend on price, the other variables that can affect quantity being held constant. No simple statement about the other variables can be made, because the analysis of supply is much more complex than that of demand. At this point, however, some of the other variables can be mentioned. (1) The prices of closely related commodities must be taken into account. The supply of hogs is affected by the price of corn. It is shown in Chapter 10 and in Chapter 12 that a firm with two outputs produces and sells them, given either the smooth or the linear-segmented production possibility curve, according to the ratio of the prices of the two outputs. If the price of one output changes, the amount of the *other* output changes. Thus, in general, where firms produce more than one product, the supply of any one product is influenced by the prices of others. The supply schedule for any one kind of labor depends on the earnings (which are also a price) this labor could obtain in another employment. (2) In short periods of time, the supply of a commodity can be dominated by the sellers' expectations of future prices. (3) Over longer periods of time, changes in technology cause changes in costs, which in turn influence supply. (4) The supplies of many commodities are affected by forces such as the weather, strikes, and other temporary and ephemeral incidents and disturbances.

A hypothetical supply schedule is shown in Table 13–1.

### TABLE 13–1

### A Supply Schedule

| Price | Quantity |
|-------|----------|
| $2.00 | 40 million bushels |
| 1.95 | 38 million bushels |
| 1.90 | 36 million bushels |
| 1.80 | 34 million bushels |

The numbers in the table can be imagined as applying to the sellers of some kind of grain in a particular market on a particular day. Notice that the higher the price, the larger the quantity. This relation generally holds in supply schedules, but not always, because there can be supply schedules where larger quantities are sold at *lower* prices. More will be said on this later.

## Supply Curves

Like demand curves, supply curves are also drawn to present a smooth continuous relation between price and quantity. They too can be straight lines and still be called curves. Figure 13–1 shows two supply curves, $S_1$ and $S_2$. They have positive slopes, that is, they go up and to the right. Consider curve $S_1$ first. One price is shown in the figure, the price $OP$. At this price, the amount sold is $PA$. The supply *at* the price $OP$ is $PA$. It is evident that more would be sold at a higher price and less at a lower price. The curve $S_2$ is there to illustrate the meaning of a change in supply. An increase in supply is a shift of the whole curve to the right — the shift from $S_1$ to $S_2$. With an increased supply, more is sold at any price — the amount $PB$ instead of $PA$, at price $OP$. The meaning of a decrease in supply is simply the reverse. (See Note 1 in the Appendix to Part Four.)

Change in Supply

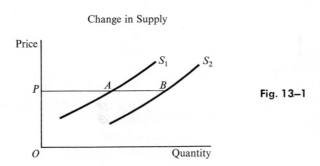

Fig. 13–1

An expression often used by economists because of its convenient brevity is "supply price." The supply price of anything is the price that will call forth a certain supply, or amount, of the commodity or service under some given circumstances. A supply price is the price corresponding to a point on a supply curve. For example, the supply price of pianists who can play cocktail music in bars is probably low, because it seems that there are always many such persons who are willing to perform for comparatively little money. On the other hand, the supply price of double the number of engineers who now specialize in one of the new exotic fields is probably very high, because additional engineers would have to be attracted away from other new, exciting, and well-paid fields.

### Elasticity of Supply

Elasticity of supply is just as important as elasticity of demand and has the same meaning. Let $E_S$ be the symbol for elasticity of supply. The definition is

$$E_s = \frac{\text{relative change in quantity}}{\text{relative change in price}} = \frac{\dfrac{\Delta Q}{Q}}{\dfrac{\Delta P}{P}} = \frac{\Delta Q}{\Delta P}\frac{P}{Q}.$$

$E_S$ is also the coefficient of elasticity of supply. Since, in general, both price and quantity go up and go down together, $E_S$ has a positive sign.

When supply is elastic, the responsiveness of sellers (or producers, depending on the context) to small changes in price is relatively great. If price changes by 10 per cent, the amount changes by more than 10 per cent. Inelasticity of supply, of course, signifies a relatively small response of sellers or producers.

Elasticity of supply can vary from one price range to another. Figure 13–2 shows a supply curve whose different slopes are probably typical of many supply curves in the short run. The different elasticities of the one

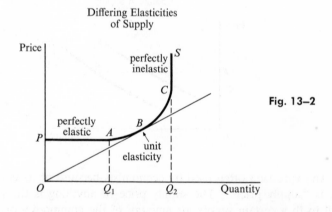

Differing Elasticities
of Supply

Fig. 13–2

curve are indicated in the figure. As is true of a demand curve, a supply curve is perfectly elastic when it is horizontal and perfectly inelastic when it is vertical. A gentle slope, as in the arc $AB$, signifies elasticity, whereas a steep slope, as in the arc $BC$, means inelasticity. An economic interpretation of the supply curve in Figure 13–2 is this: Below some price, namely $OP$, nothing at all is sold by the sellers. But if the price is in fact $OP$, they will sell any amount up to $OQ_1$ without having to get a higher price. For amounts larger than $OQ_1$, however, the price must be higher. Finally, the sellers cannot or will not sell any amount larger than $OQ_2$, no matter how high the price might be.

The geometry of the elasticity of supply is a little different from that of the elasticity of demand. The supply curve in Figure 13–2 has unit elasticity at point $B$, where the curve is tangent to a straight line drawn from the origin. When it is a straight line through the origin, a supply curve has unit elasticity over its whole length, no matter what its slope. If the straight line cuts the vertical axis, supply is elastic. And if the line cuts the horizontal axis, supply is inelastic.

An inelastic supply curve is illustrated in Figure 13–3. Let the price first be $PB$ and then change to $QC$. The elasticity of supply is the relative change in quantity divided by the relative change in price.

$$E_S = \frac{BC}{OB} \div \frac{QE}{PB} = \frac{PE}{OB} \times \frac{PB}{QE}.$$

This last term can be rewritten as $\dfrac{PE}{QE} \times \dfrac{PB}{OB}$. Because the triangles $PBA$ and $QEP$ are similar, $\dfrac{PE}{QE} = \dfrac{AB}{PB}$.

Therefore,

$$E_S = \frac{AB}{PB} \times \frac{PB}{OB} = \frac{AB}{OB}$$

Because $AB$ is shorter than $OB$, $\dfrac{AB}{OB}$ is less than one, and supply is inelastic. If $AB = OB$, so that $E_S = 1$, then the supply curve has to pass through the origin. And if $AB$ is longer than $OB$, so that $E_S > 1$, then the supply curve has to cut the price axis above the origin. (See Note 2 in the Appendix to Part Four.)

If the supply curve is a curved line, its elasticity at any point can be measured by drawing a line tangent at that point.

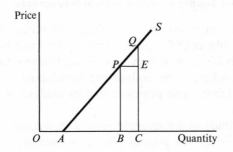

Fig. 13–3

### Time and Elasticity

Time is even more important for the elasticity of supply than it is for the elasticity of demand. The longer the period of time, the more elastic is supply likely to be.

Figure 13–4 has three supply curves pivoted around the price $P$. The curve $S_1$ is perfectly inelastic, representing supply in a very short period of time. A rise in price cannot call forth a large amount. The curve $S_2$ is the supply of the same commodity in a period of time such as the short run. Here a rise in price does call forth a larger amount. The curve $S_3$, let it be supposed, is supply when time is long enough for the fullest adjustment, as in the long run. The same rise in price results in a still larger amount.

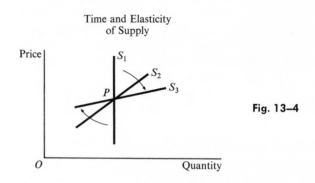

Fig. 13–4

## Supply and Costs

The complex relations between the supply of a commodity and its costs of production are taken up in Chapters 14 and 15.

## The Supply of Services from Households

The behavior of consumers, i.e., households, as buyers of commodities and services is the subject of Chapters 4 and 6. Attention now turns to the behavior of households as sellers of services to business firms. The purpose of the analysis here is to explore the foundations of the shapes of supply curves for labor. The principal tool of analysis is another set of indifference curves.

Consider the attitude of a household toward its income. In general, the more income the better. In general also, more income is to be had, in given circumstances, only by more work — only by the household's selling more services during a period of time. More work means the sacrifice of some leisure, which is also desirable. The gain in utility from more income has to be balanced against the loss of utility from less leisure.

Let it now be assumed that the members of a household can freely vary the size of their joint income by varying the number of hours per week that they work. It might be objected that this assumption is not realistic, because millions of people are employed at fixed working hours over which they have not the slightest control. Still, many such people can choose whether or not to work overtime, can take leave without pay, can play games with their allowances for sick leave, and can in fact make other adjustments. Besides, many people have two jobs. And since the economic unit here is the household, rather than one person (although some households consist of one person), it must be clear that a household of two or more persons does have some flexibility in deciding how many hours to work in a week. Shall the wife work? Part time or full time? Shall the husband take on another job in the evenings or on weekends? A few second thoughts, therefore, show the possibility of flexible choice of income even where most of the income of a household comes from salaried employment at fixed hours. Then, too, millions of other people in the American economy can and do make their own choices as to how many hours a week to work. These others are farmers, business proprietors, independent professional people, and others who are self-employed.

### Indifference Curves for Income and Leisure

The next step is to construct indifference curves to show income and leisure as substitutes. A week has 168 hours. Suppose that 12 hours a day are used for sleeping, eating, dressing, traveling to and from work, etc., so that the maximum amount of "leisure" — time not spent in working — is 84 hours a week. Figure 13–5 exhibits three indifference curves from a

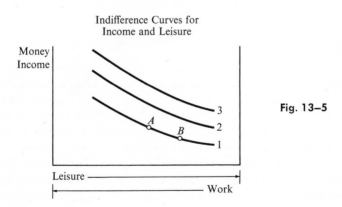

Indifference Curves for
Income and Leisure

Fig. 13–5

whole map of them. The vertical axis is money income in dollars per week. The horizontal axis, when read from left to right, shows hours of leisure per week. When read from right to left, the horizontal axis shows hours of work per week. Take indifference curve *1*. It shows combinations of income and leisure that are equally desirable. Point *A* indicates one such combination, and point *B* another. To go from *A* to *B,* the individual sacrifices income but gains enough leisure to compensate, so that he is indifferent between these two combinations and between any others on the same curve. But always, other things being equal, more income is preferable to less. Accordingly, any combination on indifference curve *2* is preferable to any on curve *1*. And curve *3* is, of course, still higher and still more desirable than curve *1*.

What about the shape of this kind of indifference curve? Observe that those in Figure 13–5 descend fast at first (i.e., on the left), and then flatten out a bit. This means that the utility of an hour of leisure is high when the hours are few, and that when the hours of leisure are many, not much income is sacrificed to get more hours of leisure. The indifference curves would be perfectly flat for someone who wanted no leisure at all. They would be very steep for someone who wanted to loaf as much as possible. Accordingly, variations in the shapes of the indifference curves can be made to describe many patterns of attitudes toward income and leisure.

Differing hourly payments — fees, wage rates, etc. — can be represented in the diagram through the slopes of straight lines, as shown in Figure 13–6.

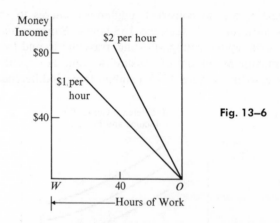

Fig. 13–6

In this figure, *OW* represents 84 hours. The line marked $1 shows the weekly income attainable by working various numbers of hours at $1 an hour. The line marked $2 shows that twice as much income can be earned with any given number of hours of work. Thus the steepness of these lines reflects the hourly rate of pay.

### The Optimum Choice

Now to solve for the optimum. The rational person, who surveys all possibilities and who coldly calculates what is best for him, wants to be on the highest reachable indifference curve. In Figure 13–7, the line *LA* represents one hourly wage rate. If this rate prevails, the highest indifference curve is curve *1*, which is tangent to the straight line at point *A*. Then the person works *LM* hours a week; if he chose to work any other number of hours, he would be on a lower indifference curve. Higher wage rates are shown by the slopes of the lines *LB* and *LC*. The points *B* and *C* are also points of tangency. The line *ABC* joins points of tangency. Its meaning is that as the wage rate rises, the individual first works more hours and then works fewer. The line *ABC* need not have the shape exhibited in Figure 13–7. The shape can be almost anything, because the shape depends on where the indifference curves touch the straight lines; this in turn depends on the shapes of the indifference curves.

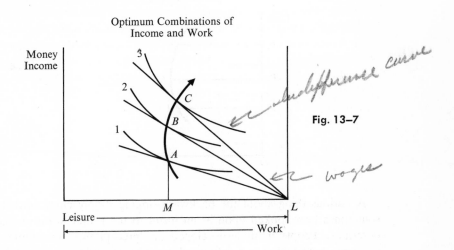

Optimum Combinations of
Income and Work

Fig. 13–7

## The Backward-Sloping Supply Curve

The information conveyed by an indifference diagram such as Figure 13–7 can be rearranged and presented in an ordinary price-quantity diagram. This is done in Figure 13–8. Here the curve *CBA* is a supply curve, one that shows the relation between wage rates (price) and the number of hours (quantity) worked at each.[1] A curve like the one in Figure 13–8 is called backward sloping, even though only part of it — the part *BC* — slopes backward, i.e., up and to the left.

[1] The curve *ABC* in Figure 13–7 and the curve *CBA* in Figure 13–8 face in opposite directions, like two boomerangs with their middles toward each other. The reason for this is that Figure 13–7 measures work from right to left, whereas Figure 13–8 measures work from left to right.

The backward sloping supply curve in Figure 13–8 is derived from Figure 13–7, and therefore is the supply curve for an individual. But the same curve can also be made to stand for a group of persons in a labor market, when the supply curves of different persons are added. All that needs to be done is to restate the numbers implied by the horizontal axis. And so far as that goes, the same or a similar curve is often used to portray the response of the entire labor force in the United States to different levels of income. Here, too, the axes are redefined — quantity becomes hundreds of millions of manhours, and price becomes average real income per gainfully occupied person.

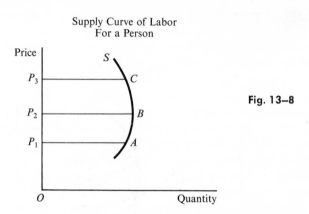

Supply Curve of Labor
For a Person

**Fig. 13–8**

A curious thing about the backward-sloping supply curve is that it has sometimes been looked upon as an insult to the people whose behavior it describes. People in underdeveloped or "precapitalist" economies sometimes are accustomed to a definite plane of living and want no more money than is needed to acquire their customary goods and services. When, therefore, such people begin to work in newly established commercial ("capitalistic") enterprises, they typically work only long enough to earn the money that is enough for them. Then they quit. Accordingly, to get more work out of people who behave this way, their wages must be lowered. But when such people begin to learn about new goods and services and abandon their old customs, they come to take on the "capitalistic" virtues — acquisitiveness, rationality, and insatiability of wants. Then their supply curves take on positive slopes.

As the foregoing indifference-curve analysis shows, however, the backward-sloping supply curve can apply to highly sophisticated as well as to simple people. It is only a question of the shapes of indifference curves, i.e., of the importance attached to income and leisure. Backward-sloping supply curves for labor are probably fairly common. When incomes are low, supply curves are positively sloped. But when incomes rise above some level, leisure begins to compete strongly with income; then supply curves alter their slopes to become backward-sloping. The steady drop in the length of the average workweek in the last several decades is just one kind of indication.

### Applications

For clear thought on economic problems, the idea of the supply curve is just as important a piece of mental equipment as the demand curve. The supply curve and its elasticity are ways of expressing the terms of availability of commodities and services. Domestic servants are no longer so easy to find as they were two generations ago. Their supply curves now can be imagined as being much higher up and much less elastic than they used to be. Why? Remember that the supply of anything depends, in part, on other prices. The same kind of people who used to go into domestic service can now earn good wages — the other prices — in more attractive occupations. Do income taxes cause people to work less? No plain answer can be given to this complex and much debated question because the answer depends mainly on the shape of the supply curves for labor. If they all have positive slopes, then the income tax does indeed reduce the number of hours of labor people want to work because the tax lowers the price (i.e., income) received. On the other hand, if all supply curves have negative slopes, the effect is the opposite: The income tax causes people to offer *more* labor, not less. But in the present state of knowledge, no one knows how many million persons have the one kind of supply curve and how many million the other. Nor does anyone know how many million persons have curves that first slope up to the right and then slope backward; the effects of the income tax depend on where these persons are on these curves. Then, too, attitudes toward leisure and income change over time, just as do the tastes for consumer goods. The effects of income taxes are therefore further complicated by changes and shifts in the supply curves for labor.

### Summary

The meaning of supply is symmetrical with the meaning of demand. *Supply schedules* and *supply curves* show relations between prices and quantities. In general, though with important exceptions, supply curves are positively sloped. *Elasticity of supply* is defined in the same manner as elasticity of demand. If a supply curve is a straight line through the origin, elasticity is unity. If the straight line cuts the price axis, supply is elastic. If instead the straight line cuts the quantity axis, supply is inelastic. The longer the period of time, the more elastic is supply likely to be. The *supply of services* sold by households to business firms depends on attitudes toward *income and leisure,* which are substitutes. These attitudes can be represented with indifference curves. With a given wage rate, the rational person chooses the combination of income and leisure (and therefore of work) that puts him on his highest indifference curve. With different wage rates, the supply curve of the labor for one person can be derived. Supply curves for labor can be *backward-sloping.*

## SELECTED REFERENCES

On the supply of services from households: W. J. L. Ryan, *Price Theory* (London: Macmillan, 1958), Chap. 6. Lionel Robbins, "On the Elasticity of Demand for Income in Terms of Effort," *Economica,* 1930. Reprinted in American Economic Association, *Readings in the Theory of Income Distribution* (Philadelphia: Blakiston, 1946).

## EXERCISES AND PROBLEMS

1. Suppose that the supply of something is inelastic and that it decreases. Explain this without using any technical terms.
2. Draw diagrams of linear supply curves with unit elasticity and prove that no matter what their slope, elasticity is still unity.
3. Use the indifference-curve analysis to derive a positively sloped supply curve for the labor of a person.
4. Draw indifference curves for income and leisure for yourself.
5. How do taxes affect the amount of work a person will perform? To get taxes into the analysis, just lower one of the straight lines in Figure 13–7. Draw diagrams to show that taxes can make a person work more and can also make him work less.

# Market and Short-Run

# Prices in Pure Competition

# 14

MARKET PRICE • EQUILIBRIUM OF THE FIRM IN THE SHORT RUN •
THE SHORT-RUN SUPPLY CURVE OF THE INDUSTRY • EQUILIBRIUM
OF THE INDUSTRY IN THE SHORT RUN • AN APPLICATION •

It is now time to bring demand and supply together. This chapter and
the next four show how demand and supply determine prices and quantities
in markets where pure competition prevails. Four simple models of
competitive[1] pricing will be constructed. Three will be partial equilibrium
models, where one commodity is considered by itself. The fourth will be
a simplified general equilibrium model, which shows the connections among
all demands, all supplies, and all prices.

No new concepts or analytical devices need to be introduced. Those
required for the theory of competitive pricing have already been described.
The demand curves of consumers and of business firms and the cost curves
of business firms have been explained and their foundations explored.

## Market Price

The first model of the process of price determination under pure competition is market price, which is the price that prevails in the market period.

[1] When used in this book, the word competitive always means purely competitive,
unless the context clearly indicates otherwise.

Other names for the model are pricing in the immediate market and the temporary equilibrium of demand and supply. The main feature of the model is that stocks of the commodity are already in existence. The market period is the period of time, or set of conditions, short enough or such that certain stocks or amounts of the commodity are taken as given. They are not in the process of being produced — they are there, on hand, in the possession of the sellers. Therefore, market supply schedules are not influenced by costs of production. Estimates of prices and of costs made in the past — weeks ago, or months ago, or perhaps even years ago — caused the quantities to be what they are today, or this week, or this month. Meanwhile, much has happened. Past estimates are usually wrong, if only by a little; past costs may or may not be recouped in today's selling price.

The market supply schedule, then, shows the amounts the sellers would sell at different possible prices. The perishability of the commodity, its storage costs if it is storable, the price it might fetch in another market if one exists — these matters, together with the sellers' price expectations and their cash positions, determine the shapes of market-supply schedules.

Market demand schedules must be defined for similarly short periods of time. The buyers are also influenced by their expectations of future prices. Is now the time to buy? Or should purchases be postponed because prices will probably fall in the next few weeks? The availabilities and prices of substitute commodities also influence buyers, as well as their cash positions.

### The Equilibrium Price

The equilibrium price in the market period is the price that equates demand and supply. At this price, the buyers are willing to buy a certain amount. The sellers are willing to sell exactly the same amount. The market is cleared, there being no surplus and no shortage. Of course, some buyers and some sellers are disappointed; the equilibrium price is too high or too low for them.

Figure 14–1 shows how to visualize the determination of the equilibrium market price. In some market in some short period of time, $D$ and $S$ are the demand and supply curves, the graphic versions of the market demand and supply schedules just discussed. The two curves intersect at point $A$, which corresponds to the price $OP_1$ and to the quantity, bought and sold, $P_1A$. At price $OP_1$, demand and supply are equal. At a higher price such as $OP_2$, demand is $P_2B$, whereas supply is $P_2C$. The excess supply of $BC$ forces the price down. The higher price can prevail only briefly because the sellers try to sell more than the buyers want to buy at the same price. Similarly, a price lower than the equilibrium can exist only briefly because the excess demand *EF* pushes the price up. The buyers try to buy more than the sellers want to sell.

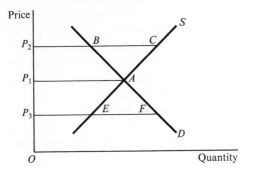

Equilibrium of Demand
and Supply

Fig. 14–1

The model displayed in Figure 14–1 is simple, but being simple it is also general. As a first approximation, the model is accordingly applicable to a wide range of markets — the organized markets in which farm products are sold, the produce markets in large cities, the stock exchanges, the government-bond market, the foreign-exchange markets where rates are free. The model is a generalization about these and similar markets. These markets differ among themselves in many ways; any one generalization about them omits much. Still, the model draws attention to the forces common and basic in all markets. It is best to think of the demand and supply curves as being in ceaseless motion so that, always, new equilibrium prices are coming into being. A diagram such as Figure 14–1 is like a snapshot of a scene of action. (Note 3 in the Appendix to Part Four gives a simple algebraic treatment of competitive equilibrium.)

Demand and Supply : No Price

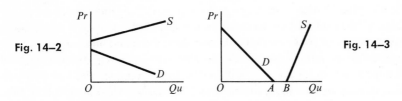

Fig. 14–2

Fig. 14–3

Do demand and supply always result in exchanges at a price? Not necessarily. Consider Figure 14–2. Here is a demand curve and a supply curve, but no price. The demand is such that the buyers are not willing to pay prices as high as the sellers insist on receiving for the smallest amounts they are willing to sell. Then look at Figure 14–3. The demand here is such that the buyers will take the amount $OA$, but no more, at a zero price. But the sellers are willing to let the buyers have the amount $OB$ without any charge. Hence this commodity can command no price when demand and supply are like this. The commodity is a free good. This might be an example: Edible wild berries grow in a summer-resort area. The owners of the land allow people to pick and eat as many as they please, i.e., the amount $OA$ in Figure 14–3. But if more people should come into the area, if the demand should increase, and if the demand curve should move far enough to the right to intersect the supply curve, then the owners would *sell* the right to pick the wild berries.

In the market period (and also in the short run and in the long run), the intersection of the demand curve and the supply curve determines quantity as well as price. Figure 14–4 gives emphasis to this important matter. In this figure, the two supply curves are perfectly inelastic, meaning that the sellers want to sell all they have and will take any price they can get. But the two supply curves stand for different amounts. With supply curve $S_2$, the larger amount $OB$ causes the equilibrium price to be lower.

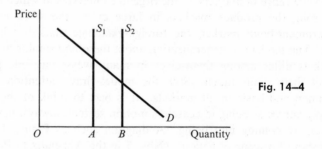

Fig. 14–4

### Changes in Demand and Supply

Changes in demand and in supply cause changes in price, or in quantity, or both. What happens to price and to quantity depends upon the magnitudes of the changes in demand and supply and upon their elasticities. Figures 14–5 and 14–6 each contain two sets of demand and supply curves. They can be paired in four ways, to represent increases or decreases in either demand or supply, or both. Thus, for example, the price is the same when $D_1$ and $S_1$ are coupled and when $D_2$ and $S_2$ are coupled. But the quantity is larger for the combination of $D_2$ and $S_2$. Notice that each of the figures shows four equilibrium prices and quantities. In Figure 14–5, where both demand and supply are inelastic, the price differences are greater than the quantity differences. The opposite is true in Figure 14–6, where both demand and supply are elastic.

## Speculation

At any one point of time, the actions of buyers and sellers in organized markets are dominated by expectations of future prices. Since many commodities bought and sold on organized markets are produced seasonally, and since some commodities are consumed seasonally, fluctuations in market prices would be wide were it not for speculation. A speculator is a trader who buys and sells in the hope of earning a net income from differences in prices. The usual belief is that the activities of speculators, who try to guess what prices will be in the future, cause market prices to be more stable over time than they otherwise would be. Certainly, gross seasonal fluctuations are prevented. Beyond this, however, neither theoretical analysis nor empirical research can establish clearly just what is the price-stabilizing effect of speculation. In the organized markets where homogeneous and storable commodities are traded, there are two sets of prices — spot and futures. Spot, or cash, prices are those paid and received for actual physical quantities of a commodity. Futures prices are prices in contracts for delivery of the commodity at some date in the future. The contracts are paper contracts; with most of them most of the time, physical delivery never takes place, the contracts being bought or sold before their delivery dates. In general, the spread between spot and futures prices of a commodity tends to be close to the costs of storing it. When they make mistakes in judgment, when they are moved by overenthusiasm or by panic, speculators can cause wild fluctuations in prices. Even when they make correct judgments, speculators can cause prices to fluctuate up and down. If, for example, prices fall, speculators who correctly predict further price declines will sell, thus strengthening the downward movement.

Many commodities are traded in geographically separate markets. Price differences between the markets are held exceedingly close to transportation costs by the activities of speculators.

### Changes in Demand and Supply

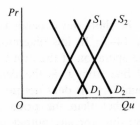

**Fig. 14–5**

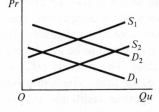

**Fig. 14–6**

## Information

In a competitive market, there can be only one equilibrium price at any one time. This statement, or some version of it, has been repeated by economists for many generations. The validity of the statement, however, depends on an assumption that so far has been implicit, namely, that buyers and sellers have "perfect knowledge." This means only that they know what the price is and what price the same thing is selling for in other markets, if there are any. Complete and accurate information is available in the highly organized markets; ticker tapes and other devices carry it. But in many other markets, information is imperfect. It is costly and troublesome to acquire. The many buyers and sellers do not know what all of the offers are. In such markets, there can be several prices at the same time.

### Equilibrium of the Firm in the Short Run

The market price of a competitively produced and sold commodity fluctuates. But the fluctuations are not capricious or random. They have a pattern, hardly ever exact and closely predictable, but nonetheless a pattern. The doctrine of short-run equilibrium price is a way of stating the level around which market prices fluctuate in the short run.

The short-run supply of an industry under pure competition is a flow of production from the firms in the industry, producing with their fixed plants and equipment and with their variable inputs. The rate of the flow depends on the price of the commodity and the cost functions of the firms. The short-run supply schedule, or curve, shows the volumes of production from the industry at each possible price. The first step in constructing this schedule is to describe the price-output adjustments of a single firm.

To any one firm under pure competition, demand is perfectly elastic at the prevailing price. The firm can sell more or less without having any effect upon the price. To the firm, price and marginal revenue are equal. Marginal revenue, it will be remembered, is the addition to total revenue by selling one more unit. The extra revenue from an extra unit is marginal revenue and it is also the price.

How much a competitive firm produces in the short run depends on its marginal cost and the price. Consider Figure 14–7. In this diagram, the price is assumed to be at a level that makes the operation of the firm highly profitable. The price is $OP$. The horizontal line from $P$ is the demand curve of the firm. The firm produces the amount $OA$. It does not produce more because additional output has a cost higher than the price. The short-run marginal cost curve — $MC$ — shows this; for any output larger than $OA$, $MC$ exceeds price. Nor will the firm produce any less than $OA$

because if it did, the firm would fail to seize the opportunity to produce and sell units whose marginal cost is less than their price.

The rectangles in Figure 14–7 show the firm's position. *Total revenue* is price times quantity, the rectangle *PA*.[2] *Total cost* is average cost multiplied by quantity, the rectangle *FA*. *Net profit* is the excess of total revenue over total cost. Net profit is the heavily shaded rectangle *PB*. *Fixed cost* is the difference between total and variable costs; fixed cost is the lightly shaded rectangle *FC*. *Variable cost* is the rectangle *OC*. *Net revenue* is the excess of total revenue over variable cost. Net revenue is the rectangle *PC*, i.e., the two shaded areas together.

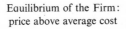
Equilibrium of the Firm:
price above average cost

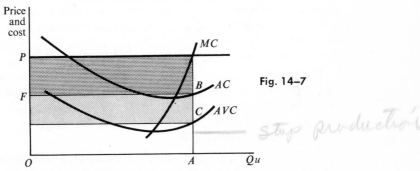

Fig. 14–7

Must the firm earn net profits if it is to produce in the short run? The answer is no. Consider Figure 14–8, which shows an unprofitable price for the firm. The price is below the firm's full costs. But the firm produces the amount *OA*, whose marginal cost equals the price *OP*. At this price, the

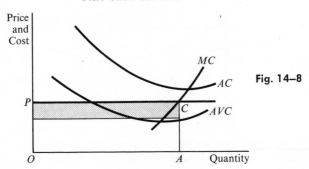
Short-Run Equilibrium of the Firm:
Price below full cost

Fig. 14–8

[2] For simplicity, rectangles will be designated by the letters diagonally opposite.

firm's net revenue is the shaded rectangle *PC*. Another look at Figure 14–8 shows that net revenue is less than fixed costs, that the firm operates at a loss. But it *minimizes* its loss. If the firm stopped producing and shut down, its loss would be equal to its fixed costs. Producing the output *OA,* the firm's net revenue *PC reduces* the loss that would equal its fixed costs. If, therefore, price is lower than full cost but higher than variable cost, output with a marginal cost equal to price gives a net revenue that reduces loss to a minimum.

Here is a simple arithmetical example of the same proposition: Suppose you have a poultry farm and that your fixed costs per week are $100. Your full costs per pound for each fryer you sell are 10 cents. Your variable costs for feed, labor, etc. are 5 cents a pound. Would you temporarily produce at a price of 8 cents? Yes, as a rational businessman you would, because if you were to shut down, your loss would be $100 a week. But if you produce at 8 cents, the 3 cents over your variable costs, multiplied by the number of pounds, recovers for you at least part of your fixed costs. A small loss is preferable to a large one.

The general principle, then, is that the firm in the short run adjusts its output so that net revenue is maximized. If this means a net profit, so much the better for the firm. If maximum net revenue means a loss, then the loss is minimized. Price must exceed average variable cost, and marginal cost must equal price.

If, however, the price is so low that it is below any point on the curve of average variable cost, the firm stops producing. If it did not, the firm would lose, besides the amount equal to fixed costs, even more — the price would not cover the unit expenses of currently purchased labor and materials.

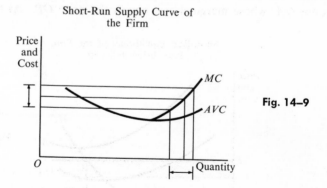

Short-Run Supply Curve of
the Firm

Fig. 14–9

The supply curve of the firm in the short run, therefore, is that portion of the marginal cost curve that lies above the average variable cost curve. Figure 14–9 shows three prices, and the corresponding equilibrium amounts for each price. The arrows indicate the association of amounts with prices.

## The Short-Run Supply Curve of the Industry

When the marginal cost curves of the firms are combined, the result is the supply curve of the industry. Thus the supply of the industry is based on the costs of the firms. At each possible price, firm A, firm B, firm C, etc. produce amounts corresponding to the equalities of their marginal costs at that price. The total of the amounts is the industry's supply at the same price.

Figure 14–10 shows a short-run supply curve for an industry. Suppose the price is $OP$. Then the output of the entire industry is $OA$ millions of units. The figure also indicates the adjustments of two of the firms.

Industry Supply and Firm Supply in the Short Run

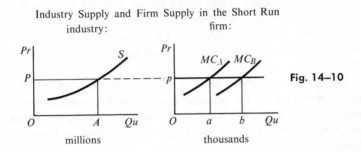

**Fig. 14–10**

Firm $A$ has short-run marginal costs of $MC_A$. Firm $B$'s are $MC_B$. Observe that firm $B$ has much lower costs for *any* output; for example, output $Oa$ is optimum for firm $A$, but firm $B$'s marginal cost is about half of $A$'s at the same output. So firm $B$ produces much more, namely, $Ob$. But observe that when both firms are in equilibrium, the marginal costs of their equilibrium outputs are equal. The *last* bushel produced on the low-cost farm has the same cost as the *last* bushel produced on the high-cost farm, because both bushels sell at the same price.

### Elasticity of Industry Supply

The elasticity of industry supply depends on two things. One is the differences of costs among the firms. If differences in costs are large, the high-cost firms are likely to stop producing at relatively low prices. When the price rises, these firms start up again and add their outputs to the larger outputs of the other firms. At lower prices, then, industry supply can be elastic. Above some price, all the firms are in operation. The second determinant of elasticity of supply is the shape of the marginal cost curves of the firms. If these curves are relatively steep, i.e., inelastic themselves, then they cause the supply curve to be inelastic. The $MC$ curves *must* be highly inelastic after some point, because this is still the short run with its *fixed* plant and equipment. At high prices, industry supply is bound to be inelastic.

The industry supply curve would be inelastic at all prices in a branch of mining, if costs differed much from mine to mine and if each one had rapidly diminishing marginal returns. Conversely, over a wide range of prices, supply would be elastic in an industry with small differences in costs among the firms and if the tendency to diminishing returns were slight.

## Equilibrium of the Industry in the Short-Run

An industry is in equilibrium in the short run when the output of the industry holds steady, there being no force acting to expand output or to contract it. A firm is in equilibrium in the short run when it maximizes its net revenue. The firm clearly does not want to change the output that yields its maximum net revenue. If all firms are in equilibrium, then so is the industry.

Demand in the short run is a flow of consumption, the volume of the flow depending on the possible prices. At the equilibrium price for the industry, demand equals supply. The rate of consumption equals the rate of production. In everyday language, consumption and production are in balance.

### Changes in Demand

Figure 14–11 shows three short-run equilibrium prices for the industry. If the demand is low — $D_1$ — then the equilibrium price $P_1$ is low. At this price, many or even most of the firms can be suffering losses. Nonetheless, $P_1$ is an equilibrium price because demand equals supply. The firms equate their marginal costs with $P_1$, and total output holds steady despite firms' losses. If demand increases in the short run to $D_2$, then the new and higher equilibrium price is $P_2$. At this price, only a few firms, perhaps, are suffering losses. Many might be earning good net profits. And at the high price $P_3$, perhaps all of the firms are earning net profits.

Short-run equilibrium, therefore, does not denote any one condition of profitability for the industry. Equilibrium is compatible with both widespread losses and widespread net profits. When demand is depressed and when the firms adjust to the lower price caused by the depressed demand, the market price falls to the short-run equilibrium level. An industry with a depressed demand and with many firms suffering losses is often called a "sick industry." In such an industry, much idle capacity exists because the firms losing money operate at less than their capacity outputs. Unemployment of labor can also be at high levels if, in the short run, opportunities to take other jobs are few. Nevertheless, it often happens that a few firms in a sick industry earn good profits. They are the firms with the newest plant and equipment, and the best management. An industry can be sick for many years — the market price continuing to hover about a low equilibrium level. On the other hand, a competitive industry can be in short-run equilibrium with a strong demand, a high equilibrium price, and large net profits for nearly all of the firms. Such a condition is not, however, likely to last for long. As other firms begin to enter the profitable industry, the short run merges into the long.

Short-Run Equilibrium Prices

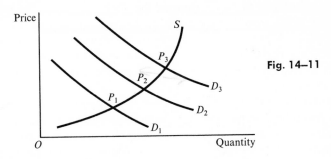

Fig. 14–11

## Changes in Supply

The short-run supply curve can shift, to the right or to the left. Two groups of causes can bring about changes in supply in the short run. One set of causes has to do with the production functions of the firms. In many industries, the physical outputs of firms depend in part upon the weather, upon the amount and the timing of rainfall, upon variations in temperature, upon the frequency and severity of storms, etc. The physical outputs of the agricultural industries also depend on how bad are the effects of insects, pests, and the diseases of plants and animals. Minor improvements in technology can also occur in the short run. Their effects are to reduce the costs of given outputs or to make possible larger outputs with given costs. Another cause of changes in short-run supply is fluctuation in the prices of the variable inputs of the firms. Their marginal cost curves can rise or fall as wage rates, fuel prices, etc. go up or go down.

## An Application

Chapter 17 contains several applications of the theory of short-run competitive price. At this point, just one application is introduced, more for its contribution to the understanding of the theory than for its usefulness in economic policy.

Suppose that a tax is imposed on the producers of a commodity, the tax being so many cents a unit for each unit they produce. Naturally, the producers wish they could pass the tax on to the consumers. But they could only do so if they could raise their prices. This is impossible in pure competition because individual producers have no control over price at all. The tax, however, is an added cost. It increases the marginal costs of the firms, thus causing them to produce less at any given price. Therefore the industry supply curve shifts to the left. The new equilibrium price is higher than the old. The tax, accordingly, *does* result in a higher price — not because of the producers' wishes, but because of the decrease in supply. The rise in price is not, however, equal to the tax.

Effect of a Tax on Equilibrium Price

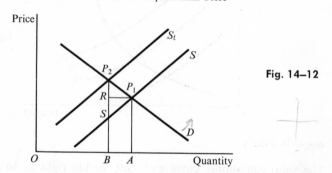

Fig. 14–12

Why so? To see this, look at Figure 14–12. The initial equilibrium is with the curves $D$ and $S$, the price being $P_1A$ and the quantity $OA$. The tax brings into existence the new supply curve $S_t$. The vertical distance between the two supply curves is the amount of the tax per unit. The new equilibrium is the price $P_2B$ and the quantity $OB$. The rise in price is $P_2R$, whereas the tax per unit is $P_2S$. The rise in price is less than the tax.[3] Just how much less depends on the elasticities of demand and supply. The more elastic the demand and the less elastic the supply, the smaller is the rise in price as a fraction of the tax. The common sense of it all is this: The more elastic the demand, the less willing are the buyers to pay higher prices for smaller quantities. The more inelastic the supply, the greater is the decline in marginal cost as output is cut back by the tax, which is then added to a lower level of cost.

### Summary

The *equilibrium market price* of a commodity bought and sold in a

---

[3] The same point is proved with simple algebra in Note 3, Appendix to Part Four.

market where pure competition exists is determined by market demand and supply schedules. The equilibrium price equates demand and supply. Equilibrium prices and quantities continually change because demand and supply curves are always in motion. The actions of speculators prevent gross seasonal fluctuations in prices. The flow of production from an industry in the short run is described by the *short-run supply curve of the industry*. This curve is the sum of the short-run supply curves of the firms. Each firm adjusts its output so that marginal cost is equal to price which, in turn, is equal to marginal revenue. The firm produces even if price is less than full cost provided that price is above average variable cost. The *supply curve of a firm* is the portion of its marginal cost curve that lies above the average variable cost curve. The *short-run equilibrium price* is determined by the equality of industry demand and industry supply. The equilibrium price can be consistent with either widespread losses or profits for the firms in the industry.

## SELECTED REFERENCES

Alfred Marshall, *Principles of Economics,* 8th ed. (London: Macmillan, 1920), Book V, Chap. 5. Jacob Viner, "Cost Curves and Supply Curves," *Zeitschrift für Nationalökonomie,* 1931. Reprinted in George J. Stigler and Kenneth E. Boulding, (eds.), *Readings in Price Theory* (Homewood: Irwin, 1952). George J. Stigler, *The Theory of Price,* rev. ed. (New York: Macmillan, 1952), Chap. 9 and 10.

## EXERCISES AND PROBLEMS

1. Draw diagrams with equilibrium market prices showing various effects of changes in demand and supply.

2. Show that price does not change if demand increases and if supply is perfectly elastic, and that quantity does not change if demand increases and if supply is perfectly inelastic.

3. Suppose both demand and supply were (1) perfectly elastic and (2) perfectly inelastic. What then?

4. Why would a firm in pure competition never want to spend any money on advertising its product?

5. Why does the firm in pure competition operate in the rising portion of its marginal cost curve? Why not the falling portion?

6. For a firm, does marginal cost determine price or does price determine marginal cost?

# Long-Run Prices in

# Pure Competition

## 15

MEANING AND RELEVANCE  •  EQUILIBRIUM OF THE FIRM  •
EQUILIBRIUM OF THE INDUSTRY  •  EXTERNAL ECONOMIES AND
DISECONOMIES • THE LONG-RUN SUPPLY CURVE • APPLICATIONS •

"In the long run," Lord Keynes once said, "we are all dead." He was talking about the need to do something quickly and boldly about serious unemployment. Keynes was also venting his impatience with those who hope that, given a little time, serious problems will go away and that eventually — in the long run — all will finally turn out well. Keynes's remark has been much quoted, with the apparent implication that the long run is far away, a never-never land, a condition of happy adjustment.

### Meaning and Relevance

The implication is not true. The essence of the idea of the long run is the growth of an industry. Industries do grow; new firms enter growing industries, adding their new capital to the expanding stock of the capital of the firms already in the industry. Some industries decline; firms leave them, and the stocks of capital shrink. Nor does the long run have to be a lengthy period of calendar time, though indeed it can be. For industries using readily available, unspecialized, and easily transferable resources, the long run is a comparatively brief length of calendar time.

The long-run equilibrium price of a competitively produced commodity has been a central interest of economic theory for two centuries. In the eighteenth and nineteenth centuries, Adam Smith, David Ricardo, and others sought to explain the "natural values" of commodities, to find the causes of the "natural" level of the price of, say, wheat, when all temporary and ephemeral forces, such as variations in the weather and the effects of wars, are set aside. Karl Marx, the founder of the philosophy of communism, devoted most of the space in *Das Kapital* (1867) to *his* theory of the values of commodities produced in a capitalist economy. Smith, Ricardo, Marx, and others gave explanations of value that looked mainly or primarily to the amounts of labor needed to produce a commodity. When it was introduced in the second half of the nineteenth century, the concept of marginal utility was put to work on the same task; theorists sought to find the ultimate cause of value in consumer demand. Alfred Marshall's contribution to economic theory is often said to consist of his having synthesized cost of production and consumer demand as mutual determinants of the value of a commodity.

Price theory used to be called "the theory of value and distribution," i.e., the theory of the exchange rates of commodities and the derived theory of the incomes of owners of productive services. In the past, those parts of price theory having to do with pure competition and the long run had strong philosophical or even ideological associations. Most of the prominent theorists have had strong leanings to conservative positions on issues of economic policy. Since the 1930's, however, price theory has tended to become a box of tools that anyone, conservative and radical alike, can use for varied purposes. As Chapter 17 shows, even socialists can draw upon price theory for help in designing a socialist economy.

Because it describes the fullest mutual adjustment of demand and supply, the doctrine of long-run price is still important in modern price theory. The demonstration of the economic advantages of free trade and many of the central propositions of welfare economics are special cases of long-run equilibrium prices in pure competition.

Of current interest are problems like these: At the end of this century, what will probably be the relative price of beef? Of petroleum products? Of lumber? Answers, in the form of estimates, to such questions are important because they can guide policy decisions in the years to come. Notice the form of such questions. The dollar price of a pound of beef in the year 2000 might reflect more than anything else the change in the general level of prices between now and then. The question asks for the *relative* price of beef — its price relative to the prices of other meats, of dairy products, of cereals. The answers to such questions will also be framed independently of temporary disturbances that might exist in the 1990's, disturbances such as unusual weather or deep depressions. The answers run in terms of the probable growth of demand and the probable changes in the conditions of supply.

## Equilibrium of the Firm

The main task of the analysis is to construct the long-run supply curve of a purely competitive industry. Here too, of course, the behavior of the industry is the collective behavior of the firms. Hence the individual firm must first be put under analysis.

The long-run cost curve of the firm is now brought forward from Chapter 11. In Figure 15–1, $LAC$ is the long-run average cost curve, with its companion $LMC$, the long-run marginal cost curve. The objective of the firm is to maximize its net profits, the excess of revenue over full cost. The firm does this by adjusting output so that $LMC$ = price. Suppose first that the price is $OP_2$. At this price, the firm adjusts the scale of its plant so as to produce the amount $OB$. Total revenue is the rectangle $P_2B$. Total cost is the rectangle $OR$. So the net profits are the shaded rectangle $P_2R$.

### Entry and Net Profits

Let it now be assumed that all of the firms in the industry have exactly the same costs. A justification of this assumption will be given shortly. If, then, all the firms in an industry are earning net profits, other firms will be attracted to the industry. In the absence of other events such as a change in demand, the added output from the new firms lowers the price. As the price falls, the net profits of the firms, both the old ones and the newcomers, diminish. When the price equals minimum average cost, net profits are zero. There is then no inducement for new firms to enter. Neither is there any incentive for firms to leave an industry when net profits are zero because all the firms are earning normal profits, which by definition are large enough to keep the firms in the industry. Normal profits, of course, are included in the cost curves.

Just how quickly new firms enter an industry where net profits are to be had is clearly a complex matter. An entrepreneur thinking of going into an industry new to him needs information on costs, prices, and net profits. He must make an estimate as to how long high net profits will continue. He must have, or be able to get, the needed know-how and financing. To build a new plant takes time. These and similar analytical complexities are set aside by the assumption that competition is pure *and perfect*. The assumptions of *perfect knowledge* and of decisions under *certainty* have been implicit all along. To them is now added the assumption of *perfect mobility*, i.e., firms enter and leave an industry quickly and without friction. These perfections greatly simplify the analysis.

### Equality of Price and Minimum Average Cost

The entry of new firms lowers the price in Figure 15–1 to $OP_1$. If the price should go below $OP_1$, the firm will continue to produce in the short

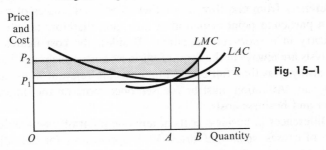

Long-Run Equilibrium of the Firm

Fig. 15–1

run provided that the price is higher than average variable cost. But in the long run, the firm will not produce at a price below $OP_1$ because any such price does not cover full cost. The price $OP_1$ is equal to marginal cost and also to the minimum average cost. And since price is the same as marginal revenue to a firm under pure competition,

$$P = MR = LMC = LAC.$$

One more thing: Observe that, at price $OP_1$, the firm's demand curve is tangent to the long-run average cost curve at its minimum point.

The importance of the equalities and of the tangency just mentioned will be explained shortly. In the meantime, consider another aspect of the long-run equilibrium of the firm: The firm's marginal cost is rising. Marginal cost *must* rise, for if it did not, there could be no equilibrium, no output with maximum net profits. Imagine that the long-run marginal cost of a firm were either constant or falling, i.e., the *LMC* curve would either be horizontal or declining downward to the right. If there is to be any production at all, the *LMC* curve would have to lie below the horizontal curve. So, if *LMC* is either horizontal or falling to the right, the firm would expand indefinitely, without limit. The more it would expand, the larger would be its net profits, which, however, would never reach a maximum. Since all this is absurd, it follows that long-run marginal cost must be rising, in the neighborhood of the equilibrium output.

Observe that this proof of rising marginal cost in the long run holds for firms in purely competitive industries. The doubts expressed in Chapter 9 about the cause of eventually decreasing returns (page 143), and in Chapter 11 about the upturn of marginal and average costs on the right-hand side of the curve (page 176) are settled at least for competitive firms.

## Equality of Full Costs

The next step is to show that the firms in an industry of pure competition can be regarded as having exactly the same costs. The equal-cost assumption is more than a helpful simplification; it rests upon reasoned premises.

Statistical studies of the costs of firms in an industry always show great differences from one firm to another. But such studies of costs are made for a particular point or period of time, and therefore the studies catch the industry in a short-run condition. Besides, the cost figures available for analysis are always in the form of business costs which, as Chapter 8 shows, are always less than full costs. Full costs are relevant in the analysis of the long run. Attention must be focused once more on the difference between them and business costs.

Differences in business costs at any one point of time are due to a multitude of causes, small and large. With opportunity for full adjustment, i.e., in the long-run, the small causes disappear or become so negligible that they can be disregarded. But the large cause that remains in the long run is the scarcity of resources. Let the scarce resource be management. In some purely competitive industries, the scarce resource could be a particular type of land or other natural resource. To point to management is to achieve a greater degree of generality, and to say that good management is scarce could hardly evoke disagreement. "Scarce" here means that in the long run the supply curve of the resource is positively sloped, not horizontal.

Assume first that management is hired by entrepreneurs. Only a few firms in the industry can have the services of the best managers. They bring about low business costs of the firms they work for. But these managers can demand and get salaries equal to the cost savings they cause. If one firm does not pay such a salary, another will. Hence managers' salaries equalize full costs.

Next, assume that the entrepreneurs do their own managing. Part of their implicit costs are the salaries they forego. The entrepreneur-managers look upon their foregone salaries as costs. If they do not earn them, they abandon that particular industry to go into another. Here, too, costs are equalized.

## Equilibrium of the Industry

When the firms in a purely competitive industry earn zero net profits, the number of firms is in equilibrium; no firms enter and no firms leave. Each firm is in equilibrium, holding its output steady. Therefore the output of the industry is in equilibrium, there being no force causing the output of the industry either to expand or to contract.[1]

In this equilibrium, all the firms in the industry produce at their minimum average costs. The firms do so more from necessity than from choice. The firms produce their profit-maximizing outputs whose costs are at a minimum.

The next step on the way to the construction of long-run industry supply curves is to take account of external economies and diseconomies.

### External Economies and Diseconomies

External economies and diseconomies are changes in the position of the long-run cost curves of firms when the changes are caused by the growth of the industry. If firms enjoy external economies, their cost curves drop along their entire lengths. Similarly, external diseconomies cause firms' cost curves to be lifted up.

Figure 15–2 has two positions of a long-run average cost curve of a firm, positions $A$ and $B$. External economies cause the curve to drop from $A$ to $B$, whereas external diseconomies lift the curve up from $B$ to $A$. In all likelihood, however, such changes in the position of a firm's cost curve would rarely be so great as they are shown in Figure 15–2.

The idea of external economies is another of Alfred Marshall's contributions. He drew a contrast with the firm's "internal" economies which are reflected in the declining, or left hand, part of the firm's $U$-shaped long-run

External Effects on a Firm's Costs

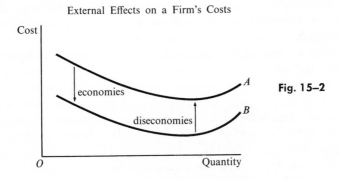

Fig. 15–2

[1] The paragraph above conforms to standard modern theory. When the industry is in long-run equilibrium, *each* firm is also in long-run equilibrium. But a moment's reflection will remind anyone that in an industry with a steady rate of output, some firms are expanding their own volumes of production, while others, the ever-present weaker ones, are cutting their outputs back. In a growing industry, some firms grow much faster than others. Every industry has its new firms, its vigorous and progressive firms, and its older and perhaps decaying firms. At stake here is not a contrast between "theory" and "reality." The issue — whether the full equilibrium of an

cost curve. When they occur, external economies, said Marshall, are the result of the growth of the industry the firm belongs to. As an industry grows, many small changes take place. If auxiliary services such as financing and transportation become cheaper, if materials and semi-finished goods bought by the firms become better and cheaper as they are supplied in larger quantities, if the skills of the labor force improve as the result of the spread of training programs paid for perhaps from public funds, if, then, these and similar cost-reducing changes happen, external economies exist. They do not flow from the introduction of major technological improvements, which also thrust cost curves downward. No, Marshall's external economies arise from the concurrence of many little things which can include the more efficient application of known technology. The many little things producing external economies as an industry grows can be summed up under two headings: (1) decreases in the prices of some inputs, and (2) increases in the physical productivities of some inputs.

Marshall did not use the expression "external diseconomies," but instead wrote about the tendency toward diminishing return. External diseconomies accompanying the expansion of an industry arise from higher input prices or from diminishing physical productivities of the firms' inputs, or from both. Input prices become higher if important inputs to the industry are available to it at rising supply prices. That is, the supply curves of the inputs slope up to the right so that as the industry grows and as its demands for the inputs increase, their prices rise. The industry can get more of such inputs only by bidding them away from other industries. Industries exploiting natural resources — farming, mining, cutting timber, fishing — run into steadily less favorable physical input-output ratios as they expand unless their expansions are accompanied by offsetting technological improvements.

Marshall's concepts are still relevant in the theory of competitive prices in the long run. They will be fitted into the theory shortly. But at this

---

industry requires the full equilibrium and the equal costs of *all* firms — is an issue between two theories, the modern theory and Alfred Marshall's. To Marshall, long-run equilibrium of the industry meant the equality of long-run demand and supply, nothing more. Some firms could be expanding, others declining, and still others holding their outputs steady. Marshall's famous analogy was the trees of a forest: The forest is growing at some rate, measured in board feet of timber; some trees are being born, some are growing fast, some are growing at the same rate as the forest, some are growing more slowly, and some are dying. A serious shortcoming of Marshall's theory, however, is that he did not demonstrate that for an industry in equilibrium, the outputs of the growing firms are equal to those of the declining firms. It is possible that modern methods of analysis, starting from Marshall's brilliant insights, will much improve the current theory of the connections between the output of an industry and the outputs of the firms in it. See Peter Newman, "The Erosion of Marshall's Theory of Value," *Quarterly Journal of Economics,* Vol. LXXIV, No. 4, November, 1960, pp. 587-600.

point, a few remarks will be made about the expressions "external economies" and "diseconomies" as they are met in other contexts.

### External Effects in Modern Analysis

In the postwar literature on welfare economies and on the development of underdeveloped economies, the expression "external effects" carries a broader meaning. In this literature, an external economy is any benefit that flows from $A$ to $B$ for which $B$ does not have to pay. $A$ and $B$ can be firms, or industries, or consumers. A standard, though unimpressive, example is the beekeeper and the fruit grower. The bees pollinate the blossoms, which furnish food to the bees; external economies here flow both ways. An external economy in consumption is exemplified by my neighbor; he keeps his house and garden neat, trim, and attractive. This pleases my eye, and might even increase the resale value of my house. But when $A$ does something to increase $B$'s costs or lower his revenue or his utilities, $A$ is inflicting an external diseconomy on $B$, whether or not $A$ intends to do so. The ill effects of smoke and pollution are examples of external diseconomies. The neighbor's noisy power mower is an external diseconomy in consumption, because my utility is reduced.

These broader external effects — another name for them is spillover effects — will be discussed more fully in Chapter 17, part of which will touch on the welfare aspects of competitive pricing. As to economic development, it suffices to say here that if a choice has to be made between introducing two new industries in a backward area, one with greater external economies than the other, the choice goes to the one yielding the greater external benefits, all other things being equal.

### The Long-Run Supply Curve

The long-run supply curve of an industry in pure competition shows a set of prices and amounts. The prices are equal to the minimum average full costs of the firms. The amounts are the equilibrium outputs of the industry at each price. Long-run supply curves can be horizontal, positively sloped, or negatively sloped. These are the curves of constant-cost, increasing-cost, and decreasing-cost industries.

### Constant-Cost Industries

Although no one knows for sure, it is probable that many, if not most, industries are subject to neither external economies nor diseconomies. Or, if both tendencies are present, they counterbalance each other. Such industries have constant costs in the long run. On a diagram, the height of the supply curve is equal to the minimum average long-run costs of the firms. Since the long-run supply curve is horizontal, changes in long-run demand cause no changes in the long-run equilibrium price. When demand increases and when the output of the industry is fully adjusted to the larger demand, the additional output comes from more firms. A doubling of the long-run equilibrium output of a constant-cost industry comes from a doubling of the number of firms in the industry.

To see why this is so, consider Figure 15–3, which shows a firm, and Figure 15–4, which shows an industry. Notice that the firm's quantity axis is measured in thousands of units and the industry's in millions of units. To begin, let both the firm and the industry be in equilibrium. The price is $OP;$ the firm (and each of the other firms) produces $Oa$. The industry produces $OB$, which is $Oa$ multiplied by the number of firms. The industry demand is $D_1$, and of course the firm demand is the horizontal line in Figure 15–3 drawn from $P$. Now let the industry demand increase to $D_2$. Suppose that the increase in demand is not slow and gradual, but comes fairly quickly. Hence the price rises. All the firms now earn net profits and can earn more by expanding production. To seize the extra net profits, they expand output with their existing plants and do so along their short-run marginal cost curves. Thus if price initially rises to $OP'$ — it could go higher — the firm increases output to beyond $Oa$. The industry's output expands along the short-run supply curve $S_1$. The high and profitable price attracts new firms to the industry. The supply curve $S_1$ shifts to the right. The additions to total output cause the price to fall. As it does, the old firms cut back production along their $SMC$ curves. If demand continues to be $D_2$, the price finally falls back to $OP$. When it does, no new firms enter. The short-run supply curve stops shifting and becomes

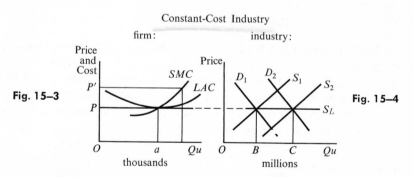

Constant-Cost Industry

the curve $S_2$. Each firm, both old and new, again produces the amount $Oa$. Total industry output is $OC$, the additional amount $BC$ coming from the new firms. The long-run supply curve of the industry is $S_L$, drawn through the points of equilibrium of $D_1$ and $S_1$, and $D_2$ and $S_2$. Should the demand increase again, firms would temporarily expand once more. When the dust would settle on the new long-run equilibrium, it would be found farther to the right on the horizontal line $S_L$.

### Increasing-Cost Industries

In increasing-cost industries, external diseconomies prevail. The expansion of such industries causes the cost curves of the firms to be pushed up. The rise in costs makes the long-run supply curve slope upward to the right.

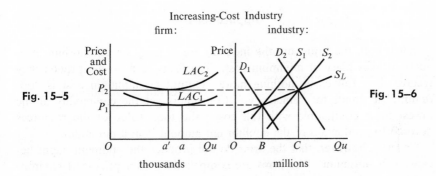

**Fig. 15–5**                                                                      **Fig. 15–6**

Figures 15–5 and 15–6 help to tell the story. Initial equilibrium of the firm and the industry is at price $OP_1$. Each firm produces $Oa$; all of them together produce the industry output of $OB$. Then let long-run demand increase from $D_1$ to $D_2$. The price goes up; firms expand along their $SMC$ curves; new firms enter; and the short-run industry supply curve shifts to the right. But costs rise. The cost curve $LAC_1$ is pushed up. In Figure 15–5, the new and higher cost curve is $LAC_2$. Thus the additional output from the new firms does not eventually cause price to go back down to $OP_1$, but only down to $OP_2$, which is the new and higher equilibrium price. The long-run supply curve $S_L$ therefore slopes upward to the right.

In Figure 15–5, the new and higher cost curve $LAC_2$ is drawn so that its minimum point corresponds to the output $Oa'$. This is a smaller equilibrium output. The higher costs force the firms to shrink a little in size. But this result is not necessary. Much depends on what the higher costs are and how the firms can adjust to them.

### Decreasing-Cost Industries

Similar reasoning and similarly constructed diagrams can show that external economies cause the cost curves of firms to fall and that therefore the long-run supply curve of the industry slopes downward to the right.

Some economic theorists have objected to the idea that an industry can have a downward sloping supply curve. The objections come in two groups. First, the importance of external economies is belittled; along with this goes the assertion that external diseconomies are always present and always have a heavier weight. An industry can expand only by bidding resources away from other industries; it can bid resources away only by paying higher prices. Secondly, some theorists say that if long-run supply curves slope downward, the stability of the equilibrium can be in doubt. The question of the stability of equilibrium is discussed later, in Chapter 18.

### Applications

When both the firms and the industry are in long-run equilibrium, production takes place at minimum cost. The firms earn no net profits; they receive their full costs, nothing more. Output at minimum cost is "optimum;" it stands for "efficiency." Consumers get the commodity at the lowest price compatible with full costs; the total value of the resources devoted to production of the equilibrium amount is at a minimum.

Observe, however, that the firms do not produce the optimum ouput because it is optimum. The firms are compelled by their price-cost environment to produce that output. In trying to maximize their net profits, the firms find themselves — in equilibrium — earning zero net profits while producing optimum outputs. If they did anything else, they would lose money.

Remember too the limitations surrounding the doctrine that, in the long run, price equals minimum cost. Competition must be pure and also perfect enough that the firms can make their full adjustments. The doctrine assumes away the effects of technological changes. Tastes and technology hold still long enough for the horizontal line of demand to the individual firms to become tangent to the minimum points on their $U$-shaped cost curves.

If the long-run equilibrium price is to be regarded as an unequivocal optimum, two more conditions must hold. Both are discussed more fully in Chapter 17. They can be mentioned briefly here. One of the conditions is that the minimum average cost, which equals the equilibrium price, is a full measure of *all* of the costs of producing the commodity. The other condition is that there be no gross disparity between the average incomes of the producers and the consumers. Many theorists would argue that if the producers are poor and the consumers are rich, or vice versa, the long-run equilibrium is not optimum.

Despite these limitations, the doctrine gives a standard of economic efficiency. As later chapters will show, the standard is used to measure the deviations from economic efficiency that occur in monopoly, monopolistic competition, and oligopoly.

### Summary

The doctrine of *long-run equilibrium price* in pure competition applies to the growth of an industry, to the fullest mutual adjustment of demand and supply. In the long run, the firm adjusts its output and the scale of its plant so as to equate long-run marginal cost with price. If price is such that the firms in an industry earn net profits, new firms enter the industry. All firms have the same costs because payments for scarce resources have the effect of equalizing the long-run average costs of firms. When the industry is in equilibrium, each of the firms is in equilibrium, with $P = MR = LMC = LAC$. Output is at minimum cost. As an industry grows in response to higher prices caused by increased demand, the firms can be subject to *external economies or diseconomies,* which cause their costs to fall or to rise. For a *constant-cost industry,* the long-run supply curve is horizontal at the level of the minimum average costs of the firms. For an *increasing-cost industry,* the long-run supply curve is positively sloped, showing rising minimum average costs of the firms owing to the presence of external diseconomies. A *decreasing-cost industry* has a negatively sloped supply curve owing to external economies. Subject to certain qualifications, the long-run equilibrium of the firms and the industry in pure competition is a condition of optimum economic efficiency.

## SELECTED REFERENCES

Alfred Marshall, *Principles of Economics,* 8th ed. (London: Macmillan, 1920), Book V. Joan Robinson, *The Economics of Imperfect Competition* (London: Macmillan, 1933), Book III.

George J. Stigler, *The Theory of Price,* rev. ed. (New York: Macmillan, 1952), Chap. 10.

From George J. Stigler and Kenneth E. Boulding, eds., *Readings in Price Theory* (Homewood: Irwin, 1952): Jacob Viner, "Cost Curves and Supply Curves;" Joan Robinson, "Rising Supply Price;" and Howard S. Ellis and William Fellner, "External Economies and Diseconomies."

## EXERCISES AND PROBLEMS

1. Draw the diagrams for the firm and the industry for decreasing-cost industries.

2. Does long-run cost *determine* price? Explain.

3. Suppose a competitive industry were given a permanent subsidy in the form of payments for each unit produced by each firm. Draw diagrams to show what would happen to the price.

4. The price of a jacket is always higher than the price of trousers of the same quality. Why?

5. Draw diagrams to show the effects of technological improvements on long-run price.

6. Compare and contrast the relations between prices and costs in the market period, the short run, and the long run.

# Price Interdependence

## and General Equilibrium

# 16

RELATIONS BETWEEN THE PRICES OF TWO COMMODITIES ·
EQUILIBRIUM BETWEEN TWO MARKETS · THE THEORY OF GENERAL
EQUILIBRIUM · USES OF GENERAL EQUILIBRIUM THEORY ·

So far, prices have been studied one at a time, each in isolation. The price of any one commodity is of course influenced by the prices of other commodities. Other prices have been let into analysis only to help fix the shapes and positions of demand and supply curves. Once being admitted, other prices have been held constant by assumption and could then be ignored. Besides, attention has been paid only to the prices of commodities closely related to the commodity under analysis. Such is the method of partial equilibrium theory, the method long followed by American and British theorists. Partial equilibrium theory is simple; it also has the great advantage of giving results applicable to a great range of uses. Partial equilibrium theory is applied in industry studies, in analyses of foreign trade and the taxation of individual commodities, and in investigations of price-support programs for farm products.

But prices are in fact interdependent. The demands, supplies, and prices of commodities are interconnected — through the substitutions that households make in their budgets and in their sales of productive services; prices are connected also through the substitutions that firms make in their purchases of inputs and in their sales of outputs. When the theorist turns his attention to the behavior of the entire system of prices, he uses the method of general equilibrium theory. Although this method is nearly a century old, it was cultivated for many decades solely by a small number of theorists on the continent of Europe. Only since just before World War II have American and British economists become interested in general equilibrium theory.

The interdependence of prices will now be examined in steps. First comes an analysis of the relations between the prices of two related commodities. Then comes a description of the equilibrium between two related markets. After this comes a presentation of a simple model of the general equilibrium of prices in an economy with pure competition in all of its markets.

### Relations Between the Prices of Two Commodities

Commodities and services are either substitutes for each other or else they are complements. The common relation between two or more commodities is that of substitution. Complementary commodities exist here and there in clusters. Much depends on how broadly or narrowly commodities are defined. If the definitions are narrow, so that there are tens of thousands of commodities, the complementary relation is widespread. But if definitions are broad, the complementary relation tends to disappear and all commodities tend to become substitutes.

The relations between the prices of two related commodities are more complex than might at first be supposed. The analysis of the relations can be tricky. Since commodities can be substitutes or complements on both the demand and supply sides of markets, there are four relations to be handled in the simplest treatment possible. The four are: (1) Two commodities are substitutes on the demand side, i.e., to consumers. (2) They are complements on the demand side. (3) They are substitutes, or rivals, on the supply side. (4) The two commodities are complements on the supply side.

The analysis to follow assumes pure competition in commodity markets. This means that the mutual responses of demand, supply, and price are clear and definite. A similar analysis can be made for commodities produced under conditions of monopoly and imperfect competition, but such an analysis yields less precise results. Demand and supply here are short run.

#### Substitutes on the Demand Side

When two commodities are substitutes to the buyers, a rise in the price of one of them causes the price of the other commodity to rise. Assume at first that the markets for both commodities, $A$ and $B$, are in equilibrium.

Obviously, if the demands for both goods increase, their prices will rise. But if the demand for $A$ alone increases, the resulting rise in the price of $A$ causes the demand for $B$ to expand, thus forcing up the price of $B$ also. Suppose, however, that there is no initial change in the demands for $A$ and $B$. Let a disturbance come from the supply side. Imagine that the supply of $A$ decreases, so that the price of $A$ goes up. The demand for $B$, being dependent on the price of $A$ as well as upon other things, then increases, and up goes the price of $B$.

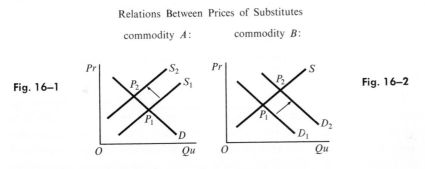

Relations Between Prices of Substitutes

commodity $A$:              commodity $B$:

Fig. 16–1                                        Fig. 16–2

Figures 16–1 and 16–2 illustrate the tendency of the prices of substitutes to rise together, even if no initial change in demand occurs. Figure 16–1 shows how a decline in supply, from $S_1$ to $S_2$, raises the equilibrium price of commodity $A$. In Figure 16–2, the accompanying expansion of the demand, i.e., from $D_1$ to $D_2$, of commodity $B$ raises its price. The demand curve $D_1$ for commodity $B$ is associated with $P_1$ of commodity $A$; similarly, $D_2$ is associated with $P_2$. The two changes in price need not of course be equal or even proportional. How the prices change depends on how close $A$ and $B$ are as substitutes and how strong a force is the decline in supply.

## Complements on the Demand Side

When two commodities are complements to the buyers, a rise in one price can cause a fall in the other price. Let $C$ and $D$ be complements. Once more imagine a disturbance on the supply side. Suppose that the supply of $C$ is reduced. The price of $C$ rises, and at the higher equilibrium price, less is bought. Therefore, less of the complement $D$ is wanted. Thus the demand for $D$ falls, causing a decline in the price of $D$. Figures 16–3 and 16–4 display these changes. The reverse would happen if the supply of $C$ would increase: The price of $C$ would fall; more would be bought, causing an increase in the demand for $D$ and a rise in its price. Notice that the opposite movements of the price of complements occurs when the change begins on the supply side. Obviously, both prices would go up and down together if the demand for both commodities together would increase or decrease.

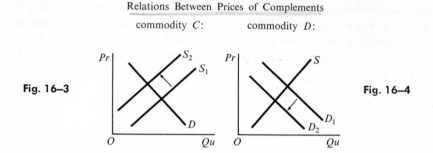

Relations Between Prices of Complements

commodity $C$:                    commodity $D$:

Fig. 16–3                                                                    Fig. 16–4

### Rivals on the Supply Side

The behavior of the two commodities that are rivals on the supply side parallels that of substitutes on the demand side. The two prices move up and down together. The two commodities are $E$ and $F$. Their production requires the same resources, so that if more go into one, fewer are available for the other. Let a disturbance come now from the demand. Suppose the demand for $E$ increases. At the resulting higher price, more of $E$ is produced. Therefore the supply of $F$ is reduced, causing the price of $F$ to go up.

### Joint Supply

When two commodities are complements on the supply side, they are said to be produced under conditions of joint supply. The larger the output of one commodity, the larger the output of the other, for some natural reason. Examples are wheat and straw, beef and hides, soda ash and calcium chloride. The proportions in which the two commodities are produced can be variable or fixed. Wool and mutton are the standard examples of variable proportions. In the long run, ranchers can change breeds so as to produce either more wool or more mutton. In the short run, they can sell more or fewer sheep for slaughter, thus altering the proportions of the flow of mutton and wool to the market. When proportions are variable, the marginal cost of each commodity can be calculated. If $G$ and $H$ are joint products, and if proportions are altered so as to produce more of $G$, the extra costs of the alteration can be matched against the extra output of $G$. Therefore, meaningful supply curves can be derived from the firm's marginal costs when proportions are variable. When, however, proportions are fixed, it is better to regard one of the commodities, at least in the short run, as a byproduct that is thrown on the market to sell for whatever it will bring. When this is so, the supply curve of the byproduct is perfectly in-elastic. Suppose now that the demand for the main product increases. Its price and its volume of output both rise. So too does the output of the byproduct. If there is no change in the demand for the byproduct, its price falls. With joint supply, then, it is possible for the two prices to move in opposite directions.

## Equilibrium between Two Markets

When reflective consumers or businessmen talk about pairs or groups of prices, they often say that the prices in question are in line or are not in line. Everyone's experience with prices, as a buyer or a seller, or both, tells him that the price of, say, L is normally above the price of M. If then he sees the price of L go down below the price of M, he expects it to come back up again and resume its normal level. All that has been said so far in this chapter is that a change in one price causes other prices to change. But what of the alignment of prices?

Equilibrium Between Two Prices

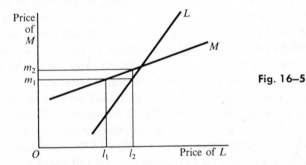

Fig. 16–5

Here too, J. R. Hicks has given an explicit treatment of the equilibrium *between* two competitive markets. This equilibrium is separate from the two equilibria *within* each market. Figure 16–5 illustrates these matters. This kind of diagram is new. The horizontal axis measures the price of a commodity L; the vertical axis shows the price of M. The two commodities are substitutes. Notice that both axes measure prices. Any point in the field stands for a pair of prices. The line L shows the equilibrium prices of L corresponding to all possible prices, whether equilibrium or not, of M. Similarly, the line M shows the equilibrium prices of M corresponding to all possible prices of L. Both lines are straight, simply for convenience. The point of intersection of lines L and M signifies the pair of prices where each is in equilibrium and both are in equilibrium together. Neither price exerts any influence on the other to cause it to rise or to fall. Suppose now that some transitory influence momentarily depresses the price of $L$. Let the price of $L$ fall to $Ol_1$. Then the reaction from the market for $M$ comes into play. The price of $Ol_1$ for $L$ causes the price of $M$ to fall to $Om_1$; this result is obtained by reading off the $M$ curve. The next reaction comes from the $M$ market on the $L$ market. The price $Om_1$ causes the price of $L$ to rise to $Ol_2$, which forces the price of $M$ to $Om_2$. So it goes, until the point of intersection is reached and the reactions cease.

### The Theory of General Equilibrium

When all prices are viewed as dependent upon one another, the theory of prices becomes general equilibrium theory. The French economist Léon Walras (1834–1910) was the first to design a model of the general equilibrium of a purely competitive economy. Others have constructed refinements of Walras's model, but no radical modifications have yet been made. Walras's general equilibrium model is simple, that is to say, the economic ideas that are its building blocks are simple; modern versions of them have been presented earlier in this book. But the building blocks are put together mathematically. To a mathematician, Walras's mathematics are not complex. But full and easy understanding of the mathematics of the general equilibrium of prices is denied to most students of economics. It is indeed quite possible to simplify the mathematics too; see Note 4 in the Appendix to Part Four. The references at the end of this chapter show where other simple versions can be found. But those who need such simplification still have trouble with the algebra and can hardly benefit much from it. The description of Walras's model now to follow is literary — a word used with scorn by the Italian economist Vilfredo Pareto (1848–1923), who also contributed to the mathematics of general equilibrium theory. The mathematics gives a vision of the interdependence of prices that is clear, precise in detail, complete, and self-checking in its logical consistency. Though the view opened by a literary exposition is a little cloudy, it is better than none at all.

Walras's model has households and firms in a self-contained economy. Pure competition prevails in all markets whose prices connect the actions of all households and firms. The firms sell commodities to the households which, in turn, sell resources, or factors of production (i.e., labor, the services of land and of equipment), to the firms. There is no unemployment of labor or of other resources.

### Households

The tastes of the households, or consumers, are assumed to be constant. Each household buys quantities of each commodity in accordance with tastes, income, the price of the commodity, and the prices of *all* other commodities. This last point is the special emphasis of general equilibrium theory. In buying any one commodity, a household assesses *all* commodity prices. A change in any one of them affects the entire budget, causing the household to reappraise and to rearrange it. For example, a rise in the price of shoes causes a change in a household's demand for butter. This is clear enough because the household buys both shoes and butter. But the higher price of shoes is traceable to changes in the prices of other commodities, those the household does not buy. In this sense, then, a household's demand for any one commodity depends on the prices of all commodities. Of course, many of the repercussions from the other prices are exceedingly small.

The households in Walras's model spend their entire incomes on consumption. Their incomes are derived from the sale of their resources, which also have prices. Thus each household's budget is also determined by the prices of resources. Any one household sells one or two resources, perhaps several of them. A change in the price of one resource causes a change in the price of another, because households can make substitutions in their capacities as sellers, just as they can in their capacities as buyers. Thus the prices of resources are connected in a network.

The demands of households for commodities depend, accordingly, on two networks of prices. One is the network of the prices of commodities; the other is the network of the prices of resources. The two networks are connected through the actions of the households.

The market, or total, demand for each commodity is the sum of the demands of the households. The market demands, of course, also depend on the same two networks of prices.

### Firms

The commodities produced by the firms sell at prices equal to full costs of production, because pure competition exists everywhere and because the context is the full adjustment of the long run. Unit costs are constant in the simple Walrasian model. Thus average costs and marginal costs are equal and constant. Because this also means constant returns to scale, the price of each commodity is the sum of its cost components. They are the amounts of each resource needed to make a unit of the commodity multiplied by the prices of the resources. Thus if a suit of clothes requires 10 minutes of one kind of labor at $3 an hour, 15 minutes of another kind at $4 an hour, etc., the price of a suit of clothes is equal to $0.50 plus $1.00, plus etc. In this example, the 10 minutes of one kind of labor and the 15 minutes of another kind are called *coefficients of production*. In the simple model, they are assumed to be fixed.

As suppliers, the firms govern their actions by the prices in the network of commodity prices. As buyers of resources, the firms govern their actions by the prices in the network of resource prices, which along with the coefficients of production determines the costs of the firms. The two networks are therefore also connected by the actions of the firms.

### Equalities of Demands and Supplies

There being no unemployment in the model, the demand for each *resource* must equal its supply. The demand comes from the firms, supply from the households. The network of resource prices is a set of prices making each demand equal to each supply, and making all of them compatible with one another. Each resource market is in equilibrium; all together are in a general equilibrium.

The demand for each *commodity* equals its supply. The demand comes from the households, supply from the firms. The network of commodity prices establishes an equilibrium in each market and the compatibilities of the equilibria in all commodity markets.

Because the two networks of prices are doubly interconnected, the equilibria in the resource markets and in the commodity markets are joined in one grand general equilibrium.

In the general equilibrium of all prices, demands equal supplies, and all households and firms are in equilibrium. For each household, the marginal utility of each commodity equals its price (Chapter 4). Alternatively, the ratio of the prices of any two commodities equals their marginal rates of substitution (Chapter 6). For each household, the marginal rate of substitution between income and leisure is equal to the price ratio between income and work (Chapter 13). For each firm, the marginal cost of each commodity equals its price (Chapters 10 and 15). For each firm, costs are at a minimum (Chapters 10 and 15).

The essence of general equilibrium is that the tastes of the households and the technologies available to the firms mutually determine the quantities of the commodities produced.

How do all the equalities of demands and supplies come about? Walras himself described the reaching of general equilibrium as a process of "groping." Imagine that the price of commodity $A$ is out of equilibrium, that the price is below the equilibrium level in the market for $A$. Then the excess of demand at that price forces the price of $A$ up. But — and here is the emphasis of general equilibrium theory — the rise in the price of $A$ causes an expansion of the demands for $B$, for $C$, etc. Besides, the rise in the price of $A$ causes a decline in the supplies of a whole group of other commodities. Therefore, other prices change too, and these changes reflect back on the demand for $A$ and the supply of $A$. During the process of groping, the price of $A$ may fall for a while. But in the end, it dances its way up to its own equilibrium, one that is consistent with those in all other markets. The simplifying assumptions in the model, and above all, Walras's mathematics, ensure this result. True enough, many of the changes in other demands, supplies, and prices that are caused by a change in the price of $A$ are exceedingly small. They are so small that for some purposes they can be ignored, just as partial equilibrium theory ignores them. The comprehensive mathematical equations do not, however, ignore small changes; they embrace the small and the large, tracing and relating all effects to the end.

### Limitations of the Model

Any model has its limitations. The simplified Walrasian model described here has several, even as a model of an economy with pure competition in all markets. The model is static — it operates with the assumptions of fixed tastes and coefficients of production, and allows for no processes of change over time. The households and the firms in the model are busy enough, but they everlastingly consume and produce exactly the same things, in exactly the same way, and in exactly the same proportions. There are no leads and lags in the relations between production and consumption, between demand, supply, and price. Everything happens instantaneously, as in electric circuits. But the efforts of theorists to construct good models of dynamic systems of relative prices have not yet been successful. Hicks and others have gone a little beyond Walras because they have investigated the "stability" conditions of the general equilibrium of prices.[1] They have developed the theory of what happens when changes occur in interlinked demands, supplies, and prices.

The simple model has other but less serious limitations. The assumption of fixed production coefficients can be removed, and, in much more intricate models, replaced with an assumption of variable coefficients. More complicated models can also be constructed to contain increasing and decreasing returns to scale, money and securities, and even certain forms of imperfect competition.

### Uses of General Equilibrium Theory

Despite their limitations, despite their air of unreality, models — even the simplest — of the general equilibrium of prices have important uses.

Such models advance the understanding of a private enterprise economy. Most of the praise and the blame strewn on private enterprise consists of

---

[1] The stability of competitive partial equilibria is discussed in Chapter 18.

repetition of phrases so worn as to retain little meaning. Those who praise private enterprise point to its efficiency, to the tendency for costs of production to be low, to the responsiveness of production to the wants of consumers. Those who have found serious fault with private enterprise include socialists and communists; they have long argued that private enterprise means production for profit, not for use, and that a private-enterprise economy is a chaotic and unplanned system.

The simple general equilibrium model is a model of a private enterprise system at rest, all of the consumers and producers having made their best adjustments. The model shows indeed that production is both efficient and responsive, and that the satisfaction of consumers' wants is maximized. In the domain of the discussion of economic and social philosophies and systems, the general equilibrium model is the strongest of the serious arguments for private enterprise and against collectivism. But remember, maximum satisfaction means no more than the maximum attainable under the circumstances, whatever they might be. The economy might be poor, with meager resources, a primitive technology, and an ill-trained labor force. But with free markets and the eager pursuit of self-interest, the poor economy would still approach the maximization of the satisfaction of the wants of its consumers.

The maximum satisfaction of consumers' wants is equivalent to maximum economic welfare, the meaning of economic welfare here being *efficiency*. When efficiency is at a maximum, as in the general equilibrium model, no resources are wasted; there cannot be more production of any one good without less production of another; and one household cannot consume more unless another consumes less. In contrast, economic welfare can also mean *equity*. That is, economic welfare can also be made to depend on the distribution of personal incomes. This meaning of economic welfare is discussed in Chapter 4 (pages 60, 61) which shows that some economists use the idea of utility to propose a redistribution of income with the aim of increasing economic welfare. Most modern economists, however, take the position that equity cannot be a proper subject of economic analysis because judgments as to equity are ethical or political judgments. Thus they leave equity up in the air, confining themselves to the narrow meaning of economic welfare as efficiency.

The general equilibrium model does achieve efficiency. It could be sadly lacking in equity because nothing in the model prevents some households from having enormous incomes and others from being ragged and hungry. The next chapter will go farther into this matter.

Some admirers of private enterprise might not like the fate of businessmen in the model. The entrepreneurs in Walras's model are drones. They control no prices; they exert no power over other persons; they fulfill no social responsibilities. In their efforts to maximize profits, they are able to earn no more than the normal profits included in their full costs. They are compelled by the system of prices to be efficient, to produce at the lowest attainable costs. In fact, if their singular function is to be innovators and risk takers, entrepreneurs do not exist at all in Walras's model. Neither do labor leaders.

General equilibrium theory has furnished the conceptual foundation for *input-output analysis* which was created by Wassily Leontief of Harvard University. Input-output analysis is the statistical measurement of the inputs and the outputs of all industries taken together in an interdependent system of commodity flows. Input-output has been developed far, lending itself well to planning for mobilization and to planning for the economic development of countries and regions.

Another use of general equilibrium theory is to give standards of efficiency for the welfare of the whole economy. The end of the preceding chapter mentions the use of the long-run competitive equilibrium as a standard for one industry, subject to certain qualifications. The same qualifications apply to the general equilibrium as a general standard of welfare. The next chapter goes into these matters.

### Summary

The prices of substitutes and of complements are interdependent. A rise in the price of a commodity causes an increase in the demand for its substitutes, and therefore advances their prices. But a rise in the price of a commodity can cause a fall in the prices of its complements. Similarly, the prices of commodities that are rivals on the supply side tend to go up and down together. The prices of commodities produced under conditions of joint supply can, however, move in opposite directions. The equilibrium prices of two commodities are aligned through the connections between their two markets. In the general equilibrium model, the demands of households for commodities depend on the prices of all commodities and of all resources. The supplies of commodities from firms depend on commodity prices, the coefficients of production, and the prices of resources. The demand for each commodity equals its supply, all demands and supplies being compatible because of their interconnections through the networks of prices. The general equilibrium model gives a standard of economic efficiency.

### SELECTED REFERENCES

On the relations between the prices of two competitively produced commodities: Alfred Marshall, *Principles of Economics,* 8th ed. (London: Macmillan, 1920), Book V, Chap. 6.

Even those with little mathematics can benefit from Léon Walras, *Elements of Pure Economics,* translated by William Jaffe and published for the American Economic Association and the Royal Economic Society (Homewood: Irwin, 1954). A modern version of static general equilibrium theory is contained in J. R. Hicks, *Value and Capital,* 2d ed. (London: Oxford, 1946), Chap. 8. An extensive treatment of the economics and mathematics of general equilibrium is to be found in Robert Dorfman, Paul A. Samuelson, and Robert M. Solow, *Linear Programming and Economic Analysis* (New York: McGraw-Hill, 1958), Chap. 13.

Several writers have expounded general-equilibrium theory with mathematics simple enough for anyone who remembers a little algebra. Among these are: Gustav Cassel, *The Theory of Social Economy,* translated by Joseph McCabe (New York: Harcourt Brace, 1924), Chap. 4; George J. Stigler, *The Theory of Price,* rev. ed. (New York: Macmillan, 1952), Chap. 16; John F. Due and Robert W. Clower, *Intermediate Economic Analysis,* 4th ed. (Homewood: Irwin, 1961), Chap. 20.

## EXERCISES AND PROBLEMS

1. Draw demand and supply diagrams to accompany the discussion of two-commodity price relations on pages 248 to 249.

2. Draw demand and supply diagrams showing the reverse of the exposition on pages 247 to 248. That is, where the text has a rise in price, show what happens when price falls.

3. Figure 16–5 on page 249 shows how the price of commodity $L$, after falling, is forced up to the joint equilibrium level by reactions between the $L$ and $M$ markets. Suppose that the price of $M$ rises. With a diagram like Figure 16–5, show how the price of $M$ is forced down again to the joint equilibrium level.

4. Take the general equilibrium model as the starting point. Then trace the effects of (a) one consumer's action in modifying his purchases because his tastes change; (b) one person's action in deciding not to work any more and to live on his relatives; and (c) one technological improvement.

# Applications of the Theory

# of Competitive Pricing

## 17

PRICE FIXING • THE PRICES OF FARM PRODUCTS • ECONOMIC
WELFARE • PRICING IN A SOCIALIST ECONOMY • MAINTAINING
COMPETITION •

Some of the applications of the theory of competitive pricing have
already been described. More are now to come. The theory does not of
course furnish immediate solutions. Practical problems always pose the
difficult tasks of getting and interpreting facts. The contribution of theory
is to give tools and methods of analysis, to provide a logical way of thinking
about problems. Theory tells what facts to look for and how to organize
them.

Applications of the theory of competitive pricing fall into two broad
classes. The theory of short-run prices casts light on the economic policies
of governments in fixing and influencing the prices of individual commodities. The theory of long-run prices gives standards for judging the
performance of the economy and for possible ways and means of improving
its performance.

### Price Fixing

The federal, state, and local governments engage in many forms of price
fixing. For the most part, price fixing by government is confined to monopolistic and to oligopolistic industries — transportation, electric power,

natural gas, telephone service, etc. But there is also some price fixing in industries that can be analyzed with the competitive model. Price fixing, i.e., the establishment of definite prices, must be distinguished from activities designed to raise or lower the prices determined by demand and supply in free markets. In practice, price fixing means that a government agency sets either maximum or minimum prices.

### Maximum Prices

Maximum prices are imposed either as one of many economic controls in a period of national emergency or as a means of redistributing income from one group of persons to another. Wartime price controls are one prominent example; peacetime rent controls are another.

To become a problem, a maximum price must necessarily lie *below* the equilibrium price of the commodity or service in question, that is, of course, the equilibrium price that would prevail in the absence of price control. In the past, the common method of fixing maximum prices was to declare them to be the prices actually being paid and received on a given date. To pay or receive higher prices after that date was unlawful.

Figure 17–1 gives a simplified illustration. Initially, $D_1$ and $S$ are demand and supply, both in the short run. Suppose that consumption and production are in equilibrium at $A$; the equilibrium price is therefore $P_m$.

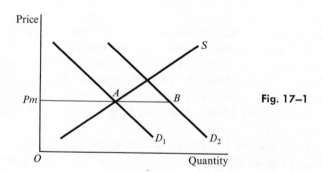

Fig. 17–1

Imagine that this price is declared to be the maximum. Then imagine that demand increases to $D_2$, the supply curve remaining constant. Production is still $P_m A$, but would-be consumption at this price is $P_m B$. Therefore, the unfilled demand, i.e., the shortage, is the quantity $AB$.

The size of the shortage when the maximum price is below the equilibrium price depends on the changes in demand and in supply, and upon their elasticities. If the shortage is not handled by the imposition of perfectly enforced rationing on the buyers, a black market is likely to spring into life. Black markets are always and everywhere the result of the setting of maximum prices by governments. An analytical question is this: Is the black-market price identical with the equilibrium price? It could be if the government made little effort to enforce its maximum, if buyers and sellers alike unhesitatingly flouted the government, and if they had the same information in the black market as in the formerly free market. The black-market price could, however, be below the equilibrium price if buyers or sellers, or both, were unwilling or afraid to trade in the black market. This can be shown by drawing black-market demand and supply curves, above the maximum price, each one to the left of the ordinary curves. Their point of intersection could, though it need not, lie below the equilibrium level.

To use the model of pure competition for the rental dwelling market is, perhaps, going a little too far. Though they are far from homogeneous, dwellings can be lumped together as "housing" in a broad-brush treatment. Rent controls are also maximum prices. They too cause shortages and networks of little black markets. In some countries, rent controls have been kept in force so long that they dried up long-run supply, i.e., the construction of new dwellings. Typically in such countries, governments have had to undertake public housing projects of great size.

So far emphasis has fallen on the excess of demand over supply at the maximum price. What of the effects of maximum prices on supply? One possible effect is to cause production of particular commodities to fall to low levels or to dry up altogether. Supply curves are interdependent. Suppose a group of competitive firms produce commodities $A$, $B$, and $C$. Imagine that the maximum prices are imposed in conditions of disequilibrium for the prices of $A$, $B$, and $C$, and that the firms were shifting resources from $A$ and $B$ to $C$ because the price of $C$ had become unusually profitable. With the imposition of maximum prices, $C$ is still profitable; resources keep on being transferred to it, away from $A$ and $B$, whose supply curves shift so far to the left that production virtually ceases.

Sometimes in the past, two maximum prices have been fixed for an industry, a lower one for the low-cost producers and a higher one for the high-cost producers. This policy was followed for commodities the government wanted produced in large quantities, even the small output of the high-cost producers being wanted. The reason for the two prices was to avoid large profits for the low-cost producers.

## Minimum Prices

When a government agency sets a minimum price for a competitively produced commodity, the result is nearly always a "surplus" of the commodity. The surplus is often called "overproduction," but this means nothing more than the excess of supply over demand *at* the minimum price.

When it results in a surplus, a minimum price is *above* the equilibrium of demand and supply. The size of the surplus depends on the gap between the minimum and the equilibrium prices and on the elasticities of demand and supply. If the minimum price is maintained at a constant figure, the size of the surplus varies from period to period as demand and supply change. In some periods, the equilibrium price may rise above the minimum so that the surplus temporarily disappears.

The disposal of a surplus is always a problem. The government agency fixing a minimum price must take some action to keep the excess supply off the market, for otherwise the minimum price cannot be made effective. One technique is for the government agency to buy and hold the surplus quantities of the commodity. Or, government can buy and destroy the surplus. Occasionally, surplus foodstuffs have been rendered physically unfit for human consumption by deliberate action. Another technique for handling the surplus resulting from a minimum price is to divert the surplus quantity to other markets. Milk is an example. In many areas of the United States, the federal government lends its auspices to the establishment of minimum prices for fluid milk. The surplus milk, whose amount has a strong seasonal fluctuation, is diverted to the markets where milk is converted into butter, cheese, ice cream, and other products.

The fixing of a minimum price, even when the control is fully effective, does not prevent the price system from working. Suppose that a minimum price is established well above the equilibrium level and that through production controls and the cooperation of the producers, there is no surplus to be disposed of. If demand increases, there are repercussions on other prices even if the fixed price is held at the same level.

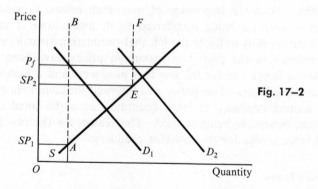

Fig. 17–2

Consider Figure 17–2. The demand is $D_1$, the short-run supply is $S$, and the price is fixed at $P_f$. The production controls cause the effective supply curve to be $SAB$, meaning that no more is actually produced than can be sold at the fixed price $P_f$. Then let demand increase to $D_2$. The effective supply curve becomes *SEF*. More is produced. As a result, less of other commodities is produced. Therefore, their prices tend to rise. The effect here is similar to the price interdependence on the supply side reviewed on page 248. In Figure 17–2, $SP_1$ is a "shadow price." With the increase in demand, the shadow price rises to $SP_2$. The increase in the shadow price, therefore, is the force causing *other* prices to tend to rise, even though the fixed price is kept at the same level.

### The Prices of Farm Products

The prices of most farm products are still determined in free markets that are close to the model of pure competition. For about half of all farm products, price "support" programs of one kind or another have been in operation. The programs differ among themselves and undergo continual modification. But, in general, it can be said that the federal government tries to raise farm prices by manipulating demand and supply.

Just *why* the federal government wants to raise some farm prices is a question too complicated to go into here. The price theory covered in this book can, however, throw some light on two of the causes of federal intervention. One cause is the extreme instability of farm prices over time. Most of that instability can be explained by the inelasticity of both the demand and the supply for farm products singly and collectively. Changes in demand and supply, when both are inelastic, cause sharp fluctuations in price. To see this, the reader can easily imagine the diagram or draw one for himself (or turn back to Figure 14–5 on page 223).

Another cause of federal intervention to raise farm prices is that adjustments on the supply side are comparatively slow. To say this is really to repeat that over periods of two to five years, supply is highly inelastic. To change from one crop to another, to alter the sizes of herds of animals, to raise fruit trees to maturity — all these and similar adjustments do take time. Such slow adjustments are obviously not peculiar to agriculture; they exist in mining and in other branches of the economy where fixed equipment is highly specialized. But, somehow, the difficulties of farmers in adjusting to changing prices command more attention and more sympathy.

Federal efforts to increase farm prices work on both the demand and supply sides. When they are successful, the efforts push demand curves to the right and supply curves to the left. Though in general little can be done to increase the demand for farm products, research is carried on to find new uses and markets for them. Only occasionally does it result in major changes for a particular product; a leading example was the introduction of frozen orange-juice concentrate which came out of federally sponsored research. On the supply side, federal policies tend to work at cross purposes. On the one hand, applied research, education, and related activities have the effect, over longer periods, of increasing supply by improving productivity, that is, by changing farmers' production functions. On the other hand, acreage allotments, marketing quotas, and other techniques of control cause short-period reductions in the supplies of the crops they are applied to. As is well known, however, reductions in acreage hardly ever cause proportionate reductions in output, because farmers take out their poorer acres and fertilize the remaining ones more heavily.

Because price-support policies apply to only about one-half of all farm products and because a few of these get much stronger support than others, the *relative* prices of farm products are changed by the actions of the federal government. Over the years, farmers shift production into the crops whose prices are raised and away from those crops whose prices receive either no support or only occasional and feeble support. The changes in *relative* prices, therefore, cause shifts in the allocation of farm resources. Two results follow. One is that "the farm problem" becomes worse — as supply curves of the favored crops shift to the right, the surpluses the government must acquire become ever larger, and the difficulties of keeping the prices up become ever greater. The other result is that land, labor, fertilizer, machinery, etc. are devoted in larger proportions to the favored crops with the higher prices.

How should the reallocation of farm resources be judged? Economists give no single answer to this question. For one thing, there is disagreement on how much reallocation has actually taken place. Let it be assumed here, however, that some reallocation has occurred and that the price-support policies have caused substantially different patterns of inputs and outputs, crop by crop, than would exist if the policies had never existed. Many economists condemn the reallocation because, they argue, it means a less "efficient" pattern of the use of resources. To argue this way is to assume that farm prices, without intervention, correspond at least roughly to the pattern of prices in the Walrasian model. Whether they do or not is difficult to say. The farm prices that can be observed are market prices; study of their behavior over the months and years gives some indication of their probable short-run equilibrium levels. Their long-run equilibrium levels cannot be measured or observed because demands, costs, and technology are continually changing.

### Methods of Subsidy

Much less controversy has prevailed on whether farmers should be subsidized somehow by the federal government. In general, the method of subsidy has been to raise prices; with inelastic demands for farm products, farmers' gross incomes are then higher. But this method is open to the objection, already noted, that resource allocation becomes less efficient.

Another method, usually called the Brannan plan, is a proposal to let farm prices be wholly free and to pay cash subsidies to farmers when free prices are "too low."

Consider Figure 17–3. Here are demand and supply for one farm commodity in one year. Demand is inelastic; supply is represented as perfectly inelastic to indicate that the farmers throw the whole crop on the

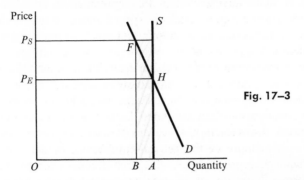

**Fig. 17–3**

market for whatever price it will bring. The equilibrium price is $OP_E$; let the support price be $OP_S$. For the support price to prevail, the government has to acquire the amount $BA$. The cost to the government is $BA$ multiplied by the support price, i.e., the rectangle $FA$. Under a policy like the Brannan plan, the price would be the equilibrium price, and the government would make up the difference. Each farmer would get a payment equal to $P_SP_E$ multiplied by the size of his own crop. The total cost to the government of this kind of subsidy would be the rectangle $P_SH$. Under the Brannan plan, the total payments by consumers are less, because they pay the lower equilibrium price and because their demand is inelastic. Under this plan, the cost to the government is higher, because under both methods, the gross income of the farmers is the same — the rectangle $P_SA$.

The higher cost to the government when the farmer is subsidized directly is not a necessarily strong argument against this method. The total cost to both consumers and taxpayers together is the same either way. But low-income consumers spend larger percentages of their incomes on food than do high-income consumers; low-income consumers pay smaller percentages of their incomes in taxes. It follows that the burden of the price-support program weighs more heavily on those with low incomes than does the burden of the direct-subsidy program.

### Economic Welfare

Later chapters describe the determination of prices and outputs in markets where monopoly and imperfect competition prevail. In general, prices and outputs in such markets achieve less economic welfare, i.e., less efficiency, than is possible under the given conditions of demand and cost. The standard of economic welfare as efficiency is taken from the long-run equilibrium in pure (and perfect) competition. This proposition is mentioned at the ends of both Chapters 15 and 16. It will now be discussed more fully, along with its qualifications and exceptions.

Theory more advanced than that contained in this book can give in elaborate and fine-spun detail the specifications of the "ideal output" that provides a maximum of economic welfare. Output is ideal if, given the scarcities and qualities of the resources, the consumers in the economy enjoy the maximum of satisfaction from the commodities produced with the resources. Any other composition of output, any other allocation of resources, would yield less satisfaction, would be less efficient.

The specifications can be stated independently of particular economic institutions. Conveniently, however, it happens that the specifications are identical with those of the general-equilibrium model, whose institutions are private enterprise, private property, freedom for producers and consumers, and the regime of universal pure competition. Again, the qualifications and exceptions have to be held in abeyance.

### The Marginal Conditions

The proof that the general-equilibrium output is ideal output usually takes the form of a review of "the marginal conditions." In much simplified form, here they are:

1. The first condition pertains to the allocation of commodities among consumers. All consumers pay the same prices for the same commodities. Each consumer makes his optimum — marginal — adjustment to each price.[1] This being so, consumers have no incentive to trade among themselves. That is, they cannot improve their satisfactions by trading. Therefore, when they all pay the same prices, the economic welfare of consumers must be at a maximum, so far as the actions of the consumers are concerned.

2. The second set of marginal conditions has to do with the maximum efficiency of production. All firms pay the same prices for the same inputs, or resources, and each firm makes its optimum — marginal — adjustment to each price. This being so, the value of the marginal physical product of an input must be the same for all firms. If it were not the same, total output (and economic welfare) in the economy could be increased by moving the input from where it is less (marginally) productive to where it

---

[1] The marginal rate of substitution for any two commodities must be the same for every person who consumes both.

is more productive. In plain language, this condition means that all firms have the same methods of production. Because, therefore, total output cannot be increased by shifts among the firms, its costs must be at a minimum.[2]

3. All firms receive the same prices for producing the same commodities, and each firm makes its — marginal — adjustment to each price. Marginal cost, minimum average cost, and price are all equal. Marginal cost to the firm equals marginal utility to the consumer because the price is the same to both. Take any two commodities A and B; in equilibrium each is produced in certain amounts. Why are these amounts proportioned so as to maximize economic welfare? Suppose one more unit of A is produced, and therefore one unit less of B. The extra unit of A has a marginal cost higher than its marginal utility. The unit of B that is sacrificed has a marginal cost less than its marginal utility. Therefore welfare has been lessened. It can be restored to its maximum by having both A and B produced and consumed in their equilibrium amounts.[3]

4. The fourth marginal condition has to do with the optimum adjustment of the supply of factors of production. For the same kinds of labor, all households receive the same rates of pay; each household makes its optimum — marginal — adjustment between work and leisure (Chapter 13).

The gist of the marginal conditions is that the last dollar of resources devoted to the production of each commodity yields the same utility to consumers. Utility cannot be increased by any transfer of resources.

For the marginal conditions to define an unequivocal maximum, rather than a minimum, marginal utilities must be declining, marginal costs must be rising, and marginal products must be declining. The relevant curves must be shaped like those earlier in this book.

The marginal conditions are all conditions of equilibrium. The several equilibria defining the optimum allocation of resources must be self-

---

[2] In the usual treatment, three marginal conditions hold for maximum efficiency in production. (1) The marginal rate of substitution between any two commodities they produce must be the same for any two firms that produce both. The firms receive the same prices; they must be at the same points on their production possibility curves (Chapter 10). If they are not, production can be increased by shifting it from less to more efficient firms. (2) The firms also pay the same prices. Therefore, the marginal rate of transformation between any input and any commodity must be the same for any two firms using the input and producing the commodity. In other words, each firm gets the same marginal product from each input. If this were not so, then again total output could be increased by shifting it among firms. (3) Similarly, each firm is at the same point on its isoquants. Because, etc.

[3] The marginal condition for the optimum adaptation of production to consumption is that the subjective marginal rate of substitution for any two commodities be equal to their marginal technical rates of substitution, i.e., an indifference curve is tangent to a production possibility curve. Equality of prices to producers and consumers, together with maximizing behavior, bring this about.

correcting, i.e., deviations from these equilibria are corrected by deliberate action of maximizing consumers and firms or by the excess of demand over supply or of supply over demand. Here is the question of the "stability" of equilibrium, one of the topics of Chapter 18.

### The Distribution of Income

Efficiency, however, is only one standard of economic welfare. As Chapter 16 shows, equity is another.

The simple Walrasian model of general equilibrium exhibits nothing specific about equity, i.e., about the distribution of incomes — the proportions of high, middle, and low incomes. Many different patterns of income distribution are indeed compatible with the model. Consider two possibilities: (1) The distribution of income could show an extreme inequality if the land, mineral resources, etc. were owned by a small number of households, if training and education were also possessed by few, and if the productive services of many households had relatively low prices. Thus the few would have high incomes and the many would have low incomes; the incomes of some households could be so low that they would have to subsist on private charity. (2) On the other hand, the distribution of income could be just moderately unequal if ownership of property were widespread, if differences in training and education were slight, and if all households possessed valuable productive services.

The equilibrium of universal pure competition yields *a* maximum of economic welfare (efficiency), accordingly, whatever the distribution of income. The economy with highly unequal incomes has *its* efficiency maximum, just as the economy with the moderately unequal incomes has *its* different efficiency maximum. If personal utilities are not comparable, as many theorists hold, the two maxima are not comparable. Can anything be said as to which is preferable? Here too, many theorists refuse to answer such a question because an answer seems to call for a statement as to the optimum combination of the standards of efficiency and equity, a combination yielding a maximum "social welfare." The main trouble is that economic logic cannot prescribe an ideal of equity — the best distribution of incomes. That is a task for social ethics and political theory. Despite all this, the position of most economic theorists is usually clear: On noneconomic grounds, they hasten to add, they favor more equity, i.e., less inequality in the distribution of incomes.

### Divergences between Private and Social Costs and Benefits

It is not far wrong to say that in the nineteenth century the question was *whether* government should intervene in the economy, and that by the middle of the twentieth century the question had become *how* government should intervene and *how far* it should go. Is there a principle or a rule that tells when government should intervene and when it should not?

The economic controls of government are exercised, of course, in the pursuit of several objectives. The only question here is the efficiency of private enterprise and whether that efficiency can be improved by government intervention.

The theory of welfare economics does have a principle of government action; it was first formulated by A. C. Pigou in his *Economics of Welfare*. Pigou's principle of intervention and of nonintervention is based on the presence or absence of divergences between the private and social costs and benefits associated with the competitive equilibrium.

Such divergences are the second major qualification to the proposition that competitive equilibrium achieves a maximum of economic efficiency.

Take an industry in long-run competitive equilibrium. Price equals minimum cost. Are *all* the costs included? Are there any other costs besides those incurred by the firms? Pigou's famous example is smoke. Suppose that the chimneys of the factories in an industry belch smoke that causes higher cleaning costs, higher medical costs, etc. to the people living in the same community. Ordinarily, these other costs are not borne by the firms operating the smoky chimneys. These other costs are not contained in the cost curves of the firms owning the factories. The cost curves exhibit the private costs. Social costs are private costs plus the other costs falling on other persons. If the industry had to bear its social costs, the cost curves of the firms would be higher. Because, therefore, the industry supply curve would then lie farther to the left, the output of the industry would be smaller. Accordingly, when social costs exceed private costs, the equilibrium output of an industry in the absence of government intervention gives an output that is "too large."

In this context, the word "social" means total — nothing more than that. Social costs are the total costs borne by all the individual persons concerned. The premises of the theory of welfare economics are wholly and solely individualistic. Some theorists carelessly write about "the costs to society," as if society were something different and apart from individuals, as if there could be tension and contrast between society and the individual.

If, then, the social costs of an industry in equilibrium exceed the private costs, the equilibrium is not a position of maximum welfare, or efficiency. It is also possible for social costs to be less than private costs, and thus for the equilibrium output of private enterprise to be too small.

In modern economics, Pigou's principle is usually put this way: Government should intervene, prima facie, when competitive equilibrium shows either external diseconomies or external economies. (These are the modern concepts, not Marshall's; see page 239.)

The presence of external diseconomies means that social costs exceed private costs, or, that social benefits are less than private benefits. Besides smoke, other examples are the pollution of rivers, uncompensated injuries suffered by wage earners, soil erosion, destruction of wildlife, etc.

Much actual government intervention can be viewed as rough approximations of the principle of correcting external diseconomies. Labor legislation, workmen's compensation, zoning laws, conservation of natural resources, and other controls are all reducible to the one principle.

The presence of external economies means that social costs are less than private or that social benefits exceed private benefits. Educational and transport facilities are examples. The significance of external economies is that the market produces too small an output of the commodities and services in question. If education and research were produced only by profit-seeking enterprise, their quantities would be far smaller than they are. In short, then, the concept of external economies is a criticism of private enterprise, a criticism in its own terms, and at the same time the concept is an explanation and justification for public subsidies to and public enterprise in a wide range of activities.

The existence of external economies and diseconomies gives only a prima facie case for intervention. Divergences are often probably small. Detection and measurement pose formidable and sometimes insuperable obstacles. Pigou's principle has intellectual appeal, but it is a frail thing in the rough and tumble of actual economic policy in the United States.

### Efficiency in Government Programs

Since the end of World War II, economists have begun the systematic application of welfare economics to certain of the large programs of the federal government. These programs contain projects for the development of natural resources — irrigation projects, electric power projects, flood control projects, and the like. The theory of welfare economics can show how these projects can be efficient — how a given object can be achieved with minimum costs or how a given budget can be allocated to attain the maximum benefits. The same theory has also been applied to national defense programs.

Some of the books listed at the end of this chapter describe the uses of price theory in contributing to greater efficiency in government programs.

### Pricing in a Socialist Economy

In a socialist economy, all material resources, or the greater part of them, are owned by government which also has unlimited powers of control. Suppose that the sole aim of a socialist government were to operate its economy so as best to satisfy the wants of its people and that the people could freely express their own wants as individuals. What would be the principles of operation of a socialist economy with consumer sovereignty?

With this aim, the socialist government would see to it that the allocation of resources would be as close as possible to the allocation of the general equilibrium model. The people in the socialist society would receive money incomes as workers as well as other money payments corresponding to social insurance benefits. Consumer goods would be sold in shops, the consumers having freedom of choice. The prices of consumer goods, the prices of intermediate goods, the prices of plant, equipment, and labor would all be fixed. They would be fixed to satisfy only one criterion — that demand would equal supply. When demand and supply would change, prices would be changed to preserve equality. The plant managers in the socialist economy would be instructed to adjust production to the prevailing prices. Plant managers would also be instructed to produce amounts whose marginal costs would equal selling prices. In the long run, this rule would assure that production would take place at minimum average costs. The plant managers would be ordered to keep the costs of any volume of output at a minimum. They would do this by choosing inputs in the same way as a competitive firm in a capitalistic economy.

Much more can be said about the allocation of resources in a socialist economy. The few points just made are enough, however, to show that a consumer-oriented socialist economy would look to the model of pure competition as its ideal. As a group of ideas and of political movements, socialism is well over a century old. But the principles of pricing in a socialist economy were not widely discussed until the 1930's.

The allocation of resources in the United States, and in countries with similar economic and political institutions, is determined not by authority, but instead by the pattern of prices. Government does directly dispose over about one-fifth of final output. The composition of the other four-fifths of gross national product results from the market-coordinated decisions of firms and households. The allocation of resources resulting from these decisions is affected in many ways by government price-fixing, taxation, and other kinds of intervention. All these forms of intervention are undertaken separately. They were adopted at different times and as responses to particular pressures and problems. The general economic policy in the United States is still to maintain free institutions and free markets.

### Maintaining Competition

One of the firm goals of economic policy in the United States is the maintenance of competition. The instruments of policy are the antitrust laws. For reasons that need not be gone into here, the antitrust laws are not enforced systematically and comprehensively. Nonetheless they have been powerful, one of their strongest effects being their role as a deterrent.

Why maintain competition? Price theory furnishes one of the interlocking elements in the explanation. With the qualifications mentioned already, nothing more need be said at this point except to draw attention once again to the efficiency attained in the equilibria of pure competition.

But many parts of the American economy do not fit the model of pure competition with its homogeneous products, its many consumers and producers, and its absence of price making by anyone. Because of this, some observers have questioned the economic foundation of the antitrust laws. If pure competition outside agriculture is actually rare, if most competition is monopolistic or oligopolistic, why maintain it? Why not seek a wholly fresh approach to the problem of policy for a free and efficient economy?

A good, though not a perfect, answer to questions like these is found in the use of the concept of *effective competition,* which has also been called workable competition. This concept has come forward in the discussions of antitrust policy since about 1940. The controversies over the fine points and over the emphasis to be given to the elements in the definition will not be gone into here. To put the definition in its barest and simplest form, an industry is effectively competitive if (1) new firms can freely enter the industry and produce at costs not markedly higher than those of established firms; (2) the firms in the industry are independent and active rivals and do not engage in collusion; (3) the number of firms is large enough so that none is dominant. When competition is effective, buyers have free choices among alternatives and firms are under constant pressures to keep their costs low.

The concept of effective competition is not so sharp and clear as the concept of pure competition. Also, the emphasis in the concept of effective competition falls on dynamic change rather than on equilibrium. Nonetheless, the concept of effective competition is a bridge between the abstract theory of pure competition and the practical task of maintaining a free and well-functioning economy.

### Summary

The doctrine of short-run equilibrium price can be used to analyze price fixing by government. When maximum prices are fixed in competitive markets, *shortages* usually arise; they are the excess of demand over supply at the fixed price. When minimum prices are fixed, *surpluses* are usually present; they are the excess of supply over demand at the fixed price. Even if a minimum price is held constant, an increase in demand can lead to advances in other prices. In general, the federal government does not fix farm prices, but tries to raise them by manipulating demand and supply.

The support-price policy has been followed; other methods have been proposed. The doctrine of long-run equilibrium price and the Walrasian model give standards of economic welfare as efficiency. The specifications of the *ideal output* of an economy are contained in the *marginal conditions* of maximum economic welfare. The efficiency maximum is subject to two qualifications. One is the distribution of incomes, which might be so highly unequal as to fail to satisfy a socio-ethical standard of equity. The other is that *social costs* might exceed or be less than private costs; if they do, external diseconomies or external economies are said to exist. Then there is a prima facie case for government intervention to improve economic efficiency. Systematic application of welfare economics to government programs has begun. A consumer-oriented socialist economy would be managed to achieve the same allocation of resources as in the general equilibrium model. The bridge between the theory of pure competition and the economic foundation of the antitrust laws is the concept of *effective competition.*

## SELECTED REFERENCES

George J. Stigler, *The Theory of Price,* rev. ed. (New York: Macmillan, 1952), Chap. 9 and 10.

On welfare economics: Howard R. Bowen, *Toward Social Economy* (New York: Rinehart, 1948). Tibor Scitovsky, *Welfare and Competition* (Homewood: Irwin, 1952).

More advanced: A. C. Pigou, *The Economics of Welfare,* 4th ed. (London: Macmillan, 1932). J. E. Meade, *Trade and Welfare* (London: Oxford University Press, 1955). Hla Myint, *Theories of Welfare Economics* (Cambridge: Harvard University Press, 1948).

Applications of welfare economics to government programs: John V. Krutilla and Otto Eckstein, *Multiple Purpose River Development* (Baltimore: Johns Hopkins Press, 1958). Jack Hirshleifer, James C. DeHaven, and Jerome W. Milliman, *Water Supply. Economics, Technology, and Policy* (Chicago: University of Chicago Press, 1960). Charles J. Hitch and Roland N. McKean, *The Economics of Defense in the Nuclear Age* (Cambridge: Harvard University Press, 1960).

On private vs social cost: R. H. Coase, "The Problem of Social Cost," *Journal of Law and Economics,* Vol. III, October, 1960, pp. 1–44.

Socialism: Oskar Lange and Fred M. Taylor, *On the Economic Theory of Socialism* (Minneapolis: University of Minnesota Press, 1938).

Effective Competition: John Maurice Clark, *Competition as a Dynamic Process* (Washington, D.C.: Brookings, 1961).

## EXERCISES AND PROBLEMS

1. Suppose that the demand for a particular farm product becomes just slightly elastic over a considerable range of possible prices. How should the price-support program for this product be modified?

2. Draw a diagram to show the magnitude of production controls (i.e., reduction in supply) necessary to achieve a high price without a surplus.

3. The application of price theory to the price-fixing activities of governments nearly always contains open or implied adverse criticism. Is such criticism justified? Why?

4. Suppose you have a free hand in setting postal rates and that you want to have the postal service operated in accordance with the criteria of economic efficiency. What would you do?

# Disequilibrium and

# Instability in Competitive

# Prices

# 18

So far, the analyses of price formation in pure competition have come
to an end with statements of the equilibria of prices and quantities. Though
one economist has protested that no shadow of approbation should be cast
over an equilibrium of price and quantity, his protests have not been
heeded. There seems to be something good about it, especially about
industry equilibrium under pure competition where equilibrium always
goes along with *equality* of demand and supply.

The spectacle of general equilibrium is awesome because of its in-
tricacy as well as its beauty and elegance, which very words indeed are
often applied to general equilibrium by mathematical economists. But
must demand and supply and all that they imply always snap into an
equilibrium? What is the magic of the intersection of the curves? Is
an equilibrium a necessary result? How do price and output get from one
position of equilibrium to another?

Prices and outputs in pure competition are, in fact, in constant motion.
Changes in tastes and in technology are principal causes. Disequilibrium,
rather than equilibrium, is the normal condition of purely competitive
markets, certainly over periods of time longer than a few weeks. The
pervasiveness of disequilibrium does not, however, make the theory of
equilibrium useless. On the contrary, understanding of the movements of

disequilibrium must rest on knowledge of the equilibrium conditions. For equilibrium is a shorthand way of referring to the *direction* of the pulling and hauling of the forces working on the prices and outputs of commodities. The forces are not random, or wholly capricious, or arbitrary. They operate within a pattern whose inner tendencies are described by the theory of equilibrium.

### Adjustments of Prices and Quantities in Disequilibrium

In the market period, both demand and supply can shift rapidly. Buyers and sellers can change their opinions about future prices, alter their trading plans, and hence bring new demand and supply schedules into being. In the short run and in the long, demand can often change much more quickly than supply. A new fad or fashion can cause a short-run demand curve to move, within a few days or weeks, to the right and to settle in a new position. Because it is a flow of production, however, short-run supply can usually change only slowly. It takes time to alter physical rates of production, to speed them up, or to cut them back.

#### Short-Run Changes in Demand

Figures 18–1 and 18–2 show the behavior of price in a purely competitive industry when demand changes. Let $D_1$ and $S$ be the short-run demand

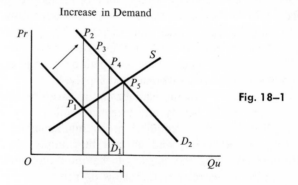

Increase in Demand

Fig. 18–1

and supply curves, and let the industry first be in short-run equilibrium. To begin with, then, price is $P_1$. Suppose that demand suddenly shifts to $D_2$. The price then shoots up to $P_2$ if the firms cannot suddenly increase their outputs. The price $P_2$ is highly remunerative because it stands far above the supply curve. The firms expand output as best they can in a scramble to earn still more net revenue. As output grows, the price now falls to

$P_3$, to $P_4$, and finally to $P_5$. Then the expansion stops. The industry is once more in short-run equilibrium.

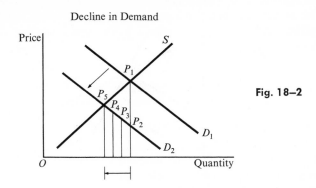

Decline in Demand

**Fig. 18–2**

Figure 18–2 shows the effect of a sudden decline in demand. Price drops from $P_1$ to $P_2$. The price $P_2$ is well below the supply curve, causing contraction to take place. As it does, little by little price rises, finally climbing to the new level of equilibrium.

### Short-Run Changes in Supply

A short-run industry supply curve can shift to the right because of reductions in the costs of the firms or because of a fall in the price of some other commodity that the firms also produce. The supply curve can be imagined as sliding to the right as the firms make their adjustments and coming to rest when the causes of the shift are exhausted. The disequilibrium price slides down the demand curve, also coming to rest in a new short-run equilibrium.

Sometimes, however, supply can change faster than demand. Suppose that the firms, because of a fall in the price of another commodity, increase the short-run supply of the commodity under examination. Imagine that the firms can make their adjustments in production quickly within, say, a few weeks. Imagine also that the demand for a period of a few weeks is less elastic than it is for the short run as a whole. Under these circumstances, price would fall below and then would rise to the new equilibrium level. Figure 18–3 shows this. The original equilibrium of demand, supply, and price is given by the positions of $D_1$, $S_1$, and $P_1$. Supply shifts to $S_2$, but while it does so, the demand curve for the period is $D_2$, which is less elastic. Price then falls to $P_2$. But as the buyers make their adjustments, demand becomes more elastic. The curve $D_2$ pivots and swings up, finally assuming the position $D_1$. In the absence of a fresh disturbance, the equilibrium price becomes $P_3$.

Changes such as these indicate the many kinds of adjustments constantly taking place in competitive markets.

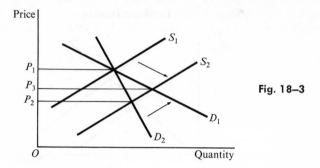

Fig. 18–3

### Disequilibrium in the Long Run

Chapter 15 describes the derivation of a long-run supply curve. The curve is a series of points *each* of which is an equilibrium. When long-run demand equals long-run supply, the industry is in equilibrium. So are the individual firms, each producing at minimum average cost.

Suppose that the demand for a commodity slowly and steadily grows because of the normal increase of population. If the industry grows at the same rate, the price will tend to its long-run equilibrium level. But there can be periods when the two growth rates are out of whack. Demand can slow down its rate of expansion in, say, a decade when population is growing at a slower rate. In possibly the same decade, the industry expands very fast, owing perhaps to overenthusiasm about technological changes. Then quite apart from its short-run fluctuations, the price can remain below its equilibrium level for many years. It is less likely that price can long remain *above* the equilibrium level because capacity in any one industry can always expand by any amount when there is sufficient time.[1]

### Unstable Equilibrium

Many equilibria have put in their appearances so far. More are to come in the theories of monopoly and of imperfect competition. The equilibrium positions of prices and quantities for consumers, firms, and industries so far presented are positions of *stable equilibrium*. If something disturbs it, a

---

[1] Price theory is vague on disequilibrium in the long run. For one thing, there is a tendency among theorists to *define* the long run so as to rule out disequilibrium. Disequilibrium in the long run seems to be a matter of the stability of the growth of an industry. The condition of price theory is surveyed in Peter Newman, "The Erosion of Marshall's Theory of Value," *Quarterly Journal of Economics*, Vol. LXXIV, No. 4, November, 1960, pp. 587–600.

stable equilibrium is self-adjusting. A billiard ball resting in a bowl on a table occupies a position of stable equilibrium because if somebody gives the ball a little push, it moves back and forth, eventually coming to rest where it was before. If the bowl is turned upside down and the ball is carefully perched on top of the inverted bowl, the ball will stay there. Now, however, it stands in unstable equilibrium because if somebody now pushes it, the billiard ball rolls down off the bowl onto the table and drops with a thud to the floor. It does not come back to where it was.

So too, a price-quantity equilibrium can be unstable. When it is, a part of the price mechanism goes awry.

## The Firm

The shorthand expression of the equilibrium output of the firm under pure competition is, of course, the equality of marginal cost and price. For this equilibrium to be stable, the firm must be motivated to return to it. Suppose the firm makes a mistake and produces an amount more than the equilibrium amount. The mistake reduces the firm's profits (or increases its losses). Thus the desire to maximize profits is the force that leads to correction of the mistake. The firm moves output back to the equilibrium level. Why is the equilibrium stable? Because marginal cost is rising in the region of equilibrium output. This point was mentioned before, but it deserves fresh emphasis.

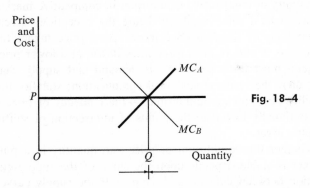

Fig. 18–4

In Figure 18–4, lines $MC_A$ and $MC_B$ are portions of two hypothetical and alternative marginal cost curves of a firm. The price is $OP$. The equilibrium output is $OQ$. Price equals marginal cost for both cost curves. The rising curve $MC_A$ means that if it expands output past $OQ$, the firm reduces its profits. In contrast, the meaning of the falling curve $MC_B$ is that the larger the output, the larger become the firm's net revenue or net profits. The prospect of ever greater profits causes the firm to expand without limit — so long as marginal cost is falling. With falling marginal cost, the output *OQ* in Figure 18–5 is *not* the equilibrium output. No, this output is, in fact, the *least* output the firm would want to produce.

The larger significance of an indefinitely declining marginal cost curve is the destruction of pure competition. The firm with such a cost curve would expand until it would produce the output of the entire industry. In other words, economies of scale over an indefinitely large range of output are incompatible with competition.

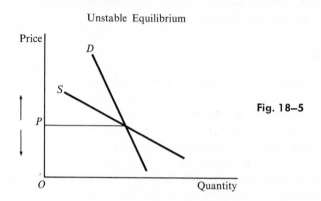

Unstable Equilibrium

Fig. 18–5

### The Industry

Stability of competitive equilibrium in competitive markets can be taken as the general rule, instability being the exception. Recall the ordinary demand-supply diagram once more. At a price higher than equilibrium, the excess of supply must force price down; at a lower price, the excess of demand must force price up. If demand and supply change (as indeed they do), the result is analytical complication; stability then becomes the stability of a moving equilibrium — the tendency of price and quantity to be continually forced to the points of intersection of shifting demand and supply curves.

Whether the equilibrium of price and quantity in a purely competitive market is stable depends upon the slope of the supply curve and on the relation between demand and supply. If the supply curve has a negative slope and if its slope is less than that of the demand curve, equilibrium can be unstable.

The negative slope of a supply curve stands for a particular pattern of sellers' responses to prices. If price falls, they want to sell more, not less. If price rises, they want to sell less, not more. This can happen, for example, to the producers of one crop, who cannot or will not grow any other crop, and who do not maximize profits, but instead try to maintain a customary income. The lower the price, the more they have to grow; the higher the price, the less effort they have to put forth. A supply curve can also have a temporarily negative slope for the traders on an organized market in the immediate market period. The sellers own stocks of the commodity and cash; suppose that their assets comprise only these. Normally, each seller maintains some preferred ration of his holdings of the commodity and of cash. Suppose next that the sellers in some market at some point of time are caught in such a state of affairs that they desperately need cash. To get it, they have to sell the commodity. The lower the price, the more they have to sell.

Equilibrium is unstable in Figure 18–5. The equilibrium price is *OP*. But if this price should temporarily rise, it will not go back to the equilibrium level but, instead, will keep on rising. It will do this because demand exceeds supply above equilibrium. Similarly, a drop in price sets up a chain reaction of more price declines because supply exceeds demand.

How far can price move away from a level of unstable equilibrium? To this question, no single answer can be given. A diagram like Figure 18–5 leaves the question open. In particular markets, instability is not likely to prevail for long. Stability of equilibrium is restored if the supply curve shifts and becomes steeper than the demand curve. If the supply curve shifts and changes to a positive slope, then of course stability also prevails.

### The Cobweb Theorem

The prices and outputs of many commodities have shown pronounced cyclical movements over long periods of time. Over the years, the prices of these commodities rise and then fall, rise and fall again in a continued wavelike pattern. Production of the same commodities has generally moved up and down in counterwaves. A general explanation for some of the cycles in commodity prices and outputs is furnished by the "cobweb theorem," as it is called. The "cobweb" name comes from the appearance of the diagrams; see Figures 18–8 and 18–10, which are on pages 282 and 283.

Commodity cycles are, of course, influenced by the forces flowing from the business cycle. Apart from this, commodity cycles have specific causes in the supply responses of producers. Suppose you raise fruit in orchards. The price of the fruit goes up. So you plant more trees. It takes several years for the trees to grow to bearing size. By the time fruit can be plucked from the additional trees, the price is low because you weren't the only one to plant more trees when the price was high.

The cobweb theorem can apply to the prices and outputs of commodities whose production is discontinuous, such as annual crops, or to commodities that take two or more years to produce, such as animals and bearing fruit trees.

The cobweb theorem has still another use because it is the simplest model of the *dynamics* of demand, supply, and price. An often-quoted definition of a dynamic theory is that of the Norwegian economist Ragnar Frisch who has said that a dynamic theory connects variables *at different points of time.*

The cobweb model shows demand and supply for a commodity produced and sold under conditions of pure competition. Production takes place in distinct periods of time; for convenience, one-year periods will be assumed here. The essential feature of the model is that output in year 2 is a response to price in year 1, output in year 3 to price in year 2, output in year 4 to price in year 3, etc. Output, then, is lagged one year behind price. The supply *curve* stays put in the model; so does the demand curve.

The one-year lag between supply and price is an assumption about the behavior of the producers. Suppose this year's price is high. As the farmers sit near their stoves in the winter making their plans for next year, each one believes that next year's price will be high too, in fact, just as high. Therefore each farmer decides to plant, grow, and harvest the size of crop associated with a high price. Each one plans to expand along his marginal cost curve to the point where it meets the *expected* high price.

### Perpetual Oscillation

The cobweb theorem comes in three standard models. The de luxe, or complicated, models are omitted here. All three standard models have price and output fluctuating around equilibrium. In the first model, price perpetually oscillates from high to low, and output from low to high; equilibrium is never attained. In the second model, price and output flap up and down, but the ups and downs become weaker, then feebler, finally ceasing as equilibrium is reached. In the third model, the movements become wilder and wilder, going always farther away from equilibrium.[2]

Now the first model with its perpetual oscillation: In Figure 18–6, the subscripts for the $P$'s and $Q$'s can be taken to mean successive years. In year 1, $OP_1$ is the price, let it be supposed. Then in year 2, the quantity $OQ_2$ is produced. But the demand curve says that $OQ_2$ can be sold only at the low price of $OP_2$. The price in year 2 then becomes $OP_2$. In year 3, the supply curve and the lag assumption say that the quantity produced is $OQ_3$. But this small quantity sells at price $OP_1$. Hence in year 3, the price is the same as in year 1. So it continues round and round as the arrows in Figure 18–7 indicate. In this example, the odd-numbered years have high prices and low outputs; the even-numbered years have the opposite.

---

[2] Algebraic versions of the models of the cobweb theorem are in Note 5 of the Appendix to Part Four.

The immediate cause of the rhythmic alternation between a high and low price is that in the perpetually oscillating model, the elasticities of demand and supply are equal.[3] It makes no difference whether they are high or low so long as the elasticities are equal. The perpetual oscillation, accordingly, is explained by the constancy of the demand and supply curves and by the identity of the kind of price responses of the buyers and producers.

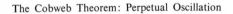

The Cobweb Theorem: Perpetual Oscillation

**Fig. 18–6**

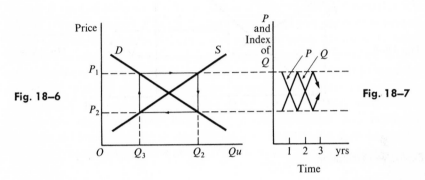

**Fig. 18–7**

Figure 18–7 is a schematic time-series diagram. The intervals of time on the diagram are years. The price scale is the same as on Figure 18–6, but quantity (in bushels or tons, etc.) is expressed by an index, so that price and quantity can be commensurate on the vertical axis.

### Damped Oscillation

The second model has the damped oscillations. Let the process start, in Figure 18–8, with $OP_1$ in year 1. In year 2, output is $OQ_2$, which sells at $OP_2$. In year 3, output drops to $OQ_3$, which sells at $OP_3$. And so on. Notice how the prices and outputs come closer and closer to equilibrium. Indeed, they finally reach it, just as a pendulum comes to rest in a vertical position.

In the model with the damping, the elasticity of supply is less than that of demand. Here too, it makes no difference whether both are elastic or inelastic. All that matters is that supply be less elastic than demand. This means that the producers respond less, relatively speaking, to changes in price than do the consumers. The producers' lesser response causes equi-

---

[3] Strictly speaking, it is the slopes, not the elasticities, of the demand and supply curves that count. But in a simple treatment of the cobweb theorem, the difference between slope and elasticity (pages 34 and 211) may be disregarded.

librium eventually to be reached, provided of course that the demand and supply curves stay put.

Figure 18–9 is also a time-series diagram showing the successive diminution of the fluctuations of price.

The Cobweb Theorem: Damped Oscillation

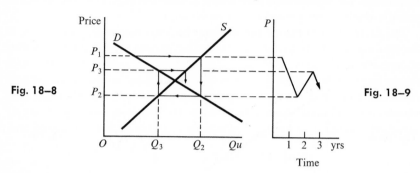

**Fig. 18–8**                                                                                    **Fig. 18–9**

## Explosive Oscillation

The third model has the explosive oscillations. The cobweb in Figure 18–10 spins outward, not inward. The fluctuations in Figure 18–11 become ever more violent. Prices and quantities move year by year farther away from equilibrium because demand is less elastic than supply. The producers' greater responsiveness to price causes the widening oscillations. The buyers always take, at a price, whatever quantity is put on the market. But the producers decide what the quantity is to be.

To the mathematical economist, the cobweb-theorem models are "beautiful." Their beauty resides in their simplicity and clarity. Though the cobweb theorem does describe something real, the simple models themselves do no more than to execute the logic of their assumptions. When seen in operation for the first time, the explosive model is likely to raise eyebrows, and raise them high. How can such things be? The explosions result from the linearity of demand and supply, from the assumption about elasticities, and from the rigidity of the assumption about the lagged-response behavior of the producers. An appropriate modification of linearity can easily muffle or banish the explosions.

## Applications

Doctrines of equilibrium, especially of general equilibrium, probably paint too cheerful a picture of the working of the price system in a private enterprise economy. Equilibrium means that the fundamental forces of wants and of scarcity are precisely balanced by the impersonal mechanism of the market. The preoccupations of theorists with equilibrium might give the impression that the actual economy is closer to the ideal of welfare economics than in fact it is.

By drawing attention to disequilibrium and instability in competitive markets, this chapter shows that prices in the private enterprise economy do not unvaryingly do their work with speed and dispatch. Disturbances of equilibrium are not promptly corrected. Some disturbances, and therefore maladjustments, can persist almost indefinitely.

The chief applications of the analyses of this chapter lie in pointing to the importance of improved institutional arrangements for the functioning of competitive markets. The instability of price and output associated with supply curves whose negative slopes are less than those of the accompanying demand curves is an instability that can probably be cured. Only brief remarks can be made here. But, in general, the cause behind a supply curve that causes troublesome fluctuations in price is the existence of one-

The Cobweb Theorem: Explosive Oscillation

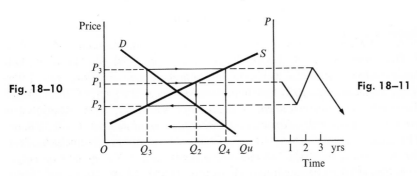

Fig. 18–10                                                          Fig. 18–11

crop cultivation by people accustomed to low incomes. Economic development programs can show such people how to grow other crops and engage in other activities, and can whet their desires for more consumer goods. If the programs are successful, supply curves swing around and take on positive slopes.

Price-output cobwebs can be smashed by more and better information and forecasts if producers act on them. Here too, government and other agencies can, through a variety of means, show producers how to make better estimates of future prices. Informational services have long existed and are steadily improving. Cobweb effects are likely to become much less important.

### Summary

Prices and outputs in competitive markets are normally in *disequilibrium,* in motion between equilibrium positions. Short-run demand can shift more quickly than short-run supply. If demand increases, prices rise high, then fall as they approach a new equilibrium. If supply should change faster than demand, prices first fall, then rise to a new equilibrium. Over long periods, price can be below equilibrium if demand grows more slowly than supply. A *stable equilibrium* is one whose deviations are corrected by the accompanying forces. The stability of the equilibrium of a competitive firm requires rising marginal cost. The stability of the equilibrium of a competitive industry requires that demand exceed supply at prices less than equilibrium. Industry equilibrium is unstable if a negatively sloped supply curve is less steep than the demand curve. The *cobweb theorem* describes price and output when supply is lagged one period behind price. In the simple cobweb model, equal elasticities of demand and supply cause a perpetual oscillation of prices above and below equilibrium. If supply is less elastic than demand, the oscillations become narrower as equilibrium is approached. If supply is more elastic than demand, the oscillations become wider, moving prices farther away from equilibrium.

## SELECTED REFERENCES

Alfred Marshall, *Principles of Economics,* 8th ed. (London: Macmillan, 1920), Book V. J. R. Hicks, *Value and Capital,* 2d ed. (London: Oxford, 1946), Chap. 5. William J. Baumol, *Economic Dynamics* (New York: Macmillan, 1951), Chap. 7. Mordecai Ezekiel, "The Cobweb Theorem," *Quarterly Journal of Economics,* February, 1938, Reprinted in American Economic Association, *Readings in Business Cycle Theory* (Philadelphia: Blakiston, 1944), Chap. 21. Paul A. Samuelson, "Dynamic Process Analysis," in Howard S. Ellis, ed., *A Survey of Contemporary Economics* (Philadelphia: Blakiston, 1948), Chap. 10.

## EXERCISES AND PROBLEMS

1. Suppose that consumers' tastes change, shifting from commodity $A$ to commodity $B$. Show how industries $A$ and $B$ are affected, immediately and ultimately.

2. Draw a diagram with a negatively sloped supply curve, but with a stable equilibrium.

3. Can the equilibrium of the consumer be unstable? Explain.

4. A firm buys an equilibrium quantity of an input. What makes this equilibrium stable?

5. See if you can draw a single cobweb diagram showing *both* explosive and damped oscillations.

6. See if you can draw a single cobweb diagram with *both* damped and perpetual oscillation.

# APPENDIX TO

# PART FOUR

## MATHEMATICAL NOTES

### Note 1.   Supply Functions

Supply functions can take many forms.  Discussion here is confined to the simplest linear form.  Let the supply function be

$$q = bp + a$$

where $q$ is the quantity supplied, $p$ is price, and $a$ and $b$ are constants. The intercept on the quantity axis is $a$, and $b$ is the slope of the supply curve.  The existence of normal, i.e., positively sloped, supply curves is assumed here.  Thus $b$ is always positive.  But $a \gtreqless 0$. If $a = 0$, the supply curve begins at the origin, which means that at zero price, the quantity supplied is zero.  If $a < 0$, then the supply curve begins at some point on the $p$ axis; that is, at some finite price, the quantity supplied is zero.  If $a > 0$, the supply curve begins at some point on the quantity axis; literally, this means that some amount will be supplied, even at price zero.

### Note 2.   Elasticity of Supply

For the same linear supply function as in Note 1, elasticity of supply is

$$E_s = \frac{p}{q} \frac{dq}{dp} = b \frac{p}{q}.$$

Page 210 describes the elasticity of a linear supply curve and also the elasticity of a tangent line to a curvilinear supply curve at the point of tangency, i.e., point elasticity.  The geometric proof on page 211 can now be supplemented: $E_s = b \dfrac{p}{q} = \dfrac{bp}{bp + a}.$

Therefore, if $a = 0$, $E_s = 1$.  The supply curve beginning at the origin has an elasticity of unity regardless of the value of $b$, i.e., regardless of the slope of the curve.  If $a > 0$, $E_s < 1$.  That is, if the supply curve cuts the quantity axis, elasticity is less than unity, again regardless of the slope. And if $a < 0$, $E_s > 1$. If the supply curve cuts the price axis, elasticity is greater than unity. Where $a \neq 0$, the value of the coefficient of elasticity is dependent on price.

### Note 3.    A Model of Competitive Partial Equilibrium

Demand and supply are now brought together in markets where pure competition prevails. What now follows is a partial equilibrium model. It holds for the immediate market, the short run, and the long run. The formal properties of the equilibrium are the same. What differs from one market period to another is the form of the demand and supply functions. Here too, discussion is limited to simple linear functions.

The demand function is now written as $D = A - Bp$. The supply function is $S = bp - a$. The sign of $a$ here is negative to signify an elastic supply. The demand curve goes down to the right, the supply curve goes up to the right. That is, $B < 0$ in the demand function and $b > 0$ in the supply function. The constants, $A$, $B$, $a$, and $b$ can all have different values.

In equilibrium, $D = S$. Therefore,

$$A - Bp = bp - a$$
$$Bp + bp = A + a$$
$$p = \frac{A + a}{B + b}.$$

Here is a hypothetical numerical example:

$$D = 30 - p$$
$$S = 3p - 10$$
$$\therefore p = \frac{30 + 10}{1 + 3} = 10$$
$$D = S = 20.$$

Suppose that demand increases, the demand function changing to $D' = 38 - p$. Then

$$p = \frac{38 + 10}{1 + 3} = 12,$$

and

$$D' = S = 26.$$

Suppose next that a tax is imposed on the producers. Let the supply prices in the supply function be the costs of the producers exclusive of tax, and let the tax be 1-1/3. For example, to produce 10 units, the supply price before the tax is 6-2/3. That is, $S = 3p - 10 = 10$. Therefore $3p = 20$ and $p = 6\text{-}2/3$. With the tax, price becomes $p + 1\text{-}1/3 = 8$

and therefore $S' = 3(8) - a = 10$ which requires $a$ to be 14 to obtain the supply of 10. Accordingly,

$$D = 30 - p$$
$$S' = 3p - 14$$
$$\therefore p = \frac{30 + 14}{1 + 3} = 11.$$

Observe that the equilibrium price has risen by less than the amount of the tax. The price increase is 1, and the tax is 1-1/3. This result accords with the geometrical demonstration on page 230.

### Note 4.  A Model of General Equilibrium

The model of general equilibrium to be described now is one of the simplest versions. It is usually called the Walras-Cassel model.[1] To conform a little more closely to the conventions associated with general equilibrium theory, several of the symbols in what follows differ from those used elsewhere in this book.

The economy described by the model has 1, 2, . . . , $n$ commodities and 1, 2, . . . , $m$ resources or productive services. The quantities of the commodities are $x_1, x_2, \ldots, x_n$. The quantities of the resources are $r_1, r_2, \ldots, r_m$.

The prices of the commodities are $p_1, p_2, \ldots, p_n$. The prices of the productive services are $v_1, v_2, \ldots, v_m$.

In this economy, the commodities are produced directly with the productive services. Intermediate goods do not appear, just as they do not in the national income and product accounts. In these accounts, the final products in the gross national product are produced with the two groups of productive services, labor and capital. To produce a unit of the $j$ th commodity, the physical quantity $a_i$ of the $i$ th resource is needed. A loaf of bread needs so many minutes of the labor time of a baker. Thus, $a_{ij}$ is called a production coefficient or an input coefficient. In the model, all the production coefficients are fixed. There are $mn$ of them.

All prices are measured in terms of the price of one commodity. Let $p_1 = 1$. Thus prices are the ratios at which commodities 2, 3, . . . , $n$ exchange for commodity 1, which Walras called the *numéraire*. The economy is really a kind of barter economy, with the *numéraire* serving as a unit of reckoning.

[1] After Walras and Gustav Cassel, the Swedish economist whose translated version was for many years the only one available in English. Treatment of the Walras-Cassel model here is adapted from Robert Dorfman, Paul A. Samuelson, and Robert M. Solow, *Linear Programming and Economic Analysis* (New York: McGraw-Hill, 1958), pp. 351–355.

## The Demand Equations

The model has two sets of demand equations. One is that of the households for commodities. The other is that of the firms for resources.

The market-demand equations for each commodity are the totals of the demands of each household for each commodity. Each household's demand for a commodity is a function of its utility, its price, the prices of *all* other commodities, and the household's income which, in turn, depends on the amounts of productive services it sells and their prices.

The market-demand equations are

$$x_1 = f_1(p_1, p_2, \ldots, p_n; v_1, v_2, \ldots, v_m)$$
$$x_2 = f_2(p_1, p_2, \ldots, p_n; v_1, v_2, \ldots, v_m)$$

(1)

$$\cdot \quad \cdot \quad \cdot \quad \cdot \quad \cdot \quad \cdot \quad \cdot \quad \cdot \quad \cdot \quad \cdot \quad \cdot \quad \cdot$$

$$x_n = f_n(p_1, p_2, \ldots, p_n; v_1, v_2, \ldots, v_m).$$

Notice that the resource prices appear in these equations. The resource prices allow for changes in demand when there are shifts in the incomes of the households.

Because the production coefficients are fixed, the demand of firms for units of resources is the sum of the quantities required for each commodity. The firms producing commodity 1, whose quantity is $x_1$, demand $a_{11}$ units of resource 1, $a_{21}$ units of resource 2, etc. The demand for resource 1 is the sum of the amounts of it used in all commodities, or $a_{11}x_1$ plus $a_{12}x_2$ etc. Then let the total supply of each resource be put equal to its demand because the model has no unemployment. Here are the equations:

$$a_{11}x_1 + a_{12}x_2 + \ldots + a_{1n}x_n = r_1$$
$$a_{21}x_1 + a_{22}x_2 + \ldots + a_{2n}x_n = r_2$$

(2)

$$\cdot \quad \cdot \quad \cdot \quad \cdot \quad \cdot \quad \cdot \quad \cdot \quad \cdot \quad \cdot \quad \cdot \quad \cdot$$

$$a_{m1}x_1 + a_{m2}x_2 + \ldots + a_{mn}x_n = r_m.$$

## The Supply Equations

All markets are purely and perfectly competitive in the model, which also has the adjustments of the long run. Therefore, the price of each commodity equals its cost per unit. Cost per unit is the sum of the payments for the quantities of the productive resources used per unit of a commodity. Production of a unit of commodity 1 requires $a_{11}$ units of resource 1 at price $v_1$, $a_{21}$ units of resource 2 at price $v_2$, etc. The equations are

$$a_{11}v_1 + a_{21}v_2 + \ldots + a_{m1}v_m = p_1$$
$$a_{12}v_1 + a_{22}v_2 + \ldots + a_{m2}v_m = p_2$$

(3)

$$\cdot \quad \cdot \quad \cdot \quad \cdot \quad \cdot \quad \cdot \quad \cdot \quad \cdot \quad \cdot$$

$$a_{1n}v_1 + a_{2n}v_2 + \ldots + a_{mn}v_m = p_n.$$

The last step is to tie the supply of resources to the prices. The supply of any one resource depends on its price, the prices of the other resources, and the prices of the commodities. The supply of hours of bakers' services depends on the wage rate, on wage rates in other occupations, and on the prices of bread, cake, cookies, etc. The final set of equations is

$$r_1 = g_1(p_1,p_2, \ldots, p_n; v_1,v_2, \ldots, v_m)$$
$$r_2 \doteq g_2(p_1,p_2, \ldots, p_n; v_1,v_2, \ldots, v_m)$$

(4)

$$\cdot \quad \cdot \quad \cdot \quad \cdot \quad \cdot \quad \cdot \quad \cdot \quad \cdot \quad \cdot \quad \cdot \quad \cdot$$

$$r_m = g_m(p_1,p_2, \ldots, p_n; v_1,v_2, \ldots, v_m).$$

There are $2n + 2m$ equations for the $2n + 2m$ unknowns $x$, $r$, $p$, and $v$. But equations (1) and (4) really contain only $m + n - 1$ independent equations. By setting $p_1 = 1$, however, the number of unknowns is also reduced by one. Thus the system of equations is determinate.

## Note 5.   The Cobweb Theorem

The mathematical model for the cobweb theorem can be expressed as follows:

$$D_t = A - Bp_t$$
$$S_t = bp_{t-1} - a$$
$$D_t = S_t.$$

Here the subscript $t$ means a time period, such as a year. Then

$$A - Bp_t = bp_{t-1} - a$$

or

$$p_t = \left(-\frac{b}{B}\right)p_{t-1} + \frac{a+A}{B}$$

$$p_1 = \left(-\frac{b}{B}\right)p_0 + \frac{a+A}{B}$$

$$p_2 = \left(-\frac{b}{B}\right)p_1 + \frac{a+A}{B}$$

$$= \left(-\frac{b}{B}\right)^2 p_0 + \left(-\frac{b}{B}\right)\frac{a+A}{B} + \frac{a+A}{B}.$$

The general solution of this difference equation gives $p_t$ in terms of $p_o$, the initial price. For any time $(t)$,

$$p_t = \left(-\frac{b}{B}\right)^t p_0 + \frac{a+A}{B+b}\left\{1 - \left(-\frac{b}{B}\right)^t\right\}.$$

### Perpetual Oscillation

If $b = B$, $-\dfrac{b}{B} = -1$ and $p_t = (-1)^t p_0 + \dfrac{a+A}{B+b}\{1 - (-1)^t\}$.

When $t$ equals zero or any even number, then

$$p_t = p_0 + \frac{a+A}{B+b}\{1-1\} = p_0.$$

When $t$ equals an odd number, then

$$p_t = -p_0 + \frac{a+A}{B+b}\{1+1\} = 2\frac{a+A}{B+b} - p_0.$$

Consequently, price alternates between these two price values and quantities alternate between the two values obtained by substitution of these prices in either the demand or supply functions. This is the model with perpetual oscillation.

### Damped Oscillation

If $b < B$, $\dfrac{b}{B} < 1$ and $p_t$ approaches $\dfrac{a+A}{B+b}$

as $t$ becomes infinite. This value for price is the same as that for the intersection of the demand and supply functions if the subscripts on price are dropped. Hence, this is the equilibrium price that is approached as $t$ is increased. Once this price is achieved, the variation in price ceases. This is the model with damped oscillation.

### Explosive Oscillation

If $b > B$, $\dfrac{b}{B} > 1$ and $p_t$ fails to converge as $t$ increases since $\left(-\dfrac{b}{B}\right)^t$

becomes infinite as $t$ increases without limit. This is the model with explosive oscillation. Each new value of price and quantity is farther from equilibrium than the preceding one.

# PART FIVE

*Monopoly*

*Pricing*

# *Monopoly Price*

# 19

THE DEFINITION OF MONOPOLY · DEMAND, MARGINAL REVENUE,

AND ELASTICITY · QUALIFICATIONS · MONOPOLY PRICE IN THE

IMMEDIATE MARKET · MONOPOLY PRICE IN THE SHORT AND IN

THE LONG RUN · COMPARISON OF MONOPOLY AND COMPETITIVE

PRICES · THE DYNAMICS OF MONOPOLY · APPLICATIONS ·

The theory of monopoly price applies to firms having freedom and independence when they decide on their selling prices. Monopolists are price makers, not price takers, as are the firms in purely competitive industries. Monopolists have freedom in price making because they sell to many consumers; they have independence because they need not fear the actions of rivals.

## The Definition of Monopoly

For centuries, men have talked and written about monopoly, usually with condemnation, often with anger. Monopoly has meant many things, each with its own shade of meaning.

In the standard definition, a monopolist is the only producer of a product that has no close substitutes. Since the output of an industry consists of products that are either perfect or very close substitutes, the monopolist is therefore the only producer in the industry. Firm and industry are iden-

tical. Because, however, the precise definition of monopoly has great practical importance, especially in the enforcement of the antitrust laws, it is
well to go farther into the problem of defining monopoly and to look at
some other definitions.

Earlier chapters show that a commodity has to be defined for the purpose
at hand; several purposes require several definitions. So too with monopoly,
and not just on general grounds. The two ideas, in fact, are linked together.
A definition of monopoly must specify the commodity that is monopolized.

The literal meaning of a monopolist as a sole seller and the dictionary
meaning of exclusive control do not help much. Sole seller of what? Exclusive control of what? When a commodity is distinct in its physical properties
and recognized by everybody as distinct, then a firm producing such a
commodity can be called a monopoly. Though rough-and-ready, this definition is none the worse for that. To be distinct, the commodity must be a
marked gap in a chain of substitutes. Its cross elasticities of demand with
other commodities must be low. In his discussion of monopoly, Joel Dean,
an authority on managerial economics, calls a monopolized product "a
product of lasting distinctiveness." Such a product has no acceptable substitutes; its distinctiveness lasts for many years.

In contrast, Edward H. Chamberlin, whose *Theory of Monopolistic
Competition* is an important contribution to price theory, is impressed by
the presence of substitutes for *any* commodity and therefore by the *competition* from them. He has advanced the concept of "pure monopoly,"
which is the control of the supply of *all* commodities and services. But
Chamberlin's is too extreme a view to be useful because pure monopoly as
he defines it could never exist. Not even the Russian government controls
the supply of *all* commodities and services; some of the food sold in Russia
is produced by peasants who cultivate little plots of land as independent
entrepreneurs.

Still another view is to define a monopolist as any firm with a sloping
demand curve. For some purposes, this definition is far too broad because
it includes all firms except those under pure competition. Yet the broad
definition does have one advantage, namely, that parts of the analysis of
monopoly price can be carried over into the theory of pricing in monopolistic competition and in oligopoly.

The essentials of a good definition of monopoly have already been mentioned: There are no close substitutes, and in making his decisions on price,
the monopolist is independent. He does not have to allow for the price
*policies* of other sellers. He does have to take other prices into account
because they, as always, help to determine the demand for his product.
The position of the monopolist's demand curve is steady, given his buyers'
tastes, incomes, and given the prices of the not-so-close substitutes. It is
steady because if the monopolist raises or lowers his price, he provokes no

change in price policy by rivals, a change that would shift the monopolist's demand curve.

One last remark about the definition of monopoly: Many a monopolistic firm sells its product in two or more separate markets. A firm can have a monopolistic position in one market, but not in another. For example, electric-power companies are monopolists in selling electric energy for lighting and for certain appliances. The same companies face intense competition as sellers of energy for cooking and heating.

### Demand, Marginal Revenue, and Elasticity

The demand for the output of a firm under pure competition is always a horizontal line on a price-quantity diagram. The demand for the output of a monopolist always has a negative slope. So do the demands for firms in monopolistic competition and in oligopoly. The purely formal properties of monopoly demand, therefore, hold for monopolistic competition and for oligopoly.

Demand, marginal revenue, and elasticity have all been explained before. What needs to be done now is to probe a little farther into the relations between them. The result will be some useful logical propositions.

The demand curve of a monopolist represents his marketing possibilities. The tastes of his customers and their incomes are built into the demand curve. So are the availabilities and the prices of the substitutes for his product. His demand curve is simply the industry demand curve described earlier in this book.

#### Marginal Revenue of a Monopolist

Marginal revenue is the addition to total revenue by selling one unit more, or the loss of total revenue by selling one unit less. It would of course be unusual, if not strange, to see a firm adjusting its sales one unit at a time, calculating the effect on its total revenue. Firms no doubt make their sales adjustments in batches, in hundreds or thousands of units at a time. But the assumptions of perfect knowledge of the market and of profit maximization require the pinpoint precision of the concept of marginal revenue.

Table 19–1 shows the relation between marginal revenue and price. The first two columns are a monopolist's demand schedule. The third column is total revenue, the numbers being obtained by multiplying those in the first two columns. The fourth column is marginal revenue, the numbers obtained by subtraction. The marginal revenue of 3 units is 6, because these units bring in a total revenue of $24, whereas 2 units bring in $18. Notice that marginal revenue is lower than price and that as price goes

**TABLE 19–1**

Marginal Revenue and Price

| P | Q | TR | MR |
|---|---|---|---|
| $10 | 1 unit | $10 | $10 |
| 9 | 2 units | 18 | 8 |
| 8 | 3 units | 24 | 6 |
| 7 | 4 units | 28 | 4 |
| 6 | 5 units | 30 | 2 |
| 5 | 6 units | 30 | 0 |
| 4 | 7 units | 28 | −2 |

down, marginal revenue goes down faster. In the numbers in Table 19–1, price goes down one dollar at a time, whereas marginal revenue goes down two dollars at a time. (See Note 1 in the Appendix to Part Five.) The same numbers can be made to say two more things. Observe that when demand is elastic, at prices *above* $5, marginal revenue is positive. When demand has unity elasticity *at* $5, marginal revenue is zero. When demand is inelastic, marginal revenue is negative.

The same relations are shown graphically in Figure 19–1. The demand curve is *D* and the marginal revenue curve is *MR*. The demand curve is linear for the sake of convenience. The *MR* curve always lies to the left of the demand curve whether or not it is linear. This is another way of saying that the marginal revenue of any quantity is less than its price. The *MR* curve is to be read this way: As quantity increases, the height of the *MR* curve above each quantity shows the addition to total revenue from the quantity. In Figure 19–1, the quantity is *OA*, with a price *PA,* and a marginal revenue of *FA*. Total revenue is the rectangle *OBPA*. Total revenue is also the area under the marginal revenue curve, *OCFA*.[1] Because each one describes the same total revenue, the two areas are necessarily equal. Therefore the two triangles — *CBE* and *EPF* — are equal. With a little help from Euclid, it can be seen that *BE* equals *EP*, so that *E* is at the midpoint of the line *BP*. To generalize: *When the demand curve is a straight line, the marginal revenue curve is also straight; it bisects any horizontal line between the demand curve and the price axis.*

This property of linear demand is convenient because it makes it easy to draw accurate diagrams and, more important that that, it simplifies the exposition of the economics of monopoly price.

---

[1] The marginal revenue of *OA* units is the line *FA*. The line that would stand just next to it on the left is the marginal revenue of *OA* — 1 units. And so on. Total revenue is the sum of these lines, that is, the area *OCFA*. Similarly, the total revenue of, e.g., 4 units in Table 19–1 can be found by adding the numbers in the marginal revenue column.

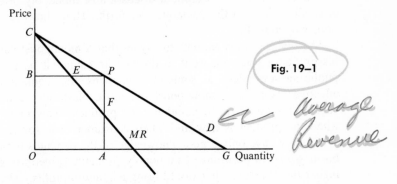

Demand and Marginal Revenue

Fig. 19–1

*average Revenue* (handwritten annotation)

## Marginal Revenue, Price, and Elasticity

A convenient formula, that will be used later, is this:

$$MR = P - \frac{P}{E}.$$

That is, marginal revenue equals price minus price divided by the coefficient of point elasticity of demand at the price in question. Suppose that $E$ is 2, then $MR = P - \dfrac{P}{2} = \frac{1}{2}P$. And if elasticity is unity, so that $E = 1$, the formula says that marginal revenue is zero.

The formula can be derived from Figure 19–1. At price $PA$, elasticity is equal to $\dfrac{PG}{CP}$. The proof for this is on page 37. Now

$$\frac{PG}{CP} = \frac{BO}{CB}$$

because the two triangles — $CGO$ and $CPB$ — are similar. Therefore,

$$E = \frac{PA}{PF} = \frac{PA}{PA - FA}.$$

But $FA$ is marginal revenue. Hence

$$E = \frac{P}{P - MR}.$$

This can be rearranged as $P = E\ (P - MR)$, and as

$$MR = P - \frac{P}{E}.$$

(For the calculus, see Note 1 in the Appendix to Part Five.)

## Qualifications

It is customary to conclude a discussion of monopoly pricing with a list of qualifications to the principles set forth. Here, however, the qualifications will come first.

The qualifications amount to saying that a monopolist cannot maximize his profits or does not want to do so. He cannot if he is regulated by a public agency unless, as sometimes happens, the regulation is wholly ineffective. Nor can a monopolist maximize his profits if he has only the vaguest notion of the demand for his product. This must often be true when the product is new and when consumer taste for it is still in flux. When they have only a poor knowledge of the demands for their products, businessmen in positions of monopoly probably sometimes set their prices higher than the level that would bring maximum profits. They are likely to do so because of the common confusion of high prices with high profits, because of the prevailing belief that demand is inelastic, and because to choose a high price may seem the safe thing to do.

Monopolists who deliberately earn less than maximum profits do so because they fear the imposition of public regulation or because they do not want high profits to count against them in a possible antitrust suit. Then, too, they might not wish to encourage potential competition.

### Monopoly Price in the Immediate Market

From now on the assumptions are that the monopolist knows his market and thus the demand for his product, knows his costs, and seeks no other goal than to maximize his profits.

First of all, consider the monopolist in the immediate market. He has something to sell, something already produced and ready for sale. Production took place in the past — weeks ago, or months ago, or even years ago. The monopolist does not let his pricing decision be influenced by his costs of production. The pricing decision must be made now. It makes no difference now whether the past costs were high or low.

In the immediate market, the monopolist sells at a price that will yield him the maximum *total* revenue. Call this price his optimum price. The maximum total revenue attainable at the optimum price might be high or it might be low, when judged by some standard such as the monopolist's earnings in the past. His demand now might be strong or weak, but whatever it is, he selects the optimum price. Suppose that the demand for the monopolist's product is $D$, in Figure 19–2. Imagine first that he has an amount $OB$ to sell. He sells this amount at the price it brings, namely, $P_2$. He can sell no more since he has none, nor would he want to sell any less because his demand is elastic (as shown by the fact that $MR$ is positive at $OB$).

Monopoly Price: Immediate Market

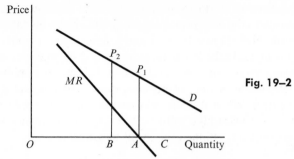

Fig. 19–2

Imagine next that the monopolist has on hand an amount equal to *OC*. He will not sell all of it because if he did, he would have a smaller total revenue than if he sold the amount *OA*. The marginal revenue of any amount larger than *OA* is negative, another way of saying that the total revenue is less. Therefore, if the monopolist has *OA* or more, he will sell the amount *OA* at the price $P_1$. The marginal revenue of this amount is zero. And since costs — for decision making — are zero, the condition $MR = MC$ holds.

What does the monopolist do with the unsold amount? If the product is something perishable, like fish or fruit, he probably destroys the excess amount or lets it rot. If the product is not perishable, he might hold it hoping that his market will improve in the future. Even a nonperishable product can be destroyed. This in fact has often happened, usually when a monopoly is not a single firm but an organization — a cartel — of firms set up to sell what they all have produced. If the organization is weak and if the firms do not fully trust each other, they might decide on destruction. But notice: When a monopoly has such a quantity that it withholds part of it from a market, perhaps destroying the amount withheld, the demand for the whole quantity is inelastic.

The demand for a monopolist's product at his selling price is always elastic, except that demand can have unit elasticity when the monopolist disregards his costs. The profit-maximizing monopolist never sells at a price where demand is inelastic.

When first encountered, these assertions seem to be wrong, somehow. It is well, therefore, to restate and to embellish their proof. Profit maximization means the equality of marginal revenue and marginal cost. Marginal cost can never be negative. It is either zero, as in the immediate market, or positive. Therefore, marginal revenue is zero or positive. Therefore elasticity is unity or greater than unity. Another kind of proof is this: Suppose a monopolist, who has no clear idea of his demand, hires consultants to study and measure it for him. Suppose that they are able to tell him, with sufficient accuracy, just what his demand is. He learns that his demand is inelastic at the price he has been charging. What does he do? He raises his price, because to do so increases his total revenue. His profits become higher owing to the larger total revenue and because his total costs are lower, since at the higher price he sells and produces fewer units. So long as his demand is inelastic, he keeps on raising his price and increasing his profits. This cannot go on forever, because if it did, the monopolist would absorb all the disposable income of his customers. His demand must turn elastic at some price. When it does, another price hike will reduce total revenue. When the next price hike would cut revenue more than it would cut costs, the monopolist has attained the profit-maximizing price.

### Monopoly Price in the Short and in the Long Run

In the short run and in the long, the monopolist is a producer who must balance his costs against his revenues. In the short run, he observes the behavior of the marginal cost of more or less output from the plant and other facilities that he has. For the long run, he makes a decision on the best size of plant to build. Since the analytical problems of the theory of monopoly pricing are on the demand side, not on the cost side, there is no need to dwell on the differences between pricing in the short run and the long.

Monopoly Price: Short and Long Run

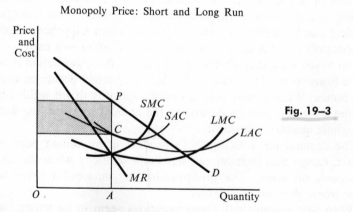

Fig. 19–3

Figure 19–3 is the conventional full-dress diagram of monopoly price. The monopolist is in equilibrium when he produces the amount *OA* and sells it at the price *PA*. His profit is the shaded area, which is his total revenue minus his total costs. Marginal revenue equals marginal cost — both long-run marginal cost and short-run marginal cost. In Figure 19–3, the monopolist is fully adjusted. His average cost, *CA*, is at a minimum, because he is on his long-run cost curve *LAC*.

If the monopolist's demand temporarily increases, he expands production with his existing plant, increasing output to correspond with the intersection of the *MR* and *SMC* curves. If there is a large and permanent increase in the demand for his product, the monopolist will build a larger
plant whose size corresponds to the intersection of the *MR* and *LMC*
curves.

If, as in Figure 19–3, the monopolist's equilibrium is on the declining
portion of the *LAC* curve, he is said to have a "natural monopoly." That
is, the cost of the output *OA* is less if a monopolist produces it than if the
same output were divided between two or more independent firms; they
would have to operate higher up and to the left on their *LAC* curves.
Many public-utility firms are natural monopolies.

### Price and Profit

It must be clear that a rational monopolist has no interest in a high price
or in a high or even a maximum profit per unit. He wants maximum profits
— maximum net revenue in the short run and maximum net profits in the
long run. But a monopolist, simply because he is a monopolist, does not
necessarily earn large profits.

The idea of monopoly usually suggests the idea of large and often ill-
gotten gains. Here too is an association of ideas, and a common one, that

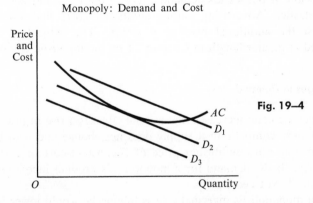

Monopoly: Demand and Cost

Fig. 19–4

has no foundation of logic. The reason for the association is probably
that highly profitable monopolies attract attention; those with slender
profits, or with none at all, are simply ignored.

The size of a monopolist's profits depends on the relation between demand and cost. Figure 19–4 shows three possibilities. In this figure, price
and the marginal curves are omitted because they are not needed for the
purpose at hand. Let *AC* first stand for a long-run cost curve. If demand

is $D_1$, the monopolist's maximum profit is large. By ordinary business standards, it would indeed be enormous because it would be about a quarter of dollar sales. If demand is $D_2$, as it could be, the monopolist receives no net profit at all. The curve $D_2$ is tangent to the average cost curve. There is only one price he can charge without losing money; this is the price corresponding to the point of tangency. Since costs are the full costs that include a normal profit, the monopolist continues to produce. He is maximizing profits, true enough, but the maximum is zero. Zero profits are bigger than negative profits, i.e., losses. If the monopolist did anything else — if he raised his price or lowered it — he would operate at a loss, because everywhere except at the point of tangency the curve $D_2$ lies below the curve $AC$. If demand is $D_3$, nothing but losses are possible. In the long run, the monopolist would not produce this product. But let the $AC$ curve now be a short-run average cost curve and suppose that $D_3$ is a temporarily depressed demand. Provided that price exceeds average variable costs, the monopolist will produce, equating marginal revenue and short-run marginal cost, so as to minimize his losses.

### Advertising

If a monopolist advertises, he tries to make his product more desirable in the minds of his actual and potential consumers. If his advertising is successful, it pushes his demand curve to the right and makes his demand less elastic. Advertising causes additional costs that must be weighed against the additional revenue it yields. The subject of advertising is treated at greater length in Chapter 21 on monopolistic competition.

### Changes in Demand

When demand increases, the normal effect is a rise in price. This is true under pure competition if supply does not change and with the exceptions of the long-run equilibrium price of a constant-cost or a decreasing-cost industry. If the demand for a monopolist's product increases, will he raise his price? Not necessarily.

If a monopolist's marginal cost is falling, he would lower his price when demand increases so long as the new equality of marginal cost and marginal revenue is compatible with a lower price. The rational monopolist is interested, of course, not in the height of his price, but in the size of his net revenue or net profits. But even if marginal cost is not falling, the monopolist can gain by lowering his price when demand increases provided that the new demand is more elastic than the old.

To prove this in the simplest way, let unit cost be constant and let the formula $MR = P - \dfrac{P}{E}$ be put to use. Suppose that the elasticity of the old demand at the old price is 2 and that the elasticity of the new demand at the new price is 3. When these numbers are fed into the formula, the result is that the old marginal revenue is 1/2 the old price and the new marginal revenue is 2/3 the new price. The old and the new marginal revenues are equal because both are equal to the same marginal cost. Therefore the new price is lower than the old. With these numbers, the new price is 25 per cent less than the old.[2] Similar results would come from any other pair of elasticity coefficients.

Figure 19–5 shows the lower price that results when a monopolist's

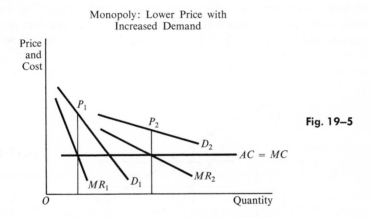

Monopoly: Lower Price with
Increased Demand

**Fig. 19–5**

demand increases and becomes more elastic. The old demand is $D_1$ and the new is $D_2$.

Similarly, if a monopolist's demand declines and if the new demand is less elastic than the old, he raises his price. Business firms in quasi-monopolistic positions have sometimes raised their prices in periods of slack demand. Public criticism is likely to say, among other things, that such firms do not act even in their own interests. The theory here shows that whatever else might be said about it, a monopolist's action in raising price in the face of a drop in demand is indeed rational if the demand becomes less elastic. In a short period of time, that is the very thing that demand is likely to do.

[2] A fuller explanation: Let the subscripts 1 and 2 denote the old and new prices, etc. By assumption, $MC_1 = MC_2$. By the rule of profit maximization, $MR_1 = MC_1$ and $MR_2 = MC_2$. Therefore, $MR_1 = MR_2$. Let $E_1 = 2$, and $E_2 = 3$. Therefore, $MR_1 = \dfrac{P_1}{2}$ and $MR_2 = \dfrac{2P_2}{3}$, and $\dfrac{P_1}{2} = \dfrac{2P_2}{3}$. Hence $\dfrac{P_1}{P_2} = \dfrac{4}{3} = \dfrac{100}{75}$.

### Changes in Cost — the Effects of Taxes

If a monopolist's costs go up, he can be expected to raise his price. If his average full costs rise by 10 cents, will he raise his price by 10 cents? Most people would unhesitatingly say yes to this question and could give plenty of examples to back up their answers. But the rational monopolist raises his price by *less* than 10 cents.

The rational monopolist looks only to the equality of marginal cost and revenue. If cost goes up, then he has a new marginal cost curve. He adjusts output and price so that his higher marginal cost is equal to marginal revenue.

There can be many causes of a rise in costs. For simplicity, assume that the cause is an excise tax of so many cents on each unit sold by the monopolist. Why the monopolist raises his price by an amount *less* than the tax per unit can be seen easily in Figure 19–6. Here, the assumptions of linear

Effect of a Tax on Monopoly Price

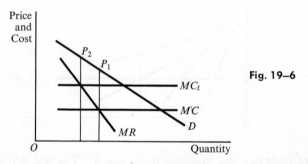

Fig. 19–6

demand and constant costs are used again. Before the imposition of the tax, the price is $P_1$. The tax raises the marginal cost curve to $MC_t$. The new price is $P_2$. The difference between $P_2$ and $P_1$ is less than the amount of the tax. With the imposition of the tax, $MC$ rises by the amount of the tax. $MR$ must rise by the same amount so that $MR = MC$. But as sales and output are cut back, price rises more slowly than $MR$ — the converse of the faster fall of $MR$ when price is declining. Therefore, price rises by less than the amount of the tax.

### Comparison of Monopoly and Competitive Prices

The standard method of comparing prices and outputs under monopoly and under pure competition is to take them both in long-run equilibrium. Imagine that an industry could either be under the control of a monopolist or could consist of many independent firms. Assume that costs are exactly the same whether the industry is monopolized or competitive. It might seem that this assumption is highly debatable, to say the least. Remember, however, that all is adjustable in the long run, that both a monopolist and a group of competitors can have the same production functions (i.e., the same technology), and that both are profit maximizers.

The simplest comparison again uses the linear-demand-constant-cost assumptions. Figure 19–7 compares equilibrium price and output in mo-

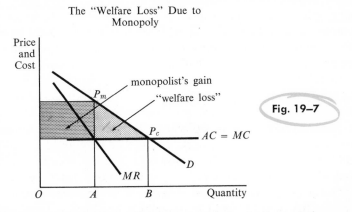

The "Welfare Loss" Due to
Monopoly

Fig. 19–7

nopoly and in pure competition. The monopoly price is $P_m$ and the competitive price is $P_c$. The constant-cost curve stands for the long-run supply curve in pure competition. The competitive price equals the long-run average and marginal costs of the firms.

With the assumptions, the monopoly output $OA$ is exactly one-half the competitive output $OB$ because the marginal revenue curve bisects any horizontal line. With other assumptions, i.e., other shapes of the demand and cost curves, the ratio of monopoly to competitive output could be more or less than one-half. Always, however, the monopolist has a higher price and produces less.

### The Net Loss of Consumers' Surplus

The monopolist obviously gains from his monopoly position. The consumers have to pay a price that exceeds cost.[3] In that sense, they suffer a loss. Which is larger — the monopolist's gain or his customers' loss?

[3] In equilibrium, monopoly price exceeds marginal cost by a factor that depends on the elasticity of demand. Precisely, $P = MC \dfrac{E}{E-1}$. This is the proof: Page 297 shows that $E = \dfrac{P}{P - MR}$. Since $MR = MC$ in equilibrium, $E = \dfrac{P}{P - MC}$. Then $EP - EMC = P$, and $MC = P\dfrac{(E-1)}{E}$, and $P = MC\dfrac{E}{E-1}$. The greater the elasticity, the closer is $P$ to $MC$, and vice versa.

Some economists hold that this question can be answered with the concept of consumer's surplus (see page 58 and Figure 4–4 on page 59). Monopoly causes a loss of consumer's surplus which is greater than the gain to the monopolist. The excess of the loss over the gain can be called "the welfare loss" due to monopoly. In Figure 19–7, the loss of consumer's surplus is the sum of the two shaded areas. But the monopolist has his net profit, his gain, which is the heavily shaded area. The loss of consumer's surplus is greater than the gain to the monopolist. The excess of the loss over the gain is the lightly shaded triangle in Figure 19–7. In other words, the consumers lose the satisfactions they would have from the amount $AB$, which can be sold at prices that more than cover full costs.

### Equity and the Distribution of Income

Some economic theorists object to this method of measuring the welfare loss due to monopoly because the method requires the addition of the utilities lost by the individual consumers. Besides, who is "the" monopolist and who are "the" consumers? The monopolist could be the sales agent for some poor farmers or fishermen, and the consumers could be wealthy people; the product could be something like, say, a rare kind of caviar. Or, to turn things round the other way, the monopolist could be a wealthy and powerful organization and the consumers a group of poor people. Accordingly, if the net loss of consumers' surplus is to have much meaning, it has to be supposed that the producer and his consumers have about the same incomes.

If they do not, then monopoly redistributes income from rich to poor, or from poor to rich. Economists who take the position that a transfer of income from rich to poor accords with the equity standard of economic welfare are then predisposed to soften, perhaps to a whisper, their condemnation of a monopoly that gives this result. Similarly, a monopoly that transfers income from poor to rich receives a charge from both barrels — this monopoly violates both standards, efficiency as well as equity.

### The Allocation of Resources

Because he produces less than would a competitive industry, a monopolist causes the allocation of resources to be distorted from the efficiency standard of economic welfare. Remember that when efficiency is at a maximum, price equals minimum average long-run cost and also marginal cost. Thus the last dollar of resources in each industry creates an incremental product value of one dollar. In monopoly, however, marginal cost is less than price; thus the last dollar of resources creates an incremental value product of more than one dollar. If a dollar's worth of resources is transferred from competitive industries to a monopoly, there is a gain. A dollar's worth of competitive output is lost, but more than a dollar's worth of extra monopoly output is achieved. Thus if a monopolist can be compelled to produce more, there is a gain in efficiency up to the point where the monopolist's price equals his marginal cost.

## The Dynamics of Monopoly

All that has been said about monopoly so far is static equilibrium theory. Change over time has been ignored. Consumer tastes and technology have been assumed to be known and given.

In a changing and growing economy, the appearance of monopoly undergoes alteration. Consumer tastes shift, technology improves, new products and new industries emerge, some older industries languish and decline. A firm with a monopoly in one period finds itself harried by competitors offering similar products in the next period; monopoly becomes transformed into oligopoly. Even the industries sheltered by public regulation become exposed in time to the inroads on their markets from other products and services. The monopolies of local transportation once enjoyed by interurban electric railways are long since gone. The railroads once had a collective monopoly of intercity transportation.

The "lasting distinctiveness" of a monopolized product hardly ever endures for long. Most such products go through a cycle. They begin their lives with their distinctiveness, being sold at monopoly prices. Then come the rival products; monopoly shades into monopolistic competition (Chapter 21) or into oligopoly (Chapters 22–24). In the end, perhaps, what was once distinctive becomes just another mail-order-house item.

Short-run monopoly is even an ingredient, though not a necessary one, of effective competition, which is mentioned at the end of Chapter 17. In an industry where several firms are rival producers and sellers of similar products, one firm can make an innovation. Suppose the innovation is an improved product the demand for which quickly increases. The innovating firm can then take advantage of its success, price as a monopolist, and earn monopoly profits — until the other firms imitate the innovation. When they do so, the temporary monopoly of the innovating firm ceases to exist.

## Applications

The great contribution of the theory of monopoly to applied knowledge is the emphasis that it gives to demand. The analyses presented in this chapter show that elasticity of demand is the key to the solution of the problem of rational pricing by a monopolist. Cost is important too, of course, but not more so for a monopolistic than for a competitive firm.

### Pricing Decisions

When a business firm has a product of lasting distinctiveness, to use Joel Dean's phrase again, and when the firm wants to maximize the profits from this product, then the firm should make the best estimate possible of the demand for its product and price according to the principle of monopoly price. The conscience of the individual firm need not be troubled with qualms about equity and the efficiency of the whole economy.

Pricing is often done by adding percentage margins, or markups, to cost. In many industries, the standard practice, however, is to calculate markups as percentages of price, not of cost. Thus, a markup of 50 per cent is 50 per cent of the price, not 50 per cent added to cost. One of the formulas mentioned earlier in this chapter can be put to work to show how to figure markups that result in profit-maximizing prices. The formula is

$$P = E(P - MR).$$

Assume that marginal cost is constant, so that marginal cost and average variable cost are equal. For maximum profits, $MR = MC$. Therefore,

$$P = E(P - MC).$$

The difference between price and marginal cost is the markup. Therefore,

$$P = E \times \text{markup}.$$

And

$$\frac{\text{markup}}{P} = \frac{1}{E}.$$

Thus, for example, if $E$ is 2, then the markup is 50 per cent. Suppose the cost is \$5.00 a unit. Then the price is \$10.00. If instead, $E$ were 3, the markup becomes 33-1/3 per cent, and the price is \$7.50. The higher the elasticity, the smaller the percentage markup. This of course is only common sense; the higher the elasticity, the closer is the competition from substitutes and the wiser it is not to be too greedy in pricing.

The only catch here is that the formula requires a precise number for the coefficient of elasticity. In practice, however, good estimates can often be made if enough thought is given to the matter.

### Marginal-Cost Pricing

The theory of welfare economics explains the conditions for an ideal allocation of resources. Applied welfare economics states rules to improve the actual allocation of resources. One of the rules, though a much controverted one, is marginal-cost pricing. Some economists have proposed that the prices charged by public utilities and by such government enterprises as public power projects be fixed so that these prices are equal to marginal costs.

The prices that the public utility companies are permitted to charge are in general based upon average costs. Profits called a fair return are added to the average business costs of the enterprises. Whether the fair returns and the average business costs are correctly computed in the normal procedure of regulation is a question irrelevant here. The point is that the existing system of regulation concentrates its attention on fair returns, on equity rather than on efficiency. Prices are fixed to bring about an equitable relation between investors and consumers. But the prices also determine volumes of production and consumption. These volumes are probably not "efficient" in the welfare sense.

The marginal-cost pricing proposal would separate the goal of fair returns to investors from the goal of improving the allocation of resources. If all public utility companies and all public enterprises were required to set their prices equal to their marginal costs, then each would be efficient in the long-run adjustment, and all taken together would be efficient. With the $P = MC$ rule, the output of each industry would be optimal and so would their relative outputs. One problem, however, would be that some of the enterprises would have falling marginal costs. Therefore, $MC$ would be lower than average cost, and the optimum price would be lower than average cost. Therefore such enterprises would operate at losses. Welfare theorists bravely say that the losses could be made up by subsidies and that the costs of the subsidies would be lower than the gain in welfare. Even so, a proposal to compel some private companies to operate at losses and then to subsidize them with public funds is likely to remain for a long time where it now is — in the ivory tower.

The existing system of public-utility rate regulation can be defended on the grounds (1) that some measure of equity is achieved; (2) that the imposition of rates, or prices, that remain constant for months or years at a time gives a strong incentive to the public-utility companies to find ways of reducing their costs; and (3) that when prices are fixed at levels corresponding to full costs as defined in this book, they are likely to be well below the monopoly levels. Thus output in fact does come closer to the efficiency ideal. This last point can easily be seen for a public utility with a steeply falling demand curve and gently falling $LAC$ and $LMC$ curves. If it is set where demand intersects $LAC$, price is far below the height defined by $MR = LMC$.

### Summary

A monopolist can set his price independently within the limits imposed by the demand for his product. When marginal revenue is positive, demand is elastic; when $MR = 0$, demand has unit elasticity; and when $MR$ is negative, demand is inelastic. A useful formula is $MR = P - \dfrac{P}{E}$. In the immediate market, a monopolist sets his price to maximize his total revenue. He sets price to maximize net revenue in the short run and net profits in the long run. The demand at any price he sets is unit-elastic or elastic. Profits depend on the demand-cost relation, not on the mere fact of monopoly. If demand increases, a monopolist lowers his price if demand becomes more elastic and if costs are constant. If costs increase, he raises his price by less than the unit rise in cost. With linear demand and constant-cost assumptions, monopoly output in long-run equilibrium is half the competitive. Criticism of monopoly is based on the net loss of consumer's surplus, possibly on grounds of equity, and certainly on grounds of efficiency. When dynamic change is taken into account, monopoly is seen to be temporary. The theory of monopoly pricing is applicable in business and in the evaluation of public-utility regulation.

## SELECTED REFERENCES

The pure theory: Joan Robinson, *The Economics of Imperfect Competition* (London: Macmillan, 1933), Books II and IV.

Theoretical and descriptive: Fritz Machlup, *The Political Economy of Monopoly* (Baltimore: Johns Hopkins Press, 1952). Donald Dewey, *Monopoly in Economics and Law* (Chicago: Rand McNally, 1959). E. A. G. Robinson, *Monopoly* (London: Nisbet and Cambridge University Press, 1941).

Business applications: Joel Dean, *Managerial Economics* (New York: Prentice-Hall, 1951), Chap. 7. Harold Bierman, Lawrence E. Fouraker, and Robert K. Jaedicke, *Quantitative Analysis for Business Decisions* (Homewood: Irwin, 1961), Chap. 18.

## EXERCISES AND PROBLEMS

1. Draw diagrams to show the effects on a monopolist of (a) a subsidy for each unit he produces, (b) a sales tax of 10 per cent.

2. What would a monopolist do if a tax were imposed on his entire net profits? Why?

3. Show the relation between elasticity of demand and the excess of monopoly price over competitive price.

4. Suppose that a monopolist's demand decreases and that $E$, which had been 1.50, becomes 1.25. Assume constant costs. By what percentage does the monopolist change his price?

5. Draw the diagram for the statements of the last two sentences just before the summary of this chapter.

# Price Discrimination

# 20

FORMS OF PRICE DISCRIMINATION • DEGREES OF DISCRIMINA-
TION • THE PRICING OF MULTIPLE PRODUCTS • OUTPUT UNDER
PRICE DISCRIMINATION • APPLICATIONS •

Price discrimination can be observed in many of the markets where the sellers are monopolists or oligopolists. In economic literature, price discrimination is a neutral term; no odium attaches to it. Neither does the expression "discriminating monopolist" convey any suggestion of approval. In general, price discrimination means that a firm charges two or more prices for the same thing at the same time. It can also mean that the differences in the prices of a firm's products are greater than the differences in their costs of production.

The theory of price discrimination throws almost the whole emphasis on the demand side. Costs, of course, must be aligned with demand, but otherwise costs play the subordinate role. In contrast, business practice usually puts the stress on differences in costs; because demand is often hard to estimate, it tends to be ignored or given scant attention.

Price discrimination is an extension of monopoly pricing, in the broad rather than in the narrow meaning of monopoly. Any seller with a sloping demand curve is a monopolist in the broad and loose sense. A firm that is a price maker can look to the possibilities of price discrimination; this is true of a monopolist who prices independently, or an oligopolist, or a monopolistic competitor.

## Forms of Price Discrimination

Price discrimination comes in so many forms and guises, and even disguises, that only the leading types and examples will be mentioned here. Of these, only the kinds intended to increase sellers' profits will be considered. Hence this discussion excludes predatory price discrimination, i.e., the temporary lowering of prices by a large firm with the intention of bankrupting smaller rivals in a particular location or line of products.

The principal forms of price discrimination, as they exist in the American economy, are listed in Table 20–1.

### TABLE 20–1

#### Principal Forms of Price Discrimination

| Main Classes | Bases of Discrimination | Examples |
|---|---|---|
| Personal | Incomes of buyers | Surgeons' fees |
| | Earning power of buyers | Royalties paid for use of patented machines and processes |
| Group | Age, sex, military status, etc. of buyers | Children's haircuts, ladies' day at baseball parks, lower admission charges for men in uniform, etc. |
| | Location of buyers | Zone prices, basing-point prices, lower export prices (dumping), etc. |
| | Status of buyers | Lower prices to new customers, quantity discounts to big buyers, etc. |
| | Use of product | Railroad rates, public utility rates, fluid milk and milk for cheese and ice cream, etc. |
| Product | Qualities of products | Relatively higher prices for de luxe models |
| | Labels on products | Lower prices of unbranded products |
| | Sizes of products | Relatively lower prices for larger sizes (the "giant economy" size) |
| | Peak and off-peak services | Lower prices for off-peak services; excursion rates in transportation, off-season rates at resorts, etc. |

### Prerequisites

The prerequisites of price discrimination are separate markets and differences of elasticity of demand between the markets. An old example is the monopoly that sells at a high price in the domestic market and at a low price in the foreign market. The two markets are kept separate by a tariff wall; domestic buyers cannot place orders abroad at the lower foreign price and import the commodity. The price is lower in the foreign market because demand is more elastic, owing to the competition from other similar products; such competition is lacking in the domestic market.

Markets are kept separate in many ways. If a firm cannot keep its markets separate, then all of its buyers will make their purchases in the market with the lowest price, thus frustrating the firm's attempt to increase its profits through price discrimination. The markets for the box seats, the orchestra seats, and the balcony seats in theaters are segregated by tickets and ushers. Because services, as opposed to physical commodities, cannot be resold, their markets can easily be kept apart. Electric power companies use meters and other devices to separate the markets for electrical energy for lighting, cooking, hot water heating, commercial uses, industrial uses, etc. Much price discrimination rests on nothing more than the imperfect knowledge and the sheer ignorance of consumers. Some degree of interdependence often exists, however, between related markets. A resort hotel, for example, might establish lower off-season rates, which might attract some of the regular patrons. This is the problem of leakages between markets, a problem whose complications will not be examined here. The discussion to follow assumes that a firm's markets are water-tight compartments.

## Degrees of Discrimination

How far can a monopolist go in charging different prices for his product? What is the limit of the increase in his net profit from price discrimination?

### First Degree

The limit is defined in the concept of discrimination of the first degree. This expression is employed by A. C. Pigou, the English economist, who created the idea of degrees of discrimination. In discrimination of the first degree, the monopolist knows the maximum amount of money *each* consumer will pay for any quantity. He then sets his prices accordingly and takes from each consumer the entire amount of his consumer's surplus (page 58). Mrs. Joan Robinson calls the same thing perfect discrimination, which is perfect, however, only from the point of view of the monopolist.

The simplest kind of discrimination of the first degree is one where, for some reason, his consumers buy only one unit each from the monopolist. Knowing exactly how willing they are, he charges each one a price so high that his consumers almost, but not quite, refuse to pay the prices. If all of his consumers have different tastes, the monopolist has a different price for each one. His lowest price is determined by his costs.

When consumers buy more than one unit of the monopolist's product, they are willing to buy more units at lower prices. The monopolist must then adjust his units of sale. Suppose that a consumer who could choose how many units he wanted to buy would buy ten units if the price were one dollar each. That is, ten units have a *marginal* utility of one dollar, though of course the *total* utility of ten units is higher. Suppose that the total utility of ten units to the consumer is 40 dollars. The monopolist makes his unit of sale the ten units; this is an all or nothing offer, and the price is 40 dollars. Consumer's surplus here is 30 dollars, i.e., 40 minus 10.

Discrimination of the first degree is the limiting, or extreme, case. Obviously, it could occur only rarely where a monopolist has only a few buyers and where he is shrewd enough to see the maximum prices they will pay.

### Second Degree

In discrimination of the second degree, the monopolist captures parts of his buyers' consumers' surpluses, but not all of them. The schedules of rates typically charged by public utilities can be regarded as a form of second-degree discrimination.

Figure 20–1 gives a simplified illustration. Let the curve $D$ be the demand of households for electrical energy in a community. The rate schedule, i.e., price list, is such that a high price is charged for the first few kilowatt

Second-Degree Discrimination

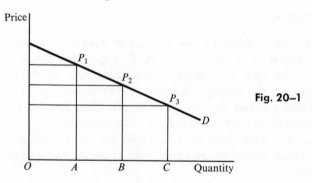

Fig. 20–1

hours (kwh) consumed per month. At the price $P_1$ in Figure 20–1, the total consumption is $OA$ kwh. Then the next block of kwh per month is sold at a lower price — the price $P_2$. At this price, $AB$ kwh are consumed.

Similarly, at price $P_3$, $BC$ kwh are consumed. Rate schedules usually have more than three blocks, or steps, which also are usually unequal in size. But the three prices, or rates, in Figure 20–1 are quite adequate for illustrative purposes.[1]

If the monopolist — the hypothetical electric-power company here — were allowed to charge only one price, and if he wanted to sell the amount $OC$, the price would have to be $P_3$. At the single price, his total revenue would be smaller. It would be the rectangle given by $P_3C \times OC$. But with the three prices, the total revenue is the sum of the three rectangles $P_3B$, $P_2A$, and $P_1O$. The monopolist in this way snatches part of consumer's surplus. The part he does *not* get is the sum of the three little triangles in Figure 20–1.

Second-degree price discrimination is necessarily practiced in markets where there are many buyers, sometimes hundreds of thousands of them. One rate or price schedule must apply to all buyers. Because tastes and incomes differ, the monopolist can seize only a small part of the consumers' surpluses of those buyers whose desires for his service are stronger, and whose incomes are higher. Second-degree discrimination is furthermore limited to services sold in blocks of small units — cubic feet of gas, kilowatt hours of electricity, minutes of telephoning — that can be easily metered, recorded, and billed.

### Third Degree: Allocation of a Given Amount

Third-degree price discrimination means that the monopolist divides his customers into two or more classes or groups, charging a different price to each class of customer. Each class is a separate market, e.g., the box seats, the reserved grandstand seats, the unreserved grandstand seats, and the bleachers.

The simplest analytical illustration of this common kind of price discrimination is that of the monopolist who sells something, already produced, in two separate markets. The problem resembles that of the monopolist selling in the immediate market; because he has some given amount to sell, his costs can be ignored. When he sells in two markets, the monopolist adjusts the amounts in each so that marginal revenues are equal. Here is another manifestation of the equimarginal principle: The last units sold in each of the two markets make the same addition to total revenue.

Suppose that the monopolist sells 1,200 units in market $A$ and 300 units in market $B$. In each market his marginal revenue is, say, \$5. If he sold

---

[1] It can be argued that the demand curve in Figure 20–1 should lie a little lower than a conventional demand curve, on which there can be only one price at one time. Because it extracts more money from the consumers, the discrimination has a small adverse effect on their incomes. The discussion above ignores the income effect, because it is almost certain to be negligibly small.

more in $A$ and less in $B$, his total revenue would be less because marginal revenue in $A$ would fall — he would transfer a unit that adds \$5 to his total revenue to a market where it would add only, say, \$4 to his total revenue. And by selling less in $B$, he would cause marginal revenue in $B$ to *rise* to \$6. There being no sense in gaining less than \$5 while losing more, it follows that optimum allocation calls for equality of marginal revenue in each market.

Though the marginal revenues are equal in the two markets, prices are unequal. The formula $MR = P - \dfrac{P}{E}$ can be put to use again.

$$\text{Since } MR_A = MR_B,$$

$$\text{then}$$

$$P_A - \frac{P_A}{E_A} = P_B - \frac{P_B}{E_B}, \quad \text{or} \quad P_A\left(1 - \frac{1}{E_A}\right) = P_B\left(1 - \frac{1}{E_B}\right).$$

Therefore, the price in market $A$, i.e., $P_A$, differs from price in market $B$ when elasticities in the two markets are unequal. If elasticities were equal, prices would be the same; hence there would be no price discrimination.

### An Example: Pricing of Milk

In practice, knowledge of demand is hardly ever so exact and complete that elasticities and marginal revenues can be precisely calculated. The best that sellers can do in practice is to increase their total revenues by price discrimination. Incomplete knowledge prevents them from raising their total revenues to the maximum that theory defines.

The pricing of milk is a good example of price discrimination in practice. In most parts of the United States, milk is sold monopolistically, by producers' associations which act as agents for the dairy farmers in each market area. The federal government lends its benign auspices to this fixing of the prices of milk. Milk is sold in two classes of markets, the markets for "fluid" milk as bought at retail in cities and the markets for "surplus" milk, which is the milk that becomes evaporated milk, butter, powdered milk, cheddar cheese, ice cream, etc. Each of the many producers' associations has a monopoly of the sale (at wholesale) of fluid milk in its own area. But in selling surplus milk, whose markets are much broader,. any one producers' association is in competition with others. Therefore, the demand for the surplus milk of any single association is highly elastic. Normally, the price of fluid milk is much higher than the price of surplus milk.

### Third Degree: Allocation of Production

When the monopolist looks into the future, planning his production and sales, he must take account of his costs as well as his revenues. Marginal revenues in each of two markets are equal here too, but they are also equal to the marginal costs of the monopolist's *entire* output. This is easy to see when marginal cost is constant over the relevant range of output; marginal revenues in both markets are equal to marginal cost and therefore to each other. But when marginal cost is a changing function of output, a diagram is needed to show the profit-maximizing division of sales between two markets.

In Figure 20–2, the monopolist has two markets, *A* and *B,* with demands $D_A$ and $D_B$. The demand in market *A* is smaller and more elastic (in the relevant range) than the demand in market *B*. The two marginal revenue curves are shown in the figure. The same product is sold in the two markets so that the one marginal cost curve suffices. The analysis holds for both the short run and the long.

Third-Degree Discrimination

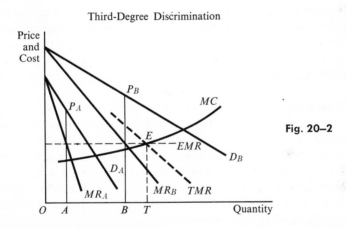

Fig. 20–2

The monopolist determines his *total* output in this way: Knowing the demands in the two markets, he calculates marginal revenue in each. Then he adds them. In Figure 20–2, the addition of $MR_A$ and $MR_B$ is found in line *TMR,* i.e., total marginal revenue. Line *TMR* is the horizontal summation of the two separate marginal revenues. The line *TMR* intersects *MC* at point *E,* which gives the total output *OT*. The line *EMR* is the line of equal marginal revenue. It then follows that *OA* is sold in market *A* at price $P_A$, and that *OB* is sold in market *B* at price $P_B$. The outputs *OA* and *OB* equal the total output *OT*. Both $MR_A$ and $MR_B$ equal *EMR,* which equals the marginal cost of *OT*. (See Note 2 in the Appendix to Part Five.)

Since $MR_A$ of output $OA$ exceeds the $MC$ of $OA$, why not sell more in market $A$? The answer is, given the sale of $OB$ in market $B$, that additional sales in market $A$ would raise $MC$ above $E$. That is, the additional sales would have a higher extra cost than the revenue they would bring. To the right of $E$, $MC$ exceeds $MR_A$, which is what would happen if sales in $A$ were greater than $OA$. Similar reasoning holds for sales larger than $OB$ in the $B$ market.

### The Pricing of Multiple Products

The theory of price discrimination just reviewed can be extended to the problem of determining the prices for the multiple products of a firm. The extension of the theory has been carried out in a well-known article by Eli W. Clemens of the University of Maryland. Most firms do in fact produce more than one product. Some produce thousands of products. The multiple products of a firm can be different sizes, models, types, styles, etc. of the same general class of thing. A firm's multiple products can also consist of physically quite dissimilar products. Each single product has a market. In the context of changing markets, changing costs, changing consumer tastes, and changing product designs, alert firms are constantly looking for new markets to invade with existing or with new products. A familiar example is the invasion of each other's markets by drugstores, variety stores, and grocery supermarkets.

What a firm has to sell, it can be argued, is not so much its product or its line of products as its capacity and know-how in production. For this statement to have meaning, certain conditions must hold. One is that the resources of the firm be readily convertible to making a range of products. This means that a good part of the equipment of the firm is general-purpose equipment and that management and labor are versatile. Another condition is that the firm normally has some idle equipment or equipment not fully utilized. This amounts to relaxing the assumptions of earlier chapters to the effect that the firm is always locked in a rigid profit-maximizing position.

In his model of the pricing of multiple products, Clemens begins by assuming that a firm has one product and that the firm's plant is being operated at 60 to 70 per cent of capacity. Marginal revenue and marginal cost for the one product are equal. With its idle capacity of plant, organization, and personnel, the firm can expand production without having to expect much increase in marginal costs. Some of the idle capacity can be used to produce a second product for a second market provided that the demand in the second market is above marginal cost. More of the idle capacity can be put to work on a third product, a fourth, and so on.

Figure 20–3 is simplified and adapted from one of Clemens's diagrams. Here the firm has four products that are sold in four markets. Actually, a firm can have dozens of distinct markets; just think of the firms that put out catalogues. But whatever holds for four can also be made to hold for any number. Figure 20–3 lines the four markets up from left to right. The first market has demand $D_1$, the second has demand $D_2$, and so on. The quantity sold in the first market is $OO_1$; in the second market it is $O_1O_2$, and so on. The firm maximizes its profits when it produces and sells quantities of each product such that their marginal revenues are equal to each other and equal to the marginal cost of total production.

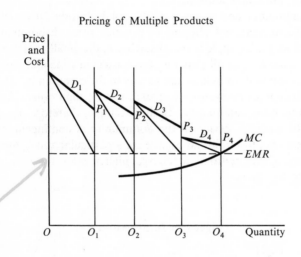

Pricing of Multiple Products

**Fig. 20–3**

The line $EMR$ is the line of equal marginal revenue. In each of the four markets, the marginal revenue curves are the lines lying below the corresponding demand curves. The prices of the four products are shown in the figure. Observe that the fourth product has a price just above marginal cost. The more elastic its demand, the closer would the price of the last, or "marginal,"[2] product approach marginal cost. For part of its output, therefore, the multiple-product firm operates like the competitive firm, bringing one of its prices close to marginal cost.

---

[2] This marginal product is not to be confused with the marginal physical product of an input, which is discussed in Chapter 9. Suppose a company producing rubber footwear finds it worthwhile, though just barely profitable, to put out a line of rubber rafts for swimming pools, etc. Then the rafts are a "marginal" product in the sense used above.

## Output under Price Discrimination

If a seller practices price discrimination, is his output larger or smaller than if he did not? The answer to this question is important, because of course one of the functions of prices is to determine the quantities of goods and services produced and sold. The answer also has to do with the relation between monopolistic and competitive outputs. But no single generalization about output under price discrimination can be made. The total output of a monopolist with two or more prices can indeed be larger or smaller than his total output if he would sell at one price. Conceivably, too, a monopolist could have an output equal to the output corresponding to conditions of pure competition.

Some commodities and services might not be produced at all if sellers were not able or were not allowed to practice price discrimination. The standard and simple example is the physician in the small community. If he charges the same fees to all patients, the physician's income would be too low, let it be supposed, to induce him to stay in the community. If, however, the physician charges his well-to-do patients more than others, he can earn enough to stay in the community. In this example, therefore, the continued availability of medical service in the community is contingent upon price discrimination. So, too, railroad service on a particular route might depend on the ability of the railroad to charge higher rates to some groups of shippers than to others.

Output with Discrimination

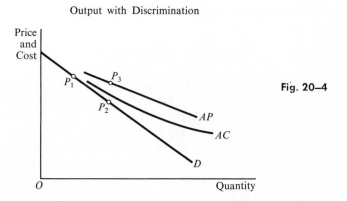

Fig. 20–4

Figure 20–4 contains an illustration. In the figure, the line $D$ is the ordinary demand, showing amounts that can be sold at prices that are the same to all buyers. The line $AP$ shows the *average* price received when different prices are charged. Thus the price $P_3$ is the average of the prices $P_1$ and $P_2$. The rest of the line $AP$ is constructed similarly. Whatever the pattern of price discrimination, the line $AP$ always lies to the right of the ordinary demand curve $D$.[3] In Figure 20–4, the cost curve $AC$ lies above $D$, but below $AP$. Accordingly, there would be no output if the firm had to select one price on $D$. But there *is* output with price discrimination, because the firm can choose an average price on $AP$, an average of discriminatory prices, which more than cover its costs.

If there were ever a monopolist able to practice the perfect discrimination described earlier, he would have an output as large as the purely competitive output with the same demand and cost functions. This is because the monopolist treats the consumers' demand curve as his own marginal revenue curve. He equates this marginal revenue with his marginal cost. Thus he equates demand with marginal cost, as in the equilibrium of pure competition.

Since discrimination of the second degree is an approach to discrimination of the first degree, it follows that output is larger than if the monopolist had a single price. When a monopolist practices third-degree discrimination, his output can be equal to, or less than, or greater than, his output at a single price. It depends on the shapes of the demand curves in the monopolist's two or more markets. If the demand curves in the separate markets are linear, then total output is the same as with a single price. With two markets, this means that the reduction in the market with the less elastic demand is equal to the expansion in the market with the more elastic demand. Proof of this is exceedingly complicated and will be omitted here.[4] In her authoritative discussion of price discrimination, Mrs. Joan Robinson comes to the conclusion that, in all likelihood, output is larger with price discrimination than without it.[5]

## Applications

The theory of price discrimination has numerous applications of varied kinds. The contribution of price theory to decisions on price discrimination, whether the decisions are for or against discrimination, is to draw attention to differences in elasticities of demand. In contrast, practical decision makers usually concentrate their thoughts on costs — on cost differences, or their absence, as justification, or the lack of justification for price differences.

---

[3] The $AP$ curve can also be derived from the total marginal revenue curve, which is the horizontal sum of the marginal revenue curves in the separate markets. Most writers designate the $AP$ curve as the average revenue curve.

[4] It can be found in Joan Robinson, *Economics of Imperfect Competition* (London: Macmillan, 1933), pp. 190–195.

[5] *Ibid.*, pp. 201, 202.

### Business Pricing Decisions

Clemens's model of multiple pricing is a leading example of how a business firm should conceptually tackle the problem of setting prices for its product line. The model, of course, is essentially simple; profits are the only objective, pricing is independent of possible reactions from rival firms, and cost complications are ignored. The lesson taught by the model is the irrationality of the common business practice of setting prices on different products by adding uniform percentages to costs. To do this is convenient. If elasticities differ, as they nearly always seem to do, then the practice of uniform mark-up pricing results in smaller profits than are attainable. In his *Managerial Economics,* Joel Dean has a long discussion of how the business firm should establish its price "differentials." He rails against uniform mark-up pricing, urging the business executive to look to the incremental costs of each product, to its actual or probable demand, and to its probable elasticity. In the short run, the firm should select the structure of prices and outputs of its several products that maximizes the excess of total revenue over total variable cost. Lack of data and the uncertainties of the future are barriers to firm estimates of demand. Still, they should not prevent analytical thought.

### Economic Policy

Price discrimination has long been a problem in American economic policy. Elaborate systems of price discrimination prevail in the rate structures of the railroads and of the public utilities. Anything smacking of first degree, or perfect, discrimination is prohibited in the pricing practices of firms and industries subject to special regulation by the federal and state governments. Such discrimination is personal. In general, classifications of buyers and of markets must meet legal tests of "reasonableness." Price differences must also be "reasonable," which usually means that they must conform to demonstrable differences in costs as measured by accounting standards. Differences in elasticities of demand are hardly ever put on an equal footing with differences in costs. The recognition given to elasticities is oblique or implicit. A regulated company may be allowed to charge a lower rate for some part of its service where it faces obvious competition, and where, accordingly, demand is more elastic. Railroads are often allowed to quote low rates on routes where they face serious competition from other common carriers.

The Robinson-Patman Act of 1936 prohibits, with certain exceptions and qualifications, price discrimination between classes of buyers when the effect of the discrimination is to injure competition. The main purpose of this law is to protect the independent retailer from the competition of the mass distributor (e.g., mail-order house) who can often buy from manufacturers at very low prices.

The rates charged by the United States Post Office are discriminatory. The pattern is based neither upon the costs of the different classes of services nor upon demand, let alone elasticity of demand. Instead, postal rates are set so as to promote the ends of policy as Congress sees them — ends such as mail service for all persons, the dissemination of knowledge (e.g., low rates for books), the subvention of advertising and periodicals, etc. If postal rates were fixed with the sole purpose of maximizing the net revenue of the Post Office Department, their structure would be far different.

During the 1930's, some agricultural economists tried to invent forms of price discrimination that would benefit farmers. If industry has discriminatory prices, they argued, why shouldn't agriculture? If government is going to raise farm prices anyway, why not work in a little discrimination? The notion was that food prices should be made higher to the rich, whose demand is inelastic, and be made lower to the poor, whose demand is less inelastic. If the gain to the urban poor and the gain to the farmers would exceed the loss to the rich, discriminatory prices for farm products would be justified. Such was the argument. All that came of it were certain programs, some of them still in effect, to make a few farm products available at low prices to selected groups of consumers. School children in many communities can buy milk at low prices; families on relief sometimes can buy "surplus" foods at low prices.

### Welfare

In the ideal economy of the welfare theorists, there would be no price discrimination. In this economy, the prevailing market structure would be pure competition under which price discrimination is impossible anyway. The natural monopolies in the ideal economy would set their prices equal to their marginal costs. Price differences between products would exactly equal differences in marginal costs, which is another way of expressing the absence of price discrimination. That consumers pay the same prices at the same time for the same products is one of the marginal conditions for maximum economic welfare.

Price discrimination takes on another hue when it is looked at in the context of a partial-welfare analysis. Partial welfare means the economic welfare flowing from one commodity or industry, considered by itself, and without regard for possible cross effects with other commodities or industries. It was shown above that demand-cost relations can be such that without discrimination a particular commodity or service will not be produced at all. Where government controls prices, it may permit or even encourage discrimination if the result is the production of something considered important — rail transportation, for example. Another general reason for government to practice or to encourage price discrimination is to reduce inequalities of personal real incomes. The equity criterion pushes aside the efficiency criterion. Tenants in public-housing projects, who must have incomes below specified levels, pay rents that are in general well below full costs. Military personnel and their families can buy groceries and other items in post exchanges at prices generally below those prevailing in ordinary retail establishments. Books in Braille are mailed free to the blind.

### Summary

The prerequisites of price discrimination by a monopolist are separate markets and differences of elasticity of demand between the markets. In *first-degree discrimination,* the monopolist captures the entire consumer's surplus of his buyers. In *second-degree discrimination,* he sets successively lower prices for successively larger quantities, seizing a part of consumer's surplus. In *third-degree discrimination,* the monopolist divides his customers into classes or groups. In the immediate market, he allocates sales between two markets so that *marginal revenues are equal.* The difference in prices depends on elasticities. In allocating production between two markets, the monopolist equates the two marginal revenues with the marginal cost of his entire output. A firm with many products maximizes profits by selling each product at a price that results in equality of marginal revenue with the marginal cost of total production. Output can be larger with price discrimination than without it. Sometimes output is possible only with price discrimination. The theory of discrimination has wide application in business decisions and in the analysis of economic policy.

### SELECTED REFERENCES

A good discussion of the many forms of price discrimination is given by Fritz Machlup, "Characteristics and Types of Price Discrimination," in National Bureau of Economic Research, *Business Concentration and Price Policy* (Princeton: Princeton University Press, 1955), pp. 397–435. Degrees of price discrimination are introduced by A. C. Pigou, *The Economics of Welfare,* 4th ed. (London: Macmillan, 1932), Chap. 17. The most rigorous treatment of the pure theory is found in Joan Robinson, *The Economics of Imperfect Competition* (London: Macmillan, 1933), Chap. 15 and 16. A less difficult though thorough discussion is in Joe S. Bain, *Pricing, Distribution, and Employment,* rev. ed. (New York: Holt,

1953), Chap. 9. The discussion of multiple product pricing is based on Eli W. Clemens, "Price Discrimination and the Multiple-Product Firm," *Review of Economic Studies,* Vol. XIX (1950–51), pp. 1–11; reprinted in American Economic Association, *Readings in Industrial Organization and Public Policy* (Homewood: Irwin, 1958). How business firms can benefit from the theory of price discrimination is explained by Joel Dean, *Managerial Economics* (New York: Prentice-Hall, 1951), Chap. 8 and 9. How dairy farmers do benefit is shown by Edmond S. Harris, *Classified Pricing of Milk,* Technical Bulletin No. 1184, United States Department of Agriculture, (Washington, D.C.: GPO, 1958).

## EXERCISES AND PROBLEMS

1. Suppose a monopolist has two markets, and that the demand schedules in them are as follows:

| Market A | | Market B | |
|---|---|---|---|
| P | Q | P | Q |
| $50 | 400 | $60 | 600 |
| 40 | 600 | 50 | 800 |
| 30 | 900 | 40 | 1,100 |
| 20 | 1,000 | 30 | 1,400 |

Suppose that the monopolist has 1,400 units to sell. What prices will he set in the two markets? Why?

2. A business firm charged with price discrimination in violation of the Robinson-Patman Act may offer a cost defense. The accused firm is exonerated if it can prove that cost differences are at least as great as price differences. Under the law, the costs are business costs, measured by cost accounting standards; roughly speaking, they are average costs. Suppose now that the law would allow *marginal* cost calculations as a defense against charges of price discrimination. What do you think the result would be?

3. Draw a diagram to illustrate third-degree discrimination in the immediate market.

4. Suppose that $E = 2$ in one market and $E = 1.5$ in the other market in which a monopolist can sell his product. What is the percentage ratio of the prices he charges?

# APPENDIX TO

# PART FIVE

## MATHEMATICAL NOTES

### Note 1.  Price, Marginal Revenue, and Elasticity

The monopolist's demand curve is

$$q = f(p).$$

That is, the amount he sells depends on the price he charges. The total revenue $(R)$ of the monopolist is price multiplied by the quantity of output he sells.

$$R = pq.$$

Marginal revenue $(MR)$ is the derivative of total revenue with respect to output.

$$MR = \frac{dR}{dq} = p + q\frac{dp}{dq} = p\left(1 + \frac{q}{p}\frac{dp}{dq}\right).$$

But $-\dfrac{q}{p}\dfrac{dp}{dq} = \dfrac{1}{E}$, where $E$ is the coefficient of price elasticity of demand.

Therefore

$$MR = p\left(1 - \frac{1}{E}\right) = P - \frac{P}{E}.$$

Table 19–1 on page 296 shows that marginal revenue declines twice as fast as price. This can be generalized for linear demands as follows:

$$p = a - bq$$
$$R = aq - bq^2$$
$$MR = \frac{dR}{dq} = a - 2bq.$$

### Note 2.  Price Discrimination

Let the subscripts 1 and 2 denote the revenues and the quantities sold in two markets. The monopolist's profit is the difference between his revenues from both markets and his total costs:

$$\pi = R_1(q_1) + R_2(q_2) - TC(q_1 + q_2).$$

$R$ is revenue, $q$ is quantity sold in a market, and $TC$ is total cost. For maximum profits, the partial derivatives are set equal to zero:

$$\frac{\partial \pi}{\partial q_1} = R'_1(q_1) - TC'(q_1 + q_2) = 0$$

$$\frac{\partial \pi}{\partial q_2} = R'_2(q_2) - TC'(q_1 + q_2) = 0.$$

Therefore, the two marginal revenues are equal to each other and to the marginal cost of the entire output. The same product is sold in both markets, and the one cost function holds. The two partial derivatives, $TC'$ above, are thus identical.

# PART SIX

*Pricing in*

*Imperfect Competition*

# Monopolistic Competition

# 21

PRODUCT DIFFERENTIATION · PRICE ADJUSTMENTS · PRODUCT
VARIATION · SELLING COSTS · APPLICATIONS ·

For some time after it was first presented in 1933, the theory of monopolistic competition seemed to be sweeping the theory of pure competition into a corner and to be taking on the task of explaining the formation of most prices. Pure competition and monopoly are the exceptions, the polar opposites, so it came to be said. Enthusiasm for the new theory ran high, because it pictures an economic world full of rival monopolists who compete with one another with their prices, with the qualities of their products, as well as with their sales promotion campaigns. The theory of monopolistic competition has turned out, however, to be something of a disappointment, mainly because no one has been able to bring it down from its high level of abstraction. Nor are there many uses it can be put to. Models of pure competition continue to have wider ranges of applicability.

## Product Differentiation

The theory of monopolistic competition is now held to the task of explaining price and output in market structures where sellers are many and where each seller has a product differentiated from those of his rivals. Monopolistic competition prevails in retailing, in the service industries, and in some branches of manufacturing. Products are differentiated by brands, trademarks, distinctive designs, packaging, and by a myriad of other devices and artifices. Even if the products sold by several sellers are physically homogeneous — e.g., fuel oil — there can still be differentiation if credit terms, promptness and reliability of delivery, etc., are important to consumers. A known and respected brand confers upon its owner a position of monopoly when he sells to customers who will buy no other brand than his. But there are other known and respected brands that furnish the competition for the purchases by consumers who shop around among the several brands of a commodity. Product differentiation, which can range from strong to weak, is effective only to the extent that it has an impact on the minds of consumers. The subjective, not the objective, features of product differentiation are what count.

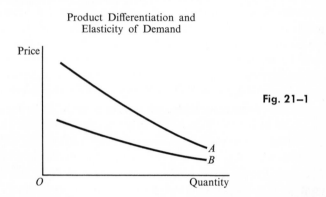

Product Differentiation and
Elasticity of Demand

Fig. 21–1

Product differentiation shapes the demand for a firm's product. Figure 21–1 contains two demand curves, *A* and *B*. Both curves are elastic because both products are in close competition with other brands or makes of the same thing. Demand curve *B*, however, is much more elastic than demand curve *A*. Product *B* is less strongly differentiated than product *A;* consumer reaction to a change in the price of *B* is greater than for product *A*.

Edward H. Chamberlin of Harvard University is the architect and the builder of the theory of monopolistic competition. In a simplified and abbreviated form, his presentation of the theory will be followed here. One of Chamberlin's achievements is to classify all of the adjustments that a firm can make under just three headings. They are price, product, and selling effort. In seeking to obtain maximum profits, the firm under monopolistic competition can review its price policy, or it can review its policy on the quality of its product, or it can review its policy on advertising or other sales effort. The three kinds of adjustments, or policies, will now be taken up in order.

## Price Adjustments

The firm under monopolistic competition is one of many. No single firm, accordingly, dominates the industry. Each firm produces and sells its product in close competition with other similar firms. The elasticity of demand for the product of each seller is high because the products are close substitutes for one another. In any group of sellers, some have succeeded in creating stronger preferences by consumers for their products, with the result that their elasticities of demand are somewhat less than those of the products of their rivals.

### The Firm

Consider first one firm by itself, without regard, for the moment, to the competitive environment of the firm. Assume that the quality of the firm's product is given and that the firm conducts no advertising. Let the context be the long run. The conclusions applicable to the long run are easily transferable to the short run; all that has to be done is to take account of the shapes of the firm's cost curves. The demand curve of the firm reflects consumers' tastes (for *its* product), their incomes, and the *given* prices of the products of the other firms. Under these conditions, the firm behaves as a monopolist, setting its price accordingly. The equilibrium of the firm, when it is viewed in isolation, is the equilibrium of a monopolist.

The firm, however, is likely to have only a small amount of pricing discretion, because its demand curve is almost horizontal. Monopolistic competition is really closer to pure competition than it is to monopoly. Though the firm in monopolistic competition possesses one of the formal properties of monopoly — the sloping demand curve — it lacks the substance of monopoly.

### The Group

Chamberlin calls the several firms whose markets are closely interwoven a "group." Though a group can be identical with an industry for some purposes, the connotation of the word is that an industry — in the everyday sense of the word — can consist of two or more groups of closely competing firms. Suppose the industry is called "books." One group of firms publishes western, detective, and adventure paperbacks; another group publishes highbrow paperbacks; still other groups produce other kinds of books. Within any one group, close competition exists, though between them competition might not be keen. Another example is gasoline retailing in a large metropolitan area. Gasoline retailing is the industry, but each filling station competes closely with those in its area. The group concept is unavoidably somewhat vague because it is hard to draw sharp lines between groups. The analysis here will proceed on the assumption that a group is definite enough to be discussed.

A supply curve cannot be drawn for a group of firms under monopolistic competition because a supply curve shows the amounts forthcoming at different prices when, as under pure competition, all firms produce the same thing and receive identical prices. Each firm in a group has a different product, and at the same time there are usually several different prices.[1]

Consequently, the behavior of a group must be reflected in the behavior of one firm. The simplest model is one embodying what Chamberlin calls his heroic assumption, namely, that each firm has identical demand and cost curves. If the demand curves are identical, it has to be supposed that the firms have equal shares of the market; if there are one hundred of them, each firm has one per cent of total sales.

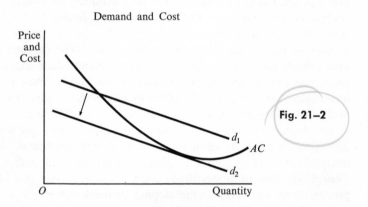

Demand and Cost

Fig. 21–2

Figure 21–2 can be made to exhibit both individual equilibrium and group equilibrium. Suppose first that each firm has the demand $d_1$ (the reason for switching the label from $D$ to $d$ will appear shortly). With long-run full costs of $AC$, each firm can make large net profits. There is no need here to draw in price, marginal cost, marginal revenue, and profits; they can be easily visualized in the imagination. Since all firms are alike, by assumption, net profits for the whole group are high. Since the context is the long run, new firms can enter and put new products on this market. As they do so, the curve $d_1$ shifts to the left, because the new products reduce the sales of the existing firms. The firms, old and new, have to lower their prices. All this goes on so long as net profits are to be had. The process

---

[1] This is formally correct. Yet if the products of the firms are very similar, as they often are, and if the price differentials are small, something like a group supply curve does make sense. For some purposes, it can be useful.

comes to an end when the demand curve slides far enough left to become
tangent to the cost curve — $d_2$ is tangent to $AC$. Another simplifying
assumption in this model is that the cost curve $AC$ stays where it is, that
the entry of new firms causes no external economies or diseconomies in
the group (Chapter 15, pages 237, 238).

In Chamberlin's theory of monopolistic competition, the solution to the
problem of group equilibrium, when the strongly simplifying assumptions
are used, is always a tangency. Tangency simply means that price equals
full costs. With tangency, the firm can neither raise nor lower its price
without suffering losses. Net profits are maximum at zero.[2] There being
no net profits, no outside firm wants to enter the group. Because full costs
include normal profits, no firm in the group wants to leave.[3] Hence the
group is in equilibrium. Notice that the tangency of the demand curve
to the cost curve is symmetrical with the tangency of demand to cost in
the long run under pure competition. The difference between monopolistic
and pure competition is that under monopolistic competition, the demand
curve slopes slightly. Because the slope is always negative, price is a little
higher and output is a little smaller.

In a rough-and-ready sense and apart from the precision of Chamberlin's
analysis, all this means that where entry is free, the long run contains a
tendency for prices to be pulled down to full costs. This is so despite the
"monopoly" each firm has of its own brand.

### Short-Sighted Price Cutting

The adjustment to equilibrium just described has taken place through
the entry of new firms. The number of firms, however, can be correct, but
the price can be higher than the equilibrium level. If so, equilibrium can be
established as the result of a price war. Consider Figure 21–3. This figure
has two kinds of demand curves. The $d$ curves, for any one firm, are drawn
on the assumption that the other firms' prices remain unchanged while
the one firm changes its price. In contrast, the $D$ curve shows what happens
to the sales of one firm when its rivals do in fact change their prices at
the same time and by the same amount. The $D$ curve is much less elastic
than the $d$ curve. The $D$ curve is also a miniature of the demand curve for
the whole group. Suppose again that there are one hundred firms. When
the amounts that can be read off the $D$ curve are multiplied by one hundred,
the result is the demand curve for the whole group.

---

[2] Tangency of the demand curve to the cost curve in pure competition is shown
on page 235, and in monopoly on page 301.
[3] This means the further assumption that firms outside the group, that could
enter it, are always earning only normal profits.

Imagine now that one of the firms is at point $A$ in Figure 21–3. Though the firm is enjoying a large net profit, it could earn still more if it could expand its sales along curve $d_1$. Imagine too that the owner of the firm is short-sighted as a businessman and believes that if he were to cut his price, his competitors would *not* lower their prices. So he cuts his price in the expectation of much larger sales and profits. But he is frustrated, because his competitors cut their prices too. The firm moves from $A$ to $B$, down the $D$ curve. Though sales at $B$ are a little larger, profits are lower. The $d$ curve has slid down from $d_1$ to $d_2$. Suppose next that the price cutting firm does not benefit from its experience, and initiates another price cut, which again the other firms promptly imitate. Once more the $d$ curve slides down. When it gets down to the position $d_3$, it can go no farther, because then more price cuts would bring nothing but losses, even for the short-sighted. This kind of price war, then, establishes the equilibrium of the firm and the group. Price equals full cost, and the curves are tangent.

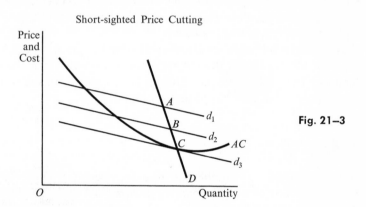

Short-sighted Price Cutting

**Fig. 21–3**

### Diversities of Demands and of Costs

Let the assumption of uniform demands and costs now be dropped. All the firms in the group now have different costs, different demands, and therefore different prices, volumes of output, and profits. Figure 21–4 shows such differences, in hypothetical form, for firms $A$, $B$, $C$, and $D$. The positions of firms $E$, $F$, $G$, etc., can easily be imagined. Though diversity exists from one firm to another, the group as a whole nearly always shows some definite pattern of profits or losses. Suppose that the group as a whole is profitable, even though a few of the firms are suffering losses. Firms outside decide that the group's markets are worth invading. They do so. As the new firms put their products on the market, the old firms suffer some losses in sales. But not all are affected equally. Perhaps firm $A$ scarcely feels the new competition at all, because its brand is solidly established. Perhaps firms *C* and *D* are hit hardest by the invading brands. Eventually the entry of new firms comes to an end, and the group's markets offer no more attractions to outsiders. Smaller net profits are now scattered about the group, but their pattern does not offer any incentive to entry.

### Product Variation

Much of the competition that is monopolistic is nonprice competition, whose two main forms are product variation and advertising. Product variation is Chamberlin's term for quality competition. In nonprice competition, the pushing and jostling among firms takes the forms of manipulating the qualities of their products and their advertising activities. While they do so, their prices remain constant for months or even for a few years at a time. Prices remain constant for many reasons: Some prices stay long at five or ten or twenty-five cents simply because these are the denominations of the common coins. Other prices stay at a dollar, or hover near it, because buyers and sellers are accustomed to this price. Still other steady prices for particular classes of products are the consequence of custom and (sometimes) inexplicable practice.

### The Firm

Take a firm selling its product at a price fixed by custom or inertia. Because it is differentiated, the product can be changed this way and that in color, or durability, or workmanship, or design, or in the services that go with it. Assume that consumers will buy larger quantities of a product that is "improved." This last word has to be enclosed in quotation marks to convey the idea that an improvement in a product might or might not be a

Differences within a Group of Firms

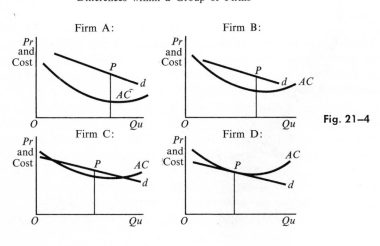

Fig. 21–4

gain in a measurable, objective sense. An improvement is whatever is intended to make consumers buy more for whatever reason, laudable or otherwise. A lurid picture on a paperback novel is there to increase sales; it probably costs more than a dignified cover. The increased revenue from larger sales must be balanced against increased costs. Hence the firm adjusts its quality so as to maximize profits. Notice the parallel with price adjustments: If it lowers its price, the firm increases its total revenue; but the firm also increases its total costs, because it sells more units.

Product Variation

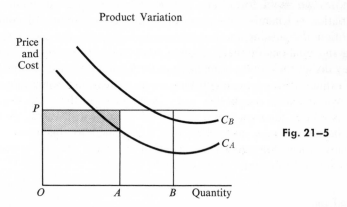

Fig. 21–5

The optimum adjustment for the firm, when its product is the variable, is indicated in Figure 21–5. The diagram is awkward, because output sold has to be inserted arbitrarily. In the figure, $OP$ is the customary price. The horizontal line drawn from $P$ is a horizontal line, nothing more. It is not a demand curve. The curve $C_A$ is the long-run, average-cost curve for variant $A$, or quality $A$, of the firm's product. When the firm chooses quality $A$, it sells the amount $OA$. The net profit is the shaded rectangle at the top. Quality $B$ of the firm's product has costs shown by cost curve $C_B$. More of $B$ is sold, i.e., the amount $OB$. But it is quite evident that the net profit from $B$ is less than that from $A$. For other qualities, $C, D, E,$ etc., the firm can calculate costs, sales, and net profits. One of the qualities must be the one that yields maximum net profits, just as when price is the variable, one of the possible prices is the optimum.

Chamberlin's product variation must not be confused with changes in quality induced by technological improvements over time. Almost any durable consumer good is better than it was ten or twenty years ago. It is likely to be better in its design and in its engineering features. This kind of product improvement comes from changes in tastes and from technical and business innovations. In contrast, Chamberlin's theory deals with the firm's use of existing techniques to modify its product in a context of existing tastes. The analogy is to hold demand and cost curves constant.

### The Group

When product is the variable, the solution of the problem of group equilibrium is also tangency, upon the assumption that all firms have the same costs and shares of the market. Suppose that all the firms in a group are alike and that all are making net profits. Then new firms will enter the group, thus causing the sales of old firms to fall off. In efforts to offset their losses of sales, the firms make further improvements in their products. As a result, their cost curves rise and keep on rising until they are tangent to the horizontal line that indicates the price. When sales adjust themselves so that they are equal to the amount corresponding to the tangency position, the firm is in equilibrium. So is the group, because here too tangency means equality of price and full costs, and, therefore, the absence of incentive of firms to enter or to leave the group.

## Selling Costs

Selling costs are incurred to increase the demand for a product. The term "selling costs" is broader than advertising because selling costs include those of salesmen, of allowances to retailers for displays, and in fact of any kind of promotional activity. Chamberlin distinguishes selling costs from production costs. The costs that must be incurred to make a product, transport it, and have it available to consumers with *given* wants are production costs. The costs of *changing* consumers' wants are selling costs. Though it is useful, the distinction cannot always be sharply made. For example, is attractive packaging a production cost or a selling cost? It probably does not matter that questions of this sort cannot be easily answered. The analysis to follow will assume that Chamberlin's distinction can always be made. Anyway, the difficulty just about vanishes when the expressions "selling costs" and "advertising expenditures" are employed interchangeably; Chamberlin himself does this.

### The Curve of Selling Costs

Advertising is a black art. Its mysteries, its great problems, are bypassed here. One of them is how to advertise and, in particular, what media give best results. Instead, let it be assumed that expenditures on advertising do increase the demand for a product, all other things — price, quality, buyers' incomes — being equal. Let the word "increase" also be understood algebraically; that is, the increase in demand could be infinitesimal, perhaps zero, or perhaps even negative if it should happen that the advertising is repellent rather than enticing. The task now is to set up a relation between the advertising expenditures of a firm and the unit sales of its product. The relationship is given in the curve of selling costs, which is another of Chamberlin's contributions to economic theory.

Figure 21–6 contains a curve of selling costs. Though in appearance it is just another $U$-shaped cost curve, the curve of selling costs has its own meaning. The curve shows the average cost per unit of selling any given amount of the product. It costs an average of $AA'$ cents each to sell $OA'$ thousands of units, $BB'$ cents each to sell $OB'$ thousands, etc. The curve first declines, because of initial economies of scale in advertising; advertising expenses that are too small are said to be wasteful. Sooner or later, after reaching a minimum somewhere, the curve must rise to indicate the mounting costliness of expanding sales. Here is one cost curve whose eventual rise can never be in doubt.[4] In all likelihood, the curve finally becomes vertical, at which volume of sales there would be the "saturation" so often

Curve of Selling Costs

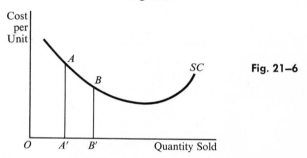

Fig. 21–6

mentioned in sales discussions. Selling costs can be very high or very low. No generalization is possible. In one year in the 1950's, a major automobile company was said to have spent $700 in advertising *each* car of its luxury make that the company was able to sell.

The shape and position of the curve of selling costs for a firm's product in a given period of time reflect the play of the other variables. They are, of course, the price of the product and of its substitutes, the quality of the product and the qualities of its substitutes, the incomes of the buyers, and their resistance, such as it might be, to having their tastes changed by the advertising. Change one or more of these variables and you change the shape and position of the curve. Raise the price, and up goes the curve, meaning that the costs of selling any quantity of the product are higher. Improve the quality and down goes the curve. If consumer tastes are veering away from the product and other similar products, the curve will curl up sooner and faster.

[4] Remember that a little doubt attaches to the eventual rise in the ordinary long-run cost curve of a firm. See page 176.

### The Optimum Advertising Expenditure

How much should a firm spend on advertising? The profit-maximizing firm spends an amount such that the combined marginal cost of production and of advertising is equal to the price the firm gets for its product. The last unit sold is just worth the cost of producing and selling it.

Figure 21–7 expresses this idea more fully. Here the firm is considered by itself. The price of the product is $OP$. The horizontal line from $P$ can be viewed as if it were a marginal revenue curve because by advertising, the firm can sell more without having to lower its price. Production costs per unit are assumed to be constant. The curve of unit selling costs is superimposed on the curve of production costs. The equilibrium amount is $OA$. Figure 21–7 indicates the production costs, the selling costs, and the net profits. Plainly the firm does not want to produce and sell more than $OA$ because if it did, the excess of marginal cost over price would reduce net profits.

Optimum Volume of Advertising

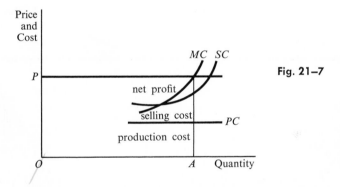

Fig. 21–7

A diagram like Figure 21–7, or an adaptation of it to the short run,[5] has some practical application. Business firms that advertise usually follow rules of thumb, such as operating with fixed advertising budgets, or spending a predetermined per cent of their sales dollars on advertising, or spending as much as their competitors spend, or spending as much as they think they can "afford." Such methods can be safe and certainly they require little thought; thus they do have their virtues, but they are not rational. The marginal approach illustrated in Figure 21–7 is rational; it aims at the profit-maximizing advertising outlay. Only rarely, however, can the relation between advertising expenditures and sales be measured with some

[5] Then the production costs are the variable costs.

degree of confidence. Yet a relation not easily measurable is still relevant. It is better to make the best guess you can of the results of the right course of action than to follow the wrong course just because it poses no problem of measurement.

### Advertising and Group Equilibrium

The perpetual controversies over advertising always throw up the question as to what part of all advertising satisfies the desire for more information and what part merely diverts sales from one product or product group to another. No attempt will be made here to answer this difficult question or even to suggest the outlines of an answer. Instead, attention here goes to competitive advertising, to advertising as a variable such as price and quality of product.

When it advertises, a firm seeks to increase its own sales. Sometimes the effect is to add to the sales of the firm's competitors, when the advertising increases the desire of consumers not so much for the firm's own product, as for the general class of product.

A simple model of advertising competition, adapted from Chamberlin, is this: Suppose the firms in a group are in equilibrium, none earning any net profits. To begin with, none of them does any advertising. Then imagine that one of them, like the short-sighted price cutter of a few pages ago, thinks that he can earn some profits by advertising, and that he believes he will be the only one to do so.

Figure 21–8 shows what happens. Let the assumption that firms are alike be used again, to keep things simple. Hence the figure stands for any one firm, thus representing all of them. The production cost curve is $PC$. The price is $OP$. The initial equilibrium is the output $OA$. Since price equals average cost of production, there are no net profits. Then one of the firms draws up an advertising plan, shown by the curve $SC_1$. This curve shows how he can increase his sales, if he alone advertises. If he is the only one to do so, he would increase his sales to $OB$, an optimum output (where marginal cost — not shown — would equal price). But the eager advertiser is mistaken. He does not achieve the output $OB$ and the net profits that go with it. His rivals follow his example and also advertise *their* products. The sales of each firm increase only a little just as they do when all firms cut their prices. Now, all of the firms are advertising some amount. Then the eager but short-sighted one tries again. It is more costly now to increase sales with more advertising. Thus the new selling cost curve is $SC_2$, which does offer the prospect of profits if the eager firm is the only one to expand advertising. Once more, however, frustration ensues. Stable equilibrium comes about only when all firms produce and sell the amount $OC$ and have selling cost curves $SC_3$. Here too tangency holds. No firm can now hope to earn profits by increased advertising, even if it were the only one to act. Notice that in this model, advertising does increase sales, from *OA* to *OC*. In the end, however, the firms are no better off for having started their advertising war.

## Applications

With the exception of the example of the optimum volume of advertising for a single firm, the theory of monopolistic competition does not lend itself to application for decision-making purposes. Nor does this theory have much to contribute to the analytic bases of economic policy. At one time, in fact, the theory seemed to be gnawing at the economic foundations of the antitrust policy. The concept of effective competition (page 270) had to be devised as the model appropriate for the policy of maintaining competition through the law.[6] Chamberlin's book contains an implicit tone of mild condemnation of the price and output equilibria attained under monopolistic competition. He repeatedly stresses the point that equilibrium price is higher and equilibrium output is lower than under pure competition.

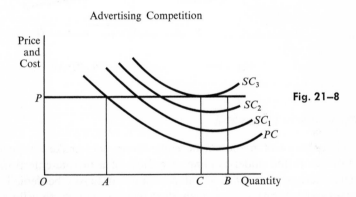

Advertising Competition

*P*

*SC₃*
*SC₂*
*SC₁*
*PC*

Fig. 21–8

*O*       *A*          *C*   *B*   Quantity

## Welfare

Earlier chapters show that the long-run equilibrium of the firm under pure competition is a point of efficiency, that it is one of the conditions of maximum economic welfare. If, then, monopolistic competition causes a deviation from that point, it reduces economic welfare. An aura of suspicion therefore falls on brands, trademarks, advertising, and all of the

[6] The distinction between definitions of competition useful for theoretical analyses and definitions useful for policy is explained in Donald Stevenson Watson, *Economic Policy: Business and Government* (Boston: Houghton Mifflin, 1960), pp. 200–207.

other means of creating product differentiation. Is the suspicion justified? No one can be sure unless he knows *by how much* price and output under monopolistic competition differ. Consider Figures 21–9 and 21–10. Both are fully compatible with Chamberlin's reasoning. In both, $P_1A$ is the price and $OA$ is the output under monopolistic competition. In pure competition, price and output are $P_2B$ and $OB$. In Figure 21–10, the difference is small. Obviously, the shapes of the curves give the two results. The steepness of the cost curve has nothing to do with monopolistic competition, only the steepness of the demand curve, because it indicates the strength of product differentiation. Many economists believe that price and output in most markets with monopolistic competition are closer to the relations shown in Figure 21–10 than to those in Figure 21–9.

Price and Output in Monopolistic
and in Pure Competition

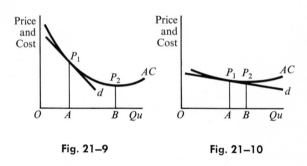

Fig. 21–9                    Fig. 21–10

### The Wastes of Competition

The theory of monopolistic competition does make an important contribution to the understanding of a facet of a private-enterprise economy. That there is some waste in the economy can hardly be denied. The waste takes many forms — too much effort devoted merely to selling things, too many brands, too many retail stores. These excesses are not negligibly small; they are normal and persistent, existing even in equilibrium conditions. They are the wastes of competition, of monopolistic competition to be more precise, of the monopolistic part of monopolistic competition, to be quite precise. Such wastes do not occur under pure competition.

Much controversy and honest doubt surround these issues. Some economists think that the wastes due to monopolistic competition are, in fact, small. Others argue that product differentiation satisfies consumers' desires for variety and breadth of choice. If pure competition prevailed everywhere, homogeneity of products would mean lower costs. Would not life then be drab? If the whole population were put into uniform clothes and made to live in uniform barracks, vast quantities of resources would be released, but what for?

From time to time, observation of events and practices in the Soviet Union can throw new light on features of a private-enterprise economy that tend to be taken for granted. In the 1950's, trademarks, brands, and advertising began to appear among the consumer goods sold in Russia. Their purpose and effect seem to be to raise standards of quality. Alternatively, quality in a socialist economy would be maintained by bureaucratic administration. Perhaps the extra costs of product differentiation are less than the cost of enforcing standards of quality. Anyway, it is arguable that American economists have taken quality in private enterprise too much for granted.[7]

### Summary

In monopolistic competition, each firm has a *differentiated product* with a highly elastic demand. When it adjusts its price, the firm prices as a monopolist does. In the simple model of the group, where all firms are alike, equilibrium comes about through the entry or exit of firms. Firm and group are in equilibrium when demand curves are tangent to cost curves. When it adjusts the quality of its product, the firm does so to maximize profits. *Product variation* is symmetrical with price adjustment. The *curve of selling costs* relates the expense of advertising per unit with the number of units sold. A firm's *optimum advertising expenditure* is such that the combined marginal cost of production and advertising is equal to price. Group equilibrium with advertising as the competitive variable is also a *tangency solution*. Long-run equilibrium in monopolistic competition is probably close to that attained in pure competition.

### SELECTED REFERENCES

The standard work continues to be Edward Hastings Chamberlin, *The Theory of Monopolistic Competition,* 7th ed. (Cambridge: Harvard University Press, 1956). The first edition was in 1933. See especially Chap. 5, 6, and 7. A collection of essays by Chamberlin is contained in *Towards a More General Theory of Value* (New York: Oxford University Press, 1957). A fascinating account of the background of his theory is presented by Chamberlin in "The Origin and Early Development of Monopolistic

---

[7] See Marshall I. Goldman, "Product Differentiation and Advertising: Some Lessons from Soviet Experience," *Journal of Political Economy,* Vol. LXVIII, No. 4, August 1960, pp. 346–357.

Competition Theory," *Quarterly Journal of Economics,* Vol. LXXV, No. 4, November, 1961, pp. 515–543.

A theory of imperfect competition, which also puts the spotlight on the firm rather than on the industry, is found in Joan Robinson, *The Economics of Imperfect Competition* (London: Macmillan, 1933). Mrs. Robinson offers a box of tools, rather than an integrated theory. Useful analyses of both Chamberlin and Robinson are contained in Robert Triffin, *Monopolistic Competition and General Equilibrium Theory* (Cambridge: Harvard University Press, 1940), especially Chap. 1.

The view that the theory of pure competition is a more useful model is presented by George J. Stigler, *Five Lectures on Economic Problems* (New York: Macmillan, 1950), Lecture 2. Chamberlin's counterargument is in *Towards a More General Theory of Value* (cited above), Chap. 15.

## EXERCISES AND PROBLEMS

1. Draw sets of diagrams, like those in Figure 21–4, to represent (a) a group of firms whose total pattern of profits and losses is such as to cause exit from the group; and (b) a group of firms with profits and losses such that the group is in equilibrium.

2. Show how a firm might increase its profits by cheapening, instead of improving, its product.

3. Construct an arithmetic table showing, for a firm, different combinations of prices, advertising expenses, and profits.

4. Draw curves of selling costs for different sets of assumed conditions.

5. Should the government establish and enforce grades and standards for ordinary branded products?

# Oligopoly — Three
# Classical Models

## 22

PROBLEMS IN THE THEORY OF OLIGOPOLY • COURNOT'S MODEL • BERTRAND'S MODEL • EDGEWORTH'S MODEL • EXTENSIONS OF THE CLASSICAL MODELS •

Many of the markets in the American economy are oligopolistic. The prices and volumes of production of several important products, such as aluminum, automobiles, heavy electrical equipment, tires, and steel, are determined by the few companies in each of the industries that produce them. Unfortunately, there is no one satisfactory theory of price and output under oligopoly. A satisfactory theory would consist of a few related generalizations commanding substantial agreement and capable of application to policy and welfare problems. Instead of this, there exists a welter of theories about oligopoly. Accordingly, it is well to look first at the difficulties that the subject of oligopoly presents to economic theorists.

### Problems in the Theory of Oligopoly

To explain the behavior of prices, the behavior of consumers and producers has to be described. This is done by setting up demand curves and cost curves. When they are brought together, equilibrium prices and quantities are determined. In a market with only a few sellers, however, the demand curves of each lose their definiteness. They do not stand still to be analyzed. They flit hither and thither. Suppose that a market has just three sellers, A, B, and C, and that their products are close substitutes. What is

*A's* demand curve? It can be imagined only by assuming that *B* and *C* charge unchanging prices for their products. If they do, then *A's* demand curve can be drawn, and as usual, it shows the different quantities he can sell at different prices. When *A* alters his price, causing *B* and *C* to change theirs, the result is different. Changes in *B*'s price and in *C*'s price immediately *shift* *A*'s demand curve either to the right or to the left. The same reasoning applies to the demand curves of *B* and *C*. The three demand curves are *interdependent,* so much so, so inextricably, that it makes little sense to try to think of them separately.

The same thing holds if a few firms compete as buyers — when there is *oligopsony*. As an example, take three research firms whose main inputs are the services of particular kinds of engineers and scientists. If one firm raises the salaries it pays to attract better technical talent, the costs of the two other firms are likely to be raised because to keep their staffs, they probably have to raise their salaries too. The cost curves of oligopsonistic firms are therefore interdependent. One of them can be clearly described only on the assumption that the others remain constant.

The theory of pure competition, the theory of monopoly, the theory of monopolistic competition — all come to clear and precise conclusions about equilibrium prices and outputs. Each of the theories is constructed with demand curves, cost curves, and the profit-maximizing assumption. Each of the theories yields equilibria that are said to be determinate, that is, the equilibria are the logical consequences of the assumptions. Some theories of oligopoly, however, yield indeterminate results — they cannot say what price and outputs are. To illustrate this point, the theory of bilateral monopoly will now be discussed. As a theoretical problem, bilateral monopoly is closely akin to oligopoly.

### Bilateral Monopoly

In bilateral monopoly a single seller faces a single buyer. The commodity traded has no close substitute; the seller has no other outlet, the buyer has no other source. The standard theoretical problem here is not that of selling the prize bull or the yacht or the painting, that is, not the problem of exchanging one unit of a commodity. Instead, the problem is that of finding what quantities of a homogeneous commodity will be exchanged, and at what price. The seller is a producing firm. The commodity is its output which it produces, in the usual assumption, at rising average cost. The commodity is an input to the buyer; its value to the buying firm depends upon its (diminishing marginal physical) productivity and upon the demand for the output that the buying firm sells in another market.

Therefore, both seller and buyer view the commodity with their price-quantity schedules. Each wants to maximize his money gain from the transaction. Suppose that the seller begins the negotiations by asking a high price. The buyer responds by offering a low price. The higgling proceeds until an agreement is reached. But it is *not* possible to say, with logical analysis based upon the assumptions, just what the agreement is. Price and quantity are indeterminate. Of course, when two firms negotiate a price and when firms and unions negotiate wage rates, they almost always do in fact come to definite agreements. Indeterminacy means that general reasoning, by itself, is unable to say even theoretically what such agreements are.

Theorists have beaten their heads against the problem of bilateral monopoly for decades. Despite their efforts, mostly mathematical, they have not succeeded in finding the principle that determines price in an exchange between two traders, who can be persons, or firms, or a labor union and a business corporation. There is a fair amount of agreement, however, that quantity is determinate in bilateral monopoly, though price is not. To confine the problem, let it now be assumed that seller and buyer can agree on a quantity and that analysis establishes the proposition that the agreed quantity is one compatible with maximum *joint* profits for the two. At this quantity, the lowest price acceptable to the seller throws the whole profit to the buyer; the highest price the buyer is willing to pay gives the whole profit to the seller.

What is the result when they confine their negotiations to price? It is too easy to take refuge in the answer that bargaining strength and skill decide the result. It is even easier to say that the particular facts of each actual transaction determine the result. But these are evasions, they are digressions from the search for valid generalizations.

The solution to the theoretical problem might come from a theory combined from economics and psychology. Sidney Siegel and Lawrence E. Fouraker have done some work along this line.[1] They have tentatively concluded that the tendency is for buyer and seller to split the joint maximum profit. The tendency becomes stronger when buyer and seller are well informed about each other. Information, then, can be a controlling force. Siegel and Fouraker also think that the "levels of aspiration" of seller and buyer also influence the result. Level of aspiration is a concept of psychology; it means the intensity of the desire to maximize. A trader who has been successful and who expects more success possesses a higher level of aspiration than one who has suffered failures.

---

[1] Sidney Siegel and Lawrence E. Fouraker, *Bargaining and Group Decision Making. Experiments in Bilateral Monopoly* (New York: McGraw-Hill, 1960). The experiments were carefully conducted and controlled. Many pairs of students at Pennsylvania State University bargained for real money.

### The Mass, the Individual, and the Group

The theories of pure competition and of monopoly, even the theory of monopolistic competition, pose no difficult problems of appropriate assumptions of human behavior. In pure and monopolistic competition, the behavior of a mass of people is handled with the profit-maximizing assumption. It makes no difference whether this entrepreneur or that one is slow to react to a rise in price, or habitually makes mistakes, or is unusually greedy. The profit-maximizing assumption blankets them all, cancels their individual differences, and gives good results. At the other extreme stands the sole individual, the monopolist. As a pure type, he too maximizes, always acting so as, in the traditional phrase, to charge what the traffic will bear.

The theory of oligopoly is a theory of group behavior, not of mass or individual behavior. There can be two in the group, or three, or four, or seventeen. Whatever the number, it is few — each one knows that anything he does will have some effect on the group. Unfortunately, there is no generally accepted theory of the behavior of a group. Do the members of a group agree on common goals? If they do, how do individual goals tie in with the common goals? Does the group have a recognized organization, however informal, with recognized rules of conduct? What are the power relations in the group? Is the group dominated by a leader? If it is, how does he get the other members to follow him? These are some, but just some, of the questions that a theory of group behavior would answer.[2]

Modern discussions of the theory of price and output under oligopoly usually take as their points of departure one or more of the classical models of oligopoly. Three of the classical models will be reviewed here. They give different results because they are built to slightly different specifications. The people in the models behave as mechanistically as clockwork dolls; they always do the same thing and are wholly incapable of learning from experience.

The classical models deal with the problem of duopoly — two sellers. There is no real difference between a theory of duopoly and a theory of oligopoly. Theorists agree that whatever is found to be true of two sellers can easily be extended to three or four or more, so long as the number remains few.

---

[2] Postwar research in the behavioral sciences has progressed rapidly. It might lead to useful models of group behavior and thus make a major contribution to the theory of oligopoly. See Almarin Phillips, "A Theory of Interfirm Organization," *Quarterly Journal of Economics*, Vol. LXXIV, No. 4, November, 1960, pp. 602–613.

## Cournot's Model

Augustin Cournot published his theory of the behavior of two competing sellers over a century ago, in 1838. But no one paid any attention to his work until the 1880's, nor did his ideas become widely known and discussed until the 1930's.

Although Cournot's is a model of duopoly, its results can be extended to three, four, etc. sellers. Hence by extension, his model can be transformed into a model of oligopoly.

Here are the assumptions for a simplified version of Cournot's model: The two producers, who shall be called Alphonse and Gaston, produce identical products and do so at identical costs. Their unit costs are constant over any range of output that would come into question. The total demand in the market they share is linear. Both Alphonse and Gaston know exactly what the total demand is — both can see every point on the demand curve.

Both producers behave in the same way. Both want to maximize the profits attainable, whatever the circumstances happen to be. They do not conspire, they do not agree, even tacitly. Each one sees what the other is doing, assumes he will continue to do the same thing, and then acts accordingly. Alphonse and Gaston adjust their outputs, not their prices.

It will be recalled that if demand is linear and unit costs are constant, the profit-maximizing monopoly output is exactly half the competitive output.[3] For present purposes, the competitive output, where of course price equals marginal (and average) cost, can be called the opportunity output of a monopolist. The monopolist never wants to produce more than the competitive, or opportunity, output because if he did, unit cost would exceed price. His optimum output, of course, is half the opportunity output.

Now let the process of price formation in Cournot's model begin. Alphose is the first to take action. He looks over the market, i.e., looks at the demand curve, and produces and sells half the opportunity amount because by doing so, he maximizes his profits. Next, Gaston appears on the scene and sees what Alphonse's output is. Gaston simply takes it for granted that Alphonse will continue to produce and sell the same volume of output. The other half of the opportunity therefore belongs to Gaston. To maximize his profits, he produces and sells an amount equal to half of the half, i.e., a quarter, of the opportunity. Then Alphonse turns his head and sees that Gaston is now selling a quarter of the opportunity. Because Gaston's action has brought down the price, Alphonse has to recalculate his position. He assumes that Gaston's output will stay at a quarter. Hence

[3] See page 305.

his chance is the other three-quarters of the opportunity. Half of this is three-eighths. So Alphonse cuts his output back. Then Gaston expands his. . . . So it goes, and at the end of it all, each one is producing exactly one-third of the opportunity, or competitive output.[4]

Table 22–1 contains an arithmetical illustration of the simplified model of Cournot. For numerical convenience, the competitive, or opportunity, output — where price equals marginal and average cost and where net profits are zero — is set at 6,400 units. Alphonse begins by selling 3,200 units. Gaston follows with 1,600 units. Alphonse keeps cutting back while Gaston keeps expanding. When they are selling equal amounts, they stop adjusting their sales. They therefore reach a stable equilibrium and a determinate result.

Cournot's two sellers produce two-thirds of the competitive output. It can be shown that three produce three-quarters and that $n$ would produce $\frac{n}{n+1}$ of the competitive output. The greater the number of sellers, the larger does this fraction become. Accordingly, as the number of sellers increases, their combined output and their price come closer and closer to the competitive level.

**TABLE 22–1**

Illustration of Cournot's Model of Duopoly

assumptions: linear demand and constant costs; competitive output is 6,400 units

| Scene | Alphonse's Output | Gaston's Output | Explanation |
|---|---|---|---|
| 1 | 3,200 units | | ½ of 6,400 units |
| 2 | | 1,600 units | ½ of (6,400 — 3,200) |
| 3 | 2,400 units | | ½ of (6,400 — 1,600) |
| 4 | | 2,000 units | etc. |
| 5 | 2,200 units | | |
| 6 | | 2,100 units | |
| 7 | 2,150 units | | |
| 8 | | 2,125 units | |
| . . . | . . . | . . . | |
| Last | 2,133 units | 2,133 units | |

[4] Just why the output of each seller becomes one-third of the competitive output is explained in Note 1 of the Appendix to Part Six. This Note also contains a mathematical version of Cournot's model.

## Bertrand's Model

Joseph Bertrand was a French mathematician who in 1883 objected to Cournot's theory of duopoly and who advanced a substitute model of his own. In his model, the competitors also produce identical products and have identical costs. They make decisions on prices, not on their volumes of output. They do not need to know exactly what the demand is. Each one can produce as much as the buyers will take at any price.

Each of Bertrand's two producers, who are Henri and Pierre, assumes that the other will not change the price he is charging. Let the assumptions about demand and cost be the same as for Cournot's model and let Henri be the first to go into business. Since he is the only one at first, he sets his price at the monopoly level. Then Pierre appears, with his assumption that Henri will continue to charge the same price. Pierre then sets a price lower than Henri's, and because he offers an identical product, Pierre seizes the entire market at that price. Henri's sales fall to zero. He, in turn, thinks that Pierre's price will stay where it is and sets his price lower. Henri, therefore, seizes the entire market. So it goes, until the price falls to the level of their costs. Neither will now lower the price because even though he could again capture the entire market, his total costs would exceed his total revenue. Since they both charge the same price, their combined output is equal to the competitive output and they are in equilibrium.

The assumptions about business behavior by both Cournot and Bertrand are similar. The two competitors in both models doggedly hold to the belief, no matter what happens, that the rival will continue to do what he was just doing. The two assumptions are not exactly the same; the one has to do with output policy and the other with price policy. Hence the two models give different results. Cournot's says that output in duopoly is less than the competitive output and that therefore price is higher. Bertrand's says that output and price in duopoly are the same as in pure competition.

## Edgeworth's Model

The English economist F. Y. Edgeworth presented another model of duopoly in 1897; his original article in Italian was not published in English until 1925. Edgeworth also shows a price war between the two competitors. By assuming that the two firms together cannot produce as much as the competitive output, Edgeworth gets results that differ from those of Bertrand. The inability of the two firms to produce as much as the competitive output can easily be imagined as existing in a short-run context.

Figure 22–1 is a modification of Edgeworth's own diagram. The two competitors are Tom and Harry. Although it is not essential in the Edgeworth model that the two have perfectly homogeneous products, because it would do if the products were close substitutes, let the assumption again be identical products. The maximum amount Tom can produce is *OB* and for Harry it is *OB'*. The two amounts are equal. Let costs also be identical. Tom's demand curve is *DT*. Harry's is *DH;* his part of the diagram has to be read from right to left. Their cost curves are *OB* and *OB';* the quantity axis can be imagined as lying below the line *HT*. Let Tom begin.

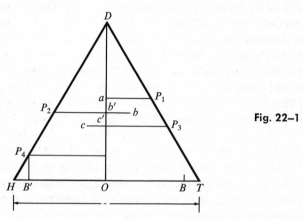

Edgeworth's Model

Fig. 22–1

He sets his price at the monopolistic level, which is indicated by $P_1$. He sells the amount $aP_1$. Harry appears, armed with the conviction that Tom will not change his price. Harry throws his whole output on the market at the price $P_2$. At this price he sells $P_2b$, which is the same amount as *OB'*. By doing this, Harry snatches $b'b$ of sales from Tom. Having lost much of his business, Tom lowers his price to $P_3$, thinking of course that Harry's price will remain at $P_2$. Tom sells all he can produce at his new price of $P_3$, namely, the amount $P_3c$ $(= OB)$. Tom invades Harry's market to the amount of $c'c$. The price cutting goes on until one of them, say, Harry is charging the price $P_4$. At this price, he is supplying half the total demand with his entire output. Tom now has no incentive to lower the price below $P_4$. He could not fill the orders if he did; he can no longer invade Harry's market. Nor can Harry invade his. Is there, then, an equilibrium when neither seller has any incentive to lower the price?

Not in the Edgeworth model. Thinking that Harry has done his worst by putting his entire output on the market, Tom raises his price all the way back up again to $P_1$. He has half the market all to himself, so he believes, and so he can price as a monopolist. Harry then follows his example, also raising his price to the monopoly level. Then the whole process begins again.

The Edgeworth model, therefore, works with a perpetual oscillation of prices. First they go down in a series of price reductions; then they jump back up to the starting point.

## Extensions of the Classical Models

It was mentioned earlier that the classical models are starting points for the investigations of oligopoly. After working on these models and on variations of them, later theorists have produced a few propositions of analytical usefulness.

### Leaders and Followers

In the Cournot model, each seller passively adapts his output to that of his rival. Each follows the other. In contrast, each of the sellers in both the Bertrand and Edgeworth models tries to seize all or part of the market for himself. Each wants to dominate, to be the leader. Obviously the kinds of behavior exhibited in the three classical models are only three possibilities out of many. Theoretical work on how sellers react to each other, on what their "reaction functions" are, has led to certain conclusions.

First, if two sellers take their cues from each other, if each thinks the other is going to behave in a definite way, and if, then, each adapts himself to the other, the result is stable levels of prices and outputs. Of course prices and outputs are not exactly the same as in the simplified Cournot model, but the follower-follower reaction yields generally similar results.

Secondly, if one firm is the leader and the other is a follower, and if each one knows this and acts accordingly, then the results are also stable levels of prices and of outputs. Price leadership is widespread in American industry. More will be said on it in the next chapter.

Thirdly, if both firms try to be the leader, the result is price war or chaos. That things do not become worse in the Bertrand and Edgeworth models is due to the assumption that both firms have the same costs. If they did not, the lower-cost firm would in the end drive the other one out of business.

### Sellers' Guesses About Each Other

In the language of part of the literature on oligopoly, the sellers in the classical models display "zero conjectural variation." This means that they don't *guess* what their rivals will do. They *know*. But suppose that firms are not sure of their rivals' actions and that they have to guess. Do they try to estimate what their rivals will *do* or what they will *think*? Can the leader be sure of the follower's actions? When each seller thinks that his price depends upon his rivals' prices in *some* way, then his conjectural variation is nonzero. By pursuing this idea, analysis grinds out another batch of models.

Guessing about the actions of rivals leads to planning courses of action, i.e., strategies. The idea of strategies, in turn, brings up the theory of games. When *The Theory of Games and Economic Behavior* was first published by John von Neumann and Oskar Morgenstern in 1944, it was widely thought that their new theory would greatly advance thinking on oligopoly. A "game" is an activity with definite rules whose outcome is controlled jointly by players with incompatible objectives. Games in this sense include the matching of coins, checkers, poker, etc., as well as military combat and the actions of oligopolistic business firms. Although game theory has developed far since 1944, its contribution to the theory of oligopoly has been a vast disappointment. The results of the great efforts to find determinate solutions of oligopolistic behavior are scarcely any better than those of, for example, Cournot.[5]

### Product Differentiation

In the classical models, the two firms have homogeneous products. When both are selling, they necessarily have the same prices, and they always divide the market exactly between them. This assumption — pure oligopoly is its usual name — does put a strain on the imagination because it requires the buyers to be wholly indifferent about the sellers as if they had no personalities at all. Products can be physically homogeneous, but sellers, when few, never are.[6] When product differentiation is introduced into oligopoly, when therefore the products become close but not perfect substitutes, much is changed. A price cut by one seller does not deprive the other of all of his sales, only of part of them.

With product differentiation, the two prices do not have to be equal. They only have to be in line. Only by coincidence would Fords and Chevrolets carry exactly the same list prices, but their prices are never far apart. Similarly, the price differential between the gasolines sold by the outlets of major oil companies and by independent distributors is normally stable. The oligopolistic interdependence of sellers sees to that.

Product differentiation also means competitive activities directed to the qualities of products and to sales promotion. Just as in the theory of mo-

---

[5] Note 2 in the Appendix to Part Six describes a simple model of duopoly as constructed in game theory.

[6] Do not wheat farmers have personalities, too? Yes they do, but purely competitive markets are so organized that in each transaction, buyers and sellers are, in Chamberlin's phrase, paired off at random. And in competitive markets, *all* sellers are "followers."

nopolistic competition, oligopolistic firms can have three variables to ma-
nipulate — price, product, and advertising.

## Uncertainty

The discussion of bilateral monopoly earlier in this chapter shows the
importance of information, i.e., the absence of uncertainty. Information
also plays a part in monopoly and in pure competition. To maximize, the
monopolist has to know at least the relevant part of his demand curve;
consumers and pure competitors have to know prices. The fluctuations described by the cobweb theorem (pages 279 to 282) are the result of producers' reliance on stale information. In oligopoly, information is even
more important because it must include knowledge of rivals and of their
courses of action. In the classical models, the sellers act with certainty because they have complete information on demand and on how their rivals
behave. When these assumptions are relaxed, uncertainty prevails. A seller
thinking of changing his price is uncertain of the consequences. He cannot
be sure what the market is even if his rivals do nothing. Nor can he be
sure whether in fact they will do nothing.

All this frays the nerves of entrepreneurs and leads to the possibility of
collusion in oligopoly. Collusion here means cooperation, or common patterns of action, rather than outright agreements on prices and outputs.

The next two chapters continue the survey of theories of oligopoly.

## Summary

The interdependence of the demand curves of the firms in oligopoly
poses serious difficulties in establishing a theory of the determination of
prices and outputs. The theoretical problem is closely akin to that of *bilateral monopoly* to which there is no agreed-upon determinate solution.
The behavior of a few competing firms is also group behavior which can
assume many patterns. The classical models give certain insights into the
actions of oligopolistic firms. In *Cournot's model,* each firm adjusts its output in the belief that the other's will remain constant. With linear assumptions, their combined equilibrium output is two-thirds of the competitive.
In *Bertrand's model,* each firm believes that the other's price will remain
constant. In *Edgeworth's model,* the price fluctuates. Thus if firms adjust
to each other, prices and outputs can be stable. But if each firm tries to
dominate, the result can be price war or chaos. Efforts to create a satisfactory theory of business strategy have not succeeded.

## SELECTED REFERENCES

On bilateral monopoly: Sidney Siegel and Lawrence E. Fouraker, *Bargaining and Group Decision Making* (New York: McGraw-Hill, 1960).

On the classical models: Edward H. Chamberlin, *The Theory of Monopolistic Competition,* 7th ed. (Cambridge: Harvard University Press, 1956), Chap. 3. An excellent and thorough presentation is in Fritz Machlup, *The Economics of Sellers' Competition* (Baltimore: Johns Hopkins Press, 1952), Chap. 12.

On the general theoretical problems raised by oligopoly: Machlup (cited above), Chap. 11. William Fellner, *Competition Among the Few* (New York: Knopf, 1949), Chap. 1.

## EXERCISES AND PROBLEMS

1. Construct your own model of oligopoly: Suppose that three new bowling alleys are opened up at the same time in the same large suburb. Assume that the owners do *not* get together to agree on the prices they will charge. Set up reaction functions, i.e., patterns of competitive response, for the three owners, and then show what happens as they compete for customers.

2. Work out a Cournot model with price, not output, as the variable.

# *Prices in Oligopoly*

# 23

THE MAXIMIZATION OF JOINT PROFITS · PRICE LEADERSHIP ·
LIMITATIONS ON THE MAXIMIZATION OF PROFITS · CARTELS ·
QUASI-AGREEMENTS · OLIGOPOLY AND ENTRY · SALES MAXIMIZA-
TION · CONCLUSION ·

The purpose of a theory of oligopoly is to explain price and output and, in particular, to explain the equilibrium relation between price and cost. The theory of pure competition shows that the long-run equilibrium price equals marginal cost as well as minimum average cost. The theory of monopoly shows that the equilibrium price exceeds marginal cost by a factor that depends on the elasticity of demand.[1] The theory of monopolistic competition shows that price is pulled toward average cost.

A theory of oligopoly should be able to show whether prices and outputs are those of monopoly or of pure competition, or whether they lie between the monopolistic and competitive levels. And it would be good to know just where between.

This requirement of the theory of oligopoly will now be put to work as the principle of selection in choosing from the long list of models to be found in the literature on oligopoly. Of these models, several will be put

---

[1] A reminder: Monopoly price equals marginal cost times $\dfrac{E}{E-1}$ (see footnote on page 305). Thus if $E$ is 2, monopoly price is twice the marginal cost of the equilibrium output.

up for inspection. First will come those saying that price and output in oligopoly are the same as in monopoly. Then will come models displaying prices and outputs close to those of monopoly. Then will come some in-between models. The last models to pass in review will be those with price and output close to the levels of pure competition.

### The Maximization of Joint Profits

When price and output in an oligopolistic industry are identical with those a monopolist would establish, the rival firms maximize their joint profits. For this to happen, certain conditions must exist.

#### Chamberlin's Model

In the clearest form, the conditions for joint maximization are found in Chamberlin's model, the model he labels as "mutual dependence recognized." Here are sellers with homogeneous products, with identical costs, and with full information. The information on total demand is complete and accurate. Each firm knows that the others have the same costs. Each firm wants to maximize and knows that the others want to do likewise.

Chapter 21 (page 336) contains a model of short-sighted price cutting by firms in monopolistic competition. In the model, a firm faces two demand curves. The first one ($d$) assumes no changes in the rivals' prices; the second demand curve ($D$) assumes that all firms move their prices up or down together. In oligopoly, however, short-sighted price cutting can hardly occur — each of the firms knows the others will meet a price cut. Therefore the only relevant demand curve is the second one. Because the products are homogeneous, the firms must charge the same price. With identical demand curves, i.e., shares of the market, and with identical costs, the common price preferred by one firm is also preferred by every other firm. Without even tacit agreement, then, the firms set identical prices, at the monopoly level, that maximize their individual profits. Thus they also maximize their joint profits. The profits, of course, need not be large because demand-cost relations might not permit large profits. Whether they are large or small, however, individual and joint profits are at a maximum.

The equilibrium in Chamberlin's model is stable, stable as granite, because each firm, in looking to its ultimate interest, never gives a moment's thought to any other possible course of action. In this model, there is no collusion in any meaningful sense. Each firm acts independently, while it recognizes the mutual dependence of all of the firms in the group.

Oligopoly is a form of competition. The significance of Chamberlin's model is that it shows the possibility that this form of competition can yield the same results as monopoly. As a representation of reality, this model is certainly not an impossibility. Noncollusive behavior of this kind, based on good if not perfect information, must sometimes occur. But there is no way of knowing empirically how important it is.

The "perfect cartel" model, which will be examined shortly, also contains the price and output of monopoly. The perfect cartel is usually looked upon as a merely temporary form of oligopoly.

### Price Leadership

Price leadership means of course that the firms in an industry follow the lead of one firm. If the products of the firms are physically homogeneous, prices are usually uniform. If the products are differentiated, prices can be uniform or can conform to a definite pattern of differentials. From time to time, the leader announces a price change, e.g., a rise of ten per cent. The next day, or the next week, the other firms raise their prices by ten per cent.

It is now customary to distinguish *barometric* price leadership from *dominant* price leadership where one firm actually dominates the industry. In barometric price leadership, one firm is simply the first to announce a price change. This firm does not dominate the others. Suppose that the industry's inventories have been piling up while consumption of the industry's product remains sluggish. A price reduction is then in order; all firms come to understand that it is due. The barometric firm is the first to announce the change. This firm does little more than to establish the prices that would, in time, be set by the forces of competition.

The bases of dominant price leadership can be the lower costs of the leader, or its larger size, or its aggressive behavior, or some combination of these. If one of, say, three firms with physically homogeneous products has the lowest costs, this firm can act as if it were a monopolist. This firm can set its price so as to maximize its profits. The other two firms must set their prices at the same level and, therefore, accept less than maximum profits. This means that they produce more than they otherwise would and that, therefore, the output of the whole industry is larger than under monopoly.

Price leadership by the largest firm in an industry is common. The other firms follow the lead with motives ranging from fear to convenience to laziness. Here, too, the leader can act as if he had a monopoly. He can maximize *his* profits. To choose the price that maximizes for him, he must be certain that the other firms will set the same price or if products are differentiated, that their prices will be in line with his. If there are several small firms in the industry, they can look upon the leader's price as given to them. If products are physically homogeneous and if the market is well organized, the small firms can treat the leader's price as if it were their marginal revenue. Then they adjust their outputs so that their marginal costs equal the leader's price and, therefore, maximize their profits.

Unless the firms in the industry have uniform costs and market shares, price leadership does not give results identical with those of Chamberlin's model. Though prices can be close to the monopoly level, the output of the industry is bound to be a little larger.

Dominant price leadership is sometimes called partial monopoly, especially when the dominant firm is large and the other firms are small. The partial monopolist is more than just a price leader. Because he wields monopoly power, he becomes a problem — a difficult one — in the enforcement of the antitrust laws.

Price leadership can sometimes be a means whereby the firms in an industry achieve a price discipline as real as if the firms entered into direct (and therefore illegal) agreement. Jesse Markham of Princeton University has called this form "effective price leadership." It is effective in suppressing active competition. Such price leadership can exist, however, only in industries having certain characteristics. They are: (1) The firms must be few in number, with strong feelings of interdependence. Very small firms must be absent, for they are likely to ignore their indirect influences on price and to engage in promiscuous price cutting from time to time. (2) Entry to the industry must be restricted, for otherwise the profitability of the prices set by the leader is under constant danger. (3) Though they need not be perfectly homogeneous, the products of the firms must be close enough substitutes to reinforce the firms' consciousness of interdependence. (4) Demand for the output of the industry is inelastic or just slightly elastic. If, instead, demand is highly elastic, the temptation of firms to reduce prices is strong. (5) The firms must have similar cost curves; if they do, conflict between low-cost and high-cost firms is absent.[2]

### Limitations on the Maximization of Profits

Up to now, the models of oligopoly passing in review have had the profit-maximizing assumption built into them. This assumption must now be relaxed and modified so that more can usefully be said about oligopoly.

Three distinct kinds of forces may prevent any firm from attaining maximum profits. Remember that maximum has no meaning apart from the relation between demand and cost; the attainable maximum can be zero profits or minimum losses. One force blocking a firm's attainment of the maximum is lack of information about prices and the market; some-

---

[2] Jesse W. Markham, "The Nature and Significance of Price Leadership," *American Economic Review,* Vol. XLI (1951), pp. 891–905. Reprinted in American Economic Association, *Readings in Industrial Organization and Public Policy* (Homewood: Irwin, 1958).

times, firms do not even have clear information about their costs. A second force can be the presence of other incentives. Chapter 8 discusses them. A monopolist who is secure in his position might prefer the quiet life to the continuous effort of adjusting his price to the profit-maximizing level. Or if he is insecure, he may keep his profits lower than they could be for fear of government regulation or of potential competition. The third force is the restraint that oligopoly itself can put on the maximization of profits by firms.

The restraints that oligopoly places on the behavior of firms in seeking profits are (1) considerations of safety, (2) desires for stable profits, and (3) tendencies toward conservative policies in large corporations where ownership and management are separated. These restraints can be stated only in a general form because specific patterns of group behavior can vary much from industry to industry and from time to time. Oligopolistic interdependence creates the urge to play it safe, the willingness to accept "reasonable" profits, and the atmosphere conducive to common courses of action.

An assumption in the discussion to follow is that less than maximum profits are associated with prices lower than monopoly prices. Figure 23–1 shows demand and cost for an industry. The optimum monopoly price is

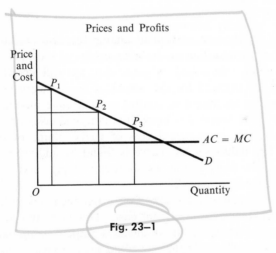

Fig. 23–1

$P_2$. The rectangle of profits drawn from $P_2$ is the largest inside the triangle bounded by demand and cost. The rectangles of profits drawn from the higher price $P_1$ and the lower price $P_3$ are much smaller. The assumption, accordingly, is that smaller profits go along with prices lower than $P_2$ in Figure 23–1. One justification for the assumption is the common practice of calculating prices on a cost-plus basis. Cost-plus pricing will be discussed a little later.

## Cartels

A cartel is an explicit agreement, usually formal, among independent firms on prices, output, and often on other matters such as division of sales territories. In general, cartels are unlawful in the United States. The exceptions are, however, not unimportant because, for example, the price of milk in many communities is fixed by associations — cartels — of producers who make their price decisions under the benevolent auspices of the federal government.

Why discuss cartels under the heading of oligopoly? Oligopoly is a form of competition. The firms in an industry either compete or they do not. If they do not, if they act in concert, should they not be analyzed as a monopoly? But the convention of treating cartels under the heading of oligopoly is firmly established. Cartels are often short-lived. Firms do have the desire for large joint profits; this desire gives the impulse to form cartels. Firms are likely, however, to quarrel over the division of joint profits; this propensity is the leading cause of the breakup of cartel arrangements. Some industries in the United States have a history of alternate periods of illegal price-fixing and of intense competition among the firms.

### Perfect Cartels

A perfect cartel is an agreement among the firms in an industry that results in the maximization of the joint profits of the member firms. The board of control, established by the cartel, has full knowledge, let it be assumed, of the demand for the output of the industry at each possible price. Therefore the board of control can calculate marginal revenue for the industry. The board also knows the marginal costs of all of the firms and can calculate the marginal cost of each volume of output for the industry. (The industry's *MC* curve is found by adding, horizontally, the *MC* curves of the firms, just as the short-run supply curve of a competitive industry is derived; see page 227.)

The board of control of the perfect cartel then sets industry marginal revenue equal to industry marginal cost. This gives the price and output for the industry. Then the board allocates output among the firms and, in so doing, allocates shares of the maximum joint profits.

Cartels are children of depressions. The impulse to joint action is stronger when demand is depressed than when it is expanding. If a cartel is established when the demand for the industry's output has fallen and when the firms have much excess capacity, the board of control might decide to tell the high-cost firms to shut down altogether, though these firms would still receive an agreed-upon share of the joint profits. The board would then allocate the industry's output so as to minimize costs. Each producing firm would then have the same marginal cost. (This point is explained in Chapter 11, page 178, for a firm allocating output between two plants.) The minimization of industry costs ensures the maximization of joint profits.

### Imperfect Cartels

In a collection of theoretical models of cartels, the perfect cartel stands as a polar extreme. It does indeed maximize joint profits. But it means the abject surrender of decision-making by the firms. A cartel is always defined as an agreement among firms that retain their identities and independence. Mutual distrust among firms and their unwillingness to give up all of their sovereignty make it most unlikely that perfect cartels could long endure.

It can be taken then that cartels are always imperfect, which here means only that though they raise prices and profits, they do not reach the levels of monopoly. Though there are many models of imperfect cartels, they will not be reviewed here. Instead, a few general remarks about them will now be made.

After fixing a price, a cartel usually has to set sales or output quotas. This does not have to be done if industry demand is growing as fast as or faster than the expansion of industry output. But, ordinarily, output quotas have to be set to maintain the cartel price. Methods of setting the quotas and of dividing the joint profits are sources of friction. If the cartel agreement is illegal besides, good ways of enforcing compliance are hard to find.

A member of a cartel can find advantage in making secret price concessions. Even if the industry demand is inelastic, the demand to any one firm at prices lower than the cartel price is highly elastic. Additional sales at covertly negotiated lower prices can therefore be profitable enough to offer strong temptation to a firm.

### Quasi-Agreements

When they knowingly behave in the same way, oligopolistic firms can be said to have entered into quasi-agreements. Other terms to express the same idea are conscious parallelism of action, imperfect coordination, collusion, and the like. Quasi-agreements can take many forms. A few of them are: Mutual adherence to the belief that price cutting is unethical, respect for one another's market shares and sales territories, the use of the same methods of calculating prices, and reliance on the continuity of patterns of prices and of competitive behavior that have gone on for some time. As a method of quasi-agreement, cost-plus pricing will now be singled out for attention. It can be called quasi-agreement if all the firms in an industry set their prices on a cost-plus basis, and if each firm believes that the others will continue to do so.

## Cost-Plus Pricing

Cost-plus pricing is a common method of determining the selling prices of products. A firm computes the selling price of its product by adding, say, 30 per cent to the average total cost of the product. Cost here is business cost, not the full cost as defined in this book. Alternatively, the firm can add, say, 60 per cent to the average variable cost of the product; the higher percentage here is to take care of overhead, as well as to earn a business profit. The percentages added to cost are called margins or markups. Thus, cost-plus pricing is also known as margin pricing and markup pricing.

The business world employs many systems of cost-plus pricing. They range from simple rules of thumb to sophisticated formulas. The simple rule of adding a customary markup seems to be common. With a sophisticated formula, a company estimates future sales, future costs, and arrives at a markup that will achieve, so it is hoped, a "target return" on the company's investment.

Economists generally regard cost-plus pricing as a practice inconsistent with the maximization of profits. Only by accident could maximum profits come from the simple rule-of-thumb method, which takes demand for granted and makes no allowance at all for elasticity of demand. Even the pricing methods that aim for a target return on the investment are a kind of satisficing rather than maximizing behavior. Cost-plus pricing need not, however, be inconsistent with maximum profits. If average variable costs are constant over the relevant range, cost plus some amount could indeed give a price identical with that determined by rational behavior (see page 308). And if shifts in demand are accompanied by no changes in elasticity, cost plus would continue to give profit-maximizing results.[3]

As a form of oligopolistic behavior, cost-plus pricing by all firms in an industry results in stable patterns of prices. In some industries, the firms use uniform systems of cost accounting. If their input prices and production functions are identical and if they add the same percentage markups, the firms can have identical prices for their products. Whether or not the firms have identical prices, their practice of cost-plus pricing also causes them to make uniform changes in prices. If excise taxes are imposed, or increased, or abolished, the firms change their prices by the corresponding percentages. They act similarly if wage rates rise throughout the industry and if materials prices go up.

---

[3] Lorie Tarshis has shown how rule-of-thumb pricing can give results very close to those of formal marginal calculations. See his *Elements of Economics* (Boston: Houghton Mifflin, 1947), p. 201.

## Oligopoly and Entry

It has been implicit all along that the number of firms in an oligopolistic industry is fixed, or given. This is so in the short run. But what of the long run? It is probably well to modify the definition of the long run for the purposes of the theory of oligopoly. Generally the long run is long enough for a firm to expand its whole plant and equipment. Now let the long run also be a period long enough for a firm to introduce a new product. Thousands of American firms are large enough and diversified enough that they can invade new fields with new products in periods of time much shorter than those needed to increase their total capacities by significant amounts.

The model of multiple-product pricing described in Chapter 20 (pages 318, 319) can be made to show one kind of entry. Portraying a common and readily observable business practice, the model shows the invasion of markets by firms with new products they can produce with their existing facilities and organization. Suppose that several firms produce and sell components for high-fidelity equipment for consumers. Suppose that their prices are established through a process of quasi-agreement. Then imagine that a large manufacturer of diversified electrical equipment designs a line of high-fidelity components and sells them at comparatively moderate prices. Such an invasion of the market for high-fidelity components can be as fully effective as if two or three new firms were to come into existence. If the manufacturer succeeds in gaining a noticeable share of the market he invades, the existing firms might be compelled to lower their prices or improve their products, or both.

Where oligopolistic markets can be invaded by the new products of firms with diversified facilities and by new firms, the result is similar to the groping toward group equilibrium in monopolistic competition (pages 336, 337). Profits are reduced. Prices may also fall. To the extent that they do, output becomes larger. With a stable total demand for the products of the firms, an oligopolistic industry can reach a low-profit or a no-profit equilibrium. Prices and outputs are by no means the same as under pure competition. But they are likely to be much closer to the competitive than to the monopolistic levels.

Entry to oligopolistic industries is often however not effective. The barriers to entry can be legal. Some public-utility industries are oligopolies; the public regulating bodies usually bar outside firms by denying them the requisite franchises or licenses. Another legal barrier can be thrown up by the operation of the patent law; the firms in an industry sometimes have patent arrangements among themselves and do not admit outsiders to them. Barriers can be illegal, too. The wide variety of means, in violation of the antitrust laws, that have been used to restrict entry is beyond the scope of discussion here. Entry to industries in which individual firms require large amounts of capital is restricted by the difficulties of raising the capital and of assembling the organization and the specialized talents essential for success. When, therefore, entry is either blocked or where the obstacles are not easily surmounted, the firms in an oligopolistic industry can have prices and outputs well above the competitive level.

The fear of potential entry often appears as a reason given for quasi-agreements that result in lower-than-maximum profits. In general, such profits accompany lower prices and larger outputs. Hence fear of entry can drive prices and outputs down from monopoly toward competitive levels. If joint profits are held down by quasi-agreements, it is still possible, by stretching a point, to say that they are "maximized" over a longer period of time. Suppose that expected joint profits in an industry are at a maximum at $50 million in year one, and that beginning in year four, the entry of new firms reduces joint profits to $10 million a year. With these assumptions, joint profits over a ten-year period are $220 million (3 × $50 million plus 7 × $10 million). But suppose that quasi-agreement holds joint profits in year one and in succeeding years to $30 million a year, and that this level attracts no new firms. Then the total profits over a ten-year period would be $300 million, a larger amount.

### Sales Maximization

A model of oligopoly in which the firm makes a compromise between dollar volume of sales and profits has been constructed by William J. Baumol of Princeton University. This model gives still another way of modifying and relaxing the assumption of profit maximization. The behavior of the firm resembles that of the megalomaniac entrepreneur in Scitovsky's model of entrepreneurial behavior (Chapter 8, pages 132, 133).

Stripped to its essentials, Baumol's model says that the firm produces and sells the output yielding the maximum revenue that is consistent with the earning of a minimum profit. The model has been criticized on the ground that Baumol does not allow for the interdependence of the prices of oligopolistic firms. To those economists who see interdependence as the key to all pricing in oligopoly, the criticism is serious because it points to a major flaw in the model. Baumol relies on his experience as a business consultant to claim an inside view of decision-making in large corporations. He argues that oligopolistic interdependence actually plays a small part in the month-by-month decisions of large firms. Anticipated reactions from competitors influence the strategy of a firm, he thinks, only when a major change is imminent, such as the marketing of a wholly new line of products or the launching of a new kind of advertising campaign. Baumol supports his contentions by pointing to the clumsy slowness of decision-making in large firms, to their reliance on the same rules of thumb, and to the prevalence of the live-and-let-live attitude.

Baumol's argument is that an oligopolistic firm looks upon its dollar sales, i.e., total revenue, as an end in itself. The executives of a large firm want dollar sales to grow. Declining sales are dreaded because of the fear that there will be trouble in arranging bank financing, that consumers will shy away from products that are losing their popularity, that the firm will lose distributors and big dealers, and that other disadvantages will ensue. Large sales mean large size which in turn, so runs a common belief, means large profits. But after some point — where marginal revenue equals marginal cost — increases in sales can be had only at the sacrifice of profits. Though it wants sales to be large, the firm also seeks a minimum level of — business — profit. Minimum profits must vary in relative and absolute size from one firm to another, from one industry to another, and from depression to prosperity. Baumol offers no one clear definition of the minimum acceptable profit. But he and other economists who have discussed the same thing point to the elements that make up an acceptable minimum. They are the funds to pay some satisfactory rate of dividends, the funds to be reinvested for growth, and the funds to ensure financial safety and the probable requirements of lenders in the capital markets. It suffices for the working of Baumol's model if minimum profits are defined as any amount less than maximum profits.

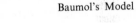

Baumol's Model

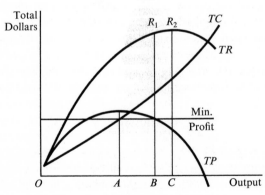

**Fig. 23–2**

Figure 23–2 presents Baumol's model; the figure is adapted from one of Baumol's diagrams. The vertical axis shows total revenues and total costs in millions of dollars. The horizontal axis shows output. Total revenue is *TR*, which the firm adjusts by changing its price. Total cost is *TC*. (Since *TC* starts from the origin, the diagram presumably shows the long run. But the diagram can easily be converted to the short run by dropping the horizontal axis by an amount equal to fixed costs.) Total profit is the curve *TP*, which states the difference between *TR* and *TC*. The horizontal line is the acceptable minimum profit. If the firm had no objective but to maximize its profits, output would be *OA*, because *OA* corresponds to the top of the *TP* curve. If the firm did nothing but maximize its total revenue, output would be *OC*, which corresponds to $R_2$, the top of the *TR* curve. Baumol's firm produces and sells *OB*, thus earning the minimum profit and setting revenue at the highest level — $R_1$ — that is consistent with the minimum profit.

Thus the firm in Baumol's model of oligopoly produces and sells more than profit maximization dictates. Just how much more depends on the shapes and positions of the curves.

Baumol's model seems to have a resemblance to cost-plus pricing, in which the firm adds a minimum profit figure to business costs to arrive at selling price. But as he shows, the resemblance is superficial because the firm in his model makes marginal calculations. The firm adjusts its output for maximum revenue subject to the profit constraint and, in doing so, prices some of its products to earn more and others to earn less than the minimum profit. In contrast, most cost-plus pricing methods are rules of thumb which cannot predetermine volumes of output.

As earlier chapters show, the profit-maximizing firm ignores its fixed costs in coming to pricing decisions. Changes in fixed costs do not affect marginal costs, which together with marginal revenue determine output and therefore price. But Baumol's firm does indeed react to a change in fixed costs, just as businessmen generally seem to do. If fixed costs rise, the result is, all other things being equal, to reduce total profit. The *TP* curve in Figure 23–2 falls, and thus the minimum profit line cuts it at a point indicating a smaller optimum output. This, in turn, means a rise in price.

### Conclusion

The models reviewed in this chapter show prices and outputs ranging between the monopoly and the purely competitive levels. For oligopoly to have the same price and output as monopoly, the necessary assumptions are uniformity of costs and products, perfect knowledge, no objective other than profit maximization, and either the mutual recognition of uniformity and interdependence or the actions of the perfect cartel. For oligopoly to have price and output identical with those of pure competition, the model must be one like Bertrand's. The significance of Chamberlin's model and of the perfect cartel model, as well as the significance of Bertrand's, seems to be only that it is conceivable, that it is not logically impossible, for the equilibrium of oligopoly to be identical with either that of monopoly or of pure competition.

Table 23–1 displays the leading models reviewed in this chapter, together with Cournot's and Bertrand's. The important models are those showing prices and outputs intermediate between the poles of monoply and pure competition. The price leadership, the imperfect cartel, and the quasi-agreement models *can* give results close to monopoly, or to pure competition. They *can* give prices and outputs between the extremes. General analysis cannot be more precise. This is unfortunate because it means that theory cannot say much that helps in assessing the performance of oligopolistic industries. The welfare aspects of oligopoly will, however, be discussed in the next chapter.

### TABLE 23–1

#### Some Leading Models of Oligopoly
#### Classified by Relation of Price to the Levels
#### of Monopoly or Pure Competition

| Equilibrium prices | Name of Model | Remarks |
|---|---|---|
| Monopoly price | Chamberlin | Products and costs must be uniform |
| Close to monopoly price | Perfect cartels<br>Price leadership<br>Imperfect cartels<br>Quasi-agreements | If firms seek maximum profits, prices are close to the monopoly level. But if they seek smaller profits, prices are closer to the competitive level. |
| Close to purely competitive price | Cournot | Price approaches the competitive level as the number of sellers increases. |
| | Long-run free-entry model<br>Baumol | Deviation from competitive price depends on elasticity of demand. |
| Purely competitive price | Bertrand | Products and costs must be uniform |

Notes: Models with indeterminate or fluctuating prices are excluded. The monopoly price maximizes individual firm and joint profits when demand and cost functions are known. The competitive price is the equilibrium price consistent with zero net profits.

### Summary

In *Chamberlin's model* of oligopoly, the prices and outputs of the firms are identical at the monopoly level, though there is no agreement among the firms. A *perfect cartel* also achieves maximum joint profits. Price leadership can be barometric or dominant. A dominant price leader can be a partial monopolist. The theory of oligopoly must take account of behavior that seeks less than maximum profits. *Imperfect cartels* can increase the profits of their members by fixing prices and production quotas; cartel agreements are likely to be temporary. When oligopolistic firms knowingly behave in the same way, they are said to have entered into *quasi-agreements.* Many patterns of uniform behavior are possible. *Cost-plus pricing* can result in stable prices. If entry to an oligopolistic industry is possible, prices and outputs can move toward the competitive level. Fear of entry can also motivate the firms in an industry to hold prices and profits at lower levels. In the *sales-maximization model,* price is set so as to maximize sales subject to the constraint of earning a minimum profit.

## SELECTED REFERENCES

Edward H. Chamberlin, *The Theory of Monopolistic Competition,* 7th ed. (Cambridge: Harvard University Press, 1956), Chap. 3. William Fellner, *Competition Among the Few* (New York: 1949), Chap. 7. Joe S. Bain, *Pricing, Distribution, and Employment,* rev. ed. (New York: Holt, 1953), Chap. 6. Fritz Machlup, *The Economics of Sellers' Competition* (Baltimore: Johns Hopkins Press, 1952), Chap. 13, 15. William J. Baumol, *Business Behavior, Value and Growth* (New York: Macmillan, 1959), Chap. 4–8.

## EXERCISES AND PROBLEMS

1. Suppose an industry has three firms of equal size, each producing the same product. The firm with the lowest costs is the price leader. Draw a diagram to show the adjustments of each of the firms.

2. Suppose that the three firms in an industry form a perfect cartel. The firms produce the same product at different costs. Draw a diagram to show how the cartel determines price and allocates output among the firms.

3. Draw a diagram to show how entry to an oligopolistic industry can cause prices to be forced down to the levels of average costs.

4. In Baumol's model, a rise in fixed costs causes the firm to reduce output. Draw the diagram. Why would a profit-maximizing firm *not* reduce its output?

5. Suppose the firms in an industry follow different methods of cost-plus pricing. Is there still a quasi-agreement that results in stability?

# Oligopoly — Price Rigidity

# and Nonprice Competition

# 24

So far, prices and outputs in oligopoly have occupied the center of attention. Once established, oligopolistic prices often remain constant for months at a time, occasionally even for a few years. A familiar example is the durable consumer good whose quoted wholesale price remains unchanged for an entire model year. Quoted prices, however, are not always the actual prices paid and received; in periods of slack demand, open or hidden concessions from quoted prices are often made.

Oligopolistic prices that long remain unchanged are said to be "rigid," in contrast to the "flexibility" of market prices in industries behaving like the model of pure competition. Rigid prices are changed infrequently and usually by small amounts. An implication of the concept of rigidity is that rigid prices are resistant to changes in demand and in costs. There can be no strong reason, from the points of view either of the profit-seeking firm or of the theory of welfare economics, that prices should move up or down with every little quiver in demand and every little flutter in costs. For a large firm, a change in prices can be expensive; new catalogues and lists have to be issued, dealers must be notified, and so on. Constancy of prices must, accordingly, be distinguished from rigidity — the lack of movement when changes occur in demand or in costs, or in both.

Perhaps the most popular of the models of oligopoly is the model with the kinked demand curve, because it offers an explanation of price rigidity under oligopoly.

### The Kinked Demand Curve

The kinked[1] demand curve and the argument that goes with it describe a pattern of business behavior such that the firm has no incentive to raise its price or to lower it. The firm's attitude rests on an estimate of what its rivals will and what they will not do. The firm believes that though its rivals will not imitate an increase in price, they will indeed follow a price reduction. Acting on this belief, then, the firm adheres to its price, seeing no reason to change until some upheaval occurs such as a major movement in demand or in costs.

Figure 24–1 shows a firm's demand curve with a kink in it. The kink is at *P,* the price at which the firm is producing and selling the amount *OQ.* Above the price *P,* the demand curve as seen by the firm is *dP.* This portion

The Kinked Demand Curve

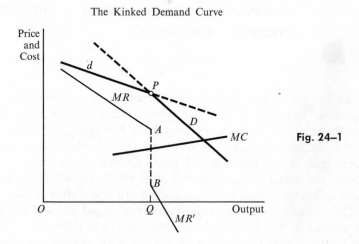

Fig. 24–1

of the curve is highly elastic; notice that the corresponding part of the marginal revenue curve *MR* is positive. The *dP* portion of the curve is elastic because the firm believes that its rivals will *not* follow suit if the firm raises its price. Thus the firm thinks its losses in sales from a price increase would be heavy, that its total revenue and its profits would fall off. The *dP*

---

[1] Kinked, rather than kinky, which means full of kinks. Though a demand curve could conceivably have several kinks, if consumers behave oddly, the essential feature of the kinked demand curve under oligopoly consists of the presence of only one kink.

curve and its dashed extension can be recognized as Chamberlin's *d* demand curve (page 336). The other part of the kinked demand curve is *PD;* this curve and its dashed extension are Chamberlin's *D* curve. The *PD* curve is much less elastic; at lower prices the *PD* curve is inelastic, as shown by the fact that its marginal revenue curve, *MR'*, is negative after a point. The firm thinks that a reduction in price below *P* will cause the rival firms to reduce *their* prices. Though the firm would enjoy some increase in sales, its profits would be smaller.

The peculiarity of the diagram of the kinked demand curve is the gap in marginal revenue, which comes from the abrupt change from the more elastic to the less elastic parts of the demand curve. The gap is shown by the dashed line *AB* in Figure 24–1. The marginal cost curve intersects the gap, which can be regarded as if it were a vertical section of the marginal revenue curve.

With its assumptions about the firm's vision of the demand for its product and of the reactions it expects from its competitors, the kinked demand curve therefore explains price rigidity. The kinked demand curve is often called subjective — it exists in the decision-maker's mind. His actual demand curve, the objective one, might be different. But the rigidity imposed by subjective demand is reinforced by cost. Look again at Figure 24–1. If the marginal cost curve rises, but not above point *A,* and if it falls, output and price do not change. This is because *MC* still crosses the vertical part of the *MR* curve. The length of the gap, i.e., *AB* in Figure 24–1 depends on the angle *dPD*. Suppose demand decreases. The decline in demand makes the firm more certain than ever of the folly of a rise in price. That is, *dP* becomes more nearly horizontal, and the angle *dPD* becomes less obtuse. The marginal revenue curve also becomes more nearly horizontal. This raises *A,* making the gap *AB* longer. Therefore, even if *MC* is declining, or changes, price holds constant. If, however, demand increases, the firm might be less sure that rivals will not imitate a price increase. Hence *dP* swings a little toward the vertical, the angle becomes more obtuse, the *MR* curve falls, and so does point *A.* If it falls far enough, *MC* crosses *MR* above *A;* an upward revision in price is then indicated. Thus the doctrine of the kinked demand curve holds that price reductions are unlikely in the face of declining demand, whereas price increases are likely when demand grows.

The kinked-demand-curve model of oligopolistic behavior gives an appearance of rationality to the maintenance of rigid prices by firms. The model has a serious flaw. There is nothing in the model to show how the rigid price is established. Nor does the model explain how a new kink forms around a new price.

## Nonprice Competition

Nonprice competition in oligopolistic industries has certain similarities to the nonprice competition in industries characterized by monopolistic competition. Conventionally, nonprice competition is divided into two forms, product variation and sales promotion. The difference between the theory of oligopoly and the theory of monopolistic competition is the stress that has to be laid on interdependence in oligopoly.

Price can be the competitive variable in oligopoly. So can quality of product. And so can be the amount and kind of sales promotion activities. Most of the models of oligopoly described in Chapters 22 and 23 could be easily reformulated by substituting "quality of product" or "volume of advertising" for "price." The reformulation would not give results different in any essential respect. Instead of waging a war of price, Bertrand's duopolists would wage a war of product improvement, or an advertising war, until neither one would have any profits. The knowledgeable and steady-nerved firms in Chamberlin's "mutual dependence recognized" model would unerringly select the qualities of products and the volumes of advertising that would maximize individual and therefore joint profits.

This point is more important than it might seem at first. A common opinion is that, though they lack price competition, the oligopolistic industries make up for the lack by vigorous rivalry in product and advertising policies. But the parallelism of price, product, and advertising competition means that any one of these variables can be manipulated to shackle the strength of competition. Chamberlin's model was just mentioned again; in the model, individual and joint profits are maximized, as in monopoly. Product or advertising can also be the key variable in a leadership model. One firm sets a standard for product design and quality, and the other firms in the industry follow. Similarly, there can be collusion, quasi-agreements, and cartels on product quality and sales promotion, as well as on price. Similarly also, a firm maximizing its sales, subject to the restraint of a minimum profit, can do so by adjusting its advertising outlays. Such a firm sells more and advertises more than if it tried to do nothing but maximize its profits. All this means that deeper exploration of nonprice competition would only follow paths of analysis parallel to those investigated in the last two chapters.

Nonprice competition, however, does raise difficult problems of welfare economics.

## Oligopoly and Economic Welfare

Since the equilibrium of pure competition provides the standard of efficiency in the allocation of resources, it follows easily that oligopoly is inconsistent with maximum economic welfare. Price seems to be higher and output seems to be lower under oligopoly, given of course the same demand and cost functions. Hence oligopoly causes a loss of economic welfare, just as monopoly does (page 306). How great is the loss? How strong is the accompanying implication that, somehow, something ought to be done about oligopoly?

Here again are questions with no certain answers, even conceptually. The welfare loss due to monopoly can be stated precisely, with the assumption of profit maximizing behavior by the monopolist. Since oligopoly can have so many shapes, no single precise statement can be made. Some help, however, can be got from the array of models of oligopoly presented in Chapter 23. These models, it will be remembered, range from those with prices and outputs identical to monopoly to those with prices and outputs approaching the levels of pure competition. The loss of welfare from oligopoly must accordingly vary from one model to another. If prices and outputs would lie between those of monopoly and of pure competition, it would follow that the welfare loss from oligopoly is less than that from monopoly.

Baumol's model of the large firm that maximizes its sales subject to the restraint of a minimum profit can be interpreted as giving a price-output result that could be close to that of pure competition. In the model, output is larger than called for by maximum profits. If the firm's output is to equal the equilibrium output under pure competition, two conditions would have to hold. One is that price would have to equal minimum *full* costs. The other is that Baumol's minimum profits would have to equal the firm's opportunity costs plus its normal profits. That is, Baumol's minimum profits are an addition, apparently, to business costs. Though it gets zero net profits in long-run equilibrium, the competitive firm does recover its full costs, i.e., business costs plus opportunity costs and normal profits. It is not hard to imagine that the firm of Baumol's model would produce *more* than the equilibrium output of a comparable purely competitive firm — if minimum profits are less than opportunity costs plus normal profits.

Figure 24–2 shows how an oligopolistic firm *could* have the price and output of a purely competitive firm. In the figure, $P_2B$ is the profit-maximizing price. The sales-maximizing price is $P_1A$. Of course, only by chance would the demand curve pass through the minimum point of the cost curve, and only by chance would the minimum profits equal opportunity costs plus normal profits.

However this might be, the comparison should not be pushed far because Baumol's model is really one of short-run behavior. The ideal output of welfare economics, and the deviations from it, are long-run adjustments. The welfare loss from oligopoly must also be conceived as the loss of consumers' satisfactions when oligopolistic industries are in long-run equi-

librium. It will be argued a little later that the welfare loss from oligopoly
is probably small.

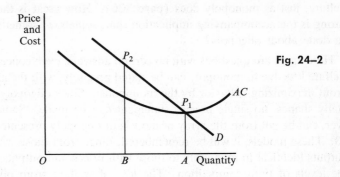

Fig. 24–2

The welfare aspects of nonprice competition in oligopolistic industries
present difficult analytical problems. Suppose that the firms in an industry
incur larger costs to produce a product of higher quality, and that the
demand for the higher quality product is larger. Suppose also that though
the price is unchanged, the result is larger profits for the firms. Hence the
firms gain. The consumers gain also; otherwise they would not buy more.
Is the gain to them as great as the additional costs incurred by the firms?[2]
Perhaps it is, but it need not be. Still another welfare problem of product
competition is the variety of products of the same type. Consumers generally seem to prefer variety — of models, designs, sizes, etc. — to standardization. Is the gain from variety greater than or less than its costs? Are
the degrees of variety optimum? That is, does the proliferation of product
types make consumer choices wider or does it confuse consumers and
make choices more difficult? Most people have strong opinions on these
and related matters. So far, however, economic theory has little to contribute.

### The Dynamics of Oligopoly

Just as monopoly changes its appearance when viewed in motion over
time, so does oligopoly. With the exception of the long-run entry model,
the theories of oligopoly reviewed here are all of the short-run variety.
They are theories of decision-making under conditions of certainty and of
perfect knowledge, and under the usual simplifying assumptions of given
demands for the outputs of each group of firms and given costs of the firms.

[2] The additional costs also represent the value of the foregone output of other
goods.

The long run is long enough for an industry to grow or to decline. The long run is also long enough for resources to move from one industry to another, for investors and for persons entering the labor force to choose among industries. In the long run also, and above all, in many of the big oligopolistic industries in the American economy, technological change occurs and consumer demands shift. New products for consumers come on the market; new machines, new processes, new materials appear in the production functions of firms. In the long run, demands are more elastic.

It follows that over longer periods of time, there is a tendency toward a uniformity of levels of business profits among industries. This of course is by no means the same thing as the universal condition of zero *net* profits in the static general equilibrium model. Still, the tendency toward uniform levels of business profits in the oligopolistic (and other) industries must prevail, given the mobility of resources over time. The tendency is rough, because some barriers to entry persist, because investors make mistakes, and because rates of growth among industries are unequal. In brief, then, the monopolistic elements in oligopoly become less important in the long run. Interindustry competition for markets and for resources in the long run shapes the short-run contexts that oligopolistic decisions are made in.

Though the complexities of dynamic change preclude rigorous proof, it can be concluded, as a matter of judgment, that the allocation of resources under oligopoly is, by and large, tolerably close to efficiency — pressures to reduce costs are strong and production is responsive to consumer demand. Islands of exception probably exist even over longer periods; deviations from the ideal of efficiency can occur in the short run. Yet the forces of the long run keep pushing price and output toward efficiency.

### Applications

There are no important applications of theories of oligopoly to problems of economic policy. This is because there are so many models of oligopolistic behavior and hence so many hypotheses about price and output. The state of theoretical and empirical knowledge does not, for example, bring agreement that there are six (or some other definite number of) models of oligopoly, that each model is determinate, and that the behavior of any oligopolistic industry can be described in general by one of the models. Consider one of the features of the theory of pure competition: Time is divided into three slices, the immediate period, the short run, and the long run. The three slices have long been accepted; there are hardly any disputes about them, and they have proved useful. Nevertheless, it would be easy to argue that this schema is too simple, that there ought to be more divisions of time; if a chorus of disagreement burst forth, theorists might begin to proliferate different systems of time periods. Still, the manufacture of models of oligopoly goes on. For each one mentioned in this book, there are several others. .

The lack of a set of agreed-upon models means that economic theory here cannot give much support to economic policy. Some of the industries regulated by government are oligopolistic. The prominent examples are radio and television broadcasting in metropolitan market areas, network broadcasting in the national market, air transportation in regional markets, and motor carrier transportation in local and regional markets. More useful models of oligopoly could be the bases from which standards of economic regulation could be derived. The lack of better models of oligopoly is also a barrier to the establishment of higher standards of antitrust policy than now exist. The antitrust laws, of course, make price-fixing ("imperfect cartels") in interstate commerce illegal; in other ways too these laws help to maintain competition. It is to be hoped that the future will bring advances in the theory of oligopoly that will give a sounder underpinning to the policy of maintaining and strengthening competition.

### Summary

The prices set by oligopolistic firms tend to be rigid. An explanation of price rigidity is offered by the hypothesis of the kinked demand curve. The firm facing such a curve has no incentive either to raise or to lower its price because of its estimate of its rivals' actions. Nonprice competition in oligopoly functions in about the same way as price competition; quality of product or volume of advertising can also be the competitive variables. How nonprice competition affects economic welfare is a difficult analytical problem. Over longer periods of time, oligopoly takes on a different hue, just as monopoly does; the long-run allocation of resources probably does not deviate far from standards of efficiency. The unsatisfactory condition of the theory of oligopoly makes it a poor foundation for analyses of economic policy.

### SELECTED REFERENCES

George J. Stigler, "The Kinky Oligopoly Demand Curve and Rigid Prices," *Journal of Political Economy,* Vol. LV, 1947. Reprinted in George J. Stigler and Kenneth E. Boulding, eds., *Readings in Price Theory* (Homewood: Irwin, 1952).

On nonprice competition: Fritz Machlup, *The Economics of Sellers' Competition* (Baltimore: Johns Hopkins Press, 1952), Chap. 14. Joe S. Bain, *Pricing, Distribution, and Employment,* rev. ed. (New York: Holt, 1953), Chap. 6.

On the dynamics of oligopoly: Joseph A. Schumpeter, *Capitalism, Socialism, and Democracy,* 3rd ed. (New York: Harper, 1950), Chaps. 7 and 8.

## EXERCISES AND PROBLEMS

1. Draw a kinked demand curve. Then draw a decrease in demand and prove that a price reduction will not occur.

2. Draw an increase in demand for a demand curve with a kink. Show that a price rise can happen.

3. Would the standardization of the essential features of differentiated products improve economic welfare? Standardization ought to reduce costs and, eventually, prices. Consumers would gain from lower prices and would lose by having less variety of choice. Which would be the greater, the gain or the loss?

4. Annual model changes are often criticized. Would consumers benefit if annual model changes were eliminated?

5. Price theory judges oligopoly by the criteria of levels of prices and output. Should other standards be brought in too? What are they?

# PART SIX

## MATHEMATICAL NOTES

### Note 1.   Cournot's Model of Oligopoly

In Chapter 22, page 352, both of Cournot's producers are in equilibrium when each produces exactly one-third of the opportunity, or competitive, output.

Alphonse begins with $\frac{1}{2}$, then cuts back to $\frac{3}{8}$, then to $\frac{11}{32}$, etc. This can be written as

$$1 - \tfrac{1}{2} - \tfrac{1}{8} - \tfrac{1}{32} \cdots$$

which is the same as

$$1 - (\tfrac{1}{2} + \tfrac{1}{8} + \tfrac{1}{32} + \cdots).$$

The numbers in parentheses are an infinite series, whose sum to the limit is $\dfrac{a}{1-r}$, where $a$ is the first term and $r$ is a constant ratio, less than 1. Therefore

$$\frac{a}{1-r} = \frac{\tfrac{1}{2}}{1 - \tfrac{1}{4}} = \frac{2}{3}.$$

Therefore, Alphonse's equilibrium output is $1 - \tfrac{2}{3} = \tfrac{1}{3}$.

Gaston starts with $\frac{1}{4}$, then expands to $\frac{5}{16}$, then to $\frac{21}{64}$, etc. His infinite series is $\frac{1}{4} + \frac{1}{16} + \frac{1}{64} + \ldots$, whose sum to the limit is

$$\frac{a}{1-r} = \frac{\tfrac{1}{4}}{1 - \tfrac{1}{4}} = \frac{1}{3}.$$

There are many modern versions of Cournot's model. The simple one now to follow is adapted from William Fellner.[1]

First, let the demand function be linear and let costs be zero, as they could be in Cournot's example of water from mineral springs. Let the market demand function be $p = a - bQ$, where $p$ is price, $Q$ is the total output of two duopolists, and $a$ and $b$ are positive constants. The outputs of the two duopolists are $q_1$ and $q_2$. Therefore, $p = a - b(q_1 + q_2)$. Duopolist 1 treats $q_2$ as a constant, and vice versa.

[1] William Fellner, *Competition Among the Few* (New York: Knopf, 1949), pp. 60n.–62n.

The total revenue of duopolist 1 is $pq_1 = aq_1 - bq_1^2 - bq_1q_2$. He equates his $MR$ and his $MC$ so as to maximize his profit. Because $MC_1 = 0$

$$MR_1 = \frac{dpq_1}{dq_1} = a - 2bq_1 - bq_2 = 0.$$

Similarly, the profit-maximizing output of duopolist 2 is given by the equation

$$a - 2bq_2 - bq_1 = 0.$$

The solution of these two similtaneous output equations yields $q_1 = q_2 = \frac{a}{3b}$. Then total output is $q_1 + q_2 = \frac{2a}{3b}$. If there were $n$ producers instead of two,

$$Q = \frac{na}{(n+1)b}.$$

The monopoly output is found by setting $q_2 = 0$ in the equation $a - 2bq_1 - bq_2 = 0$. Thus the monopoly output is

$$q = \frac{a}{2b}.$$

The competitive output is found by setting price = costs. Since costs are zero, $p = 0$. Therefore $a - bQ = 0$. The competitive output is then

$$Q = \frac{a}{b}.$$

Thus with the linear functions, the monopoly output is half the competitive, as is also shown on page 305.

If constant costs $C$ are introduced, then the foregoing has to be modified by writing $a - C$ instead of $a$.

With nonlinear demand functions, the results are about the same. The duopoly output is less than the competitive, but greater than the monopoly output. The larger the number of producers, the larger the output of oligopoly.

### Note 2.  Game Theory

The theory of games has contributed little to the advancement of knowledge about oligopolistic behavior. The theory does offer some simple models, one of which will be described here.[2]

---

[2] This note is based on the discussion in Robert Dorfman, Paul A. Samuelson, and Robert M. Solow, *Linear Programming and Economic Analysis* (New York: McGraw-Hill, 1958), Chap. 15, and in William J. Baumol, *Economic Theory and Operations Analysis* (Englewood Cliffs: Prentice-Hall, 1961), Chap. 18.

The subject of game theory is rational behavior in situations of conflict — parlor games, military combat, and the struggles of firms for profits. Games have definite rules, known to and adhered to by the participants. The method of analysis of game theory gives good results only for the "two-person, constant-sum" game. For the economic application, this means a pair of duopolists who compete for some *given* total profit. What one of them gains the other loses.

Each of the two firms has its "strategies," which are all of the courses of action, the moves and countermoves, that one firm can take in the light of what the other firm does. The strategies of the two firms are aligned in a table called a "pay-off matrix."

### TABLE A–6–1

### A Pay-Off Matrix

| *Strategy of* *Firm A* | | | | | |
|---|---|---|---|---|---|

| *Strategy of* *Firm A* | 1 | 2 | 3 | . . . | *n* |
|---|---|---|---|---|---|
| 1 | $a_{11}$ | $a_{12}$ | $a_{13}$ | . . . | $a_{1n}$ |
| 2 | $a_{21}$ | $a_{22}$ | $a_{23}$ | . . . | $a_{2n}$ |
| 3 | $a_{31}$ | $a_{32}$ | $a_{33}$ | . . . | $a_{3n}$ |
| . . . | . . . | . . . | . . . | . . . | . . . |
| *m* | $a_{m1}$ | $a_{m2}$ | $a_{m3}$ | . . . | $a_{mn}$ |

Table A–6–1 is the general form of a pay-off matrix. Firm $A$ has $m$ strategies, listed vertically in columns. Firm $B$ has $n$ strategies, listed in rows. The entries in the body of the table are the profits of firm $A$. Thus, if firm $A$ selects its strategy 3, and if firm $B$ selects its strategy 2, the table says that firm $A$'s profits will be $a_{32}$.

The pay-off matrix is set up from the point of view of firm $A$. The profits of firm $B$ are some constant minus firm $A$'s profits in the table. Firm $A$ would like the maximum number in the table. Firm $B$ would like the minimum number in the table because that would mean the maximum profits for firm $B$.

Table A–6–2 gives hypothetical data for a pay-off matrix in duopoly. The strategies of the firms are their choices of how many units of their products to sell. In the table, each firm can have three strategies — to sell 100, or 200, or 300 units of its product. The dollar figures are the profits of firm $A$ for each combination of strategies.

What will the two competing firms do? They will each offer 100 units for sale. Such happens to be the solution of this duopoly problem. Here is a "strictly determined" game.

### TABLE A–6–2

#### Pay-Off Matrix for Two Rival Firms

| Strategy of Firm A | Strategy of Firm B 100 units | Strategy of Firm B 200 units | Strategy of Firm B 300 units | Row Minimum |
|---|---|---|---|---|
| 100 units | $4000 | $5000 | $4500 | $4000 |
| 200 units | $3000 | $3500 | $3800 | $3000 |
| 300 units | $2000 | $2500 | $2800 | $2000 |
| Column Maximum | $4000 | $5000 | $4500 | |

Why do both firms choose the strategy of selling 100 units? The profits of firm *A* are $4000. Firm *B* also sells 100 units and thus prevents firm *A* from getting any more than $4000. With firm *B* selling 100 units firm *A* has no incentive to sell 200 units or more, because to do so would lower profits.

Formally, this game is strictly determined because the "maximin" is equal to the "minimax." (They are also called maxmin and minmax.) The maximin is the greatest row minimum, and the minimax is the smallest column maximum.

Firm *A* follows a maximin strategy. That is, it seeks the maximum of the minimum pay-offs. Firm *B* follows a minimax strategy of holding its rival to the minimum of the maximum pay-offs.

The strategies are conservative. They mean that each firm assumes the worst and acts accordingly. The solution, where the maximin equals the minimax, is an equilibrium solution. Both firms are motivated to adopt and to hold to the mutually compatible strategies.

But the maximin does not have to be equal to the minimax. Nor do firms necessarily employ such cautious strategies. Nor is it usually true that two firms fight over a pot of profits of a fixed size. In more complicated games, where the number of players, or firms, is greater than two, and where the prizes, or profits, do not add to a constant sum, the conclusions reached by game theory are much less definite.

# PART SEVEN

*Incomes*

*as Prices*

# The Pricing of Factors

## of Production

**25**

In modern economic theory, the factors of production are labor and capital. The factors of production are also known as "productive services," or "resources." In much economic literature they are also called "inputs." In this book, however, the word "input" means all of the things bought by the firm — fuel, raw materials, etc., as well as labor and capital.

### Factors of Production

Early in the nineteenth century, economists distinguished three factors of production, namely, land, labor, and capital. The owners of the factors of production were landowners, wage earners, and capitalists whose incomes were rent, wages, and profits. Thus the theory of factor pricing was the theory of the determination of three kinds, or three functional forms, of income. In nineteenth-century England, the landowners, the capitalists, and the wage earners were more than economic groups. They were also distinct sociological and political classes — upper, middle, and lower. Late in the nineteenth century, economists added a fourth factor of production. This was enterprise; profits then became the incomes of entrepreneurs, and interest became the income of the owners of capital.

Whether there are two, or three, or four factors of production does not matter very much. Classification is a matter of convenience and relevance. The British class system with its three kinds of incomes was never relevant in America. Conflict and discussion in this country have centered on the division of total income between labor income and property income, on the supposed tension between "human rights" and "property rights" as if the owners of property were not human beings, too. Another important reason for holding to two factors in price theory is that macroeconomic theory operates with two factors. In its special and narrow sense as a component of gross national product, the national income is the sum of factor incomes — of (1) the compensation of employees, and (2) the incomes of proprietors of farms and unincorporated businesses, together with the incomes of the owners of rental properties, of fixed-income securities, and of the stocks of corporations. The incomes of millions of Americans, who are both workers and owners, are combinations of labor incomes and property incomes.

As every student of economics knows, the gross national product consists of the values of final or finished goods and services only. To avoid double counting, the values of intermediate products are excluded. After the exclusion of depreciation and of indirect business taxes, the value of national product thus reduces to the value of the services of the factors of production. Similarly, "value added" by a firm or an industry is its dollar sales minus its purchases of intermediate products from other firms or industries. Value added is thus the value of the services of the workers and of the owners in the firm or industry.

The structure of the theory of factor pricing will now be briefly sketched. The structure has four main parts. (1) As Chapter 10 shows, each firm uses inputs and factors in such amounts that the money values of their marginal physical productivities are equal to their unit costs to the firm. (2) Each firm has a demand curve for factors of production, the curve sloping downward because of diminishing marginal physical productivity. When the demands of the firms are added, the result is the demand functions for factors in each market and in the economy as a whole. (3) The supplies of factors, at various prices, are determined by decisions as to quantities of the factors offered by their owners. Factor prices are determined by demand and supply. (4) The theory of product prices (Chapters 14–24) and the theory of factor prices are parts of one whole. The costs of firms depend on factor prices as well as on technology. The demands of consumers depend on their tastes and on their incomes, which they receive from the sale of their factors, i.e., their productive services.

*factors - inputs ?*

Consumer demands, in turn, along with technology, determine the marginal productivities of factors. Accordingly, the combined theory of product and factor prices shows how, within the limits imposed by technology and the tastes of consumers, the factors of production are directed into their many uses by their prices.

The theory of factor pricing is generally known as the marginal productivity theory of distribution. This name is not fully descriptive because the idea of marginal productivity comes in only on the demand side. And in every pricing process, supply is just as important as demand.

The first step is to define the demand for factors of production. This will now be done in two stages, first in pure competition and second in monopoly and imperfect competition. Although all factors of production are put in two classes, labor and capital, there are many kinds of each. In the discussion to follow, the word "factor" is to be understood as meaning one of several kinds of labor or of capital.

### The Demand for Factors in Pure Competition

Some of the ideas developed in Chapter 10 can now be brought forward and adapted for present purposes. The emphasis in Chapter 10 is on the quantities of inputs and factors that the firm buys. The emphasis here goes to the demand curves for factors.

#### Demand of the Firm

Let $A$, $B$, etc. stand for factors. Let $MPP_A$, $MPP_B$, etc. stand for the marginal physical productivities of factor $A$, factor $B$, etc. The prices of $A$, $B$, etc. are $P_A$, $P_B$, etc. Marginal cost is $MC$, and $P_o$ is the price received by the firm for its output. On page 154 it is shown that

$$\frac{P_A}{MPP_A} = \frac{P_B}{MPP_B} = \cdots = MC = P_0.$$

This equation, or statement, says in effect that the firm minimizes costs and maximizes profits when it adjusts quantities of each factor so that the value of its marginal physical product ($VMPP$) equals the price paid for it. That is, $\dfrac{P_A}{MPP_A} = P_o$, and therefore $P_A = MPP_A \times P_o = VMPP_A$.

In the short run, the competitive firm might be in a position where only one factor is variable in amount; this could be, for example, unskilled labor. When this is so, the firm's demand curve for the one variable factor is identical with the curve of the value of the marginal physical product ($VMPP$).

In Figure 25–1, price is on the vertical axis, and quantity of factor $A$ is on the horizontal axis. The curve $VMPP$ is the demand curve of the firm for $A$. The firm buys (or hires) the amount $OQ$ of the factor when the price is $OP$. The amount $OQ$ is the amount for which $OP = VMPP$ (i.e., $MPP_A \times P_o$). At a lower price, the firm would use a larger amount of $A$. At a higher price, less would be used.

Firm's Demand for One Variable Factor

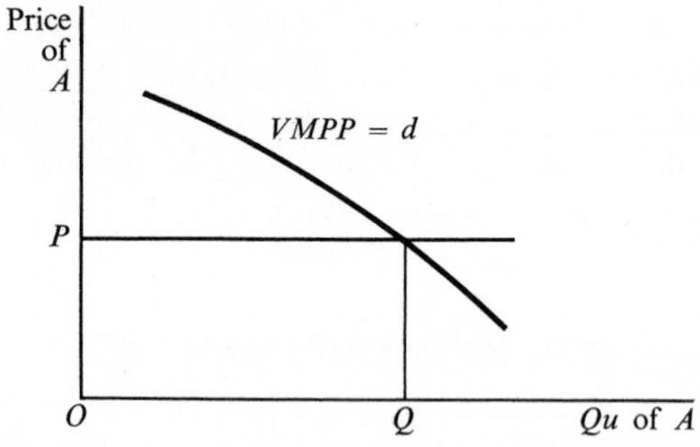

Fig. 25–1

Assume next that the firm has several variable factors. The task now is to derive the demand for $A$, when both $A$ and other factors $B, C, D$, etc. are variable. If the price of $A$ falls, more of it is used. The other factors complementary to $A$ will also be used in larger quantities, with the result of *increasing* $A$'s $MPP$. The substitutes for $A$ will be used in smaller quantities; this too has the effect of increasing the $MPP$ of $A$. Suppose, for example, that an earth-moving contractor finds that he can lease large power shovels at a lower rate. So he plans to employ more of them. If he also hires more operators (the complements) and uses fewer small power shovels (the substitutes), he will get more work (a higher $MPP$) out of the larger power shovels than if he simply leased more with no change in his work force and line of equipment.

In Figure 25–2, let the price of $A$ at first be $P_1$. The firm is in equilibrium, using the quantity $OQ_1$. Then the price of $A$ falls to $P_2$. The changes in the quantities of the other factors shift the $VMPP$ curve to the right. It becomes $VMPP_2$ instead of $VMPP_1$. The firm then equates $P_2$ and $VMPP_2$, to arrive at the amount $OQ_2$ of factor $A$. The curve $d_A$, joining the points defined by $P_1Q_1$ and $P_2Q_2$, therefore describes the demand for one factor when the quantities of others are also variable.

Firm's Demand for One Factor:
Other Factors Variable

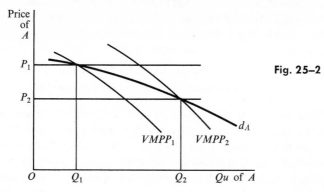

Fig. 25–2

## Demand of the Industry

The demand curve of an industry for a factor of production is the sum
of the demand curves of the firms in the industry. Here, too, another adjustment has to be made. If the price of a factor falls, the firms use more.
Other things being equal, their outputs expand as their costs fall. The
supply curve of the industry drops down, with the result that the equilibrium price of the product decreases. Hence, *VMPP* has to be revised
downward. Suppose, for example, the price of fertilizer falls. The farmers
use more, produce more, and so receive a lower price for their grain. The
fertilizer still has the same marginal *physical* product in bushels per season,
but because a bushel now sells for less, the *value* of the *MPP* is less.

In Figure 25–3, the demand curves $d_{2.00}$ and $d_{1.75}$ are constructed in the
same way as the demand curve $d_A$ in Figure 25–2. The 2.00 and the 1.75
are product prices in dollars per bushel (or other physical unit). The firm's

Firm's Demand for One Factor:
Industry Adjustment

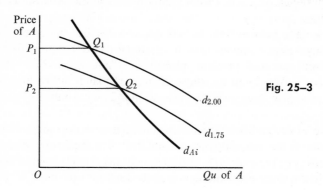

Fig. 25–3

demand for a factor is less when the price of the product is lower, because *MPP* is multiplied by a smaller number. The curve $d_{Ai}$ is drawn to show the firm's demand when changes in the price of the product are allowed for. The demand of all of the firms of the industry is the sum total of the $d_{Ai}$ curves of each of the firms.

## The Demand for Factors in
## Monopoly and Imperfect Competition

Firms producing and selling in monopoly and in imperfect competition generally have some control over their selling prices. Sometimes they have some control over the prices they pay. The unregulated profit-maximizing monopolist calmly chooses his optimum price. Many regulated monopolists must, however, sell at given prices, fixed by public authorities. Oligopolists also commonly sell at rigid prices. The firms in many industries characterized by monopolistic competition likewise sell at prices dictated by custom. Certainly in the short run, therefore, many firms *not* in pure competition can share a feature of competitive firms, namely, given product prices. To avoid more complication, this matter will henceforth be overlooked. It will be assumed that firms vary their selling prices, that they know their demands, and that they maximize.

### Variable Prices for Products and Factors

To sell more of its product, a monopoly firm as well as one in imperfect competition has to accept lower prices. Instead of a given price, the firm instead faces a schedule of prices. Thus the demand curve for the firm's product comes into the calculations, and so does its marginal revenue. Accordingly, when the firm produces more by adding more units of a variable factor, the additional (i.e., marginal physical) product must be multiplied by the additional revenue it brings. *Marginal revenue product* is the name for marginal physical product multiplied by the corresponding marginal revenue.

Since marginal revenue equals price to the firm under pure competition, it follows that marginal revenue product (*MRP*) equals the value of the marginal physical product (*VMPP*). That is, *MRP = VMPP*, where *MR = P*. But for firms whose product demand curves are sloping, *MRP* is always *less* than *VMPP*, because marginal revenue is always less than price.

The price paid for a factor or an input can also vary with the level of activity of the firm. Suppose a small firm in a small town has 10 employees at work on the same task and that each has a daily wage of $15. Suppose that if the firm hires another man to do the same kind of work, circumstances are such that the firm has to pay all 11 men $16 a day. Ten men at $15 equals $150, and 11 men at $16 equals $176. The extra wage cost of 11 men is $26. The extra cost of one more unit of a factor is called *marginal factor cost*. In this example, marginal factor cost rises if the firm buys more units of the factor, and rises faster than average factor cost — $26 versus $16. On the other hand, marginal factor cost can fall. Suppose the firm can rent trucks, which are driven by its own employees, and that the rental per truck is lower the larger the number of trucks. If one truck is $20 a day and two are $18 each, then the marginal factor cost for two trucks is $16 ($36 minus $20). When marginal factor cost declines, it goes down faster than average factor cost.

If the price paid for units of a factor is the same regardless of the amount bought by a firm, then average factor cost and marginal factor cost are identical. Figures 25–4 and 25–5 show average and marginal curves for

Average and Marginal Factor Cost

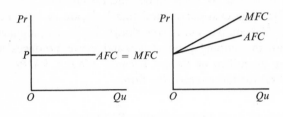

Fig. 25–4                    Fig. 25–5

two factors as one firm would see them. The average factor cost curves are really supply curves to the firm. In Figure 25–4, factor *A* is available to the firm at a constant supply price *OP*. In Figure 25–5, factor *B* is available at rising supply prices, shown by the curve *AFC*.

A firm facing rising supply prices for a factor (or any input) is often called a *monopsonist*. The literal meaning of this word is of course sole buyer; so to label such a firm carries no more meaning than to say that any firm with a downward sloping demand curve is a monopolist.

## Demand of the Firm

If the firm has just one variable factor, its demand curve is the curve of marginal revenue product for that factor. If two or more factors are simultaneously variable, the firm's demand curve for a single factor is constructed in the same way as that of the competitive firm. Thus in Figure

25–2, which is back on page 393, *MRP* curves can be substituted for *VMPP* curves.

Assume first that average and marginal factor costs are constant to the firm. When it is in equilibrium, the firm with a sloping demand curve pays each of its factors less than the values of their marginal physical products. Suppose that a firm in equilibrium has 200 employees, and that the 200th employee adds one unit of the firm's product per hour. Suppose the price of the firm's product is $5 and that marginal revenue is $3. Then, $MPP = 1$, and $VMPP = \$5$. But $MRP = \$3 =$ hourly wage cost. In other words, the 200th employee is paid $3 an hour during which he helps produce something the firm sells for $5. In contrast, a purely competitive firm in profit-maximizing equilibrium pays a unit of a factor an amount equal to the factor's *VMPP*. If its wage cost is $3 an hour, and if its *MPP* is also 1 unit per hour, the competitive firm's product price (in full equilibrium) is $3.

Earlier chapters show that a firm with a sloping demand curve produces less and sells its product at a higher price than a competitive firm. The comparison, of course, is made under the assumptions that both types of firms have the same cost curves and that both are in full (i.e., long-run) equilibrium. The comparison is now drawn for the employment of factors. The firm with the sloping product-demand curve produces less and employs smaller quantities of factors because $MRP < VMPP$. In contrast, $VMPP = MRP$ for the competitive firm.

Employment of a Factor by a
Monopsonistic Firm

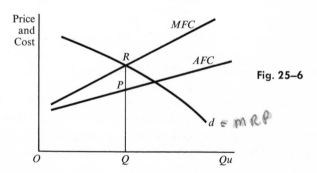

Fig. 25–6

Assume next that average factor costs are rising to a firm with a sloping demand curve. When this is so, the firm pays the factors less than their marginal revenue products. This is shown in Figure 25–6. Here the demand *d* is either *MRP* directly or derived from it by the adjustment previously described. The *AFC* curve is the supply curve to the firm of a factor; the curve *AFC* exhibits the actual prices the firm has to pay for different quantities. The firm employs *OQ* units of the factor, paying the price *PQ*. The marginal revenue product of *OQ* units is *RQ*. The firm does not employ more than *OQ* units because if it did, the extra units have an extra cost higher than their revenue productivity. Beyond *OQ,* as can be seen in Figure 25–6, $MFC > MRP$.

When factor price is less than marginal revenue product, "monopsonistic exploitation" is said to exist. Owing to its implications, this is a silly expression, though it is common in the literature. Further consideration of "exploitation" is postponed until the next chapter.

### TABLE 25–1

#### The Demand for Factors of Production

| Firm or Industry | Factor | Demand | Supply of Factor | Equilibrium |
|---|---|---|---|---|
| Firm in pure competition | one variable factor | demand curve = *VMPP* | *AFC* = *MFC* | *VMPP* = *AFC* = *MFC* |
| | several variable factors | demand for one factor equals its *VMPP* adjusted for effects of changes in quantities of other factors | *AFC* = *MFC* | adjusted *VMPP* = *AFC* = *MFC* |
| Industry in pure competition | | industry demand is sum of firms' demands further adjusted for changes in product price caused by variations in employment of factors | | |
| Firm with sloping demand curve | one variable factor | demand curve = *MRP* curve | *AFC* = *MFC* <br><br> *MFC* > *AFC* | *MRP* = *AFC* = *MFC* <br><br> *MRP* = *MFC* |
| | several variable factors | demand curve for one factor equals its *MRP* curve adjusted for effects of changes in quantities of other factors | *AFC* = *MFC* <br><br> *MFC* > *AFC* | adjusted *MRP* = *AFC* = *MFC* <br><br> adjusted *MRP* = *MFC* |

The gaps between *VMPP* and *MRP* and between *MRP* and *AFC* have consequences for the allocation of factors, or resources. "Monopolistic" firms do not employ resources in quantities as large as do competitive firms, all other things being equal. "Monopsonistic" firms put an additional brake on their uses of resources. Thus the price system fails, on the factor side, to allocate resources in accordance with the conditions of "ideal output" (Chapters 16 and 17). Here, of course, is the other side of the coin of monopoly as a cause of loss of economic welfare.

Table 25–1 shown on page 397 summarizes the discussion so far.

### The Firm's Demand for Capital

In modern analysis, the theory of capital and interest belongs in both microeconomics and macroeconomics. Since the publication of Keynes's *General Theory* in 1936, economists have devoted much more effort to the macroeconomic aspects of capital and interest. They have done so because of the importance of business investment for the stability of the whole economy and of the rate of interest as an instrument of stability policy. Discussion of capital and interest here will be kept brief and confined to a partial equilibrium analysis. Because capital is a factor and interest a cost to the firm and the industry, the basic theory has already been covered. It remains only to point to the special features of capital.

#### Discounting Future Yields

The special feature of capital goods is that their yields are available over a period of time. The services of buildings and of machinery extend over many years, depending on how durable they are and on how quickly technological change makes them obsolescent. In deciding on the purchase of a capital good, the firm looks to the stream of outputs that will be produced in the future with the aid of the capital good. The stream of outputs will be sold in year 1, year 2, year 3, etc.; thus the firm visualizes a stream of gross dollar yields in successive years in the future. From the stream of future gross yields, certain costs are deducted to arrive at the net yields. Interest and depreciation are not included in these costs; interest appears elsewhere in the calculations, in which depreciation is ignored so as to avoid double counting. Suppose the capital good is a motel. The owners can expect some average rate of occupancy, some average price per room, and some expenses of operation. Uncertainty as to the future, of course, beclouds any estimates made in the present. But the complications, theoretical and practical, of uncertainty will be bypassed here.

The future net yields must be *discounted* to the present. A dollar that will not be received for 5 years is not as good as a dollar that will be received in one year. The present value of the future net yields is calculated at the going or market rate of interest by a standard formula.[1] For example, the present value of $10,000 a year for 10 years discounted at 5 per cent is $77,217.35. The market rate of interest enters the calculations because if the firm borrows the money to buy the capital good, future net receipts must exceed or at least equal interest payments. If the firm buys the capital good with its own funds, it sacrifices the interest income it could earn with these funds.

The next step is to compare the present value of the expected net yields from a capital good with the cost, or the supply price, of the capital good. If the cost is less than present value, it pays the firm to acquire the capital good. If cost and present value are equal, it just barely pays.

Observe the three elements in the firm's decision on adding another capital good — its cost, the expected net yield, and the rate of interest. The first and third elements are given to the firm. That is, they are in perfectly elastic supply. This statement might not hold for very large firms which sometimes face rising costs of borrowed funds and perhaps rising costs of capital goods.

### Calculating the Optimum

The firm's demand schedule for capital goods is based on diminishing (revenue) productivity of additional capital goods. Take the motel example again. To get precise marginal calculations, suppose that the unit of decision is not an entire motel, but a room. Then the problem is how many rooms to build. The cost of building and equipping a room is so much. The stream of future net yields from a room depends on the number of rooms. The number of rooms could be 100, 101, 102, etc. After some number, because of the fixed factor of the location, the stream of future net yields from an additional room diminishes. Given this diminishing revenue productivity, and given the cost of a room, the profit-maximizing number of rooms depends on the rate of interest. At 7 per cent, so many rooms are built, at 6 per cent, more are built, at 5 per cent, still more, and so on.

When the rate of interest is picked out as the key variable, the future return from the capital good is expressed as a percentage yield over cost.

---

[1] If $y_1$ is the net yield in year 1, $y_2$ in year 2, etc., and if $r$ is the rate of interest expressed as a decimal, then the discounted present value $PV$ of the stream is

$$PV = \frac{y_1}{(1 + r)} + \frac{y_2}{(1 + r)^2} + \frac{y_3}{(1 + r)^3} + \cdots \frac{y_t}{(1 + r)^t}.$$

Year $t$ is the last year of the planning period, e.g., the 10th year or the 20th. Given $y_1$, $y_2$, etc., as well as $r$ and $t$, $PV$ can be found from prepared tables.

The larger the number of the capital goods added to the existing stock, the lower the percentage yield. Equality of the rate of interest with the percentage yield determines the optimum capital stock.

When, however, the cost of buying the capital good is the strategic variable, the future return from the capital good is expressed as the present value of the discounted future net yields. The more units of capital goods, the lower the future net yields per unit and, hence, the lower their discounted present value at a given rate of interest. Equality of cost and discounted present value determines the optimum number of units of capital.

**TABLE 25–2**

| Units of a Capital Good | Yield[a] | Interest in per cent | Present Value[b] in dollars | Cost per unit |
|---|---|---|---|---|
| 7 | 8 | 6 | 12,000 | 10,000 |
| 8 | 7 | 6 | 11,000 | 10,000 |
| 9 | 6 | 6 | 10,000 | 10,000 |
| 10 | 5 | 6 | 9,000 | 10,000 |

[a] Percentage yield over cost (purchase price and operating costs), excluding interest.
[b] With discount at 6 per cent.

Table 25–2 gives hypothetical data to illustrate the two methods of calculating the optimum number of units of capital a firm should acquire. The first two columns on the left say that the more units of capital, the lower are their percentage yields. The equilibrium number is 9 units, whose yield equals the rate of interest. The last two columns on the right say that the more units of capital, the lower are the present values of their future dollar yields. The equilibrium number is 9 units, whose present value per unit equals cost of acquisition.

### The Supply of Factors

The supply functions of factors *to the firm* have already been discussed. In general, factors are available in perfectly elastic supply to individual firms, competitive and noncompetitive alike. Rising or falling supply curves to firms are the exception, though they are by no means rare.

The supply of labor is discussed in the next chapter, whose subject is the theory of wages. Much of the material on the supply of capital and on the rate of interest now belongs to the domain of macroeconomics. All that can be said about the supply of factors, when their natures are not made specific, comes under the heading of elasticity of supply.

To the industry and to the economy, elasticity of factor supply takes on an aspect different from elasticity to the firm. Imagine a large area devoted to varied farming activities. Suppose that much of the land is leased on annual terms and that there is a market for the leases. Acres of land could, therefore, be in perfectly elastic supply to any one farmer; by paying the going rate, he can lease as many additional acres as he wants. But for an industry, i.e., all the farmers who grow the same crop, supply is less than perfectly elastic. If the price of their crop rises, and if the farmers all bid for more land, its lease value will rise because the land is transferred from other crops. Suppose next an increase in the demand for *all* of the farm products produced in the area. Because the total amount of farm land is fixed once and for all, its supply is perfectly inelastic.

Supply of Factors

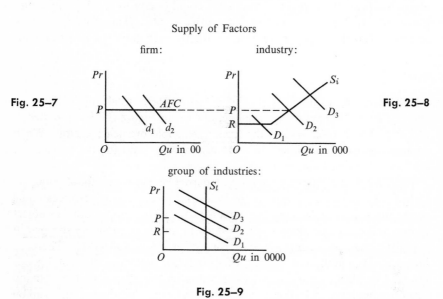

Fig. 25–7

Fig. 25–8

**Fig. 25–9**

The same factor, then, can have supply curves ranging from the horizontal to the vertical, depending on which demand curve is coupled with supply — the demand of the firm, of an industry, of a group of industries. Figure 25–7 displays an increase in the demand of one firm, the increase coming, for example, from an improvement in technology. Because the factor is in perfectly elastic supply to the firm, the price of course does not rise. Notice that the quantity axis in Figure 25–7 is scaled in hundreds. The same axis is scaled in thousands in Figure 25–8, which shows supply to the industry and demand from the industry. The price $OP$ to the firm is the industry equilibrium price, given by the intersection of the supply curve and demand curve $D_2$.

The supply curve in Figure 25–8 is perfectly elastic, however, for a small range of quantities at price $OR$. This means that if the industry is small, with e.g., demand $D_1$, the industry can get more of the factor without paying more per unit. The meaning of the price $OR$ is that other industries use the same factor. Figure 25–9, with quantities in the tens of thousands, shows group demand $D_1$ and supply resulting in the equilibrium price $OR$.

If industry demand increases, as in Figure 25–8, the price of the factor rises, as more of the factor is employed by the industry. The horizontal $AFC$ curves of the firms rise in step with the industry price. But when group demand increases, as in Figure 25–9, price goes up and quantity remains constant.

In general, the supply price of a factor to an industry is equal to or above the price the owners of the factor could obtain in an alternative employment. In Figure 25–8, the other price is $OR$. This other price can also be called the opportunity cost, or the transfer earnings, of the factor.

### Rents

The foregoing example is that of a factor whose total amount is fixed and cannot be increased. Its total supply ($S_t$ in Figure 25–9) is perfectly inelastic. Land, of course, is the leading example of such a factor. When demand increases, the long-run equilibrium price paid for the services of land rises without limit, with nothing to check the rise.

In contrast, the long-run supplies of particular kinds of capital goods — to firms, to industries, to groups of industries — are elastic at prices equal to the full cost of producing the capital goods. This proposition is subject to one major qualification: Capital goods produced in monopolistic or oligopolistic industries can have long-run prices above full costs. There is, however, no limitation on supply; whether larger quantities of capital goods are sold at higher or lower prices depends on the shapes of the demand functions and the cost functions in the industries producing the capital goods.

The incomes of owners of factors in less than perfectly elastic supply are called "rents." In this sense, the word "rent" is not confined to land, nor does it have anything to do with leasing things or hiring them. The factor owner can receive rent from land, or from capital under certain conditions, or from labor under certain conditions.

The essence of the idea of rent is that rents cannot be competed away. This is clear for land. When demand for the services of land grows, rents rise. Nothing on the supply side makes them fall, even in the long run. In contrast, more capital goods can always be built in the long run. An increase in demand for office space, for example, leads in the long run to the erection of more office buildings. When, however, the demand for particular capital goods *in the short run* increases, the incomes of the owners of existing capital goods rise. Nothing on the supply side makes these incomes fall because by definition of the short run, the short-run supply of capital goods is perfectly inelastic or nearly so. Because their short-run behavior resembles the behavior of the rent of land in the long run, the incomes of the owners of capital in the short run are called "rents," or "quasi-rents."

The net revenues of firms in the short run are mentioned often in earlier chapters, especially in Chapter 14. These net revenues are quasi-rents, but they are not so referred to earlier in this book; there is no need to do so, and it has to be admitted that the term "rent" can easily cause confusion. Anyway, given a firm's plant and equipment, i.e., its capital goods, the size of its net revenue or quasi-rent depends on current demand. If demand is high, quasi-rent is high, and can be far, far above the earnings that had been expected when the plant and equipment were built. Quasi-rent can also be low if demand shrinks much. Quasi-rent, in short, is at the mercy of short-run demand, just as the income from land in the long run depends on long-run demand.

### Rents and Profits

What is the difference between rents and profits? It is this: Rents cannot be competed away, whereas profits can. Rents are present in the long-run equilibrium of pure competition; (net) profits are not. Recall the long-run equilibrium of the competitive firm and the industry (Chapter 15). The firms earn zero net profits. The adjustments of the firms and the entry and exit of firms to the industry cause net profits to be zero. But the firms all have the same cost curves (page 236). They are the same because costs are equalized by the firms' payments — rents — for the services of scarce managers.

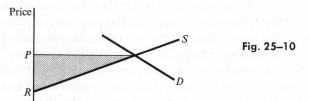

Supply and Rent

Fig. 25–10

In Figure 25–10 the *S* curve is the long-run supply curve for managers in a particular industry. The demand for managers depends on their productivity. In the long run, given adequate information and mobility, the managers all receive the same salary, which is *OP*. The supply curve says that all but one of them are willing to work for less than *OP*. No one, however, would work for less than *OR*. The shaded area in Figure 25–10 is the total rent element in the incomes of the managers. Rent is the excess of the incomes they receive over the minimum incomes they would accept if they had to, the minimum incomes being determined by what they can earn elsewhere. If the supply curve were flat, the shaded area would disappear. There is no rent when supply is perfectly elastic.

Net profits, the excess of total revenue over full costs, are the result of disequilibrium and monopoly. When they are negative, i.e., when there are losses, net profits are also the result of disequilibrium. Monopoly here means monopoly in the broad and loose sense — the sloping demand curve. As Chapter 19 demonstrates, monopoly can, but it does not have to, result in profits. When monopoly is temporary, and is brought into existence by a firm's innovation that is later imitated by other firms, then net profits, which are also temporary, arise from innovation. The existence of uncertainty has been assumed away in this book because of the formidable theoretical complexities that uncertainty causes. Some theorists link profits with the entrepreneurial function of bearing uncertainty.

### The Allocation of Factors

Their demands, supplies, and prices mutually determine the allocation of factors among all their possible employments. Suppose that a change in consumers' tastes cause the demand for a consumer good to increase. Whether or not its price rises, which depends on the kind of competition in the industry, more of the consumer good is produced, the demand for factors increasing. Some of the factors are of unspecialized types, employed in many industries. Except perhaps in the short run, such factors are available in perfectly elastic supply to the expanding industry. Their prices do not go up, but the increase in demand allocates more of them to the industry. Other factors are scarce, their supply curves rising, even in the long run. The larger demands for the scarce factors cause their prices to rise, to the expanding industry, as well as to other industries. These higher prices lead to substitutions among factors, causing still more changes in factor demands, supplies, and prices. So it goes — just one shift in consumer demand results in a ripple of changes in the allocation of factors.

### An Application

The theory of factor pricing surveyed in this chapter has the traditional name of the marginal productivity theory of distribution. The theory has been embroiled in much controversy, mainly over the social ethics of the pattern of incomes in a private-enterprise economy. Most of the controversy has had to do with wages. Further consideration of the marginal productivity theory of distribution is therefore postponed to the next chapter.

### Capital Budgeting

One of the important decisions that periodically confront the executives of a business enterprise is how to allocate their investment funds among the many projects that are always proposed. Which projects for expansion are needed most?

The idea of the need for capital expansion is, however, just as useless as the idea of a consumer's need for a commodity. "Need" conveys nothing about intensity. But the concept of demand does do so, both for the consumer and the firm. The concept of the firm's demand for capital can be applied as a useful device in capital budgeting.

### TABLE 25–3

#### A Firm's Demand Schedule for Capital

| Estimated Yield in per cent | Proposed Investments | Cumulated Demand |
|---|---|---|
| | thousands of dollars | |
| over 50 | 200 | 200 |
| 35–50 | 800 | 1000 |
| 25–35 | 1200 | 2200 |
| 15–25 | 1800 | 4000 |
| 10–15 | 2500 | 6500 |
| 5–10 | 5000 | 11500 |
| less than 5 | 7000 | 18500 |

Consider Table 25–3 which ranks the proposed investments of a hypothetical firm at some point of time when decisions have to be made on investments in new capital. The several proposals up for examination and decision are arrayed by estimated yield and size. A few have high yields, whereas many offer low yields. The planning period is, say, two years. Suppose next that the firm has, from internal sources on which it alone relies, funds for capital expenditure amounting to $4 million. A glance at Table 25–3 shows that only proposals promising 15 per cent or more should be acted on. The cut-off rate of return is 15 per cent.

(Why does the firm not rush out to sell its bonds at, say, 5 per cent, and expand its new investments to $11.5 million? Here again are the difficult problems raised by the profit-maximizing assumption and by the uncertainties surrounding the estimates of future yields. Then too, borrowing alters a firm's financial structure, making for still more complications.)

Suppose that a wholly new investment proposal comes up in the deliberations of the firm. If its estimated yield is below the cutoff rate, the new proposal can be summarily rejected. If, however, the new investment has a yield higher than the cutoff, it can displace other investments that had been decided on.

## Summary

The prices of the factors of production are connected with the prices of consumer goods through the actions of firms and households. The demand curve of a competitive firm for one variable factor is the curve of the value of the marginal physical product of the factor. The firm's demand for one factor, when several are variable, is found by adjusting *VMPP* to allow for changes in the employment of other factors. Still another adjustment has to be made to allow for variations in the price of the product as the industry expands or contracts. The demand of firms with sloping demand curves is based on *marginal revenue product.* Factors can be available to firms at rising or falling supply prices. Then the rational firm looks to *marginal factor cost,* equating it with marginal revenue product. A firm's demand for capital is based on the present value of expected net yields. The optimum capital stock is found by equating the cost of capital goods with the present value of future net yields or by equating the rate of interest with percentage yield over cost. A factor can have supply curves ranging from the horizontal to the vertical, depending on time and on whether demand is from a firm or an industry or a group of industries. *Rent* is the name for the income to the owners of a factor in less than perfectly elastic supply. The net revenues of firms in the short run are *quasi-rents* because the supply of capital is inelastic in the short run. Rents cannot be competed away, whereas net profits can.

## SELECTED REFERENCES

General: American Economic Association, *Readings in the Theory of Income Distribution* (Philadelphia: Blakiston, 1946).

Edward H. Chamberlin, *The Theory of Monopolistic Competition,* 7th ed. (Cambridge: Harvard University Press, 1956), Chap. 8. Joan Robinson, *The Economics of Imperfect Competition* (London: Macmillan, 1933), Book VII.

William J. Baumol, *Economic Theory and Operations Analysis* (Englewood Cliffs: Prentice-Hall, 1961), Chap. 14. George J. Stigler, *The Theory of Price,* rev. ed. (New York: Macmillan, 1952), Chap. 11.

On the allocation of factors: Richard H. Leftwich, *The Price System and Resource Allocation,* rev. ed. (New York: Holt, Rinehart and Winston, 1960), Chap. 15.


## EXERCISES AND PROBLEMS

1. Upon what does the elasticity of demand for a factor depend?

2. Describe the effect on the prices and on the allocation of factors of a decline in the demand for a consumer good.

3. Describe the effect of a technological improvement on a firm's demand for capital.

4. Make up a set of numbers to show the relation between quantities of a factor and of a firm's product. Calculate the marginal physical product. Make up a demand schedule for the firm's product. Calculate marginal revenue product. Assume a price for the factor and find the amount the firm employs. Show why the firm would not use more, or use less.

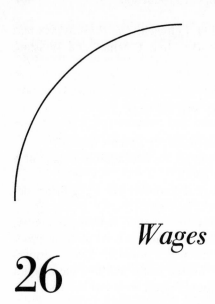

# *Wages*

## 26

THE SHARE OF WAGES IN THE NATIONAL INCOME · THE SUPPLY
OF LABOR · WAGES IN DIFFERENT OCCUPATIONS · WAGES AND
THE FIRM · COLLECTIVE BARGAINING · MINIMUM WAGES ·

The title of one of the popular essays of a French economist of the last
century, Frédéric Bastiat, was "Things Seen and Things not Seen." That
price theory looks more to things not seen than to things seen must now be
fully evident. In particular, the theory of wages describes many things not
seen.

The theory of wages deals with the slowly changing underlying forces,
with the background. In the foreground stand the day-to-day practical
problems that must be dealt with by employers, personnel administrators,
workers, and union officials. The theory of wages describes the forces
causing different levels of wages. Practical men take the levels for granted
while they wrestle with problems such as systems of wage payments — time
wages, piece wages, incentive wages, overtime wages, bonuses, length-of-
service increases, etc. Other problems include wage inequities within plants
and between plants operated by the same company. Wage disputes often
turn on fringe benefits, which must be considered as additions to wages, and
which include vacations with pay, paid sick leave, paid travel time, clothing
allowances, pensions, health and other insurance, as well as recreational
facilities.

Thus "wages" can mean many different things in different contexts. The word "wages" will be used here in the comprehensive sense of labor cost to the employer, per unit of time, or per unit of output. This usage therefore means that the current values of fringe benefits and of similar costs to the employer are included. The word "wages" here is also assigned its customary meaning in economics as the one expression for payments for personal services, embracing alike the salaries and bonuses (etc.) of the corporation executive, the fees of the surgeon, the income of the entertainer, the pay of the soldier, and the earnings of the unskilled manual worker.

As a branch of the theory of prices, wage theory has the purpose of explaining persistent differences in wages as well as the role of wages in allocating human services among occupations, industries, and areas. Wage theory is also a part of macroeconomics, where one of its main tasks is to explain the relations between the aggregate level of wages and total employment. The fact that wages are incomes enters into price theory only in the description of the general equilibrium of prices. Partial equilibrium analysis ignores the role of wages as incomes, because even if the employees of a firm or an industry are consumers of the product, their contribution to demand is negligibly small.

The marginal productivity theory of wages applies to a firm and to an industry. And when all labor and all capital are regarded as if they were homogeneous, the theory applies to the whole economy, giving an explanation of the share of wages in the national income.

### The Share of Wages in the National Income

Statistical estimates of national income in the United States go back many decades. A remarkable fact is the relative constancy of the ratio of wages to the total of national income. In most years, wages have been about 75 per cent of the national income of the private domestic economy. How can this relative stability be explained?

A favorite hypothesis is based on the marginal productivity theory with the accompanying assumption that the production function for the whole economy is "linear and homogeneous;" that is, returns to scale are constant. If the quantities of labor and capital each increase by 10 per cent, output and income increase by 10 per cent. Labor and capital are combined in such a way that their contributions to income (i.e., their marginal physical products) have a constant ratio of about 3 to 1, i.e., 75 to 25. Because the ratio of the prices paid to factors is equal to the ratio of their marginal physical products, it follows that the incomes of labor and capital are in the same constant ratio.

This hypothesis, based on the Cobb-Douglas production function (page 136), does have some empirical foundation. If the hypothesis is valid, notice that the influence of unions on the ratio of aggregate wages to other incomes reduces to zero, that the presence of monopoly and imperfect competition does not affect the result, and that changes in technology must improve the efficiency of labor and capital about equally.

John Kendrick's study[1] of productivity trends in the whole economy is a macroeconomic analysis that does *not* assume constant ratios of labor and capital. For the period from 1948 to 1957, for example, Kendrick estimates that labor's share of national income in the private domestic economy increased from about 76 to about 81 per cent. The share of capital therefore decreased from about 24 to about 19 per cent. Total real output expanded from 1948 to 1957, at an annual average rate of 3.5 per cent. During this same period, the average annual increase in the employment of capital was much greater than the increase in the employment of labor. The combined productivity of labor and capital grew, mainly because of innovations in the use of capital. The price of labor relative to capital increased. Accordingly, with *relatively* more capital and *relatively* less labor, the real income of a unit of labor rose in 1948–57, while the real income of a unit of capital fell. This result, too, is in rough accordance with the marginal productivity theory.

### The Adding-Up Controversy and Euler's Theorem

Quarrels between labor and capital still go on, but among theorists the great controversies over the meaning of the division of income between labor and capital have long since subsided. One of the controversies over the marginal productivity theory of distribution, when it first became widely discussed about two generations ago, was whether capital received a share of total income greater than that corresponding to the value of its marginal product. Suppose that each of the two factors is paid an amount equal to the value of its marginal product. Does the sum total of labor's income and of capital's income then equal total income — which is the same as total product? Or is there something left over after both factors are paid the values of their marginal products, some income that falls into the hands of exploiting capitalists?

A proposition known as Euler's theorem, after Leonhard Euler (1707–1783) the Swiss mathematician, states that

$$\text{Total product} = L \times MPP_L + C \times MPP_C.$$

That is, total product (of a firm, an industry, or the entire economy) equals the quantity of labor, $L$, multiplied by the marginal physical product of

[1] John W. Kendrick, *Productivity Trends in the United States,* National Bureau of Economic Research (Princeton: Princeton University Press, 1961), Chap. 5.

labor, $MPP_L$, plus the quantity of capital, $C$, multiplied by its marginal physical product. In this equation, the price of the product is omitted. To do so is customary because the price just multiplies all the terms in the equation by the same number.

Euler's theorem is valid in the equilibrium of pure competition, and when the production function is linear and homogeneous, when returns to scale are constant. The proof of Euler's theorem is a simple matter of the differential calculus. Another kind of proof, following Stigler,[2] is this: Assume a simple production function, total product $= \sqrt{LC}$. In this function, capital and labor are substitutes and are measured in labor hours and machine hours. If, for example, total product $= 40$, then $\sqrt{LC} = \sqrt{40 \times 40} = \sqrt{80 \times 20} = \sqrt{64 \times 25} =$ etc. To illustrate constant returns to scale, let the quantities of both labor and capital be doubled. Then $\sqrt{2L2C} = 2\sqrt{LC} = 2 \times$ total product.

Suppose next, for arithmetical convenience, that 100 units each of labor and capital are employed. The marginal product of labor is the increase in total product from one more unit of labor. That is, $\sqrt{(L+1)C} - \sqrt{LC} = \sqrt{101 \times 100} - \sqrt{100 \times 100} =$ approximately 0.499. The marginal product of capital, similarly, is the same. When these marginal products are substituted in Euler's equation, the result is

$$100 \times 0.499 + 100 \times 0.499 = 99.8,$$

which is close enough to $\sqrt{100 \times 100} = 100$.

Euler's theorem, then, states that the total product is the sum of the marginal products of the two factors. No one is exploited — in competitive equilibrium with constant returns. The controversies over the theorem mostly centered about the legitimacy of the constant-returns assumption. If firms have constant returns to scale, a competitive equilibrium is impossible (Chapter 15, page 235). The rejoinder here is that in long-run competitive equilibrium, price equals minimum average cost, the firm's cost curve *at that point* being horizontal. The momentary constancy of unit cost corresponds to a momentary constancy of returns to scale at the point of equilibrium. Thus, at the exact point of equilibrium, it can be argued that constant returns exist.

### Marginal Productivity and Social Ethics

In the past, the marginal-productivity theory of distribution was both defended and attacked owing to its implications for social ethics. Because

[2] George J. Stigler, *The Theory of Price,* rev. ed. (New York Macmillan, 1952), pp. 136, 137.

it says that a man's income is equal to (the marginal productivity[3] of) what he produces, the theory was defended by some as exhibiting the justice of the working of free markets. Workers and owners deserve what they get; markets mete it out to them. This accords with the ethics of private property — that a man is justly entitled to the fruits of his labor. Early in the twentieth century, some economists pushed the doctrine of marginal productivity too far, however, making it into almost a natural law.

Opponents of the doctrine protested that it is cruel and harsh, because it puts a stamp of approval on low wages, and because the doctrine is incompatible with distributive justice — the principle that people have a just claim to income according to their needs. It is true indeed that many persons — the aged, the blind, the disabled, for example — have low or zero productivities. It is also true that in industries and areas where the supply of labor is large relative to the demand for it, the marginal product of labor can be low and result in wages far beneath standards of needs.

In the present age, however, the problem of low incomes is met by government programs that include social insurance, public assistance, and other social-service activities. The principle of distributive justice is in actual operation, although economists would agree that the operation has many a shortcoming. Most incomes are determined in markets where marginal productivity governs the demand for labor and other productive services. The social justice inherent in market-determined incomes continues as the widely accepted criterion. Thus both principles reign in the present age, each in its place. Violent and divisive controversy has subsided. The marginal-productivity theory of wages has become a neutral instrument of analysis.

### The Supply of Labor

Supply curves for labor can have almost any shape. The shapes depend on whether the context is the short run or the long and on whether the labor is that of one person, or of a group, or of all employed persons. Chapter 13 (pages 215, 216) shows the possibility of a negatively sloped supply curve for labor.

### The Aggregate Supply of Labor

The aggregate supply of labor is often identified with the labor force, which is officially defined as the total, in any one week, of all persons, 14

---

[3] This terminology is customary in this context. Strictly, it should be marginal revenue productivity, which, when $MR = P$, includes the value of the marginal physical product.

years of age and older, who are self-employed, or employed by others, or are unemployed, or are in the Armed Forces. Of this total, many millions are independent owners and entrepreneurs. What is the probable shape of the short-run supply curve for the labor force? The supply curve can be visualized as a relation between average real wage and the number of hours of work offered in a year. To express the quantity in hours is to make allowance for part-time and seasonal employment, as well as for those persons who hold more than one job. Economists who have speculated about the short-run supply curve for the labor force have generally concluded that this curve has a negative slope. Figure 26–1

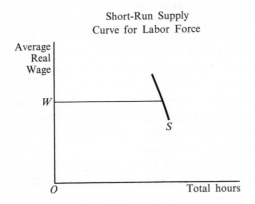

Short-Run Supply
Curve for Labor Force

**Fig. 26–1**

exhibits a supply curve for the labor force in the short run. At an average real wage above $OW$, the number of hours offered is smaller than at $OW$, signifying such responses as earlier retirement, shorter work weeks, longer vacations, longer periods of schooling, fewer hours worked by women, etc. The growth of the labor force can be represented by the rightward shift of the supply curve in Figure 26–1.

## Wages in Different Occupations

One of the traditional jobs of the theory of wages is to explain persistent differences among the wages paid to different groups. Analysis here can begin with the exercise of just a little imagination, so as to see what conditions would have to hold if all wages were to be exactly equal.

If all wages were to be exactly equal, then (1) all occupations, industries, and employers would have to be equally attractive; (2) perfect mobility of labor would have to prevail, with no costs of mobility; (3) labor would have to be homogeneous; and (4) pure competition would have to exist everywhere. Each firm in each industry would face the same horizontal supply curve. Differences in demand would not have any effect at all on the level of wages. Demand would, however, determine the numbers of persons employed in each occupation; demand would perform the allocating function.

These conditions will now be examined. By the attractiveness of an occupation is meant its nonmonetary advantages, with advantages having an algebraic meaning, i.e., the net of the occupation's positive and negative attractions. To cut through a maze of sociological considerations, let it be said simply that people have different tastes for occupations, just as they do for consumer goods and services. The supply prices in the more attractive occupations are lower. But the supply prices in all occupations are rising, at least after some point. This means, of course, that to attract more people to any one occupation, the wage rate has to be higher. With rising supply prices, it follows that differences in demand do indeed help to cause differences in wage rates. These differences are usually called "equalizing differences because such wage differences equalize the attractiveness of all occupations — the money advantage (or disadvantage) offsets the nonmonetary disadvantage (or advantage).

Consider next the mobility of labor. Mobility means transfer from one occupation, industry, etc. to another. Although it attracts attention, geographical mobility is only one form, and not everybody has to move when wages change. To act as an equalizer, mobility need only bring about adjustments at the margin. Less than perfect mobility is more pronounced in the short run than in the long. But even in the long run, less than perfect mobility is another cause of differences in wages, a cause operating on the supply side. In the nineteenth century, the English economist J. E. Cairnes (1823–1875) advanced the concept of *noncompeting groups* as part of the explanation of observable differences in wages that continue generation after generation. According to this idea, the whole labor force can be divided into groups such as professional and executive employees, clerical workers, skilled manual workers, unskilled manual workers, etc. Just how such groups should be defined and how they should be classified are complicated matters. Happily, there is no need to go into them here. The point is that mobility is high *within* each group, but low *between* them. Still on the assumption that labor is homogeneous, intragroup mobility tends to uniformity of wages within groups, modified only by differences in the attractiveness of occupations. Intergroup immobility results in differences of wages between groups.

In a society composed of socio-economic classes with rigid barriers between them, intergroup wage differences would be permanent and perhaps large. In the United States, the barriers between groups are not rigid, and there is much socio-economic mobility. Nonetheless, this mobility is so far short of perfect mobility that the thesis of noncompeting groups can still be held to apply. Even though they have been steadily diminishing, unequal educational opportunities continue to be a principal cause of self-perpetuating noncompeting groups.

Next, let the assumption of homogeneity be dropped. Each worker is a unique human being. In any group of workers, there are nearly always differences in efficiency among them. (The productivity of a worker is his capability as he works in a complex of machinery and equipment. In contrast, his efficiency is his personal skill, his diligence, his speed, his reliability, etc.) But if this idea is emphasized enough, the labor of every individual worker would have to be regarded as a separate factor of production. If the workers in a group are not of equal efficiency, then the marginal product of labor cannot be defined at all. Because marginal product is the loss of output by removing one man, the loss would depend on which one is removed. To take account of the uniqueness of each worker means, therefore, that no generalizations are possible. Instead, the way to proceed is to divide large groups into smaller and to assume that the persons within the small groups have equal efficiencies as workers. This means more supply curves coupled with more demand curves and therefore still more differences in wages.

Dropping the assumption of pure competition means, among other things, dropping the companion assumption of freedom of entry to occupations. Within any one noncompeting group, freedom of entry to some occupations is barred or limited by, for example, the policies of some labor unions, the licensing requirements of governments, the prejudices of some employers. These and similar barriers alter the shapes of supply curves, making them less elastic; by so doing, the barriers tend to raise wages in some occupations.

### Wages and the Firm

Because Chapter 25 surveys the theory of the firm's employment of factors, all that needs to be done here is to draw attention to certain special features of the firm's employment of labor. For all firms under pure competition and for many firms under imperfect competition, wage rates are given and thus beyond the control of the firm. The wage rates are determined by industry demand curves and industry supply curves. To the firm, the various types of labor are available in perfectly elastic supply at the going rates of wages. Imperfections of labor markets can make it possible or necessary, however, for a firm to pay a little less or a little more than prevailing rates of wages.

### Some Features of the Firm's Demand for Labor

Although the shorthand version of the theory of wages holds that a wage rate depends on the marginal-revenue product of labor, it is possible for the line of causation sometimes to run the other way. Marginal-revenue product can, under unusual circumstances, depend on the level of wages. Consider Figure 26–2. Suppose initially that the demand for labor is $D_1$

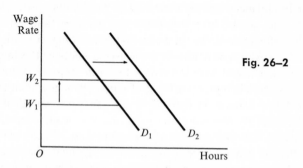

Fig. 26–2

and that the wage rate is $W_1$. Then imagine that something happens to cause the wage rate to rise to $W_2$. The higher wage rate can *cause* the demand curve to shift to $D_2$. If it does, there need be no decline in employment, but instead, as in Figure 26–2, a slight gain in employment. Several different combinations of circumstances could produce such a result. Just to indicate: In the short run, the higher wage could result in an improvement in the morale of the workers and, thus, in their productivity. In the long run, a rise in wages from a low level could mean, among other things, better health and physical vigor and, hence, greater productivity.

This feedback effect, from wages to productivity, must be distinguished from the "gospel of high wages," as it was often called in the 1920's. A single employer who pays more than the rates of wages prevailing in a labor market can be more selective in hiring and can choose the more efficient of the workers attracted by his higher wage. Employers also differ in their efficiencies. The more efficient of them can get higher marginal products from workers of superior efficiency. Employers of lesser abilities cannot pay higher wages to superior workers.

The demand for labor by business firms is a derived demand, derived from the consumers' demands for the firms' products. This proposition deserves repetition lest its significance go unnoticed. Differences in product markets can cause substantial differences in wages. At least they can in the short run. In the same city at the same time, the hourly wage rates established in negotiations with the same union for the same kind of labor can differ widely. The hourly wage for a truck driver in one industry can be twice as high as the hourly wage for a truck driver in another industry. Some industries are expanding while others are standing still or contracting. Product demand-cost·relations differ at any one time from one industry to another. Differences in wage rates for the same kind of labor in the same market area tend to persist. They are not so much the result of market imperfections as they are of continuing differences in product markets.

One of the points of criticism of the marginal productivity theory of wages has been that employers do not, so it has been argued, adjust the numbers of their employees when wages rise or fall. When such criticism is based on actual observation, the facts that are seen might not be the kind relevant for testing the generalizations of theory. The employers in question are perhaps not ardent profit seekers; perhaps they do not have all the information they need for rational decisions. In short, a business firm at any one point of time is by no means necessarily in a position of profit-maximizing equilibrium.

If a business firm fails to adjust employment in face of a rise in wages, its behavior need not, however, be inconsistent with the theory — certainly not in the short run. It is enough to recall the proposition that demand in the short run is always less elastic. A firm's demand for labor in the short run can easily be perfectly inelastic, or nearly so. The short-run demands for the products of firms in imperfect competition are less elastic and can be inelastic. For an oligopolistic firm with a kinked demand curve, the relevant portion of the marginal revenue curve is vertical (page 374). The possibility of substituting capital for labor in the short run is likely to be small and is often zero; office equipment, however, is an example where short-run substitution is relatively easy. If, then, a firm's short-run demand for labor is highly inelastic, a change in wages causes little change in employment.

### The Monopsonistic Firm

When it faces a rising supply curve of labor, the firm is said to be in a position of monopsony. Firms are sometimes also in positions of oligopsonistic interdependence, i.e., the amount of labor available to one firm at a given wage rate also depends on the wage rates being offered by rival firms.

The wage paid by the monopsonistic firm is determined by the intersection of the marginal wage cost with the firm's demand curve for labor. Analytically, this is the same point covered in Chapter 25 on page 396.

In Figure 26–3, the supply of labor to a firm is shown by the curve $S$, which is the same as the curve of average factor costs discussed in Chapter

25. The curve $M$ is marginal to the curve $S$; that is, the curve $M$ shows the extra wage cost of an extra man; it is the same as the curve of marginal factor costs. The demand curve for labor is $d$, and is based on the marginal revenue productivity of the labor. The optimum for the firm is to hire $OA$ units of labor and to pay the wage $OW_1$. For one more unit of labor, marginal wage cost exceeds marginal revenue productivity. Notice that the wage rate is lower than the competitive level, where $S$ and $d$ intersect. (Strictly, the point of intersection of $S$ and $d$ is competitive only if $d$ is based on $VMPP$, instead of $MRP$.) Notice also that the monopsonistic wage is also lower than the marginal revenue product. That is, $OW_1$ is lower than $AR$.

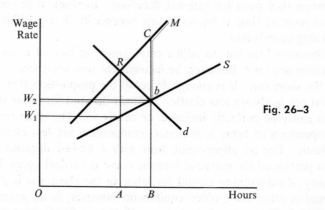

A Monopsonistic Firm

Fig. 26-3

Suppose that an external force imposes a higher wage rate on the monopsonistic firm. The force could be a union or government through a minimum wage law. In Figure 26–3, let the imposed higher wage be $OW_2$; let it be assumed that only coincidence makes $OW_2$ correspond to the intersection of $S$ and $d$. The imposition of the higher wage alters the supply curve of labor to the firm. For $OB$, or $W_2b$, of labor the firm must pay a wage of $OW_2$. For a larger amount, the firm has to pay a higher wage. Thus the supply curve becomes $W_2bS$. The marginal wage cost curve then becomes $W_2bCM$. It has a discontinuity from $b$ to $C$. So the firm increases employment to $OB$. Any other imposed wage — higher than $OW_1$ and lower than $AR$ — will cause the firm to increase employment.

## The "Exploitation" of Labor

For more than a century, most of the critics of capitalism have had something to say about the exploitation of labor. One form of exploitation is the payment of low wages. How low do wages have to be if labor is exploited? The English economist A. C. Pigou advanced the argument that to pay a worker a wage less than the value of his marginal physical product of labor is to exploit him. In this view, labor is not exploited in industries where pure competition prevails, but is exploited in monopolistic industries. Yet it is easily possible for wages in industries approaching the model of pure competition to be much lower than wages in monopolistic industries.

In imperfect competition, the equilibrium earnings of *both* labor and capital are less than the value of marginal physical product. Since it is not helpful to say that both labor and capital are exploited, economists interested in exploitation shifted the definition to say that labor is exploited if its wage is less than its marginal revenue product. It was shown earlier that wages are less than marginal revenue product for the monopsonistic employer. Such a definition would blanket in as "exploited" many employees whose wages, by any other standard, are high. There must be other employees, in the competitive industries, who are not so exploited, but whose wages are among the lowest paid.

The concept of exploitation deserves no place in the theory of wages. The concept belongs in the domain of investigation of market imperfections. Exploitation can be said to exist when employers deliberately take advantage of their workers' ignorance, when employers practice wage discrimination, by paying different wages to workers of equal efficiency, etc.

### The Supply of Labor to a Firm

Just how important is monopsony in labor markets? The supply curve of labor to a large firm is usually drawn as a rising curve, like the supply curve in Figure 26–3. A rising curve states that to get more workers, the firm must pay higher wages or that the number of workers potentially available to a firm is an increasing function of wages. It can be argued, however, that a rising curve exists only when the level of unemployment in the market area is exceptionally low. Normally, the level of unemployment is such that a firm can expand its work force, without changing its wage rate, simply by hiring more of the people who daily apply for jobs. Over some range, then, the firm's supply curve is more likely to be horizontal than rising in the short run.

### Collective Bargaining

Collective bargaining between a union and an employer is the leading form of negotiation between one seller and one buyer. The theory of bilateral monopoly is accordingly the theory relevant to collective bargaining. Chapter 22 shows that, despite the intellect lavished on it, the theory of bilateral monopoly does not give a determinate solution. General reasoning based on the profit-maximizing assumption cannot say exactly what price and output will be in transactions between one buyer and one seller. At best, theory can point to a range of outcomes, a range within which bargaining decides the actual outcome.

So, too, with collective bargaining. In practice, of course, the thousands of collective-bargaining agreements encompass thousands of details, ranging from seniority rules to grievance procedures to conditions of work, as well as to details of wage scales. Relevant to price theory is the collective bargaining over the general or average level of union wages in a firm or industry. If the demand for a firm's product increases and if, as a result, the curve of marginal revenue product of the firm's labor shifts to the right, the union may then demand an across-the-board wage increase. Given the new demand, what will be the rise, if any, in wages that will be negotiated in collective bargaining? This kind of question cannot be given an exact theoretical answer, even if, let it be noted, all the pertinent information is assumed to be known.

Just as economists have constructed many models of oligopoly, so also have they designed many of collective bargaining. Here, too, no single model or any set of models commands agreement. The problem peculiar to models of collective bargaining is how to set up the hypothesis for the goal of the union. Are unions economic, or political, or politico-economic organizations? Do they try to maximize some quantity? Of the many possible hypotheses, three can be mentioned here because they have forms that make it possible to analyze them with the usual methods of price theory. (1) It can be assumed that the union acts in the same way as a business monopoly, that the union is a sales agent for the services of its members. If this were so, the union would try to set an optimum wage which would maximize the income of its members. Because the short-run demand for labor is generally inelastic, it seems likely that the union would strive for a high wage to increase the total income of the members of the union. But if demand is elastic, as it can be — when payroll is a large part of total costs, when capital can be easily substituted, and when product demand is elastic — the rational union has a modest desire for a higher wage level. (2) Another possible kind of behavior is that the union tries to maximize the number of its members. It can be supposed that at each wage rate the union can negotiate, there are so many persons who will belong to and owe allegiance to the union. The higher the wage, the larger the number; thus a special kind of supply curve (a "membership function") can be imagined. Upon the assumption that the union knows the demand curve for the services of its members, the wage sought is at the intersection of the demand curve and the supply curve as just defined.

(3) Still another way of defining the behavior of a union is to imagine it as seeking an optimum combination of wages and employment. Different combinations of wages and employment can be represented through families of indifference curves. To develop this analysis would be to go too far afield here, but some of the results of the analysis can be presented. The analysis can give an exact theoretic basis to the common view as to a union's reaction to a change in the demand for an employer's product. If this demand increases and if, therefore, the demand curve for labor shifts to the right, the union will seek a wage increase. The union *could* seek the gains of more employment for its members, but it *prefers* to get a wage increase, accompanied by perhaps only a small amount of additional employment. On the other hand, the union's reaction to a decline in demand is to resist a reduction in wages even if wage cuts would mean laying off fewer workers.

For employers also, systems of indifference curves or preference functions can be constructed, showing profit levels related to wages and output. When the indifference curves of a union and of an employer are brought together, a range of bargaining can be defined. But only a range. Theoretical reasoning cannot specify a determinate wage. In some of the models, however, the range within which bargaining takes place is narrow; this result confirms the general opinion as to the complementary interests of unions and employers.

### Minimum Wages

Does the imposition of a minimum wage rate cause unemployment among the workers for whose benefit the minimum is established? No single valid answer can be given to this question. Much controversy has centered over the applicability of theoretical models to this problem. Economists who have argued that minimum wages do in fact cause unemployment have sometimes drawn conclusions too hastily from the theoretical models. Not that the models are wrong. They might be irrelevant to some problems. In any event, many qualifications must be introduced when models are applied.

Take the simplest case, the imposition of a minimum wage on a competitive industry. If all the firms are in equilibrium, each one equates $VMPP$ with the wage of the type of labor in question. A higher wage means riding up and to the left on the $VMPP$ curve; at the new equilibrium, less of the labor is hired. Therefore, some unemployment ensues; its amount depends on how high the wage is raised, the slope of the $VMPP$ curves, and on the number of workers and firms. Even in this simple case, qualifications have to be brought in. At the time when a minimum wage is introduced, the competitive industry might be expanding in response to a higher price caused by growing demand. If so, the *VMPP* curves are shifting to the right. In the same period of time, many of the firms might be improving their methods of production, and this too would shift the *VMPP* curves. It is quite possible, therefore, for the imposition of a minimum wage to be accompanied by more, not less, employment. The minimum wage does, however, have the effect of putting a brake on the expansion of employment.

It was shown earlier in this chapter that the short-run demand of firms for labor can be highly inelastic. This, too, means that the short-run effects of a minimum wage are likely to be slight. In the long run in a dynamic economy, innovations shift the demand curves for labor.

A minimum wage causes a monopsonistic firm to *increase* employment, as is shown on page 418. This result is analogous to the imposition of a maximum price on a monopolist. His response is to produce and sell more.

Still another effect of a minimum wage deserves brief mention. In Chapter 25, pages 392 and 393 explain the derivation of a firm's demand curve for a factor of production when more than one factor is variable. Suppose a firm employs two kinds of labor, skilled and unskilled, that the two are substitutable, and that the minimum wage affects only the unskilled workers. If, in consequence, fewer of them are employed, the productivity of the skilled workers increases, i.e., their *VMPP* (or *MRP*) curves shift to the right. Hence, more skilled workers are employed. The substitution of more efficient for less efficient workers is, in fact, an often observed effect of minimum wages.

## Summary

The marginal-productivity theory of wages offers an explanation of the relatively constant share of wages in the national income, when it is assumed that the production function for the whole economy has constant returns to scale. With the same assumption, it can be shown with the aid of *Euler's theorem* that the sum of the marginal products of labor and capital is equal to total product in the equilibrium of pure competition. The marginal-productivity theory can be aligned with the social ethics of private property; the theory conflicts, however, with the principle of distributive justice. The supply curve for the whole labor force probably has a negative slope. Persistent differences in wages are due to the unequal attractiveness of occupations, to the imperfect mobility of labor, to the nonhomogeneity of labor, and to imperfect competition. The demand for labor by business firms is derived from the demands for the firms' products. The short-run demand for labor is likely to be highly inelastic. A higher wage imposed on a monopsonistic firm causes it to increase employment. Theory cannot give a meaningful definition of exploitation. Nor can it state the wage rate that is the outcome of collective bargaining. Though they can cause some unemployment, minimum wages do not always yield this result.

## SELECTED REFERENCES

On the share of wages in the national income: Lloyd A. Reynolds, *Labor Economics and Labor Relations,* 3rd ed. (Englewood Cliffs: Prentice-Hall, 1959), Chap. 17. Allan M. Cartter, *Theory of Wages and Employment* (Homewood: Irwin, 1959), Chap. 11. William J. Baumol, *Economic Theory and Operations Analysis* (Englewood Cliffs: Prentice-Hall, 1961), Chap. 14.

On the levels of wages: J. R. Hicks, *The Theory of Wages* (London: Macmillan, 1932), Part I. John T. Dunlop, ed. *The Theory of Wage Determination* (London: Macmillan, 1957), Parts I and IV. K. W. Rothschild, *The Theory of Wages* (New York: Macmillan, 1954), Parts One and Two.

On wages and the firm: Allan M. Cartter, cited above, Chap. 4 and 5.

On the theory of collective bargaining: Allan M. Cartter, cited above, Chap. 7, 8, and 9. John T. Dunlop, ed., cited above, Parts III and V.

## EXERCISES AND PROBLEMS

1. Draw diagrams to show how a union can raise the wage level in an industry by influencing the supply of labor.

2. Show how a union can increase wages by influencing the demand for labor — by encouraging employers to increase the degree of mechanization (for example, the bituminous coal industry in the postwar period).

3. Why are men often paid more than women for doing the same kind of work?

4. Why are wages low in some of the most disagreeable of occupations?

5. Suppose that a high (e.g., $2.00 an hour) minimum wage were imposed on *all* employers. Trace the short-run and long-run effects on employment, on capital-labor ratios, and on the composition of output of consumer goods and services.

# Index of Authors

# Index of Subjects*

* Numbers in italics refer to subjects in the mathematical notes.